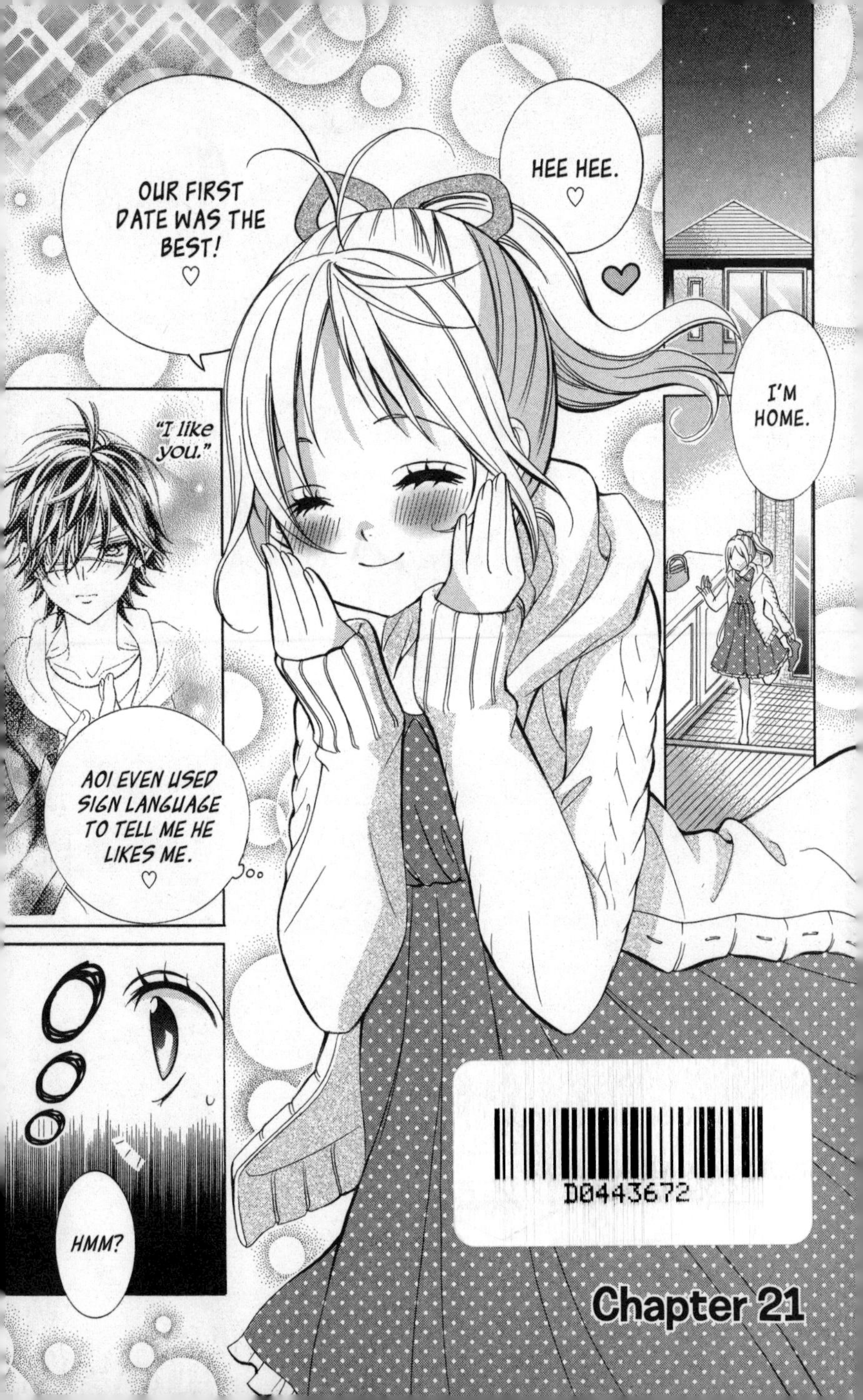
I'M HOME.
HEE HEE. ♡
OUR FIRST DATE WAS THE BEST! ♡
"I like you."
AOI EVEN USED SIGN LANGUAGE TO TELL ME HE LIKES ME. ♡
HMM?
Chapter 21

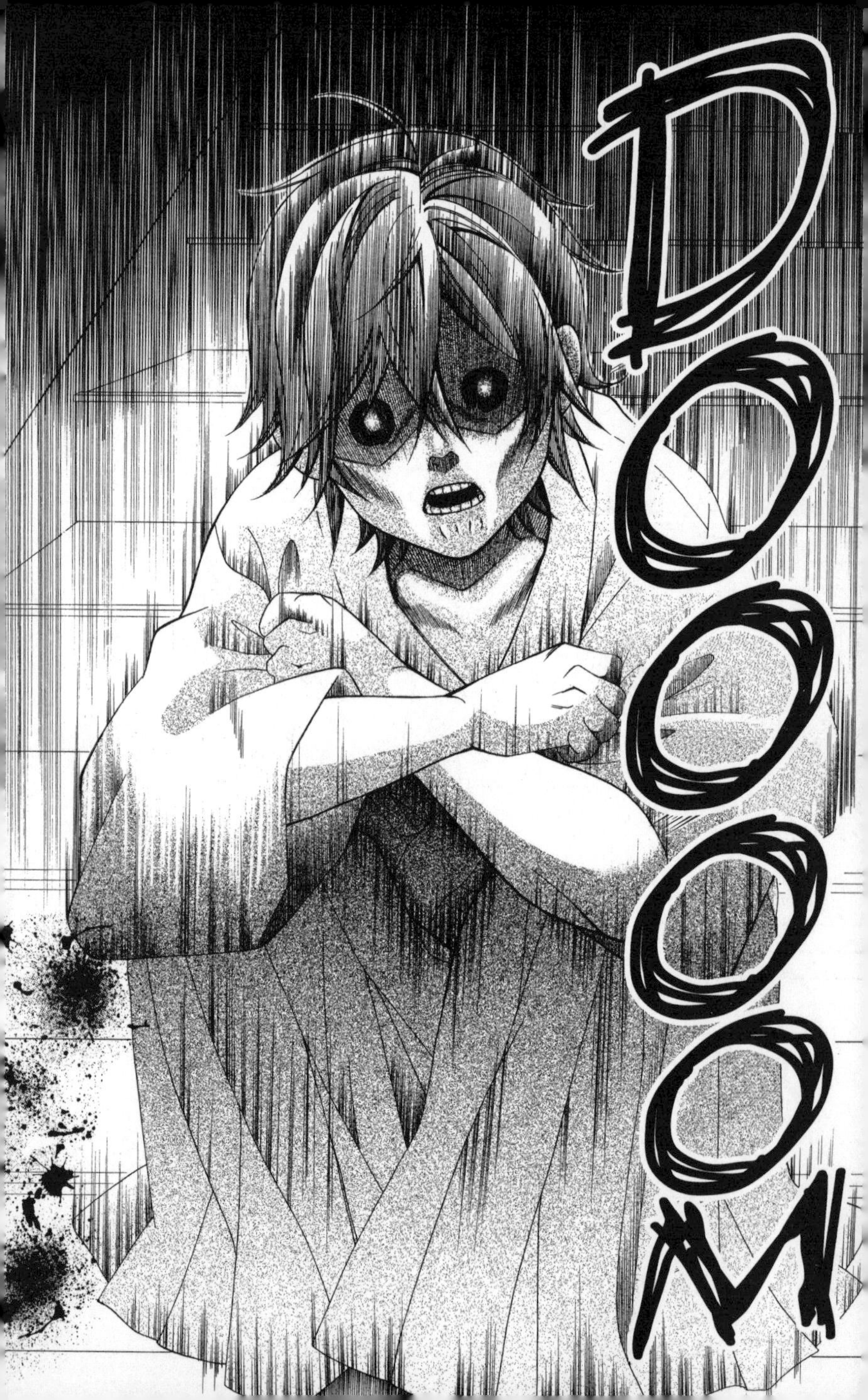
DOOOOM!

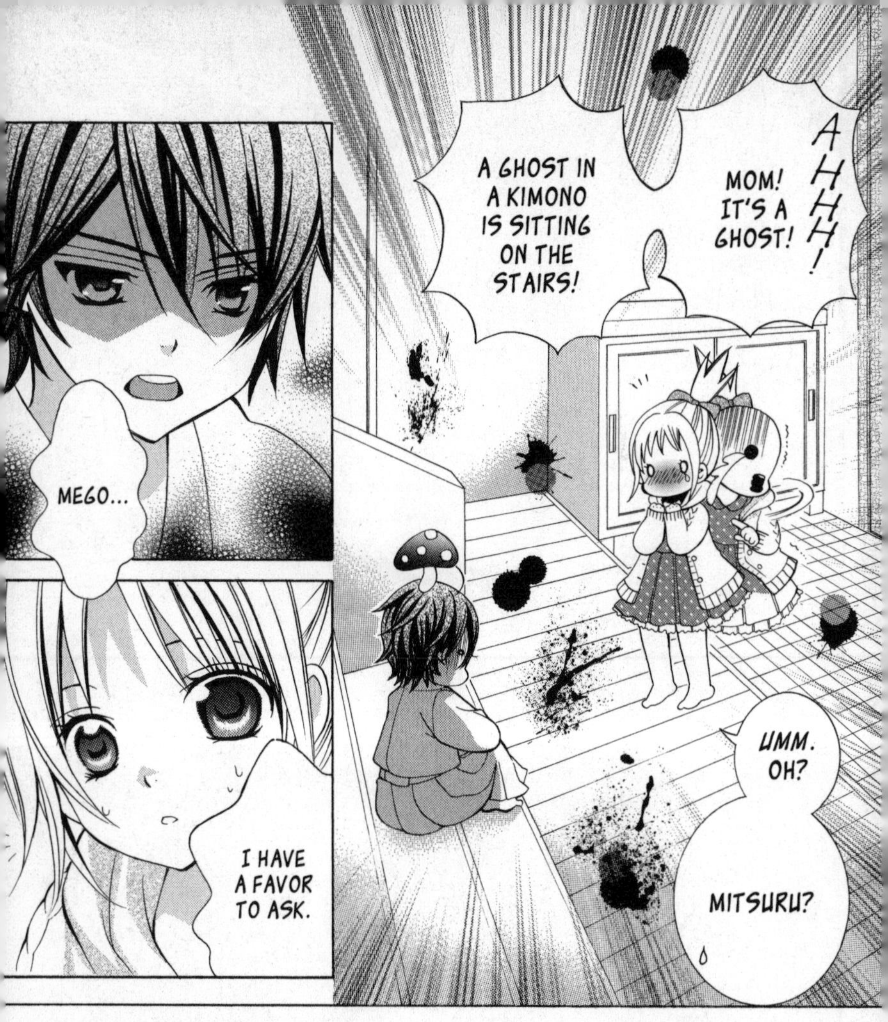
AHHH!
MOM! IT'S A GHOST!
A GHOST IN A KIMONO IS SITTING ON THE STAIRS!
UMM. OH?
MITSURU?
MEGO...
I HAVE A FAVOR TO ASK.

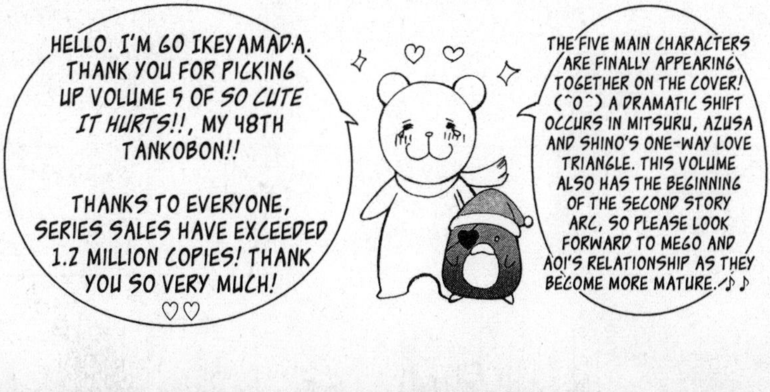
THE FIVE MAIN CHARACTERS ARE FINALLY APPEARING TOGETHER ON THE COVER! (^O^) A DRAMATIC SHIFT OCCURS IN MITSURU, AZUSA AND SHINO'S ONE-WAY LOVE TRIANGLE. THIS VOLUME ALSO HAS THE BEGINNING OF THE SECOND STORY ARC, SO PLEASE LOOK FORWARD TO MEGO AND AOI'S RELATIONSHIP AS THEY BECOME MORE MATURE.♪♪
HELLO. I'M GO IKEYAMADA. THANK YOU FOR PICKING UP VOLUME 5 OF *SO CUTE IT HURTS!!*, MY 48TH TANKOBON!!
THANKS TO EVERYONE, SERIES SALES HAVE EXCEEDED 1.2 MILLION COPIES! THANK YOU SO VERY MUCH! ♡♡

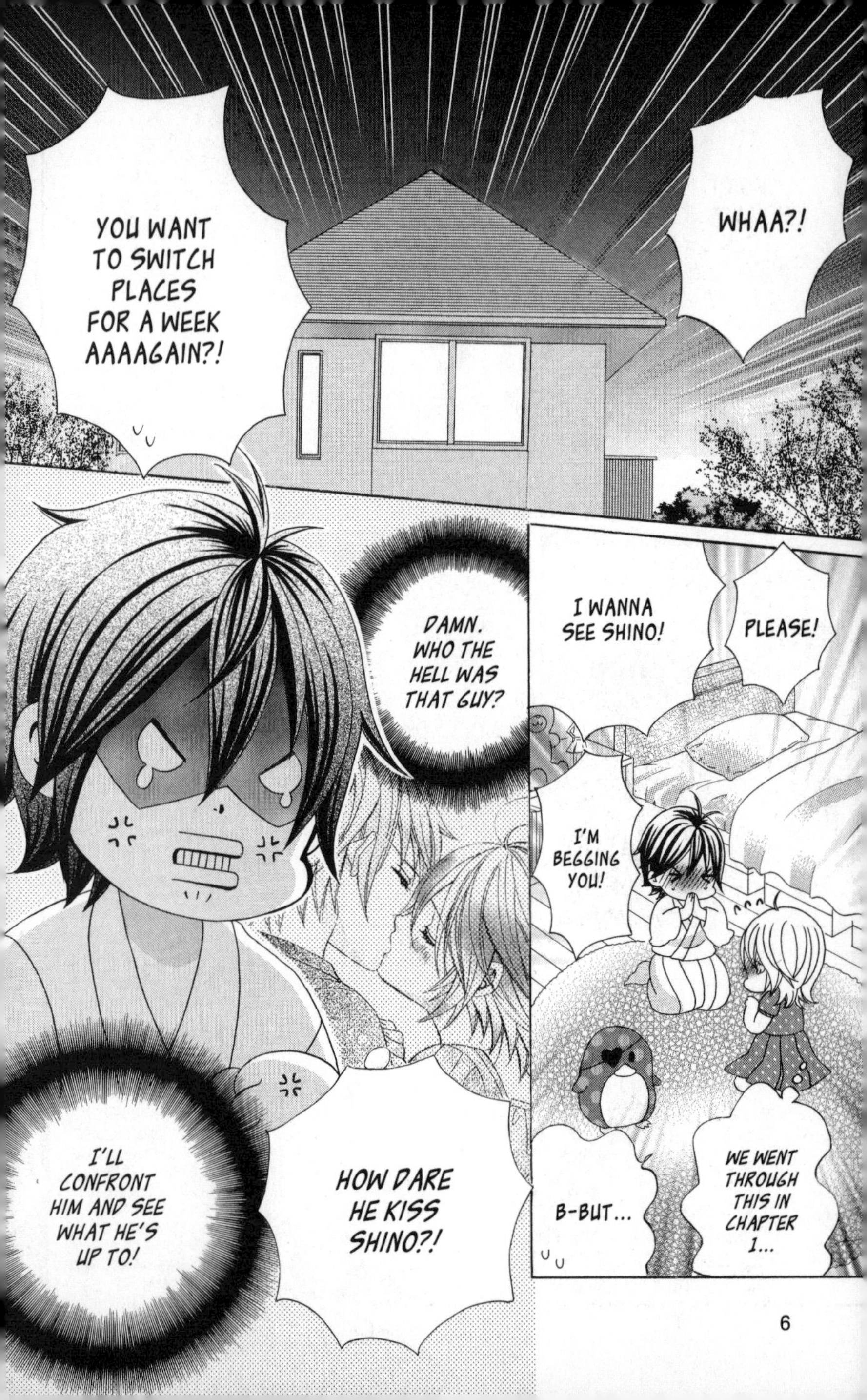
WHAA?!
YOU WANT TO SWITCH PLACES FOR A WEEK AAAAGAIN?!
PLEASE!
I WANNA SEE SHINO!
I'M BEGGING YOU!
WE WENT THROUGH THIS IN CHAPTER 1...
B-BUT...
DAMN. WHO THE HELL WAS THAT GUY?
HOW DARE HE KISS SHINO?!
I'LL CONFRONT HIM AND SEE WHAT HE'S UP TO!

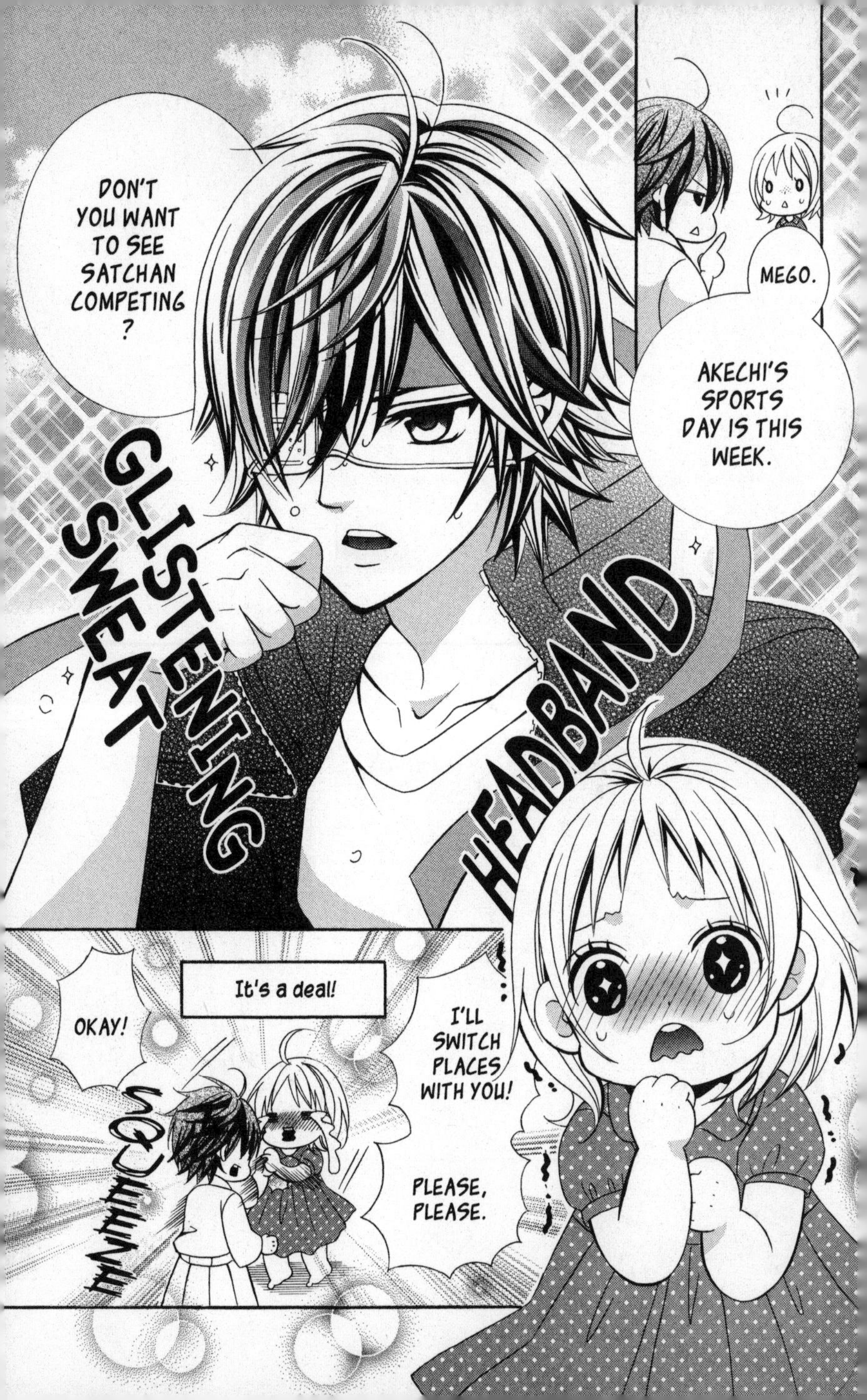
MEGO.
AKECHI'S SPORTS DAY IS THIS WEEK.
DON'T YOU WANT TO SEE SATCHAN COMPETING?
GLISTENING SWEAT
HEADBAND
I'LL SWITCH PLACES WITH YOU!
PLEASE, PLEASE.
It's a deal!
OKAY!
SQUEEEE

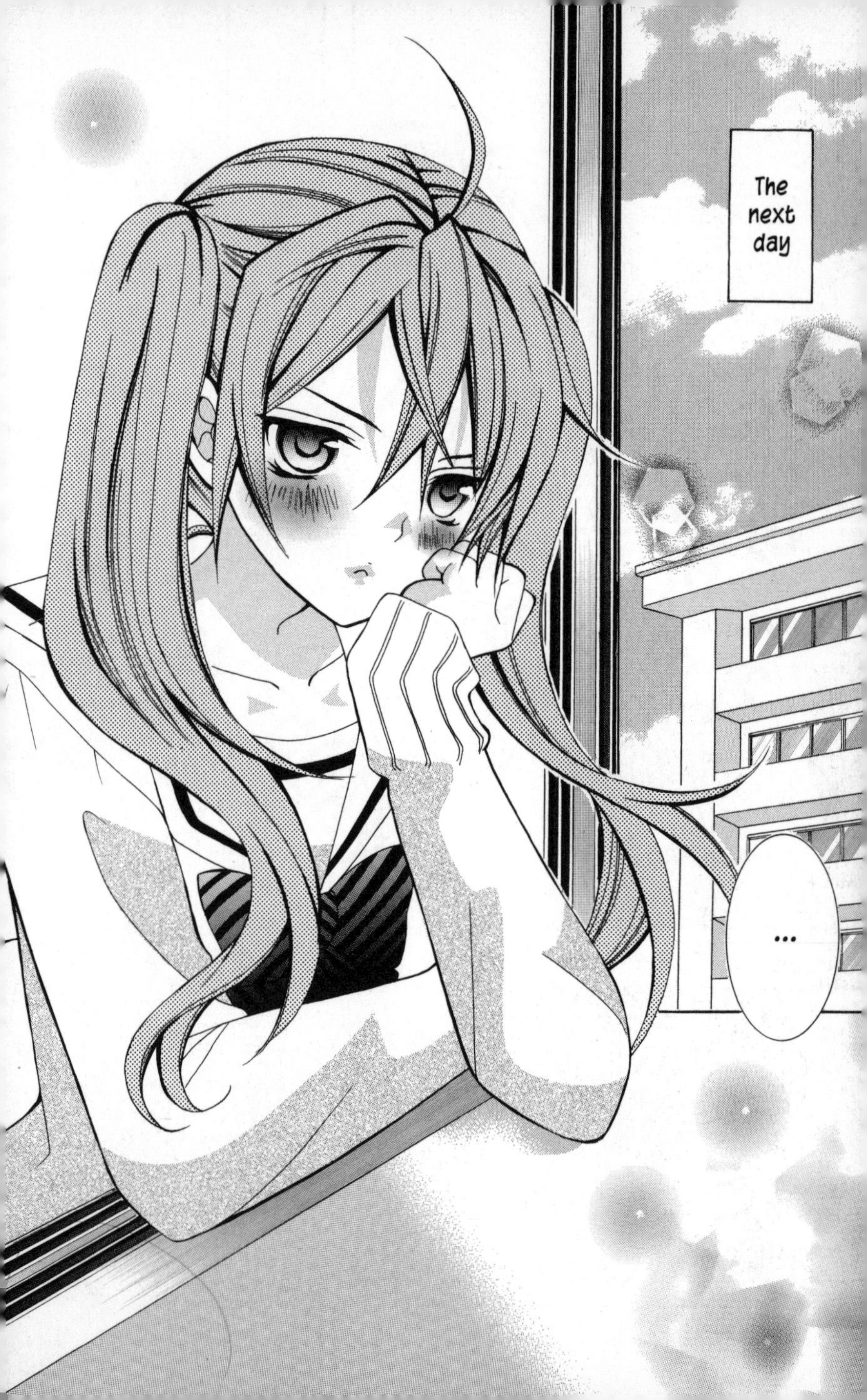
The next day
...

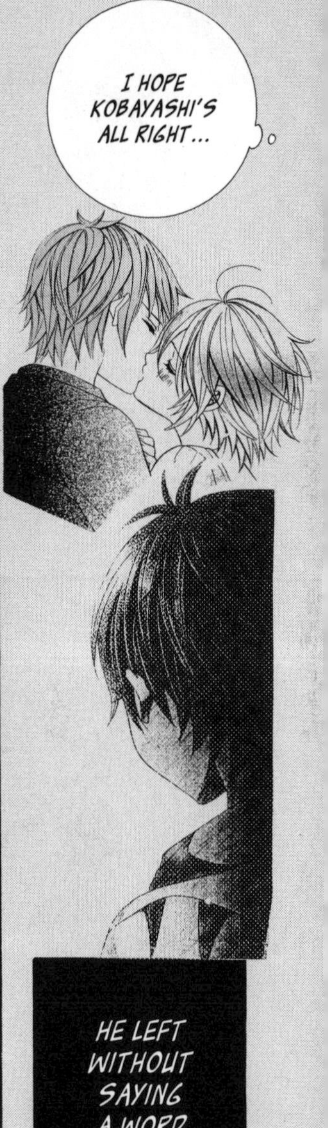
I HOPE KOBAYASHI'S ALL RIGHT...
HE LEFT WITHOUT SAYING A WORD YESTERDAY ...

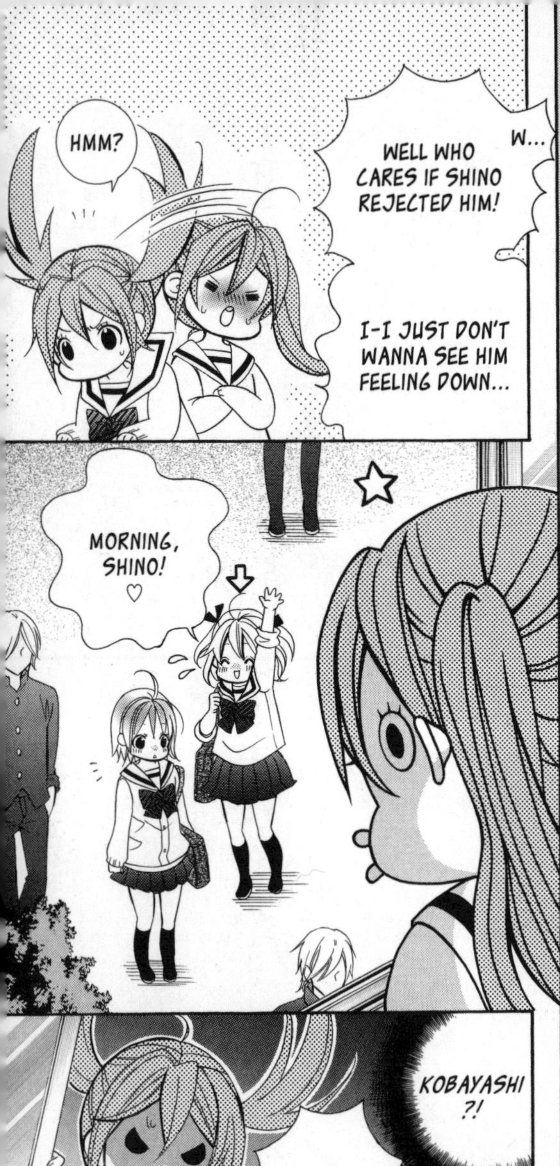
W...
WELL WHO CARES IF SHINO REJECTED HIM!
I-I JUST DON'T WANNA SEE HIM FEELING DOWN...
HMM?
MORNING, SHINO! ♡
KOBAYASHI ?!
HE'S HERE AGAIN?!

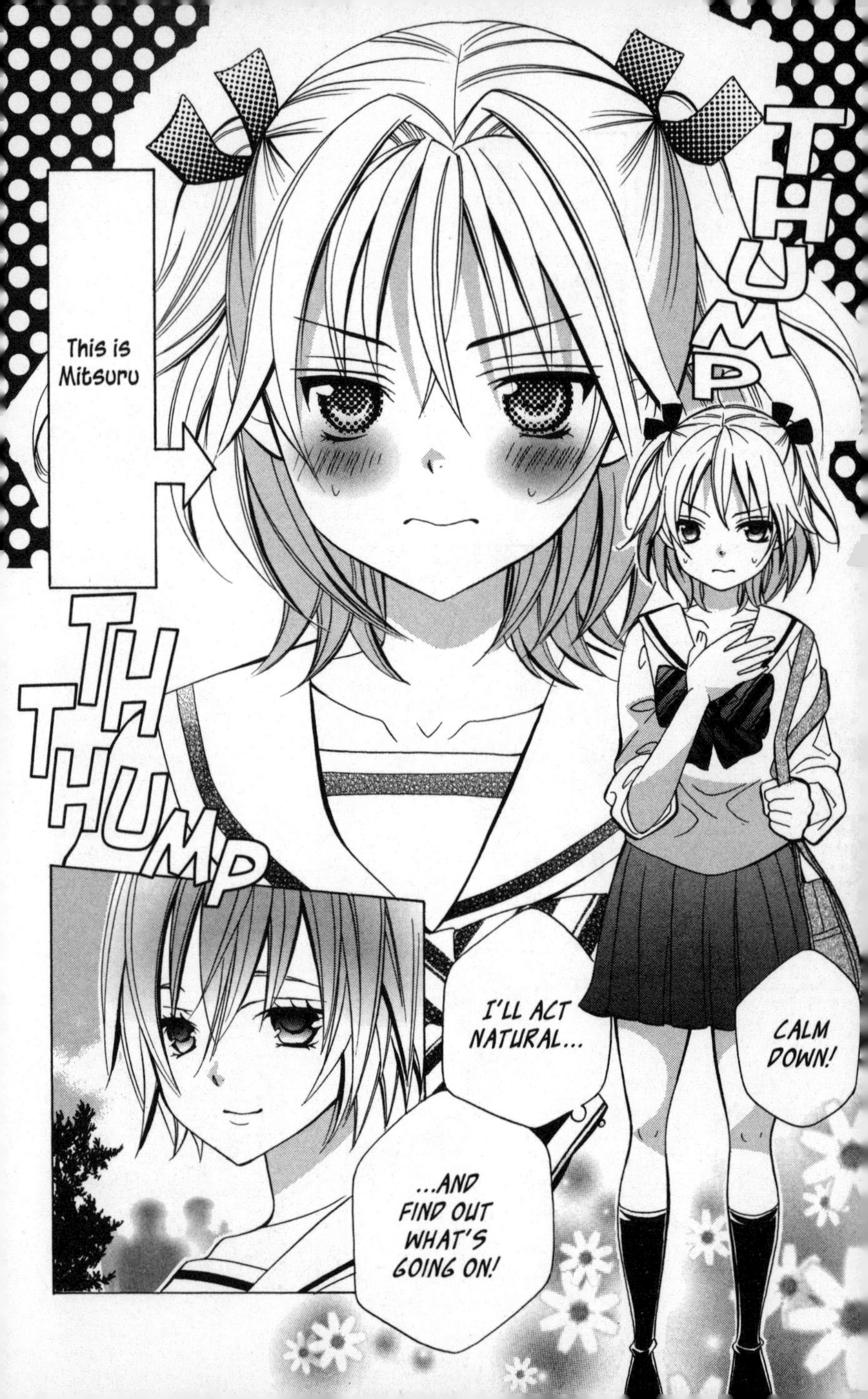
THUMP
This is Mitsuru
TH THUMP
CALM DOWN!
I'LL ACT NATURAL...
...AND FIND OUT WHAT'S GOING ON!

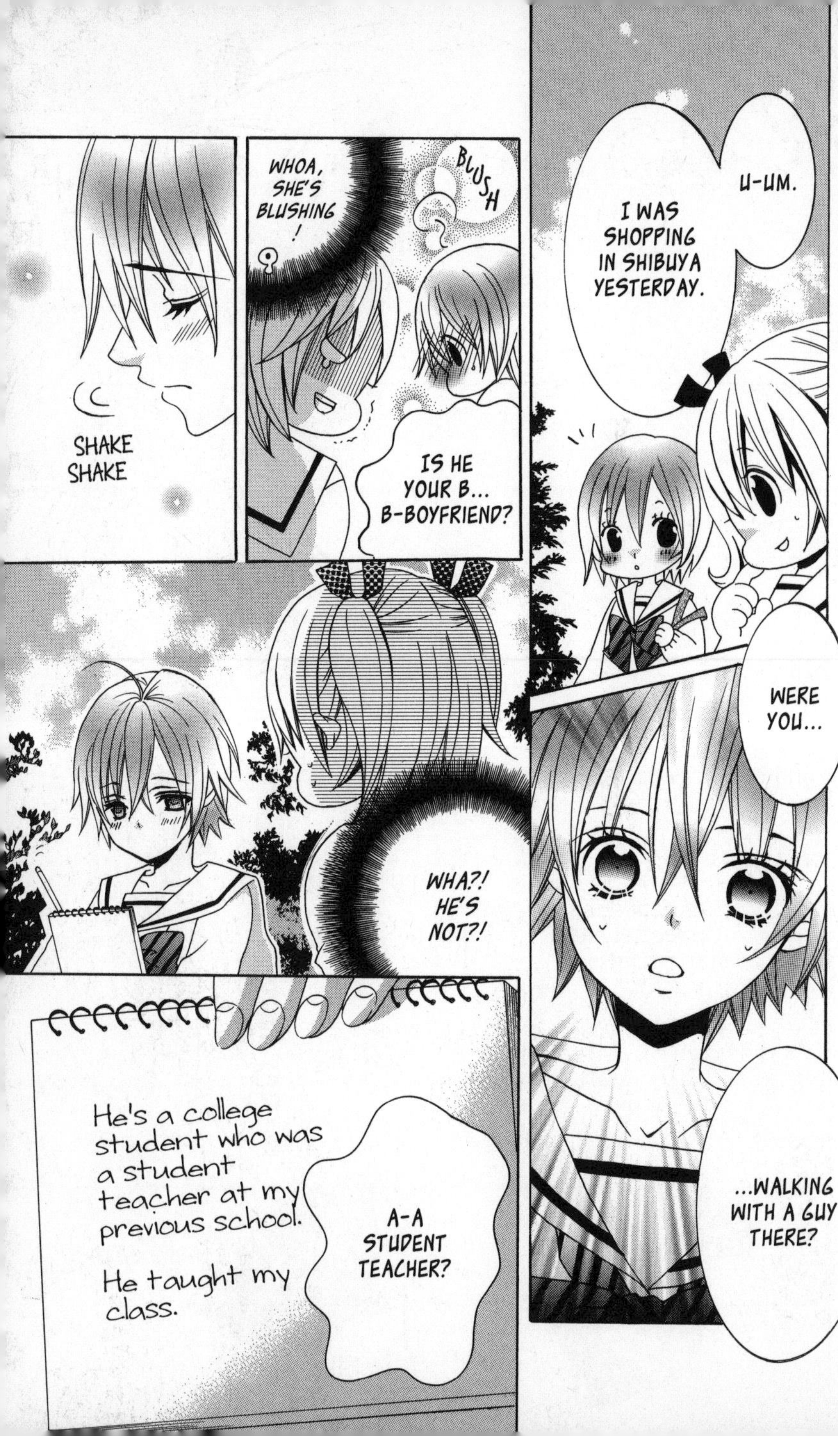
U-UM.
I WAS SHOPPING IN SHIBUYA YESTERDAY.
WERE YOU...
...WALKING WITH A GUY THERE?
BLUSH
WHOA, SHE'S BLUSHING!
IS HE YOUR B... B-BOYFRIEND?
SHAKE SHAKE
WHA?! HE'S NOT?!
A-A STUDENT TEACHER?
He's a college student who was a student teacher at my previous school.
He taught my class.

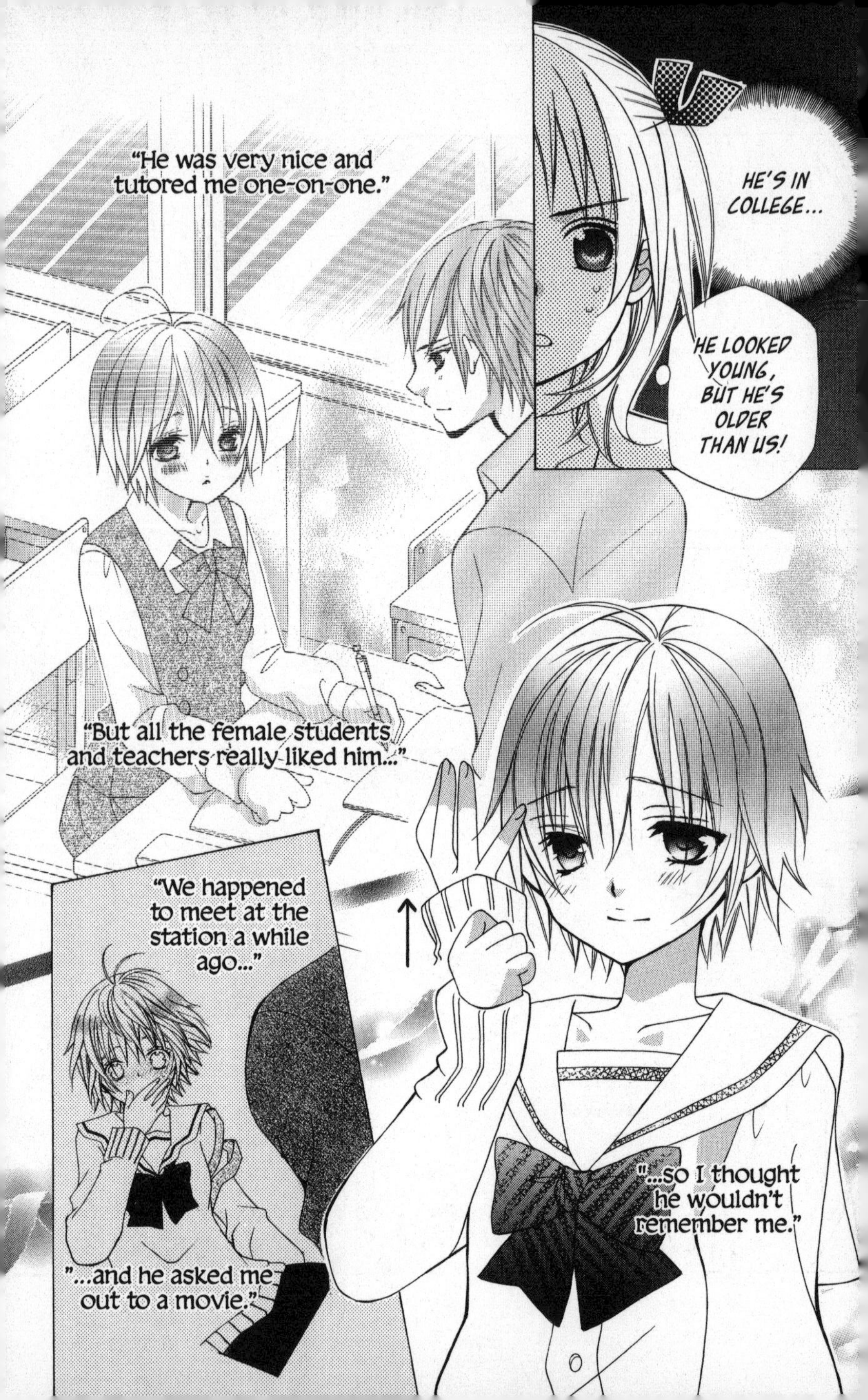
HE'S IN COLLEGE...
HE LOOKED YOUNG, BUT HE'S OLDER THAN US!
"He was very nice and tutored me one-on-one."
"But all the female students and teachers really liked him..."
"...so I thought he wouldn't remember me."
"We happened to meet at the station a while ago..."
"...and he asked me out to a movie."

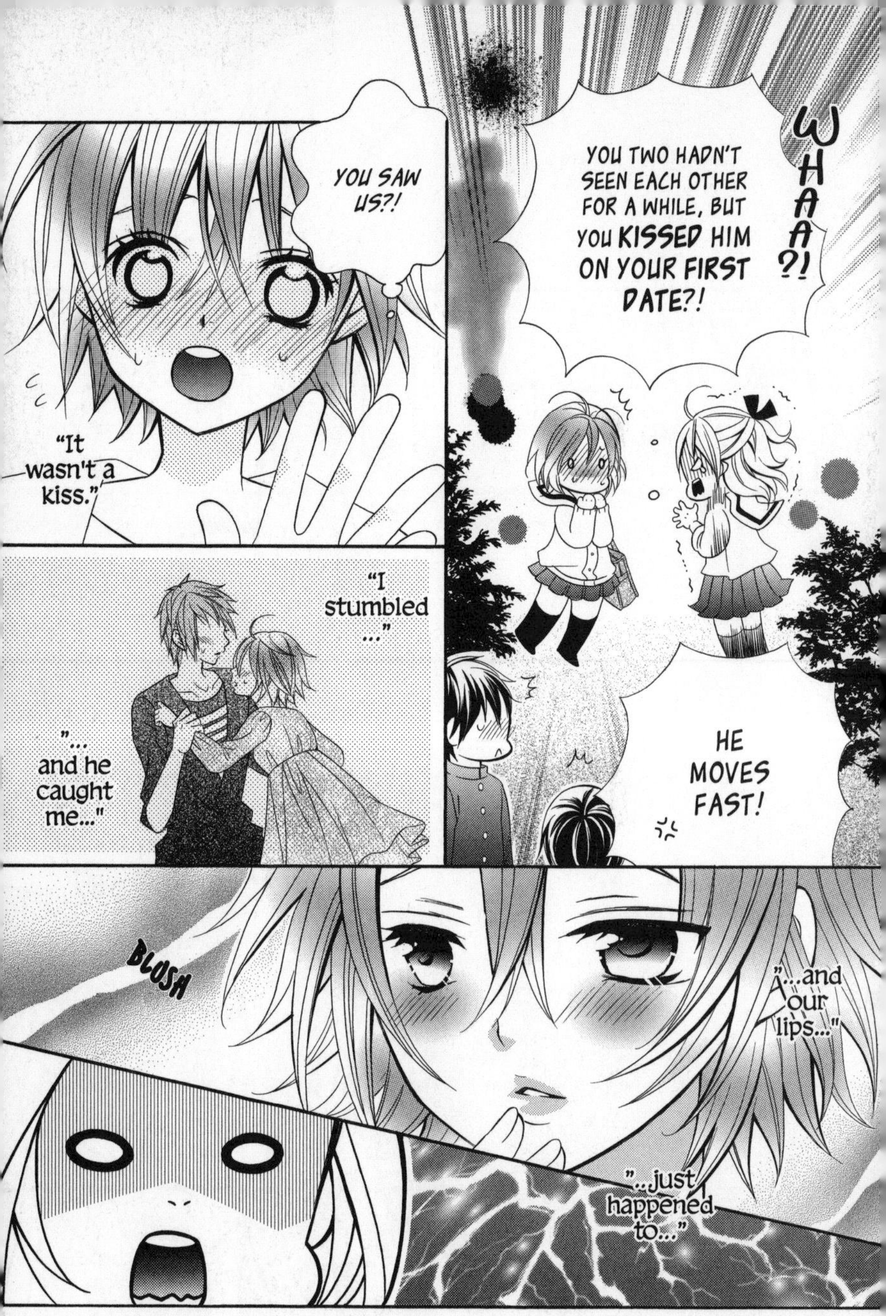
WHAA?!
YOU TWO HADN'T SEEN EACH OTHER FOR A WHILE, BUT YOU KISSED HIM ON YOUR FIRST DATE?!
HE MOVES FAST!
YOU SAW US?!
"It wasn't a kiss."
"I stumbled..."
"...and he caught me..."
BLUSH
"...and our lips..."
"...just happened to..."

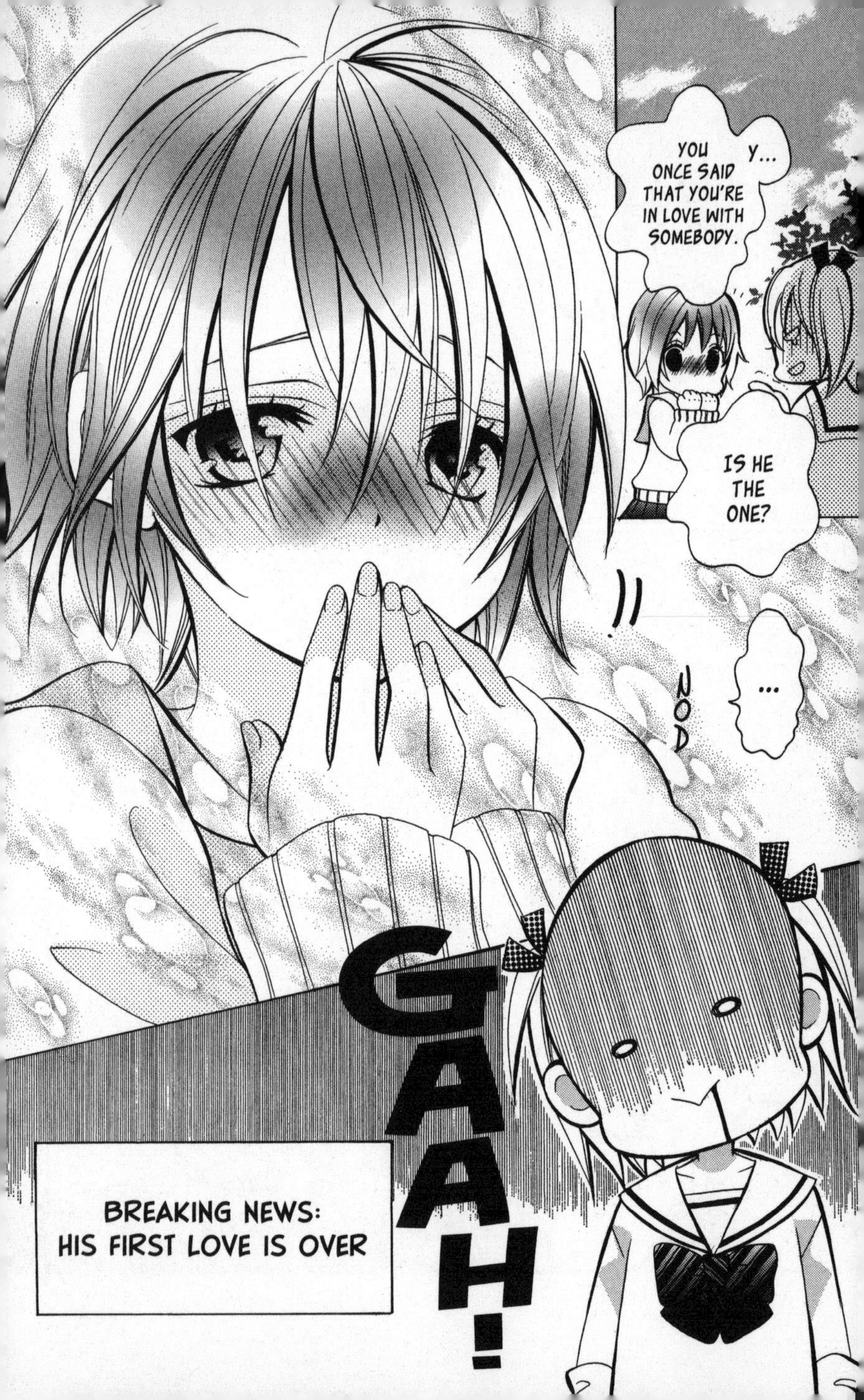
YOU Y... ONCE SAID THAT YOU'RE IN LOVE WITH SOMEBODY.
IS HE THE ONE?
!!
...
NOD
GAAH!
BREAKING NEWS: HIS FIRST LOVE IS OVER

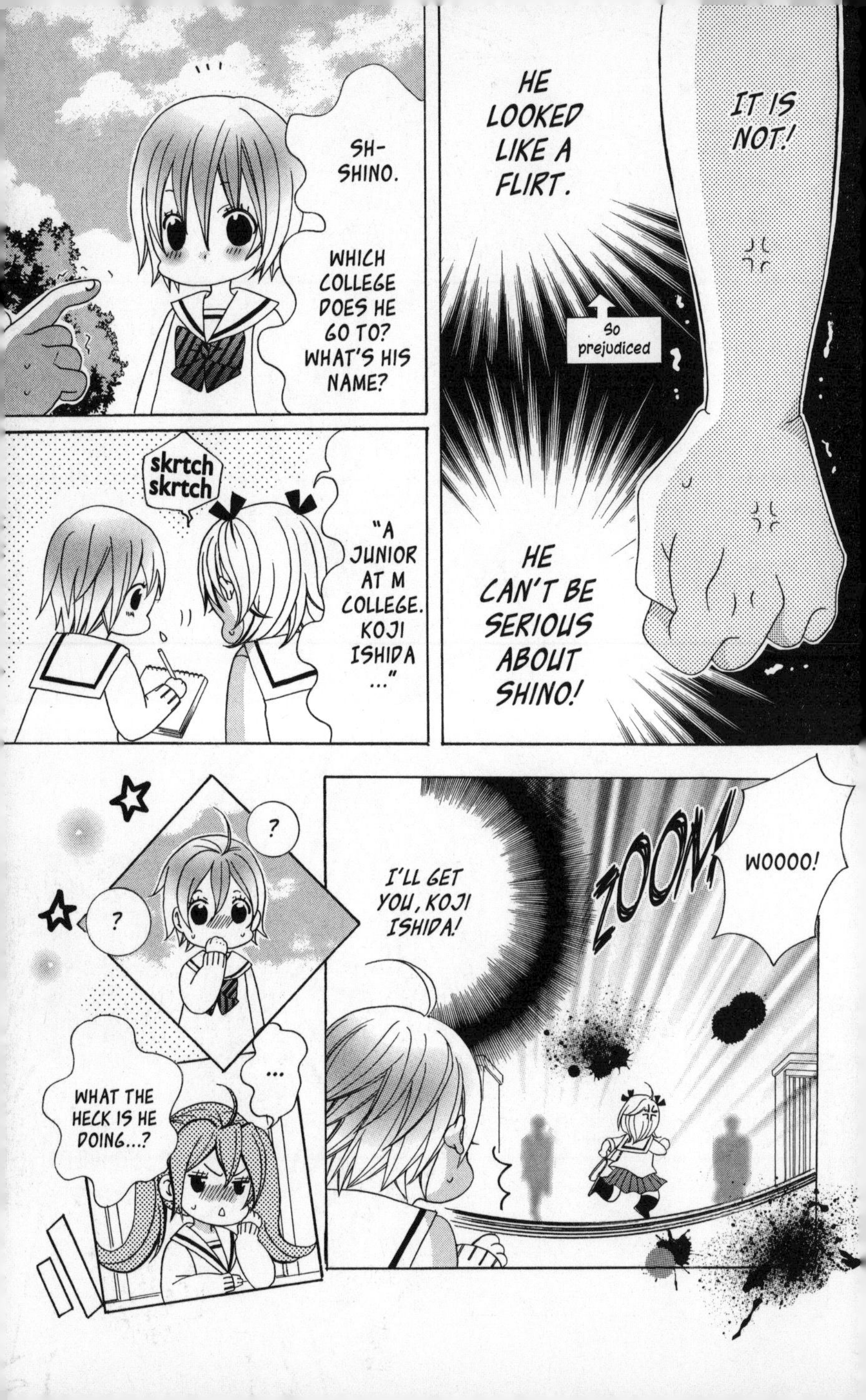
IT IS NOT!
HE LOOKED LIKE A FLIRT.
So prejudiced
HE CAN'T BE SERIOUS ABOUT SHINO!
SH-SHINO.
WHICH COLLEGE DOES HE GO TO? WHAT'S HIS NAME?
"A JUNIOR AT M COLLEGE. KOJI ISHIDA ..."
skrtch skrtch
WOOOO!
ZOOM
I'LL GET YOU, KOJI ISHIDA!
?
?
...
WHAT THE HECK IS HE DOING...?

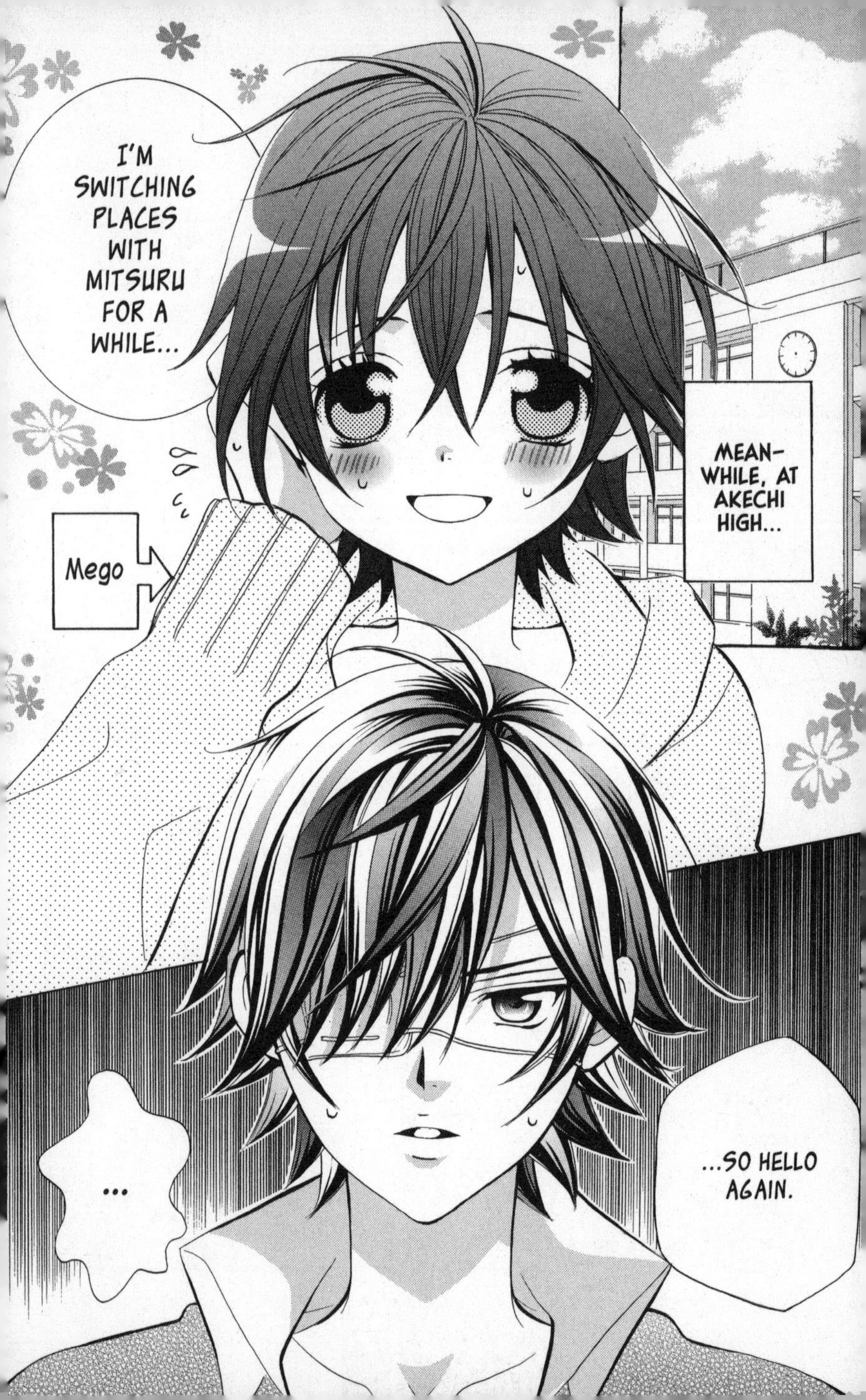
MEAN-WHILE, AT AKECHI HIGH...
I'M SWITCHING PLACES WITH MITSURU FOR A WHILE...
Mego
...SO HELLO AGAIN.
...

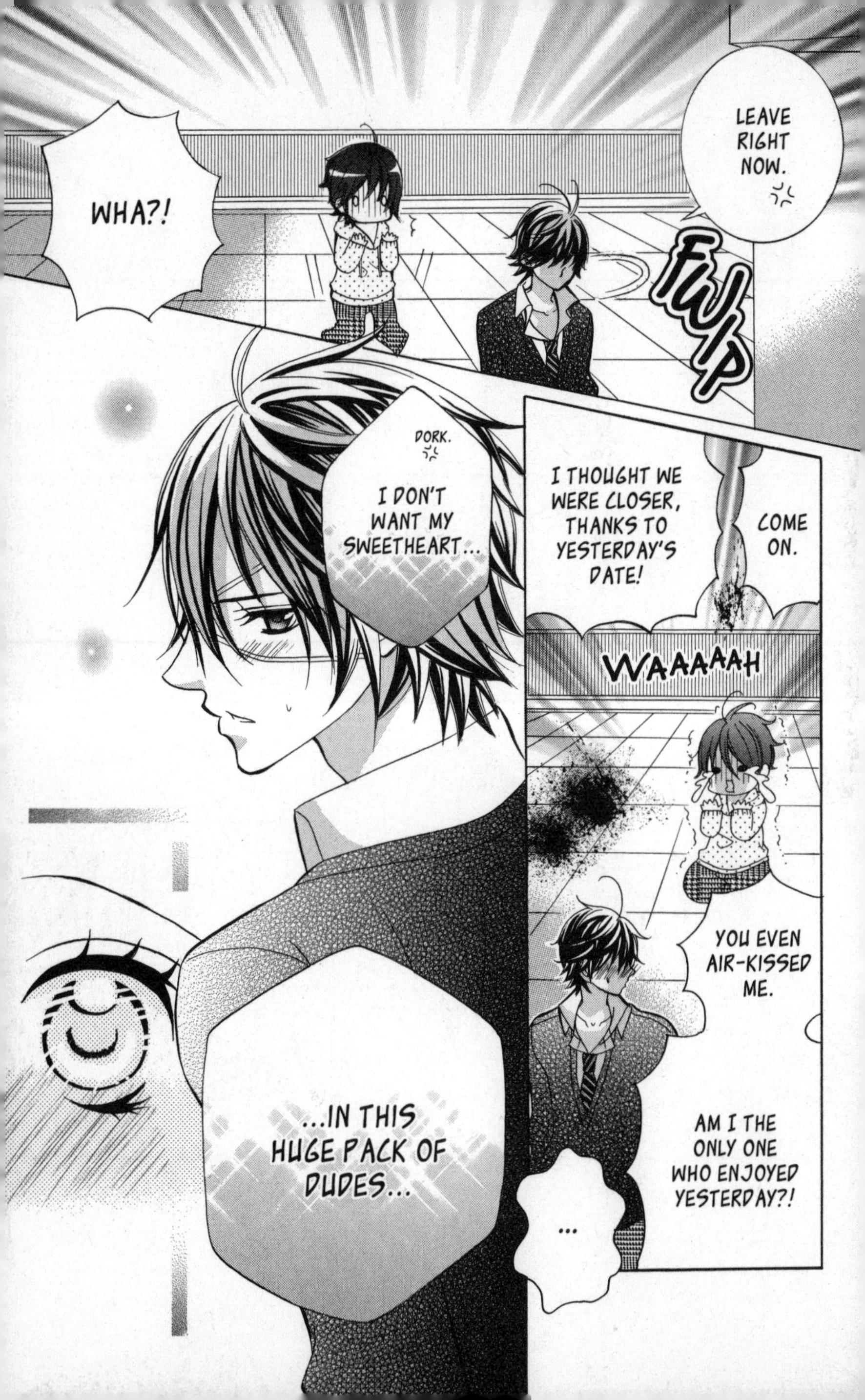
LEAVE RIGHT NOW.
FWIP
WHA?!
COME ON.
I THOUGHT WE WERE CLOSER, THANKS TO YESTERDAY'S DATE!
WAAAAAH
YOU EVEN AIR-KISSED ME.
AM I THE ONLY ONE WHO ENJOYED YESTERDAY?!
...
DORK.
I DON'T WANT MY SWEETHEART...
...IN THIS HUGE PACK OF DUDES...

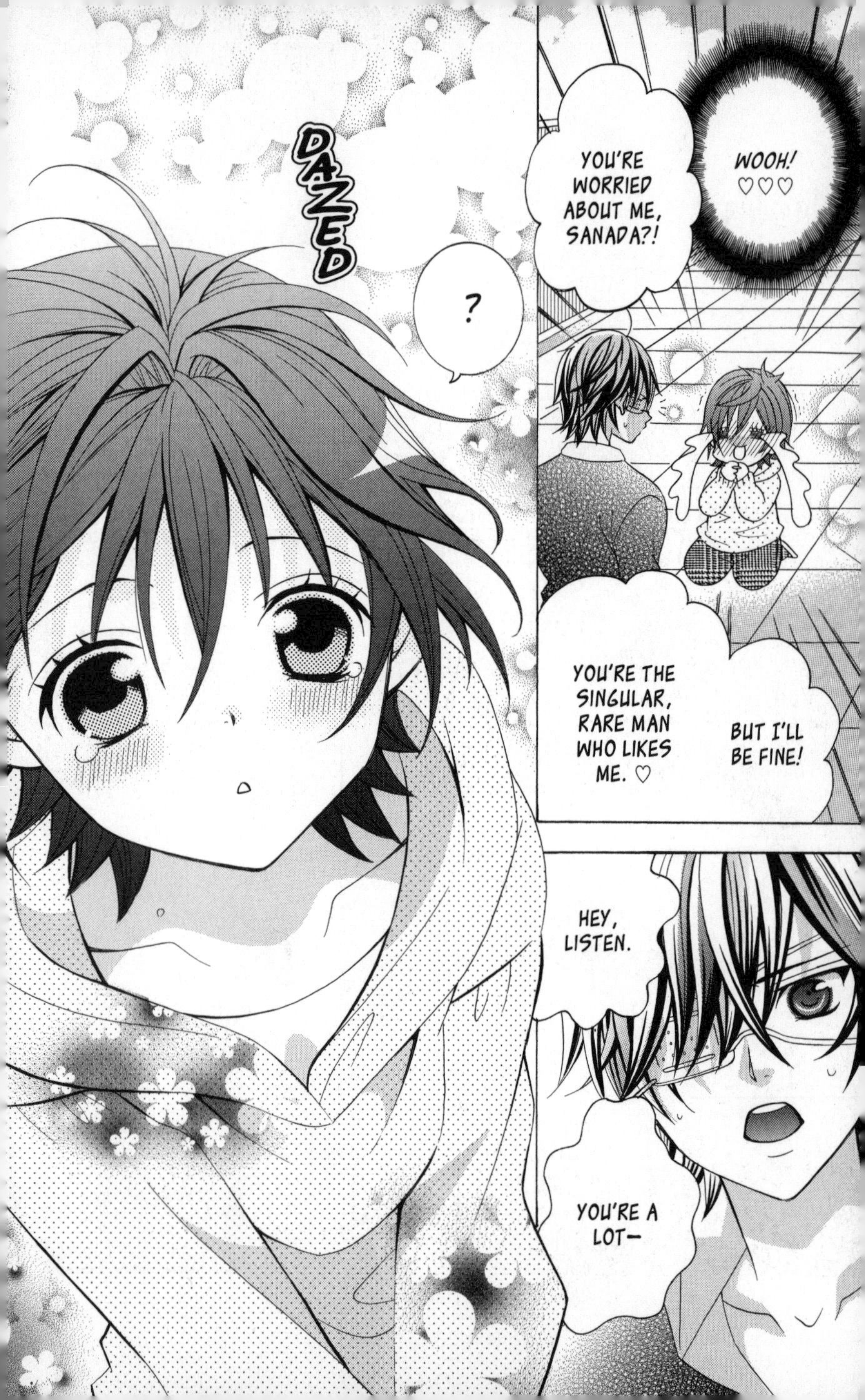
WOOH! ♡♡♡
YOU'RE WORRIED ABOUT ME, SANADA?!
BUT I'LL BE FINE!
YOU'RE THE SINGULAR, RARE MAN WHO LIKES ME. ♡
HEY, LISTEN.
YOU'RE A LOT—
DAZED
?

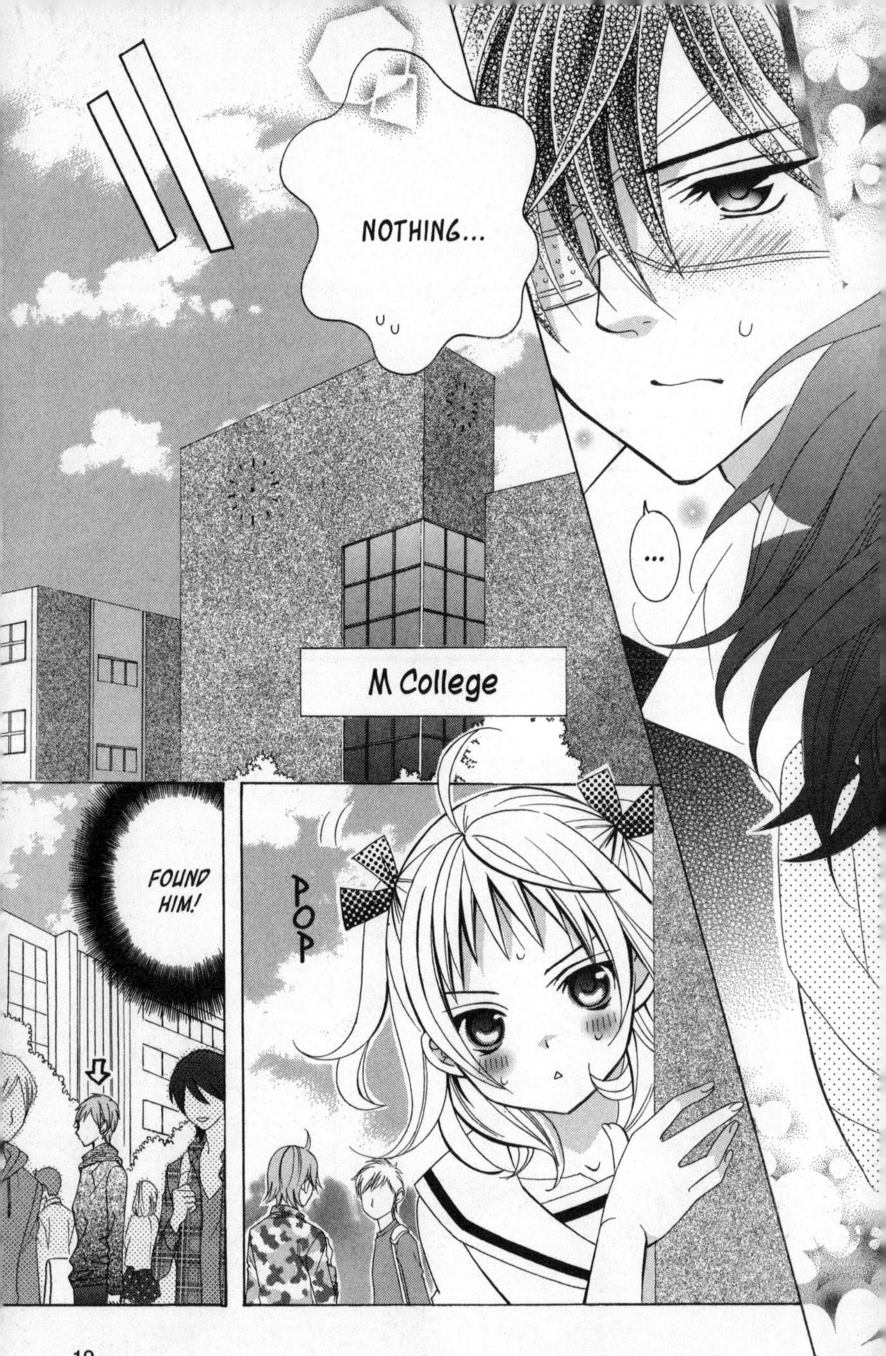
NOTHING...
...
M College
POP
FOUND HIM!

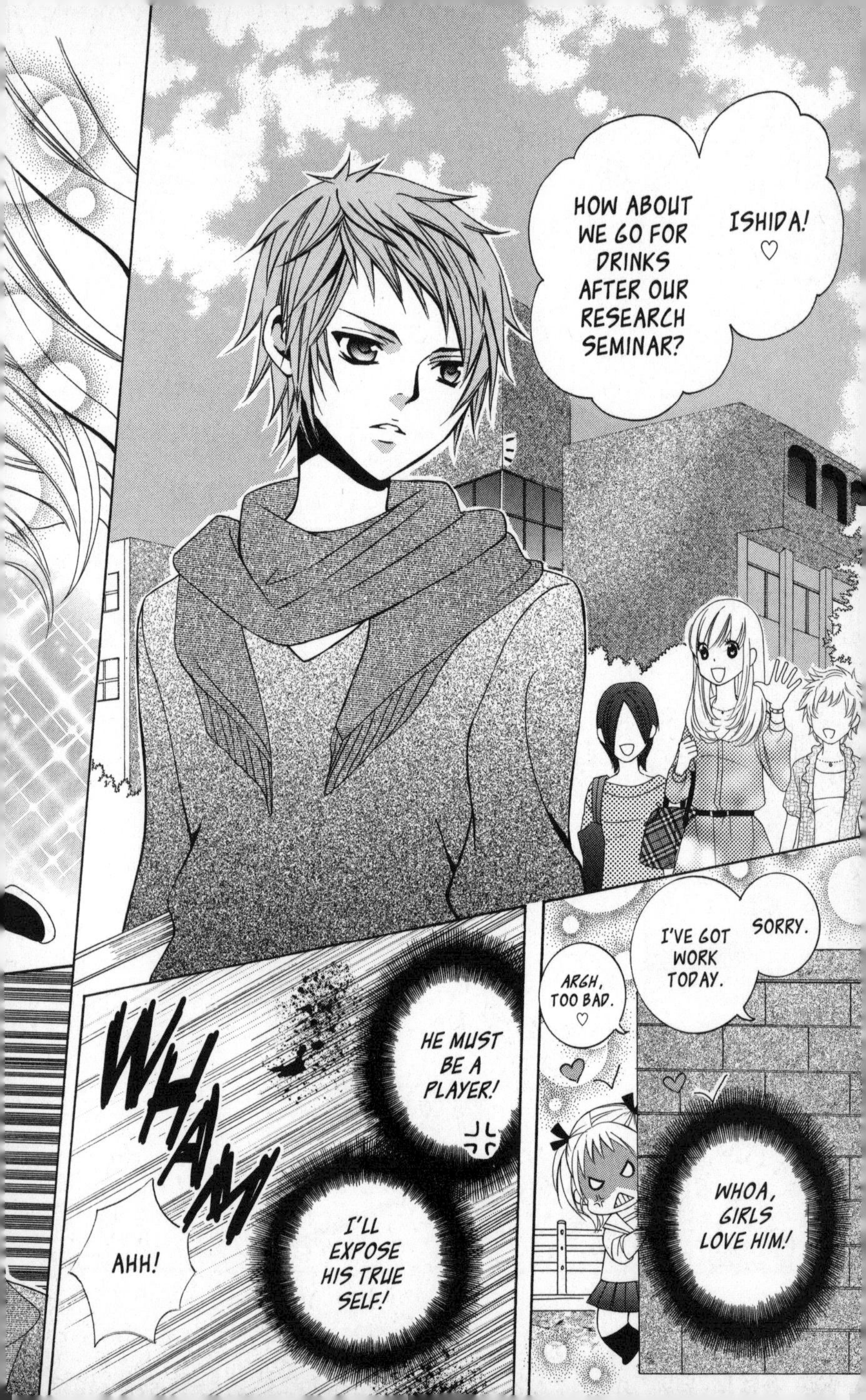
ISHIDA! ♡
HOW ABOUT WE GO FOR DRINKS AFTER OUR RESEARCH SEMINAR?
SORRY.
I'VE GOT WORK TODAY.
ARGH, TOO BAD. ♡
WHOA, GIRLS LOVE HIM!
HE MUST BE A PLAYER!
I'LL EXPOSE HIS TRUE SELF!
WHAM
AHH!

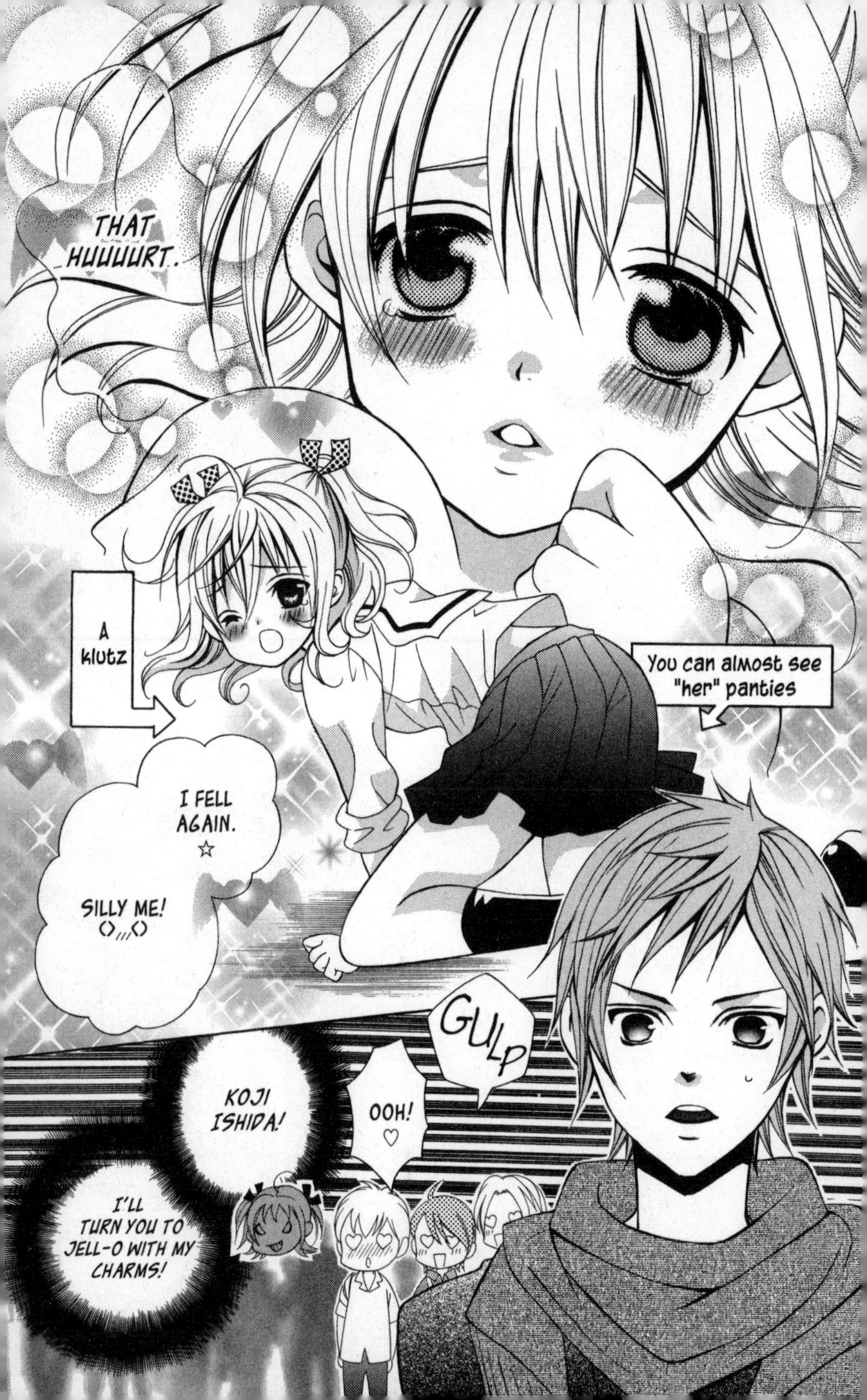
THAT HUUUURT..
You can almost see "her" panties
A klutz
I FELL AGAIN. ☆
SILLY ME!
GULP
OOH! ♡
KOJI ISHIDA!
I'LL TURN YOU TO JELL-O WITH MY CHARMS!

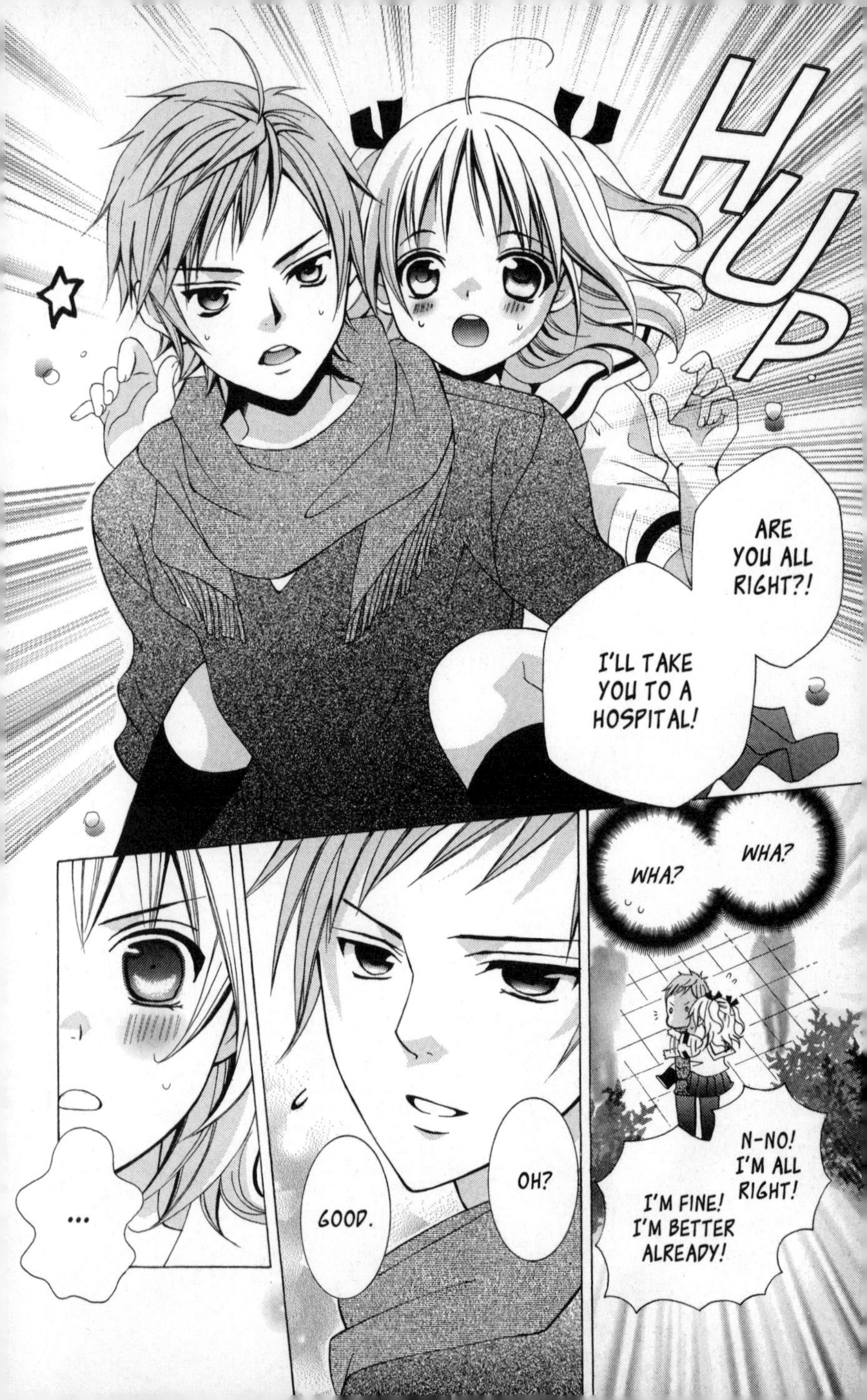
HUP
ARE YOU ALL RIGHT?!
I'LL TAKE YOU TO A HOSPITAL!
WHA?
WHA?
N-NO! I'M ALL RIGHT!
I'M FINE! I'M BETTER ALREADY!
OH?
GOOD.
...

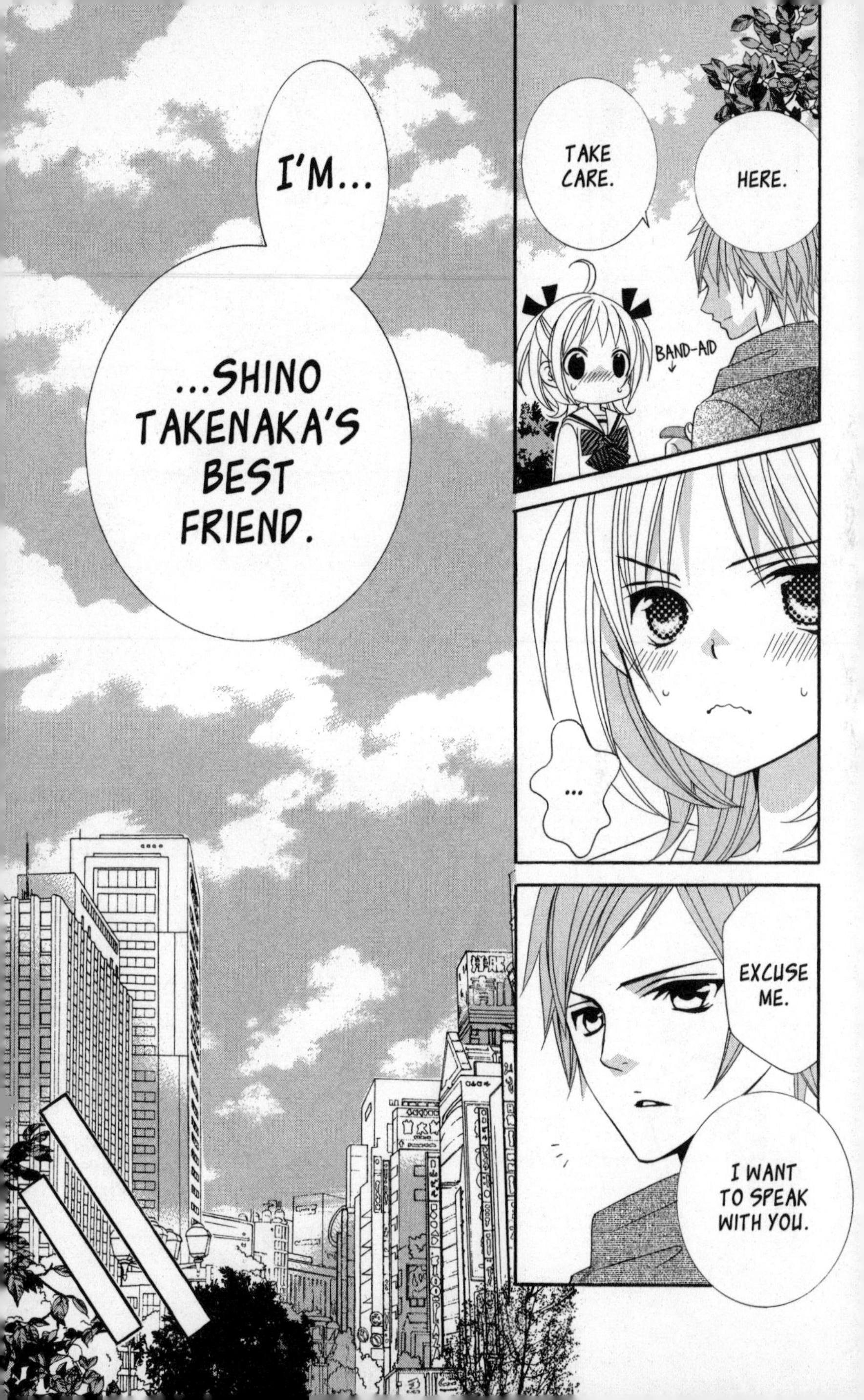
HERE.
TAKE CARE.
BAND-AID
...
EXCUSE ME.
I WANT TO SPEAK WITH YOU.
I'M...
...SHINO TAKENAKA'S BEST FRIEND.

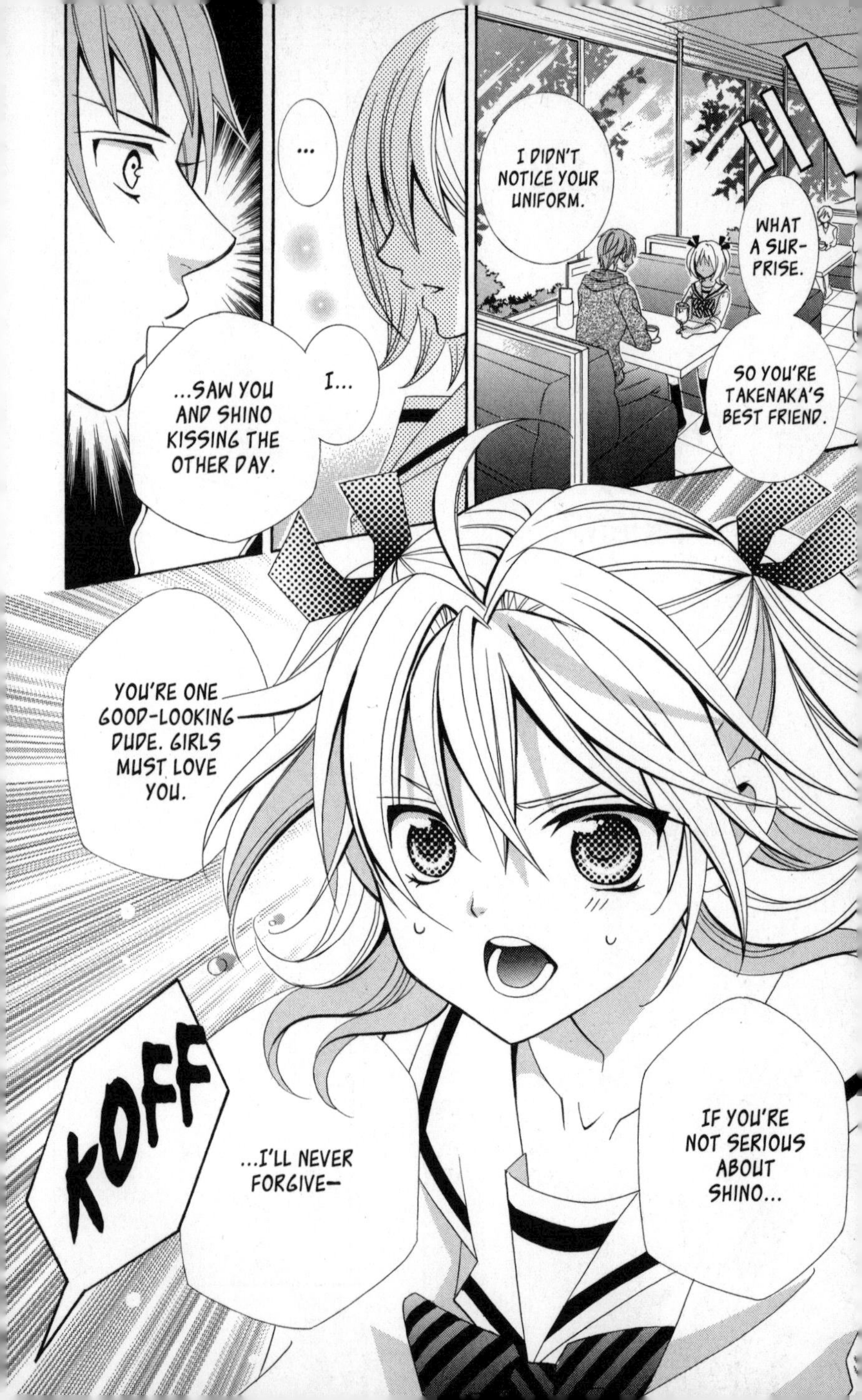
I DIDN'T NOTICE YOUR UNIFORM.
WHAT A SUR-PRISE.
SO YOU'RE TAKENAKA'S BEST FRIEND.
...
I...
...SAW YOU AND SHINO KISSING THE OTHER DAY.
YOU'RE ONE GOOD-LOOKING DUDE. GIRLS MUST LOVE YOU.
IF YOU'RE NOT SERIOUS ABOUT SHINO...
...I'LL NEVER FORGIVE—
KOFF

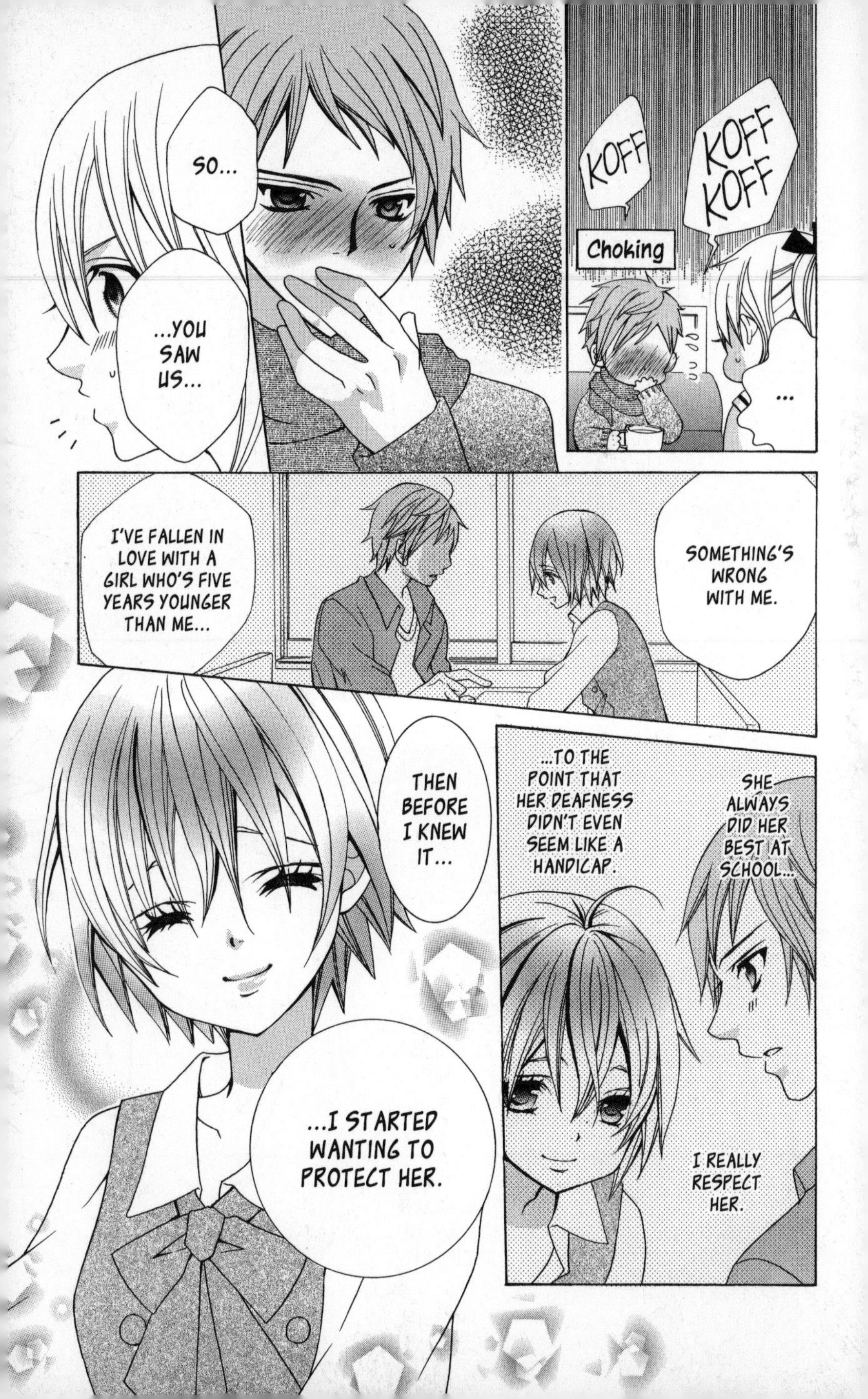
KOFF KOFF
KOFF
Choking
...
SO...
...YOU SAW US...
SOMETHING'S WRONG WITH ME.
I'VE FALLEN IN LOVE WITH A GIRL WHO'S FIVE YEARS YOUNGER THAN ME...
SHE ALWAYS DID HER BEST AT SCHOOL...
...TO THE POINT THAT HER DEAFNESS DIDN'T EVEN SEEM LIKE A HANDICAP.
I REALLY RESPECT HER.
THEN BEFORE I KNEW IT...
...I STARTED WANTING TO PROTECT HER.

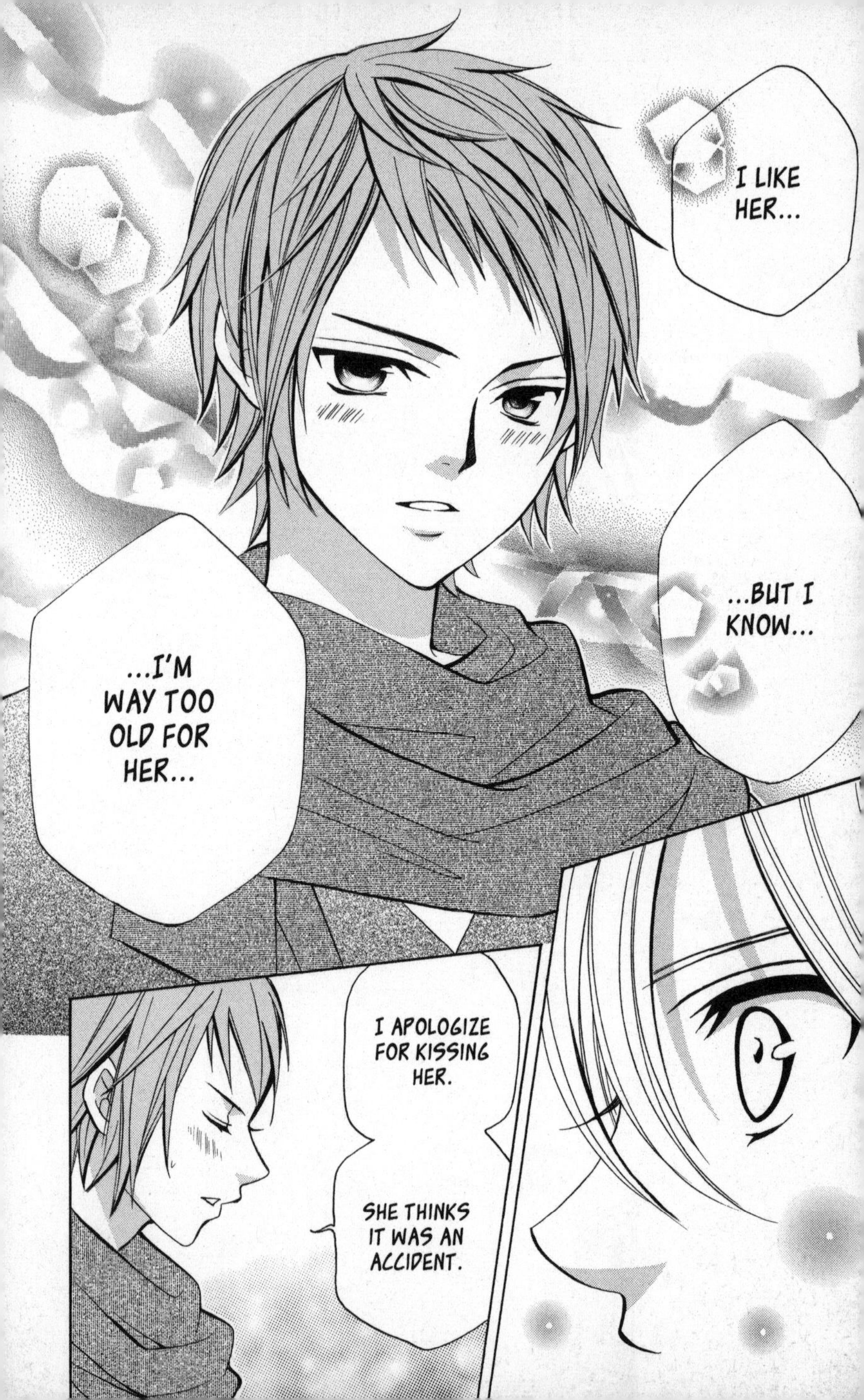
I LIKE HER...
...BUT I KNOW...
...I'M WAY TOO OLD FOR HER...
I APOLOGIZE FOR KISSING HER.
SHE THINKS IT WAS AN ACCIDENT.

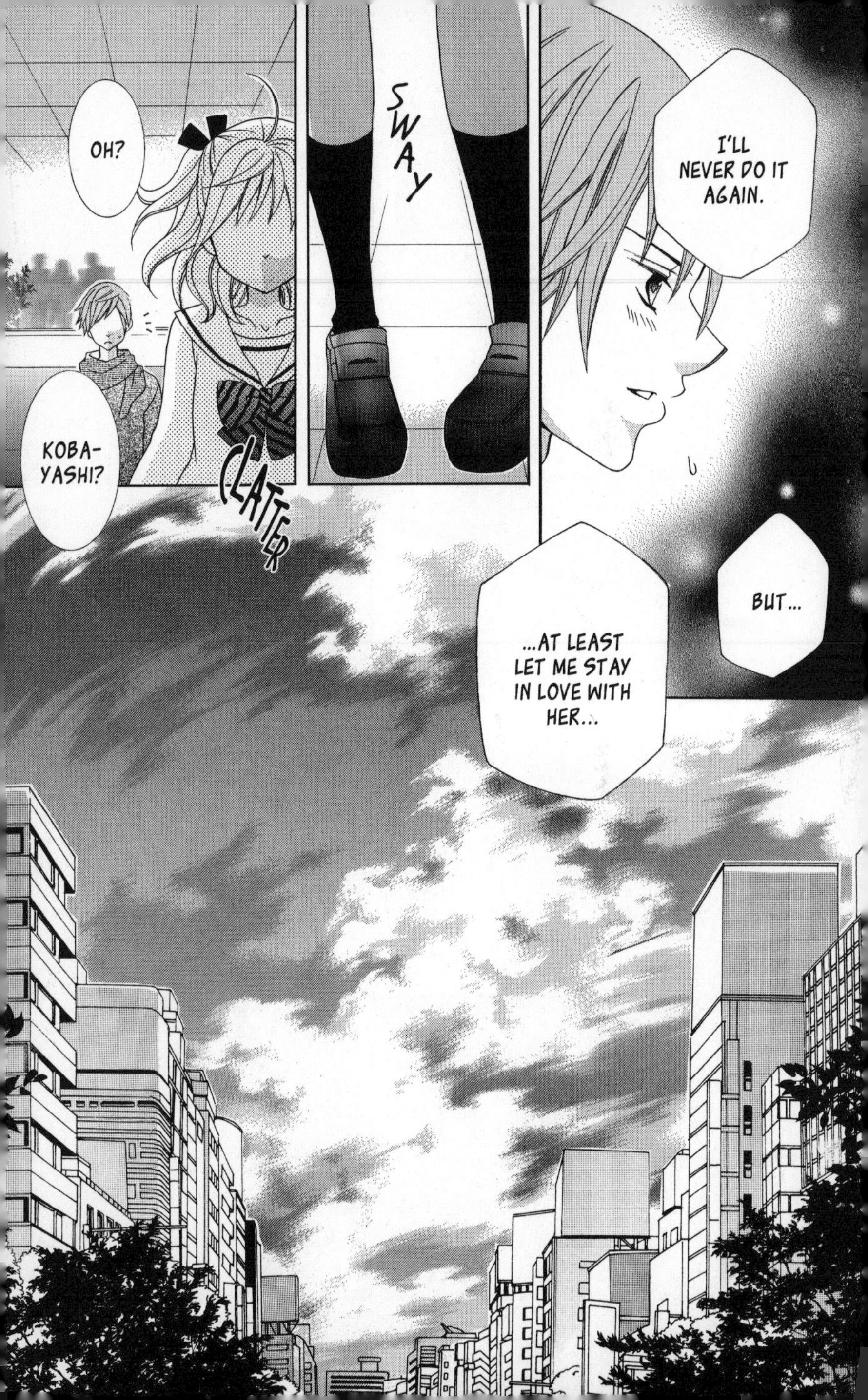
I'LL NEVER DO IT AGAIN.
BUT...
...AT LEAST LET ME STAY IN LOVE WITH HER...
SWAY
OH?
KOBA-YASHI?
CLATTER

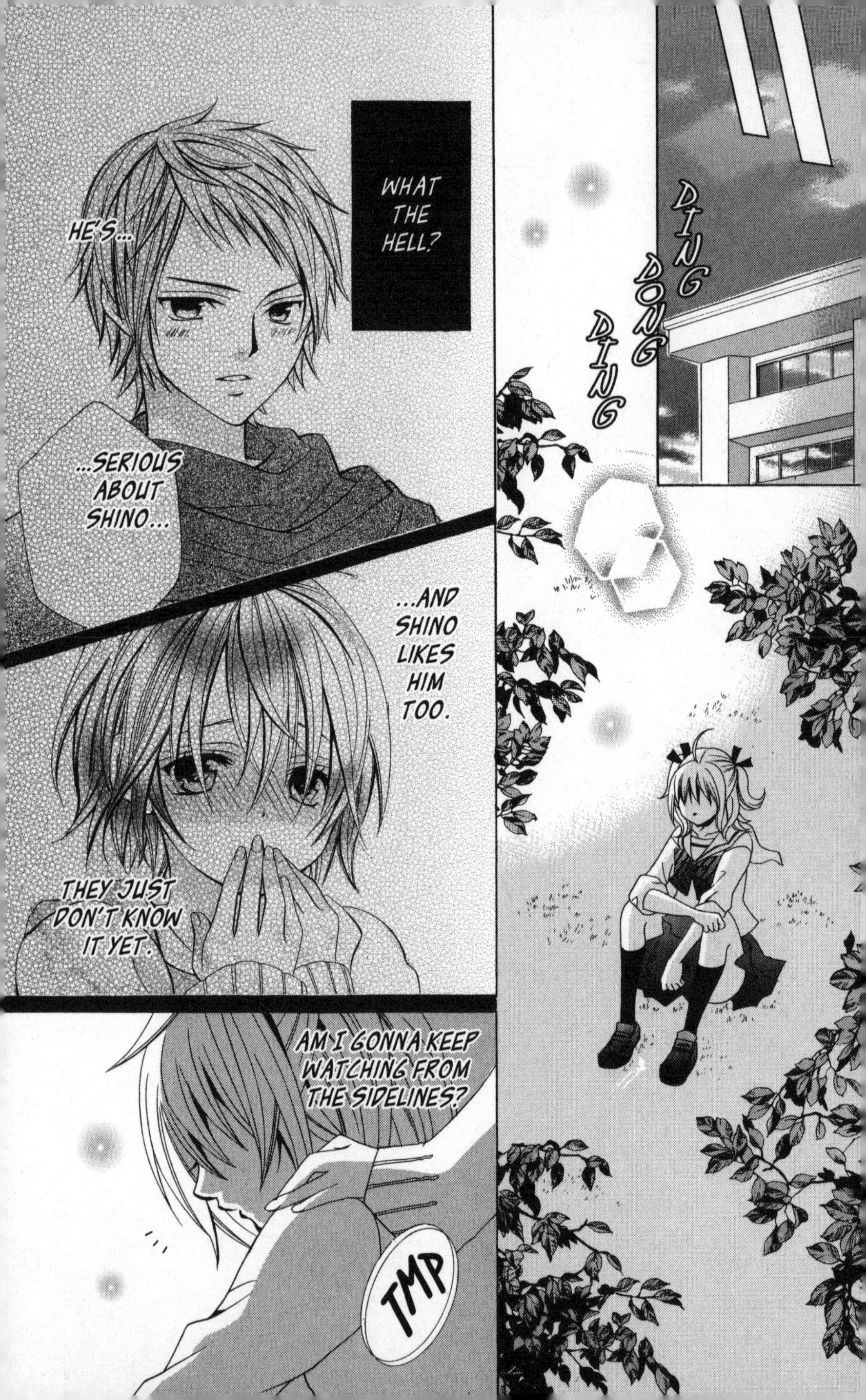
DING DONG DING
WHAT THE HELL?
HE'S...
...SERIOUS ABOUT SHINO...
...AND SHINO LIKES HIM TOO.
THEY JUST DON'T KNOW IT YET.
AM I GONNA KEEP WATCHING FROM THE SIDELINES?
...
TMP

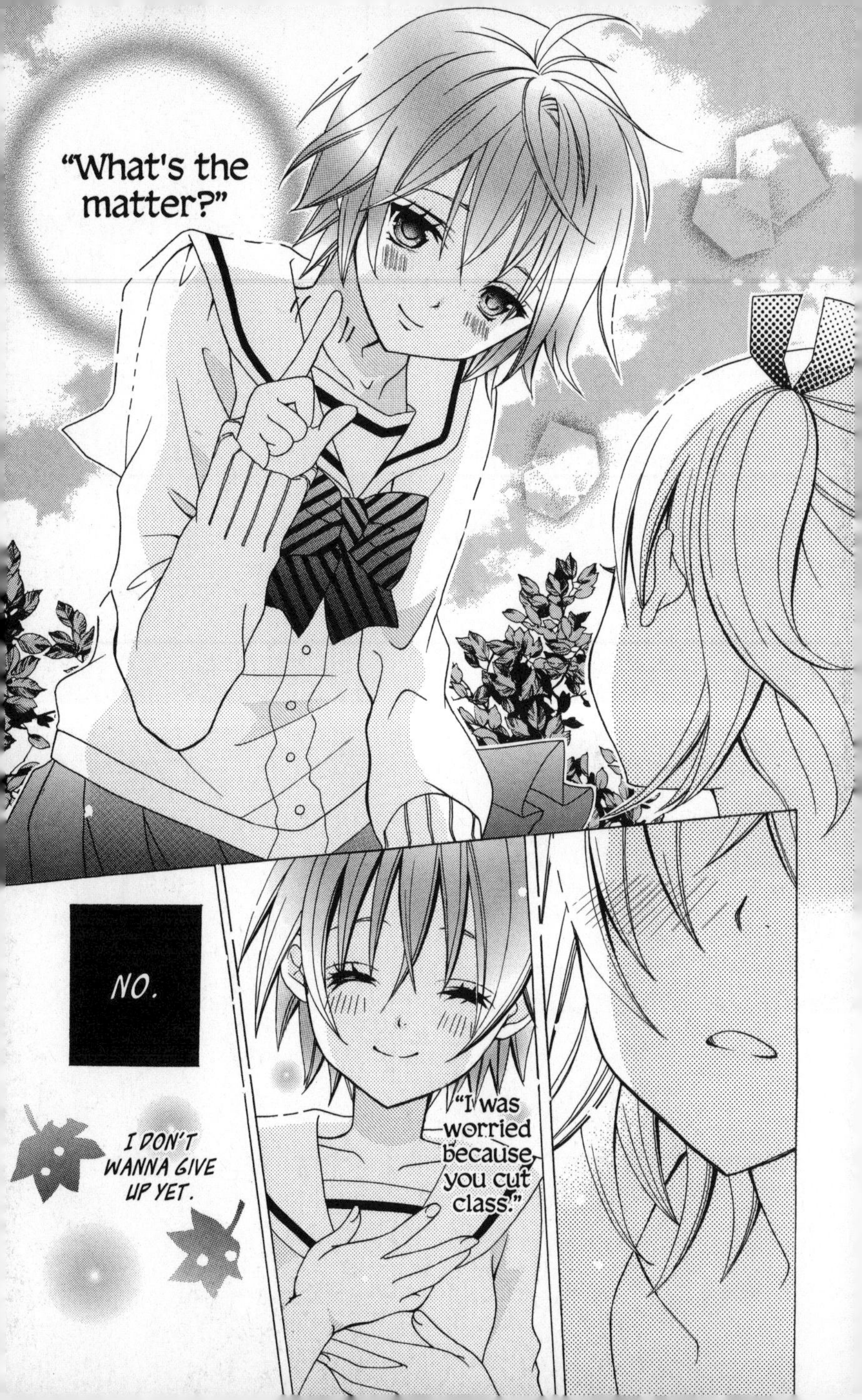
"What's the matter?"
"I was worried because you cut class."
NO.
I DON'T WANNA GIVE UP YET.

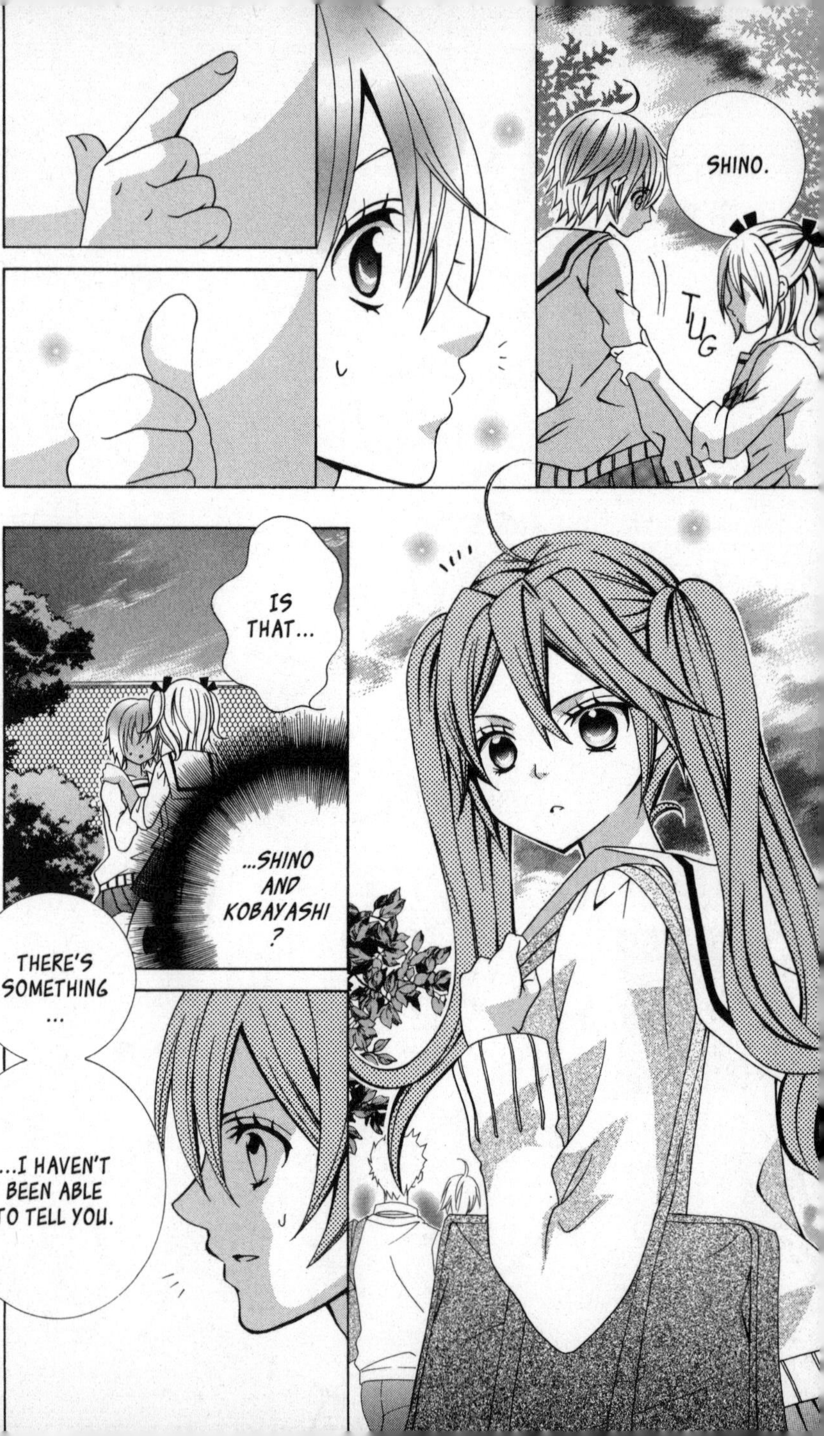
SHINO.
TUG
IS THAT...
...SHINO AND KOBAYASHI?
THERE'S SOMETHING...
...I HAVEN'T BEEN ABLE TO TELL YOU.

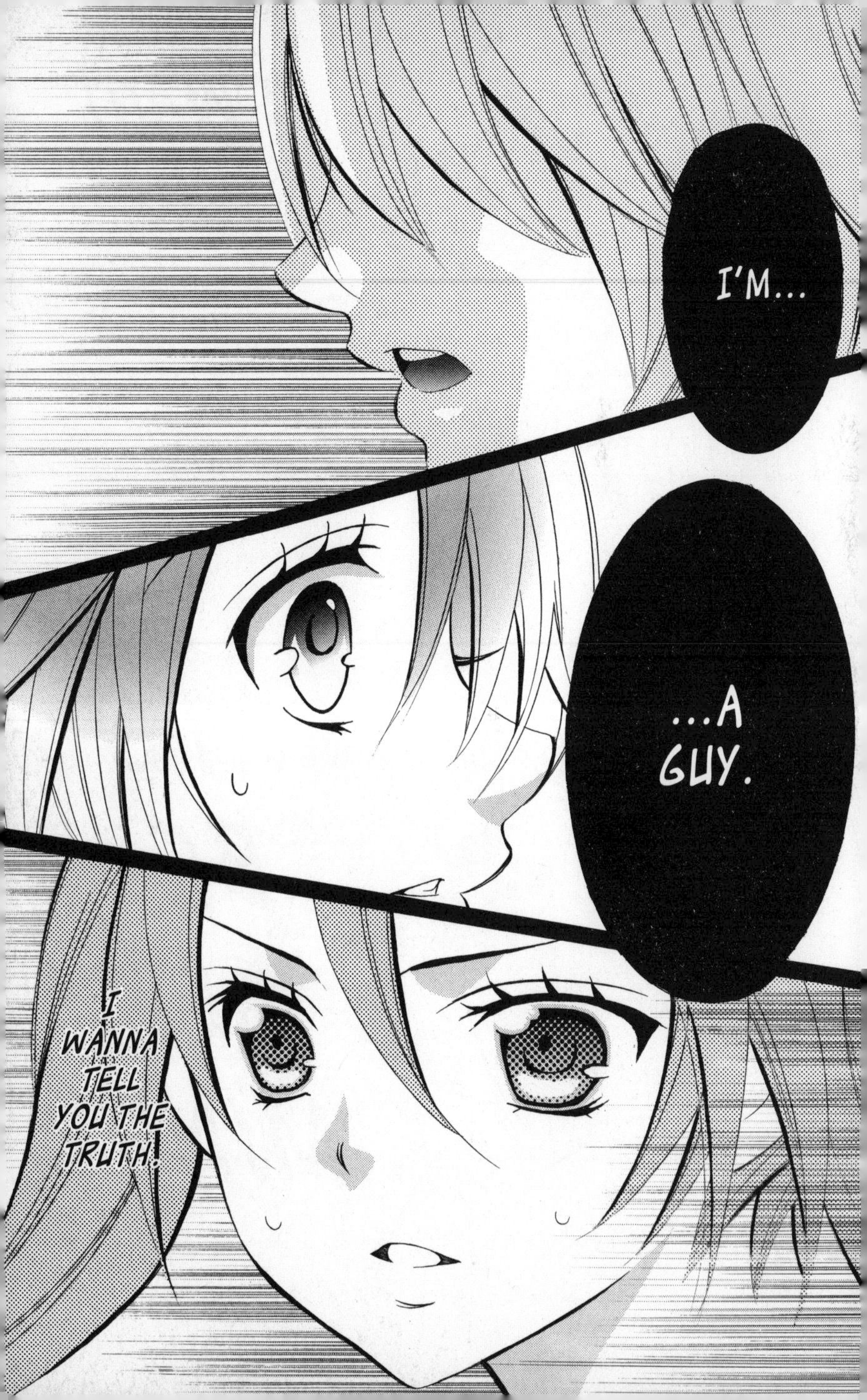
I'M...
...A GUY.
I WANNA TELL YOU THE TRUTH!

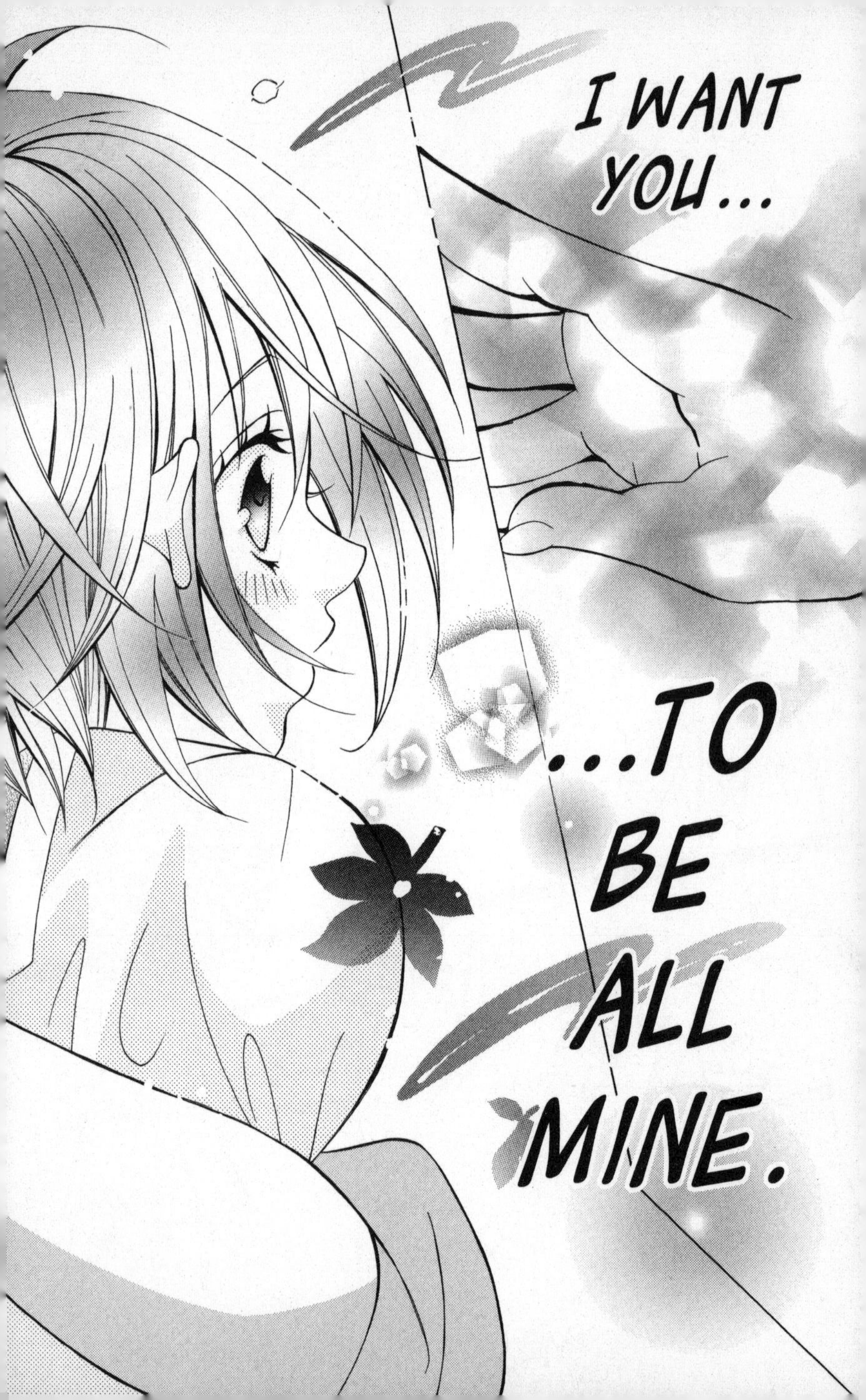
I WANT YOU...
...TO BE ALL MINE.

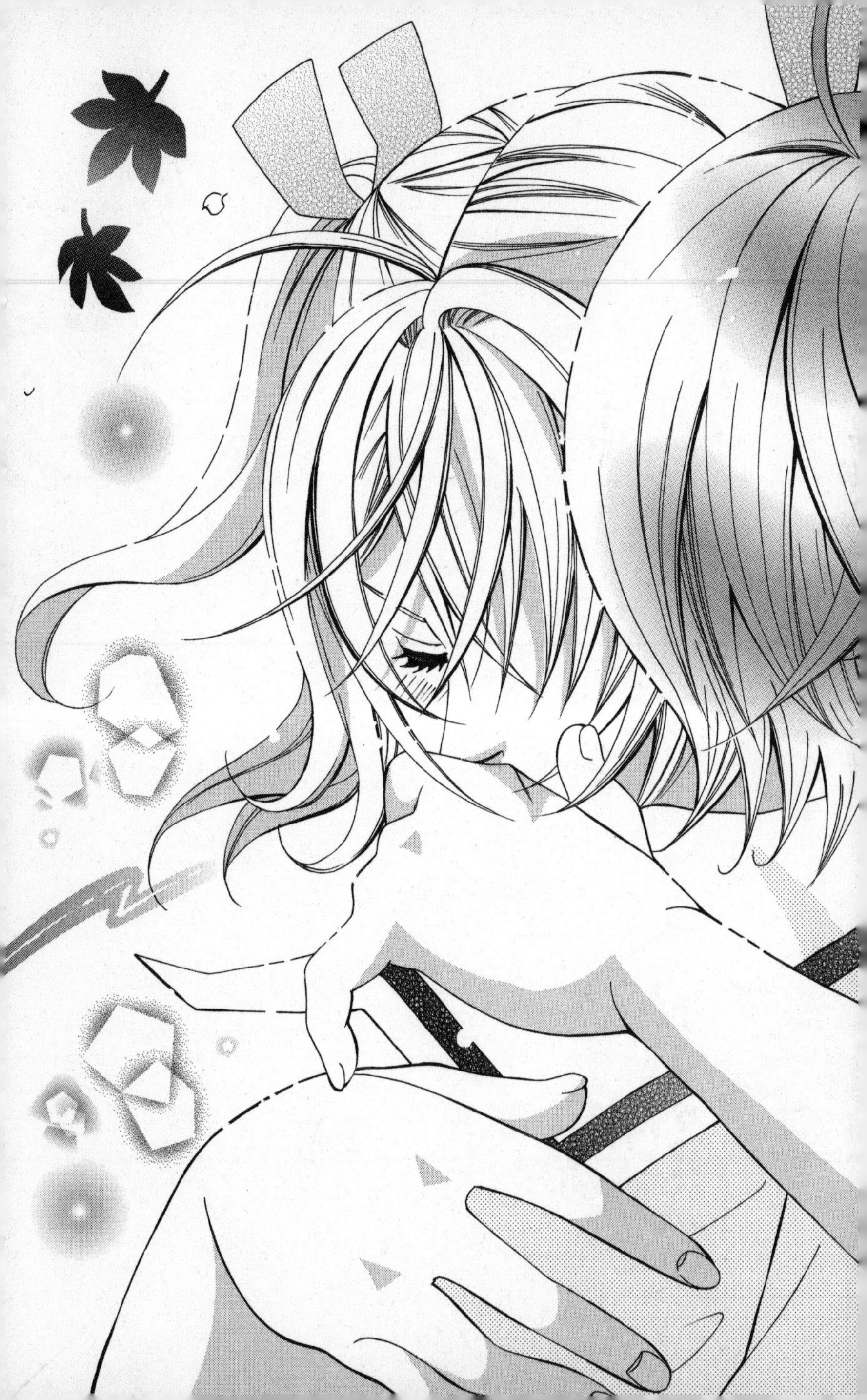

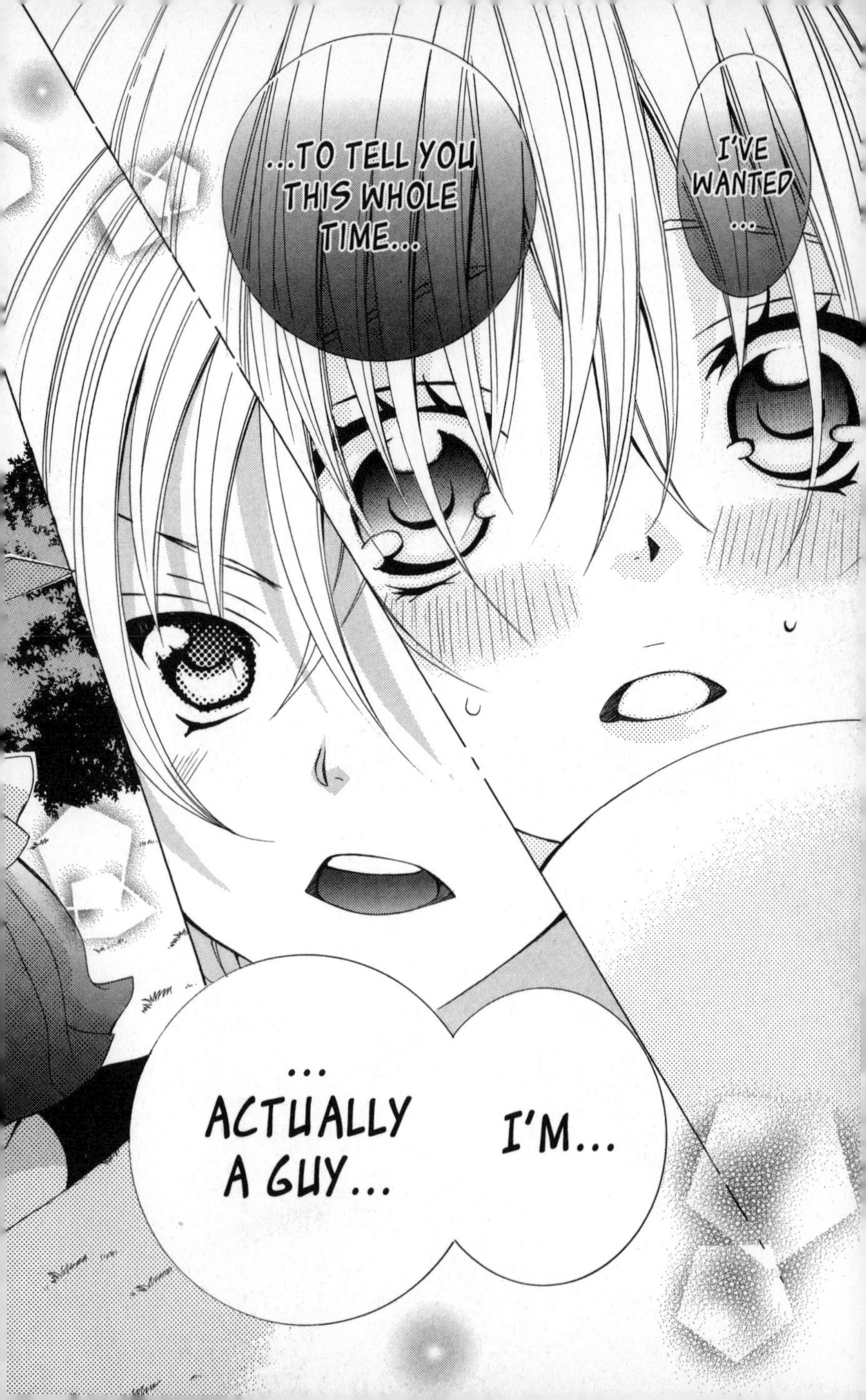
I'VE WANTED ...
...TO TELL YOU THIS WHOLE TIME...
I'M...
... ACTUALLY A GUY...

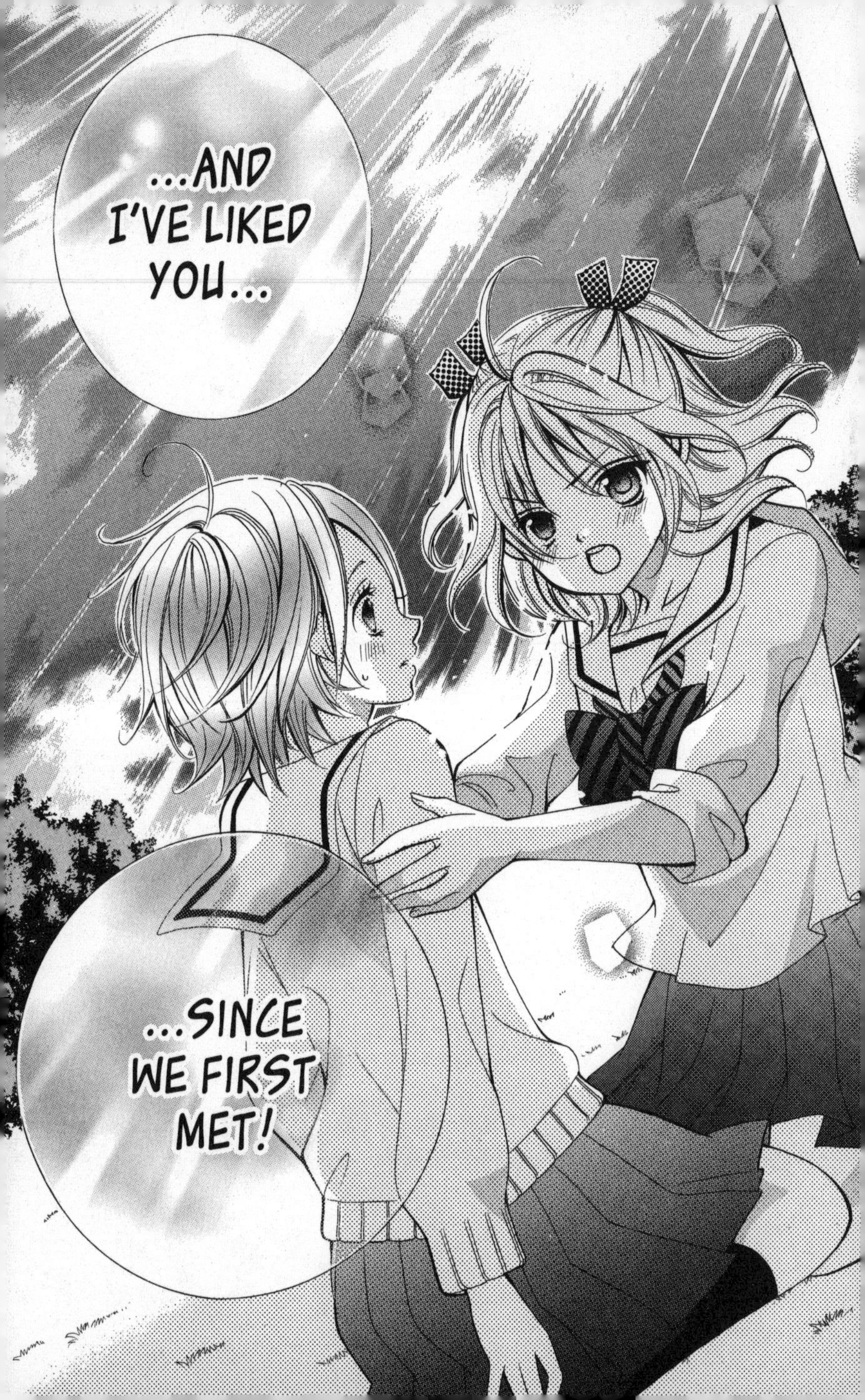
...AND I'VE LIKED YOU...
...SINCE WE FIRST MET!

So Cute It Hurts!! (>_<)

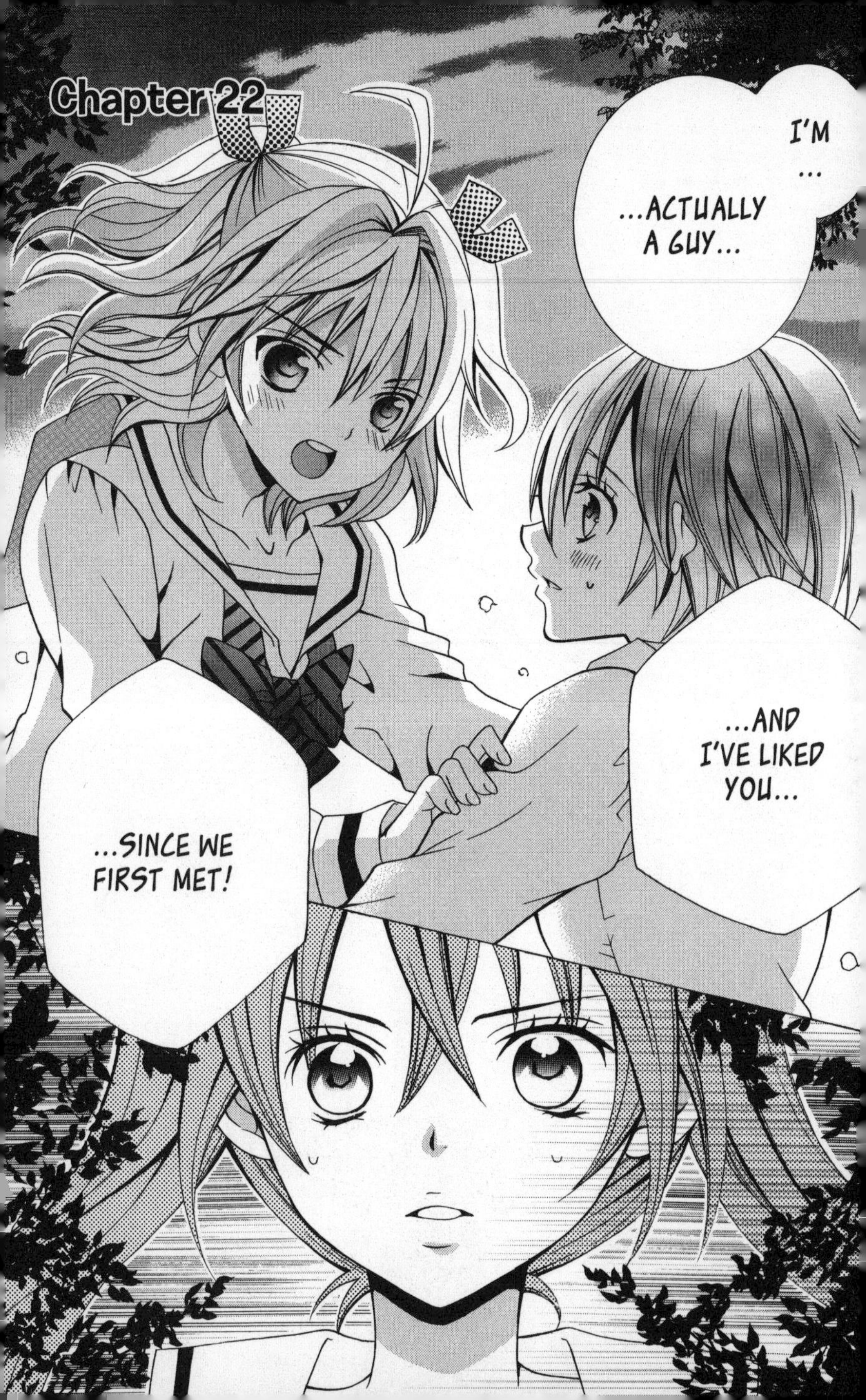
Chapter 22
I'M ... ...ACTUALLY A GUY...
...AND I'VE LIKED YOU...
...SINCE WE FIRST MET!

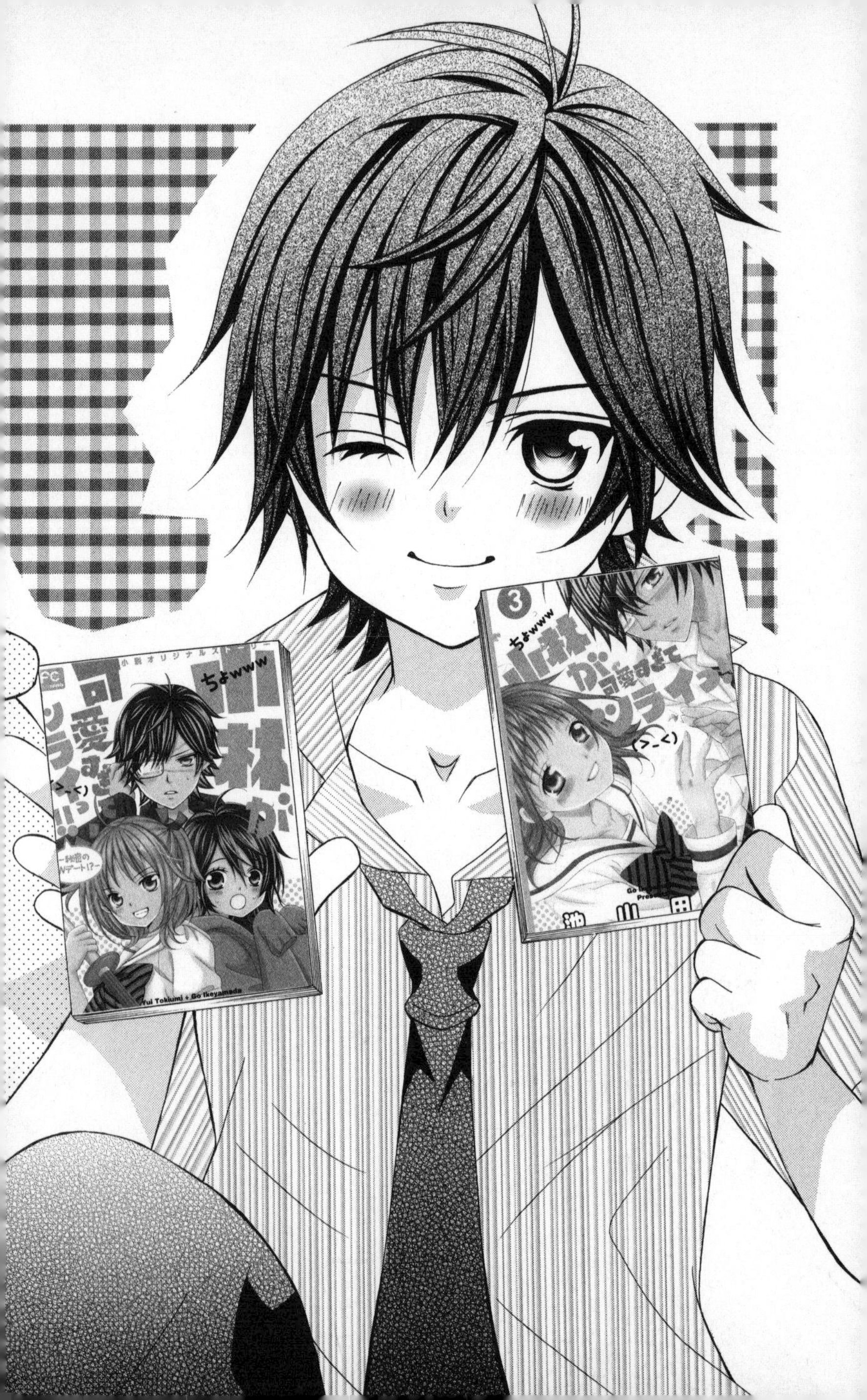
3
ちよwww
(>_<)
小説オリジナルストーリー
ちよwww
(>_<)
〜秘密のWデート!?〜
Yui Tokiumi + Go Ikeyamada

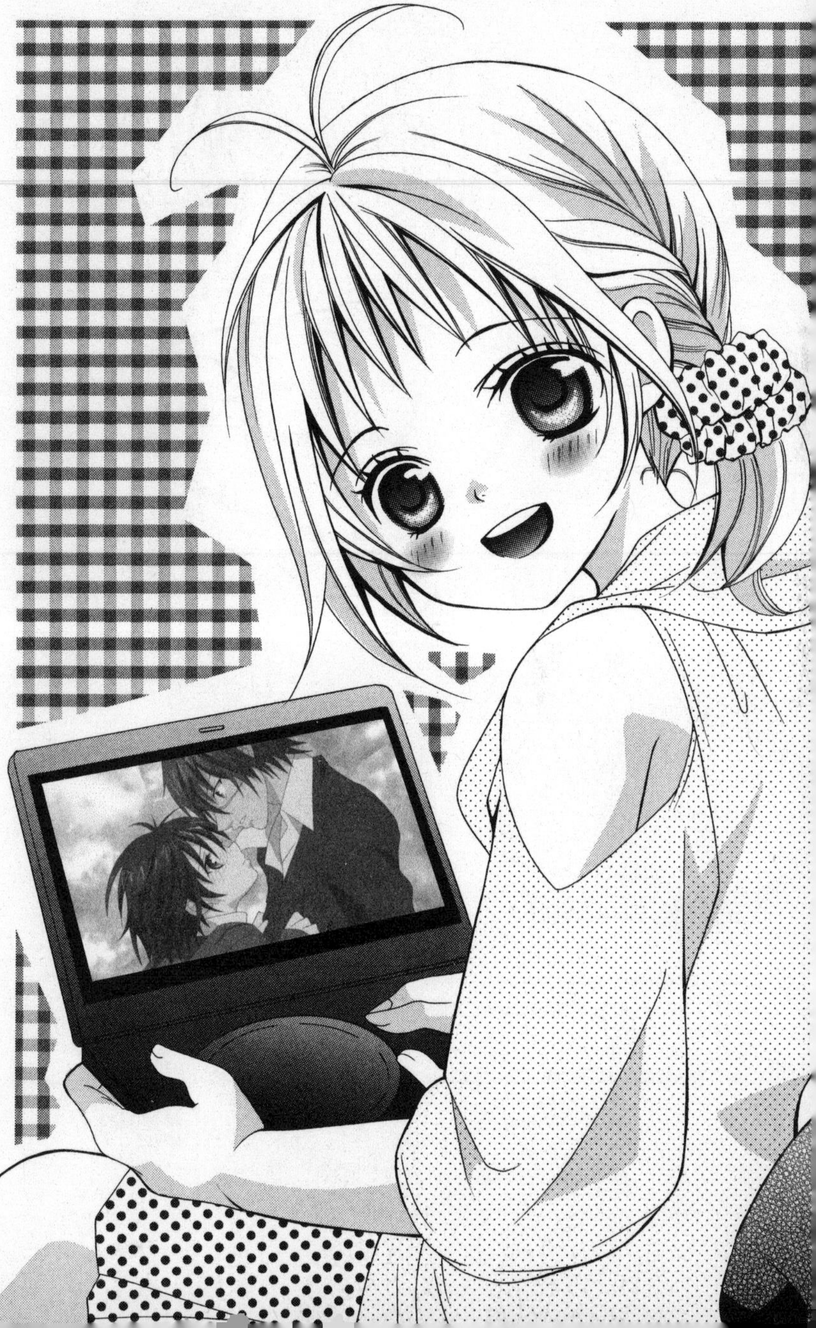

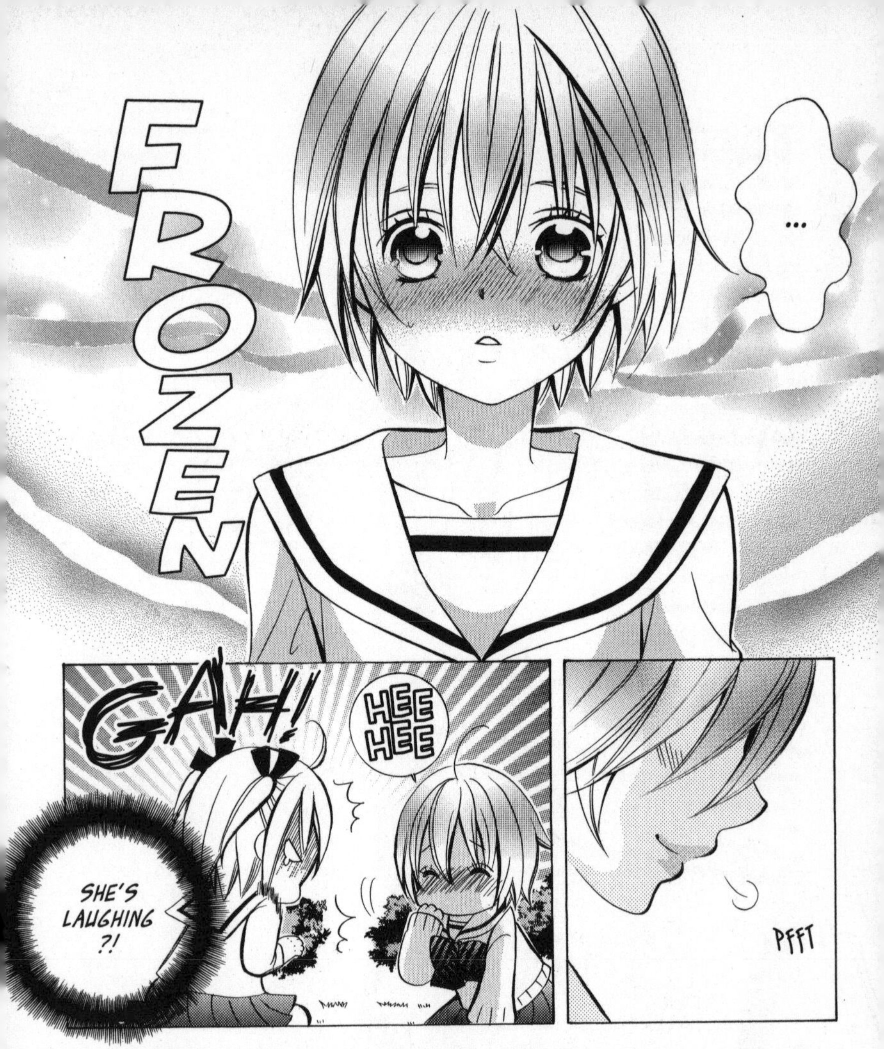
...
FROZEN
PFFT
GAH!
HEE HEE
SHE'S LAUGHING ?!

THANK YOU FOR SENDING ME LOVELY LETTERS AND DRAWINGS. ♡♡
IT'LL MAKE ME HAPPY IF YOU SEND YOUR THOUGHTS AND DRAWINGS AFTER READING VOLUME 5. ♡

GO IKEYAMADA
C/O SHOJO BEAT
VIZ MEDIA, LLC
P.O. BOX 77010
SAN FRANCISCO, CA
94107

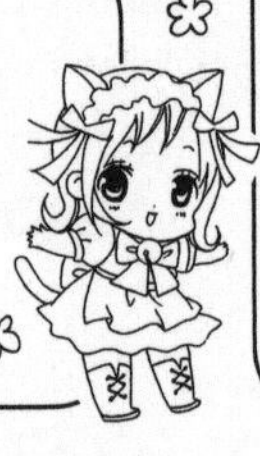

THE MANGA NOW HAS AN OFFICIAL TWITTER ACCOUNT! ↓
@KOBAKAWA_INFO
SO ♡ TAKE A LOOK! ♡

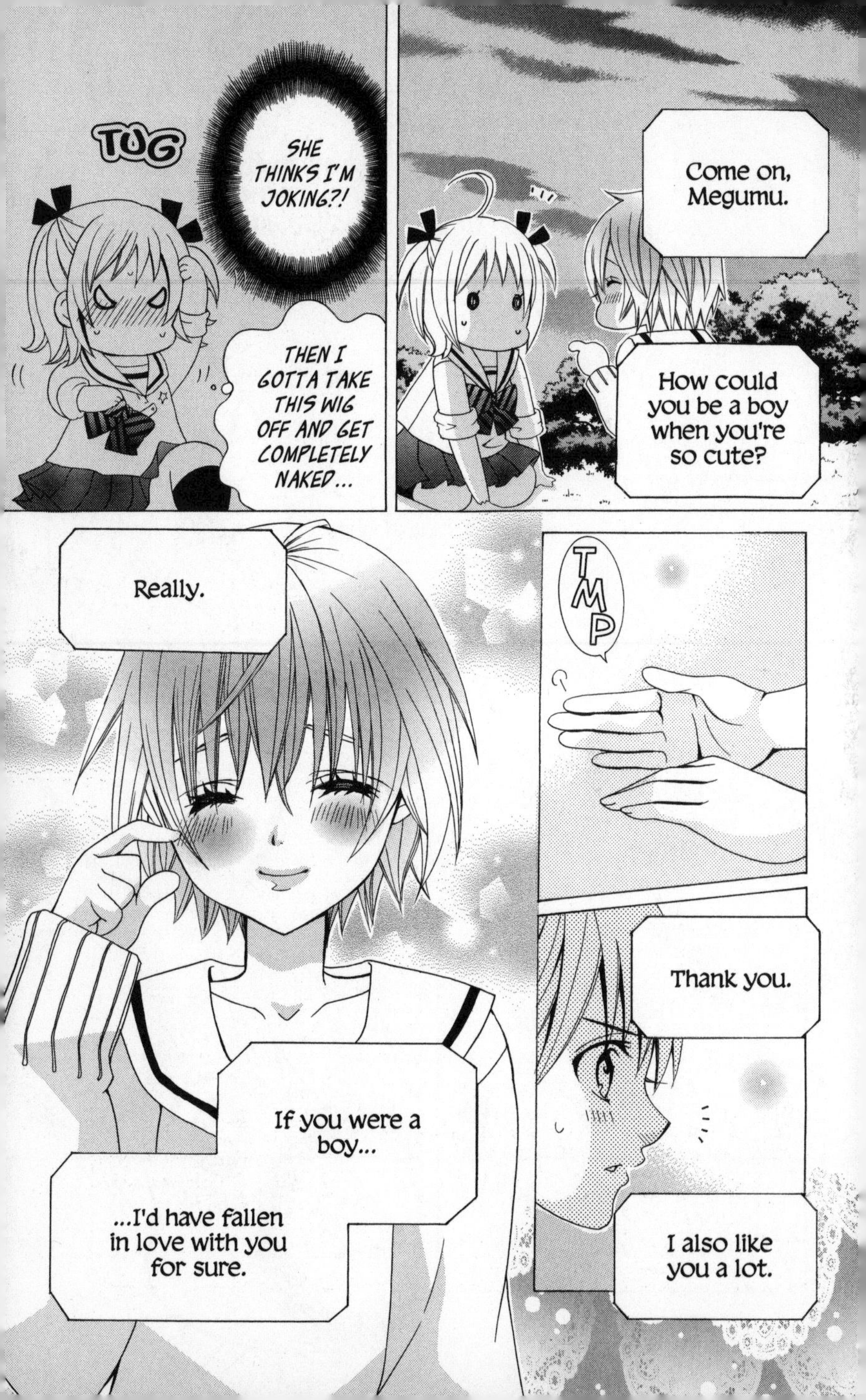
Come on, Megumu.
How could you be a boy when you're so cute?
TUG
SHE THINKS I'M JOKING?!
THEN I GOTTA TAKE THIS WIG OFF AND GET COMPLETELY NAKED...
TMP
Thank you.
I also like you a lot.
Really.
If you were a boy...
...I'd have fallen in love with you for sure.

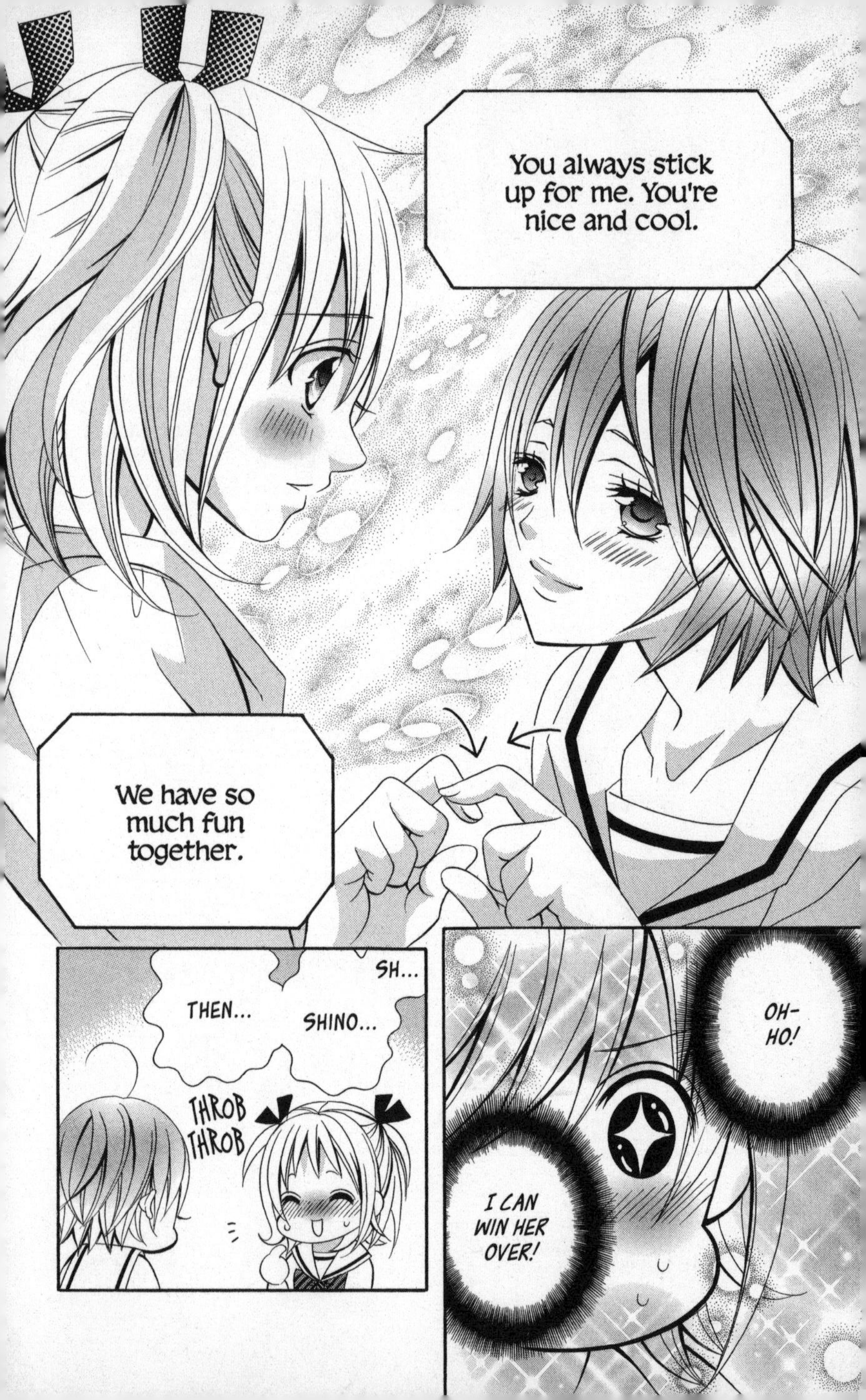
You always stick up for me. You're nice and cool.
We have so much fun together.
OH-HO!
I CAN WIN HER OVER!
SH...
SHINO...
THEN...
THROB THROB

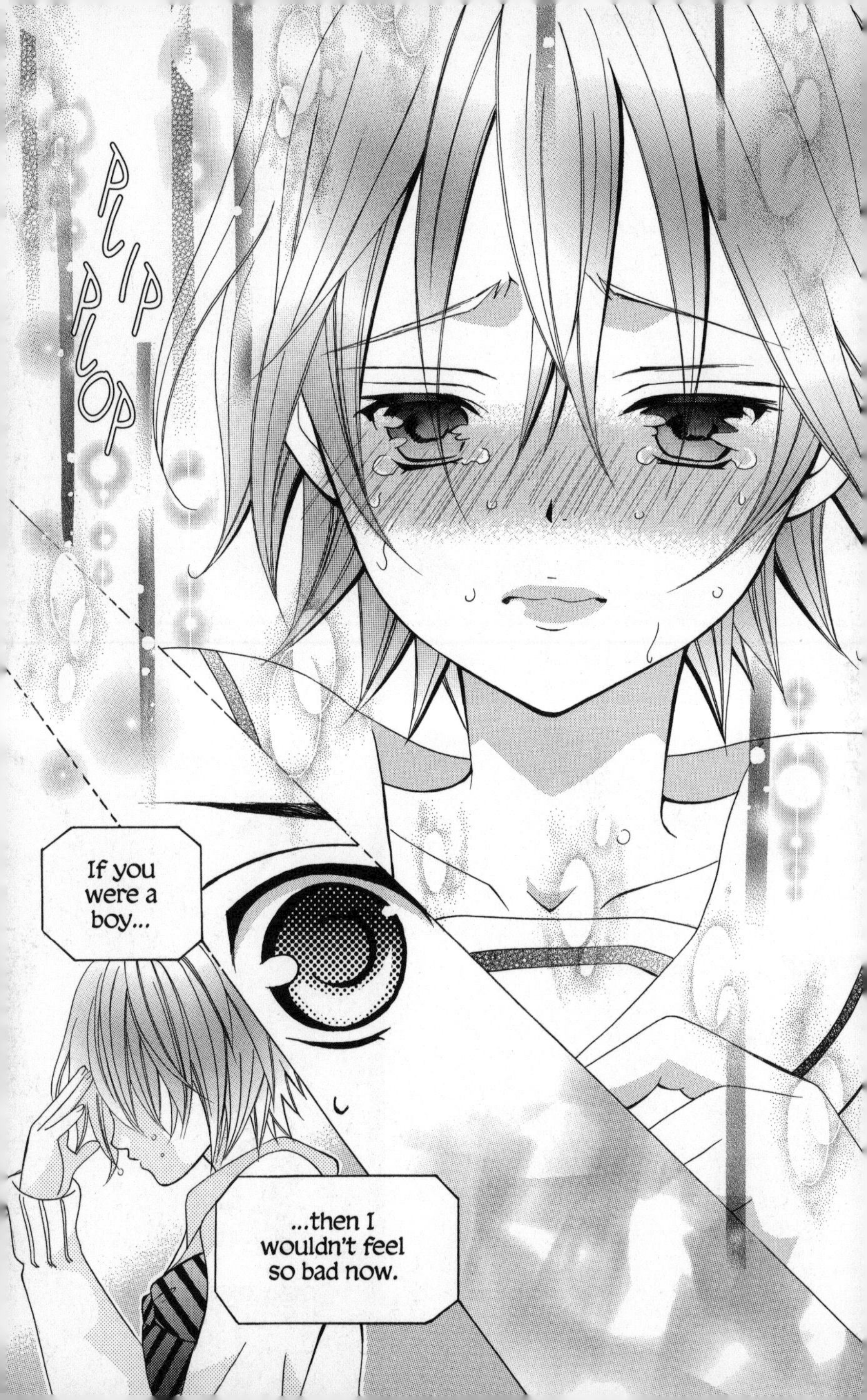
PLIP PLOP
If you were a boy...
...then I wouldn't feel so bad now.

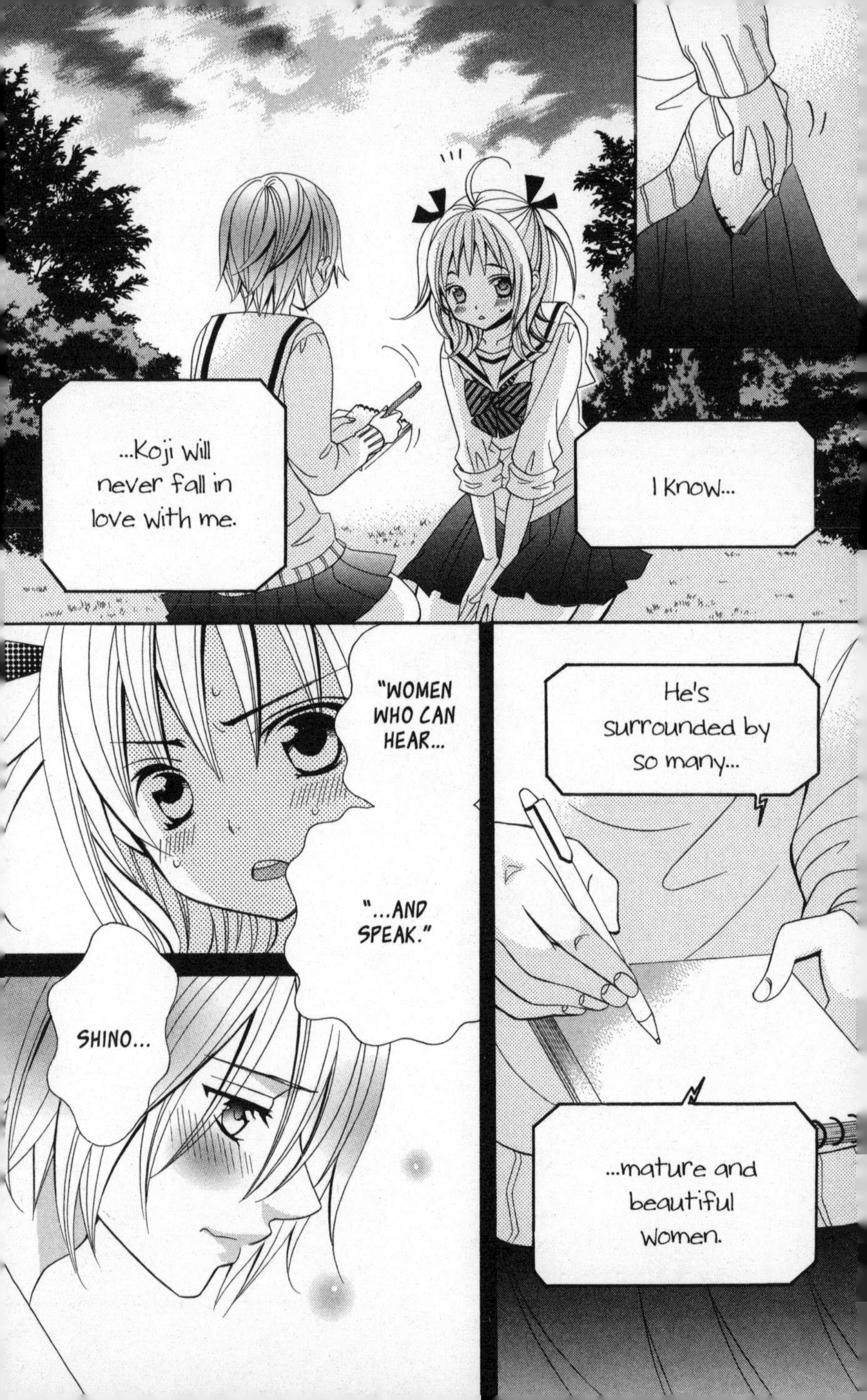
I know...
...Koji will never fall in love with me.
He's surrounded by so many...
...mature and beautiful women.
"WOMEN WHO CAN HEAR...
"...AND SPEAK."
SHINO...

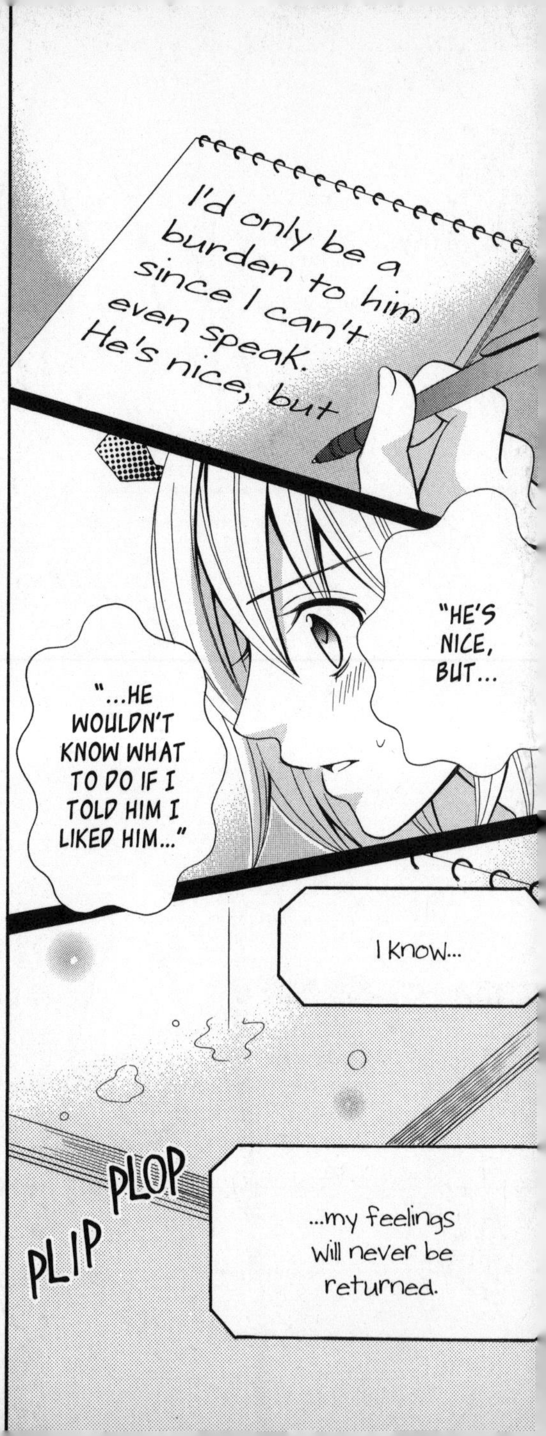
I'd only be a burden to him since I can't even speak. He's nice, but
"HE'S NICE, BUT...
"...HE WOULDN'T KNOW WHAT TO DO IF I TOLD HIM I LIKED HIM..."
I know...
PLIP PLOP
...my feelings will never be returned.

SPECIAL THANKS

Yuka Ito-sama, Rieko Hirai-sama, Kayoko Takahashi-sama, Kawasaki-sama, Nagisa Sato Sensei.

Rei Nanase Sensei, Arisu Fujishiro Sensei, Mumi Mimura Sensei, Masayo Nagata-sama, Naochan-sama, Asuka Sakura Sensei and many others.

Bookstore Dan Kinshicho Branch, Kinokuniya Shinjuku Branch, LIBRO Ikebukuro Branch, Kinokuniya Hankyu 32-Bangai Branch.

Sendai Hachimonjiya Bookstore, BOOKS HOSHINO Kintetsu Pass'e Branch, Asahiya Tennoji MIO Branch, Kurashiki Kikuya Bookstore.

Salesperson: Hata-sama

First salesperson: Honma-sama

Previous editor: Nakata-sama

Current editor: Shoji-sama

My sincere gratitude to everyone who picked up this volume!

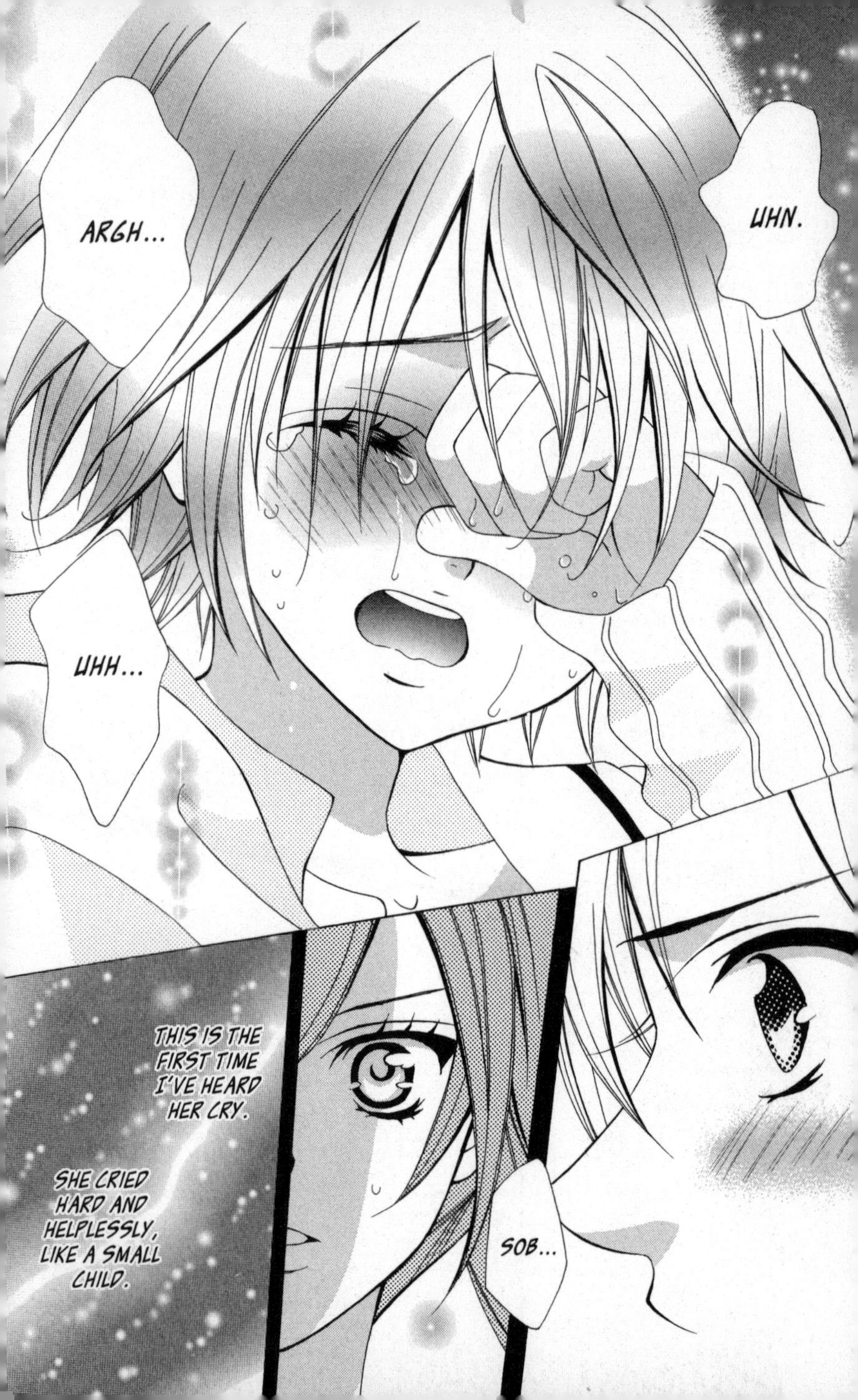
UHN.
ARGH...
UHH...
SOB...
THIS IS THE FIRST TIME I'VE HEARD HER CRY.
SHE CRIED HARD AND HELPLESSLY, LIKE A SMALL CHILD.

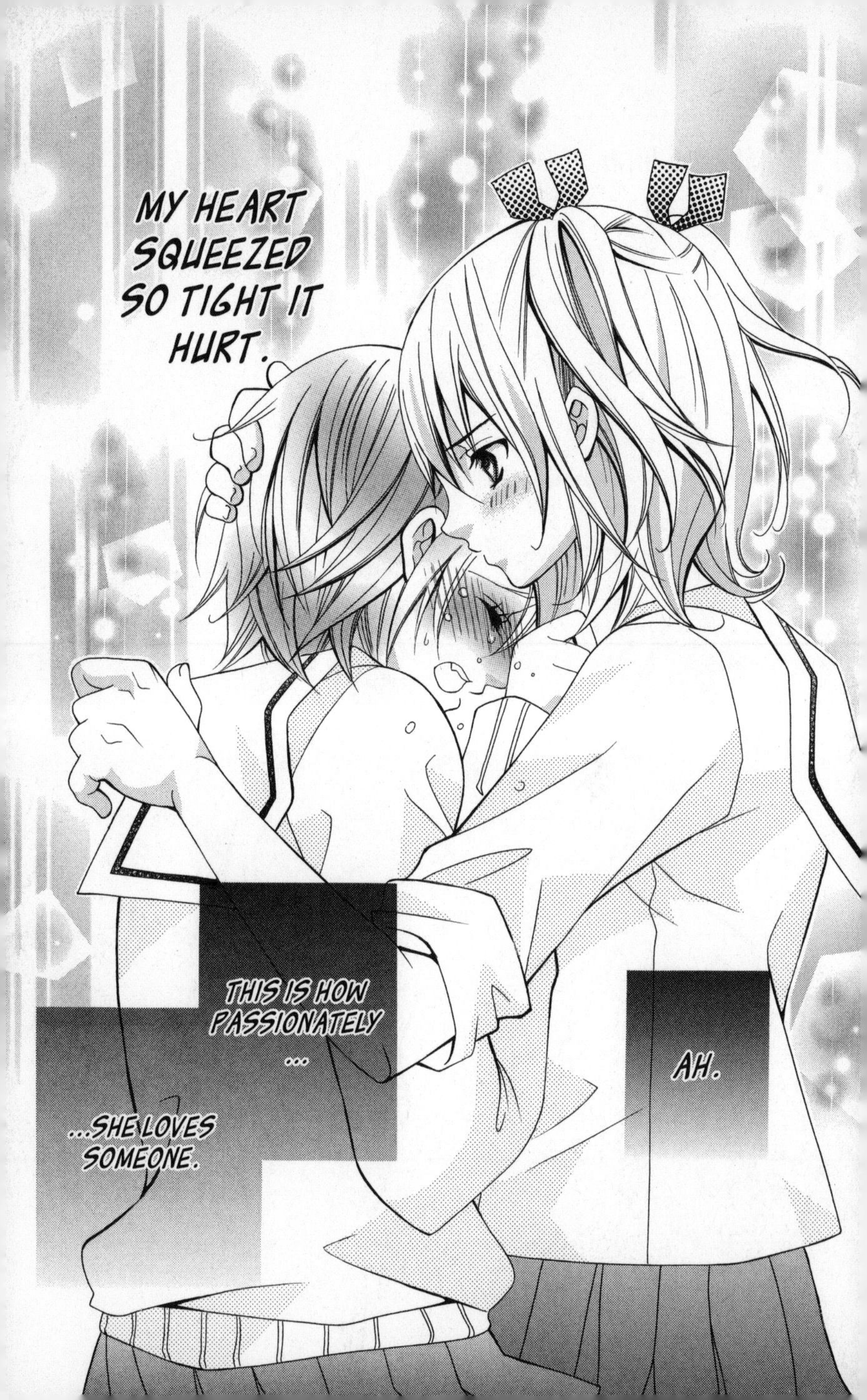
MY HEART SQUEEZED SO TIGHT IT HURT.
AH.
THIS IS HOW PASSIONATELY ...
...SHE LOVES SOMEONE.

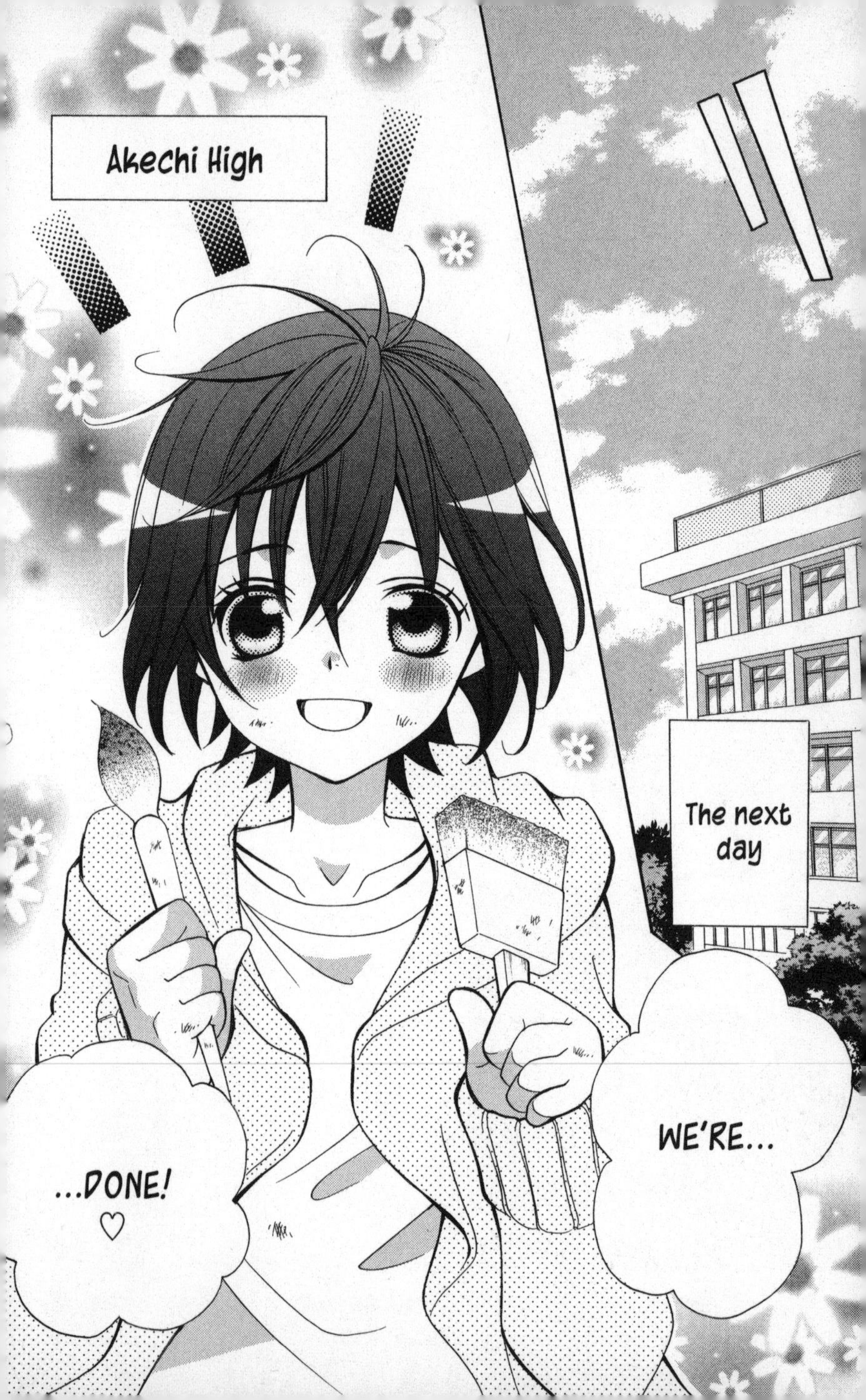
The next day
Akechi High
WE'RE...
...DONE! ♡

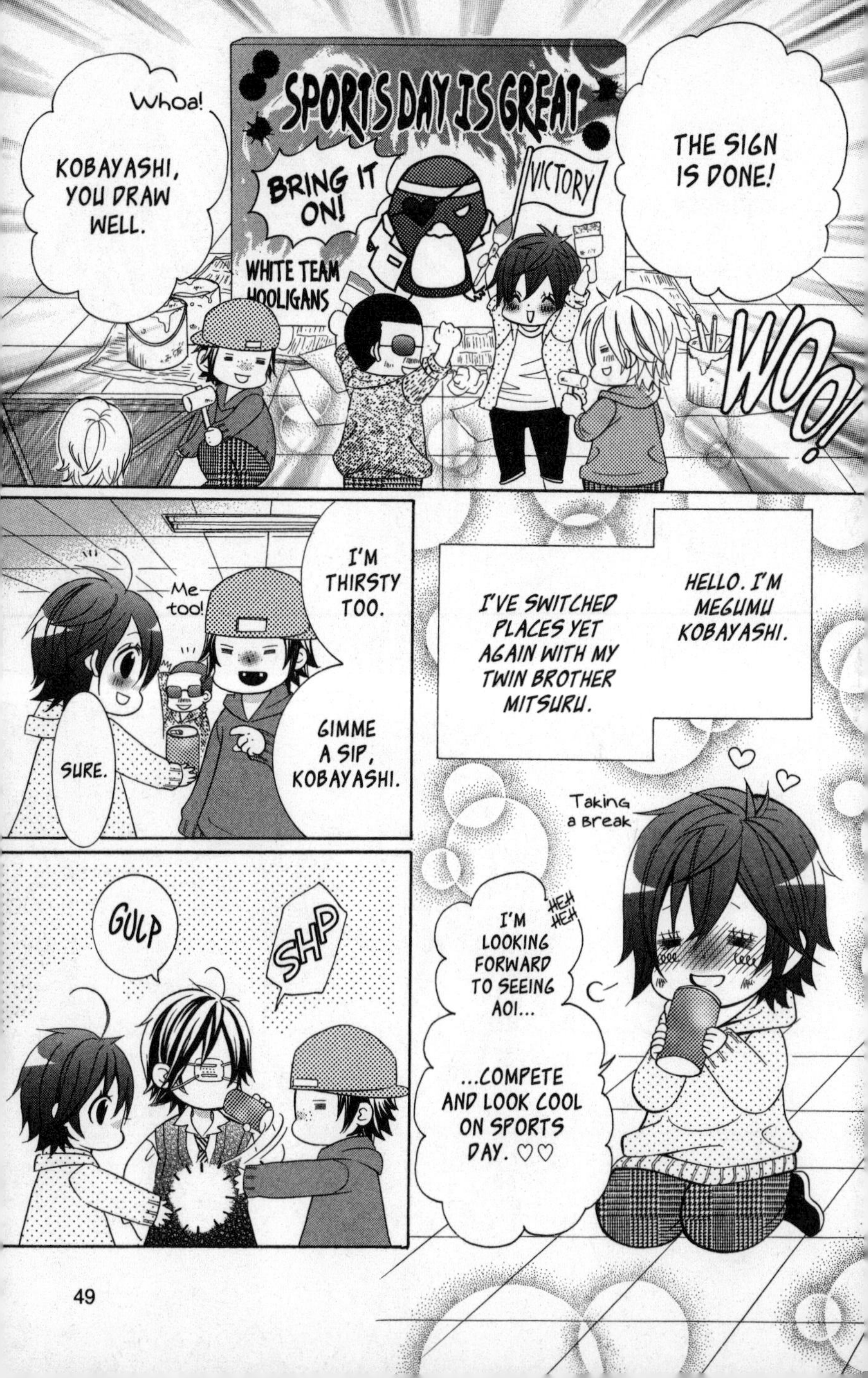
THE SIGN IS DONE!
WOO!
SPORTS DAY IS GREAT
VICTORY
BRING IT ON!
WHITE TEAM HOOLIGANS
Whoa!
KOBAYASHI, YOU DRAW WELL.
HELLO. I'M MEGUMU KOBAYASHI.
I'VE SWITCHED PLACES YET AGAIN WITH MY TWIN BROTHER MITSURU.
Taking a break
HEH HEH
I'M LOOKING FORWARD TO SEEING AOI...
...COMPETE AND LOOK COOL ON SPORTS DAY. ♡♡
I'M THIRSTY TOO.
Me too!
GIMME A SIP, KOBAYASHI.
SURE.
SHP
GULP

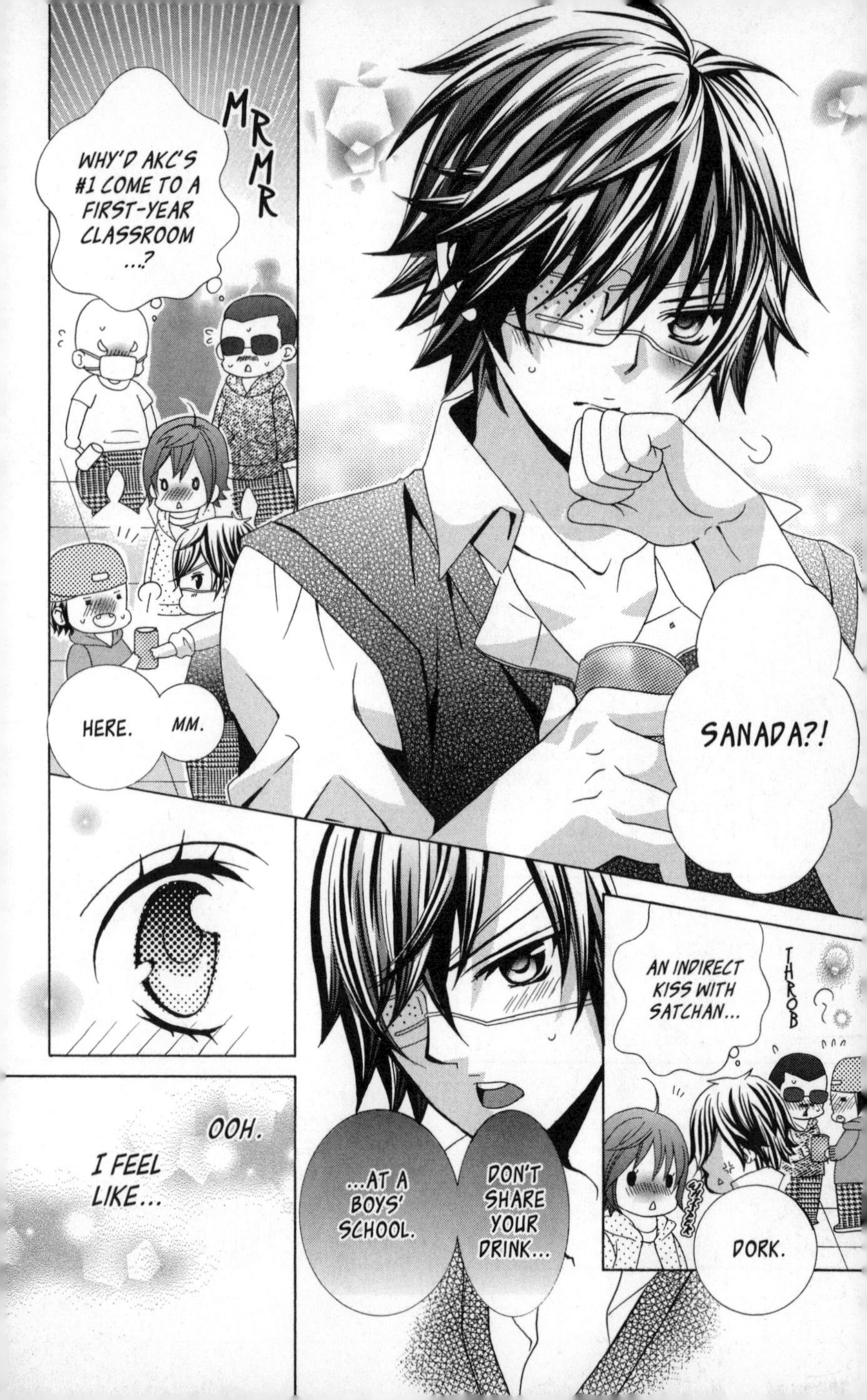
SANADA?!
MRMR
WHY'D AKC'S #1 COME TO A FIRST-YEAR CLASSROOM ...?
HERE.
MM.
AN INDIRECT KISS WITH SATCHAN...
THROB
DORK.
DON'T SHARE YOUR DRINK...
...AT A BOYS' SCHOOL.
OOH.
I FEEL LIKE...

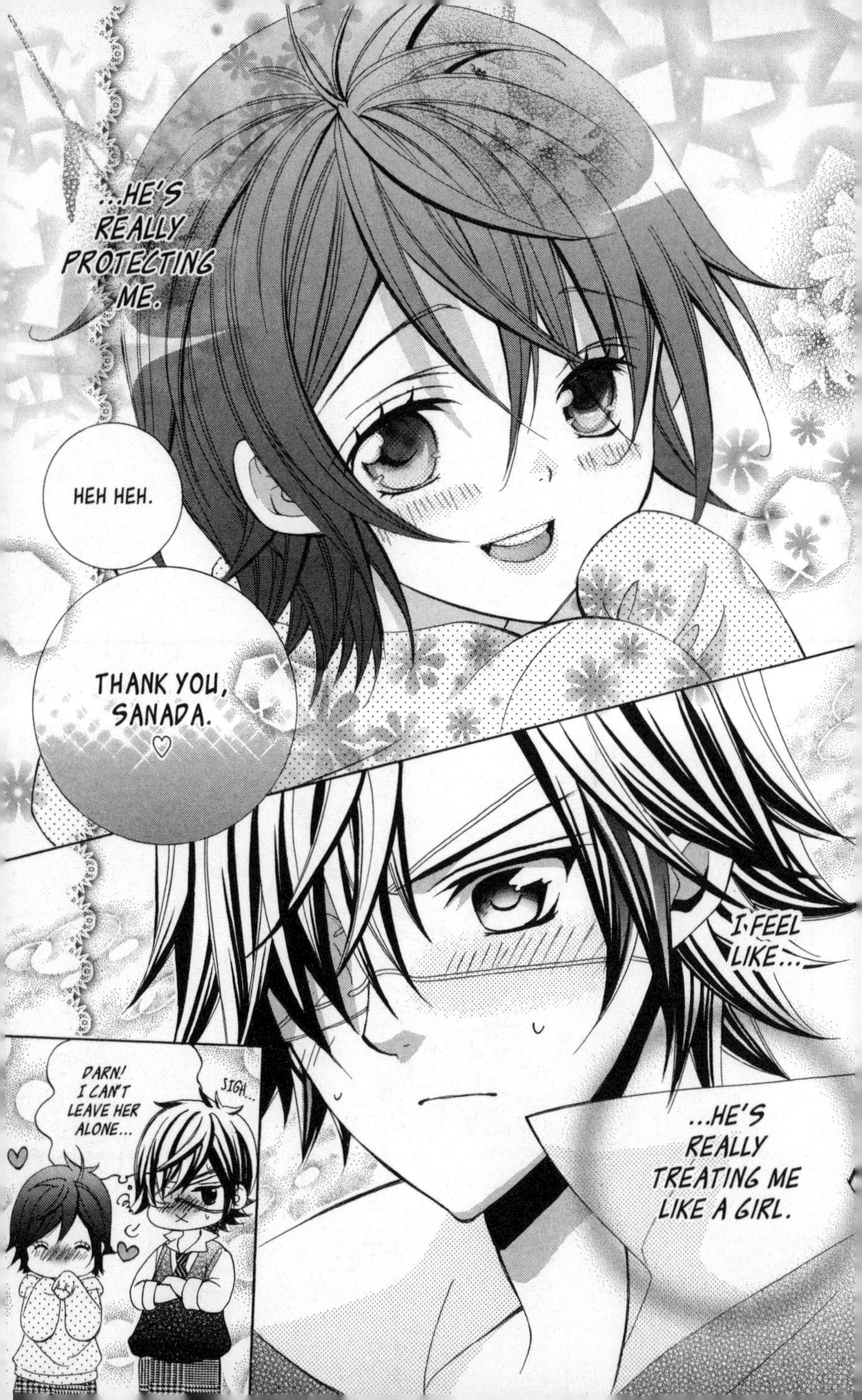
...HE'S REALLY PROTECTING ME.
HEH HEH.
THANK YOU, SANADA. ♡
I FEEL LIKE...
...HE'S REALLY TREATING ME LIKE A GIRL.
DARN! I CAN'T LEAVE HER ALONE...
SIGH...

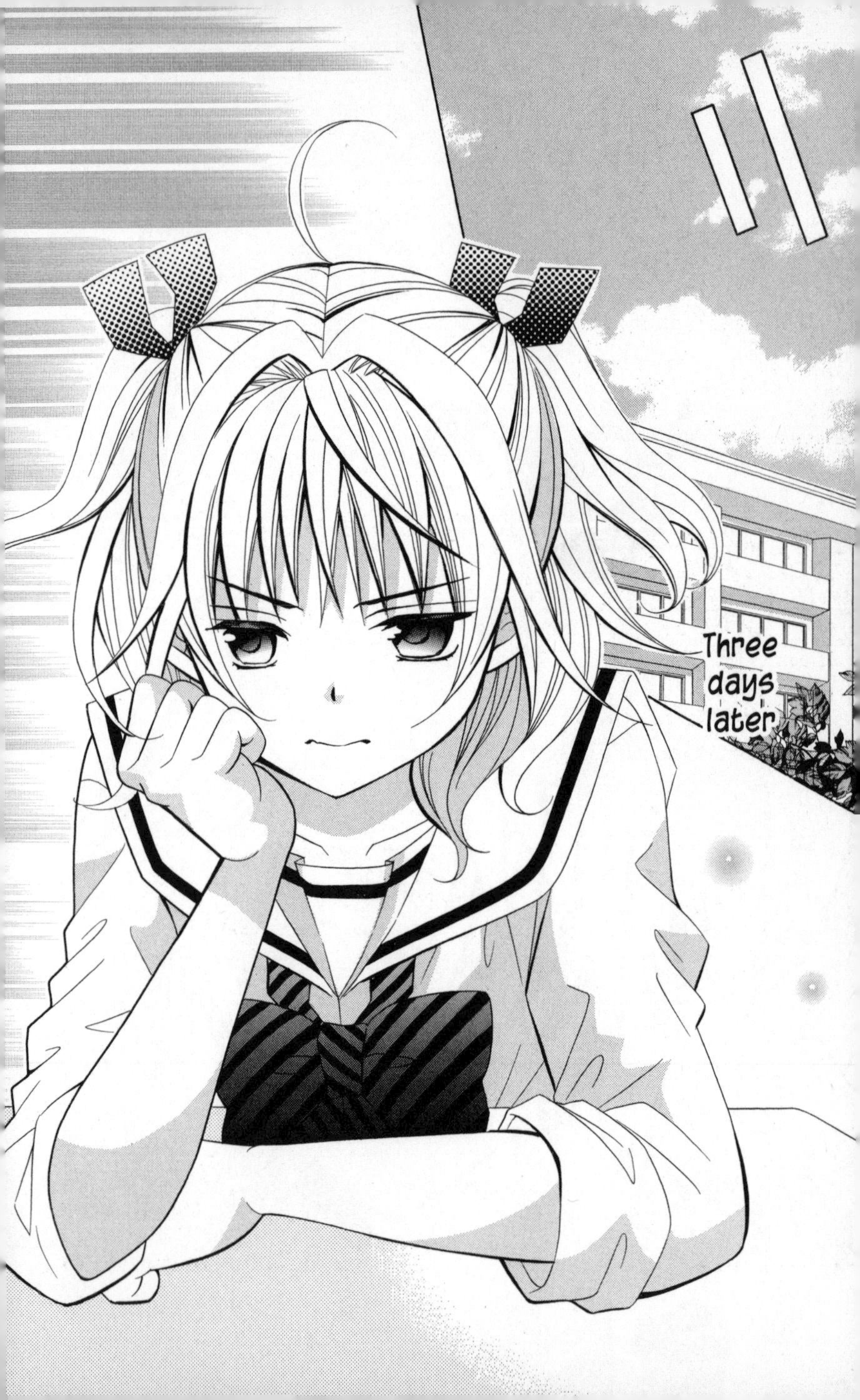
Three days later

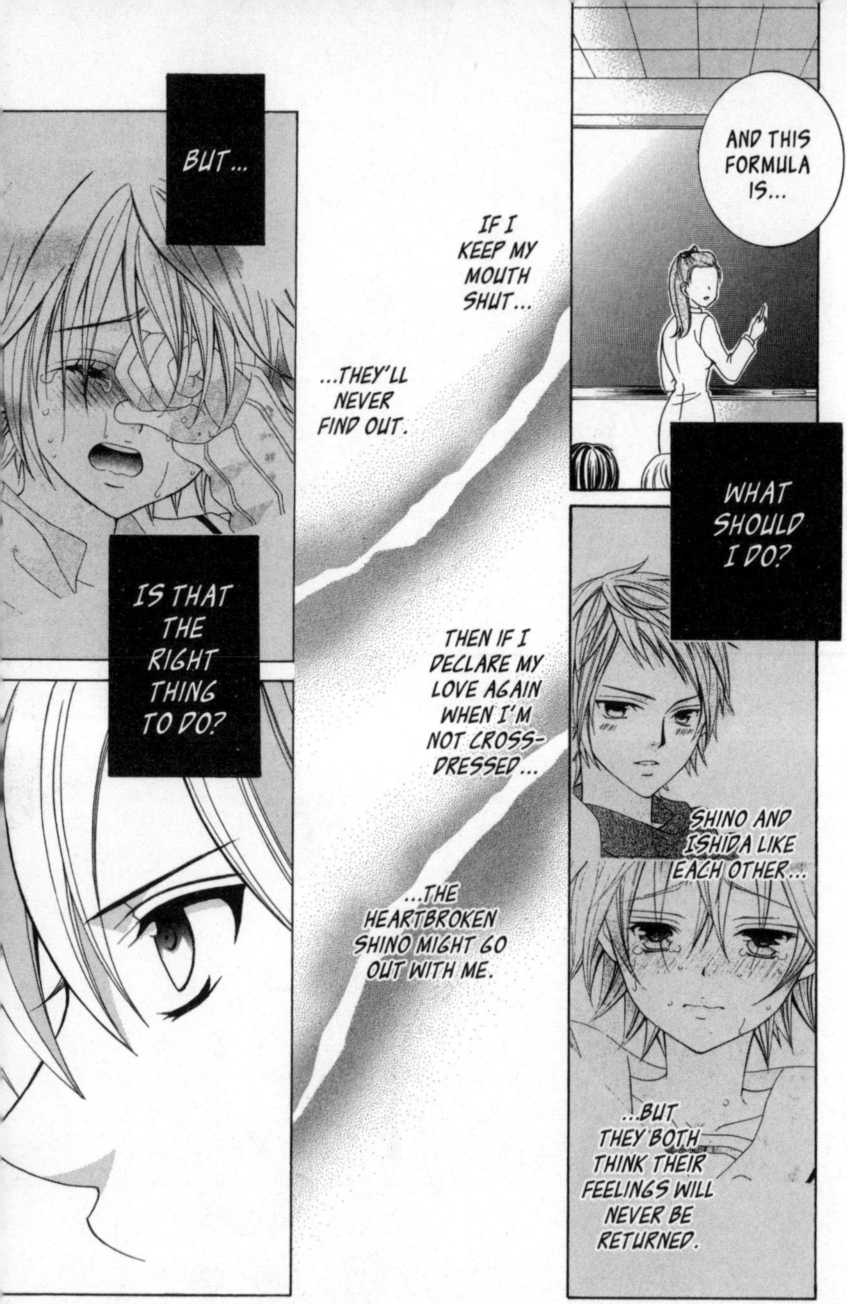
AND THIS FORMULA IS...
WHAT SHOULD I DO?
SHINO AND ISHIDA LIKE EACH OTHER...
...BUT THEY BOTH THINK THEIR FEELINGS WILL NEVER BE RETURNED.
IF I KEEP MY MOUTH SHUT...
...THEY'LL NEVER FIND OUT.
THEN IF I DECLARE MY LOVE AGAIN WHEN I'M NOT CROSS-DRESSED...
...THE HEARTBROKEN SHINO MIGHT GO OUT WITH ME.
BUT...
IS THAT THE RIGHT THING TO DO?

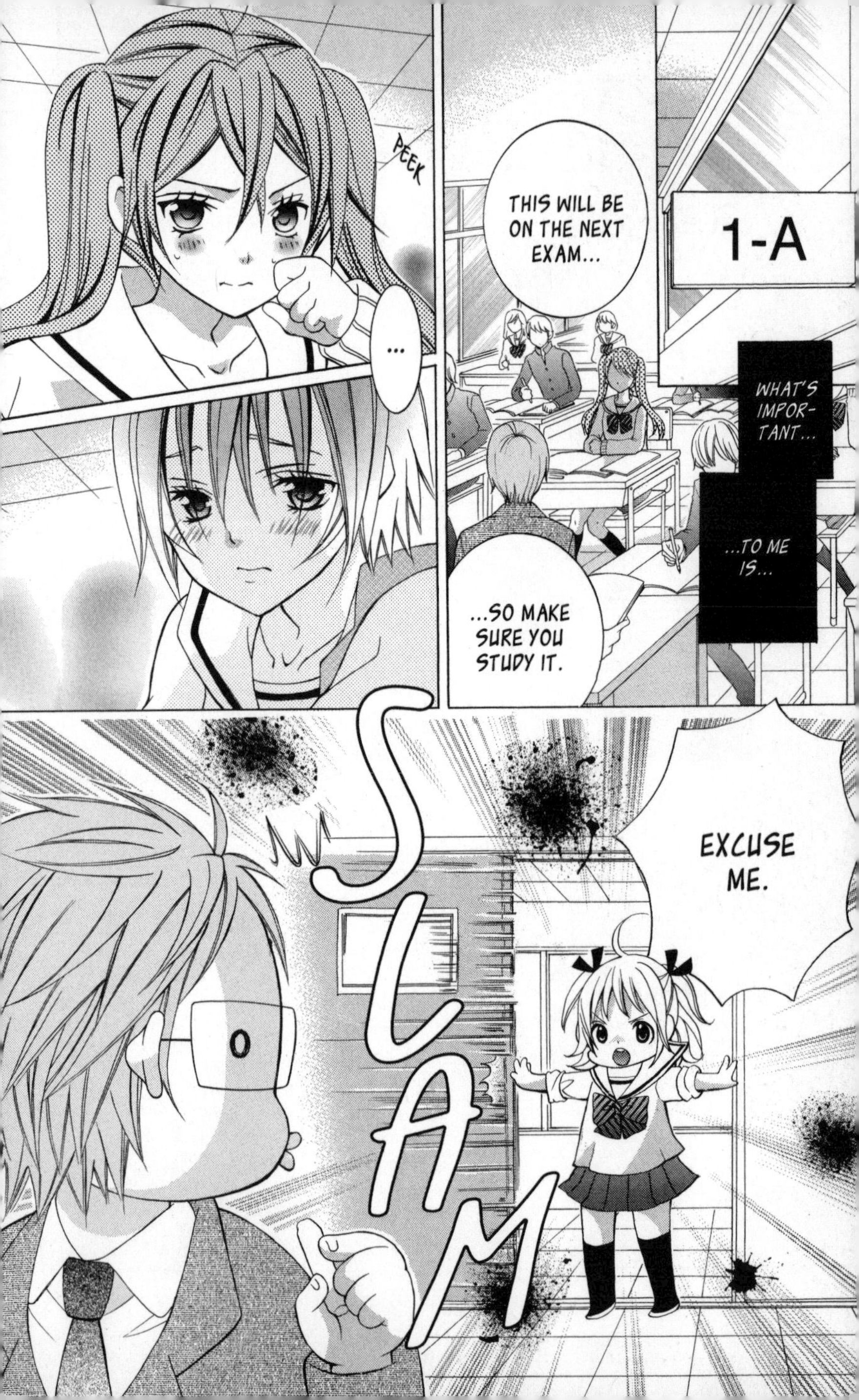
1-A
THIS WILL BE ON THE NEXT EXAM...
WHAT'S IMPORTANT...
...TO ME IS...
...SO MAKE SURE YOU STUDY IT.
PEEK
...
EXCUSE ME.
SLAM

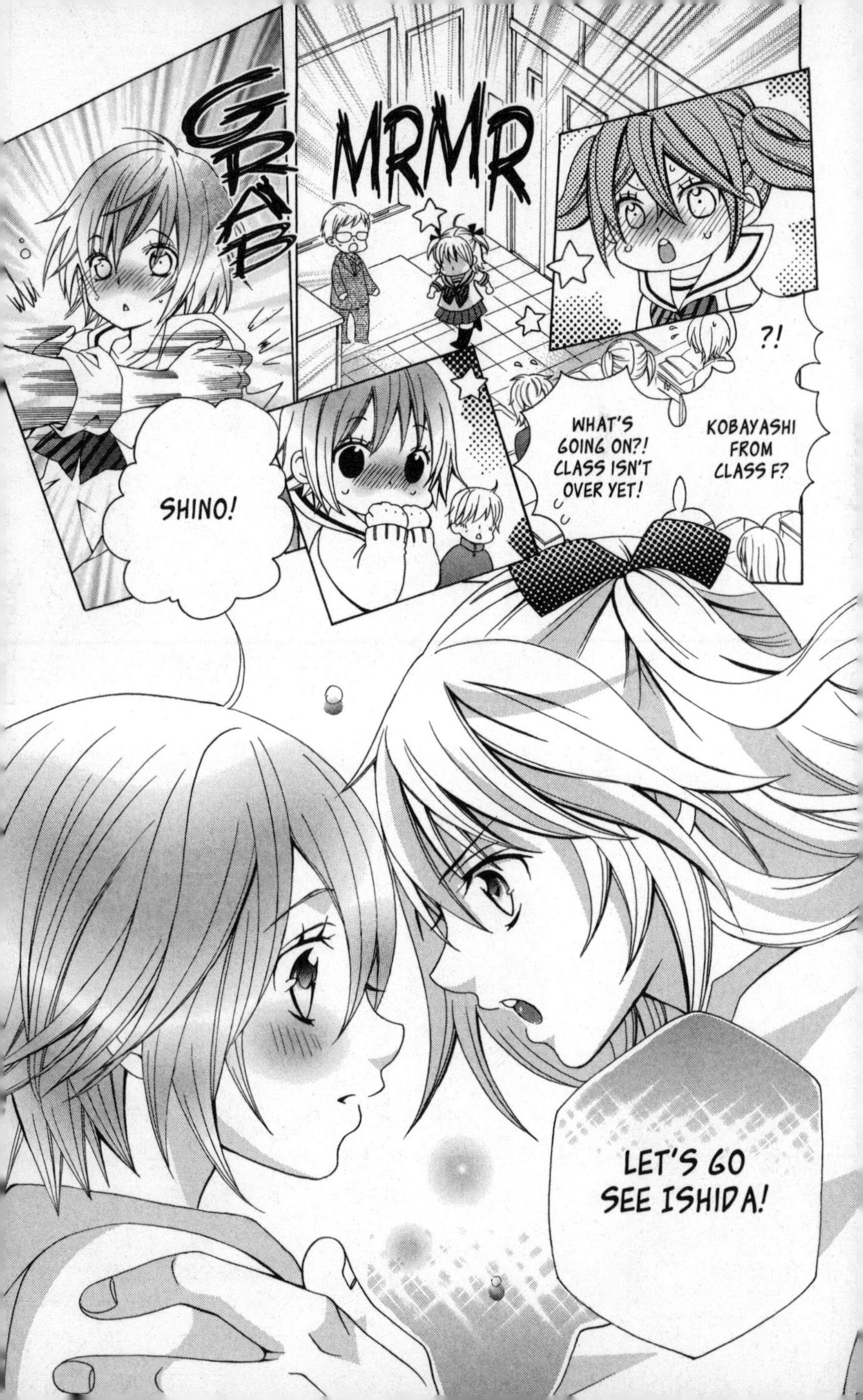
?!
MRMR
GRAB
KOBAYASHI FROM CLASS F?
WHAT'S GOING ON?! CLASS ISN'T OVER YET!
SHINO!
LET'S GO SEE ISHIDA!

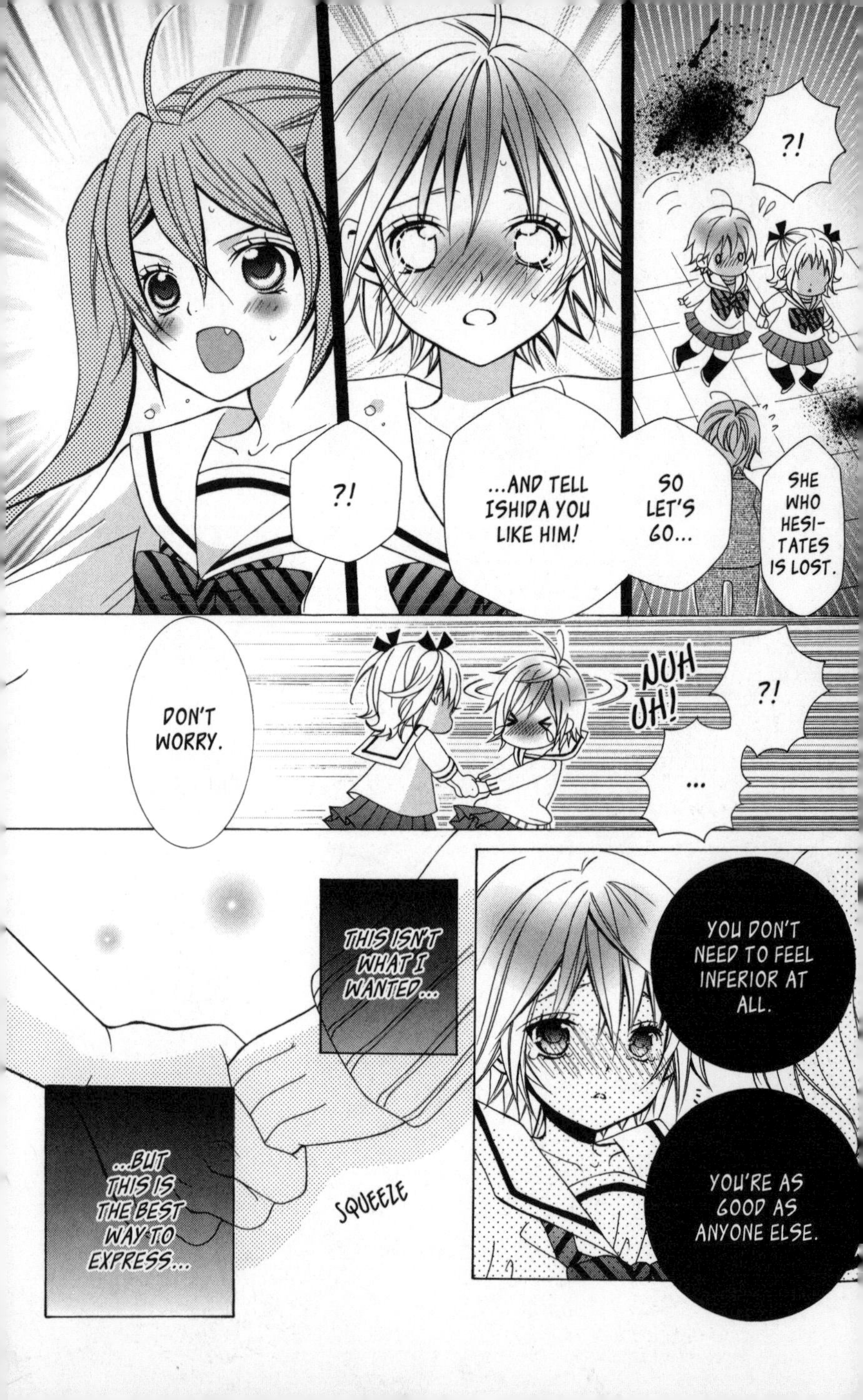
?!
SHE WHO HESI-TATES IS LOST.
SO LET'S GO...
...AND TELL ISHIDA YOU LIKE HIM!
?!
?!
...
NUH UH!
DON'T WORRY.
YOU DON'T NEED TO FEEL INFERIOR AT ALL.
YOU'RE AS GOOD AS ANYONE ELSE.
THIS ISN'T WHAT I WANTED...
SQUEEZE
...BUT THIS IS THE BEST WAY TO EXPRESS...

...MY FEELINGS FOR YOU...
CHIN UP.
YOU'RE THE MOST BEAUTIFUL GIRL IN THE WHOLE WORLD.
I LIKE YOU SO MUCH.

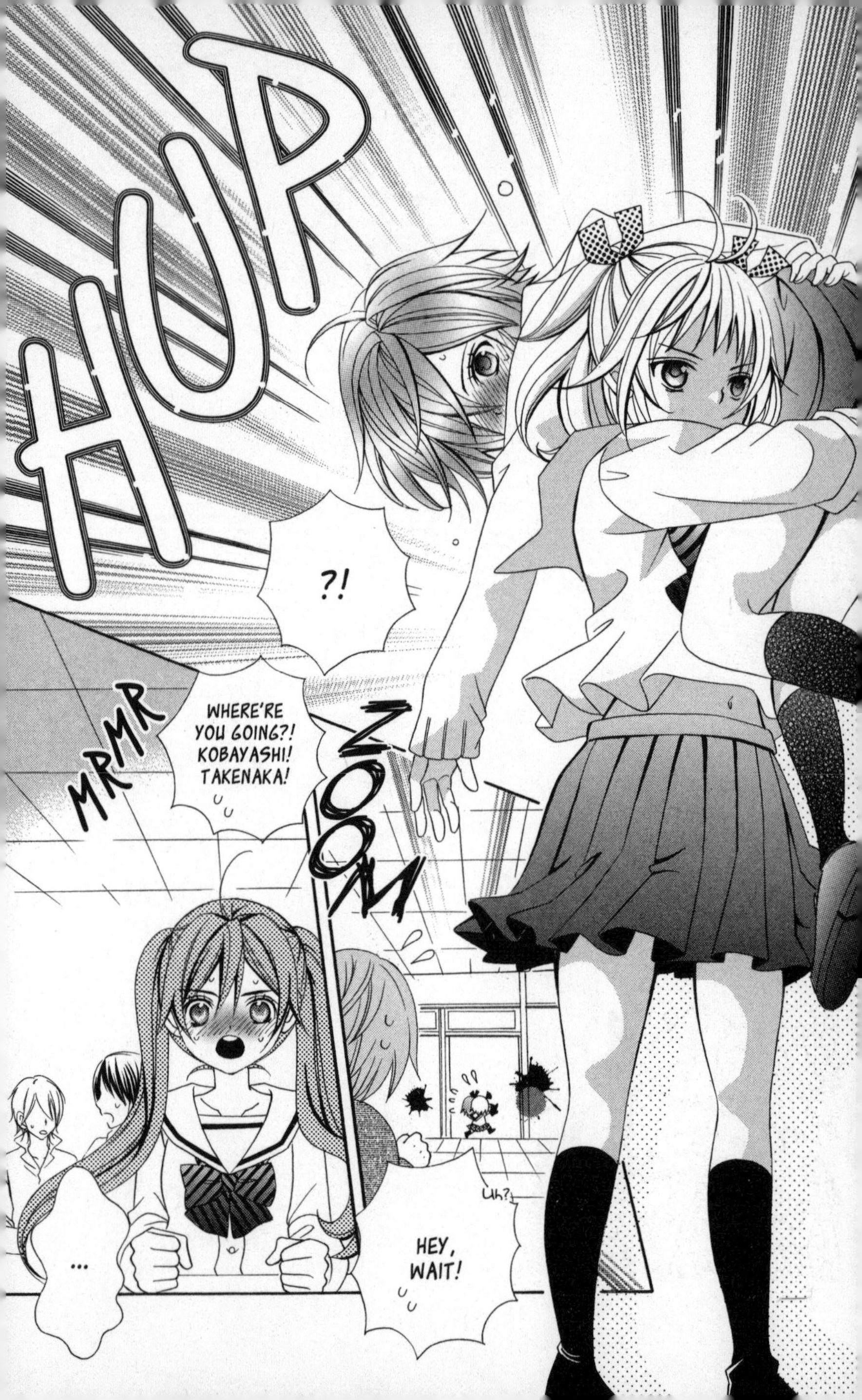
HUP
?!
ZOOM
WHERE'RE YOU GOING?! KOBAYASHI! TAKENAKA!
MRMR
Uh?!
HEY, WAIT!
...

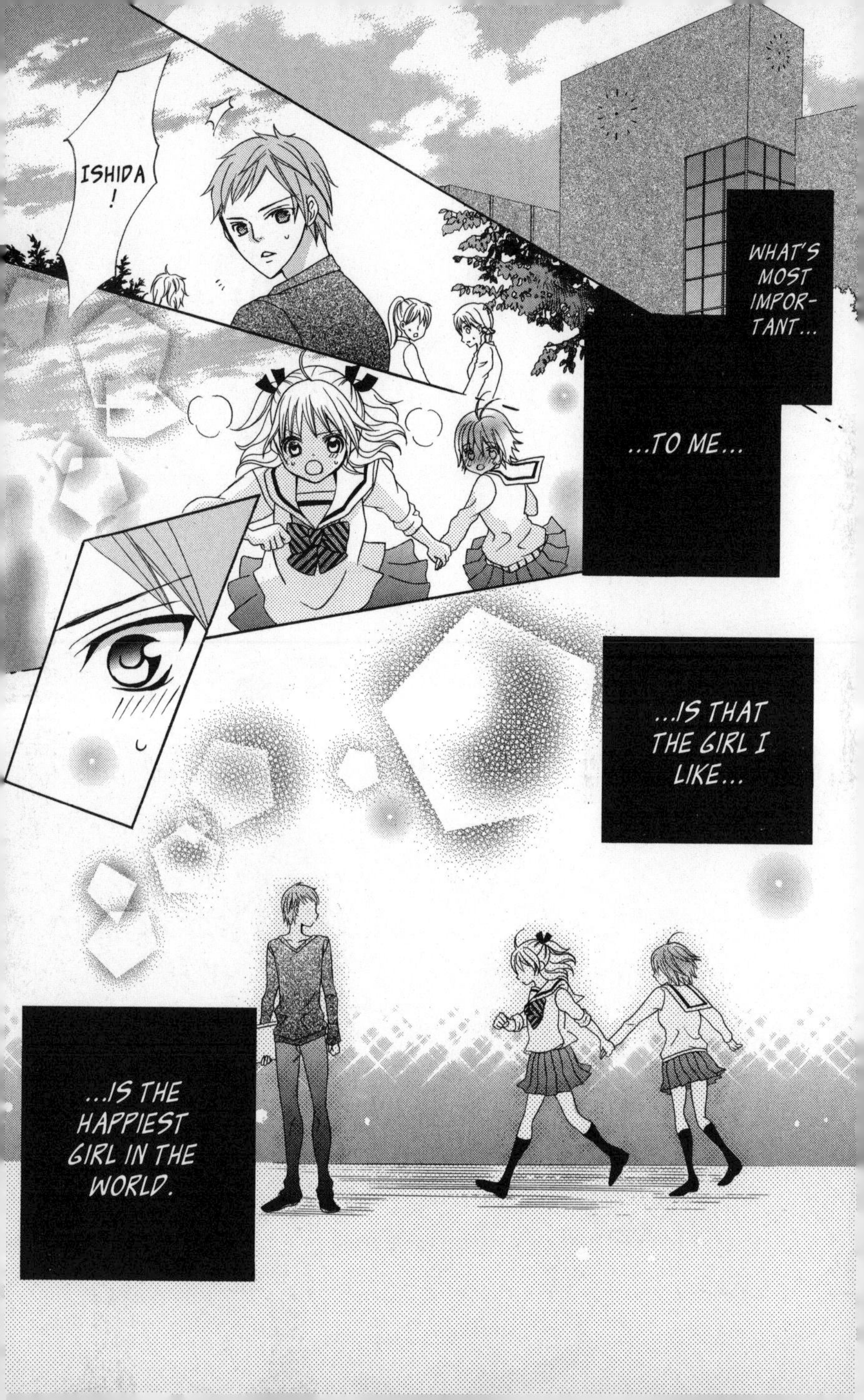
WHAT'S MOST IMPORTANT...
ISHIDA!
...TO ME...
...IS THAT THE GIRL I LIKE...
...IS THE HAPPIEST GIRL IN THE WORLD.

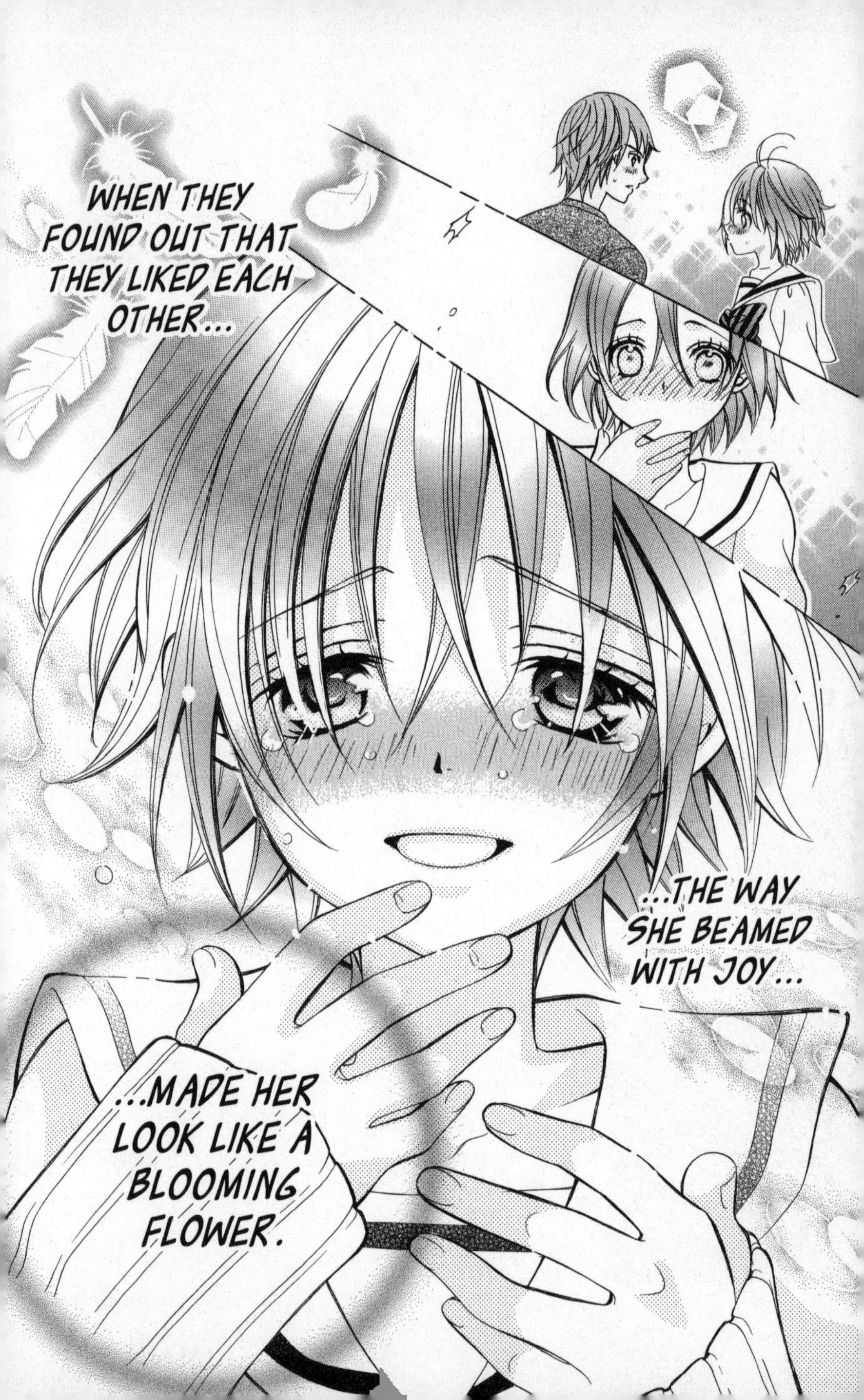
WHEN THEY FOUND OUT THAT THEY LIKED EACH OTHER...
...THE WAY SHE BEAMED WITH JOY...
...MADE HER LOOK LIKE A BLOOMING FLOWER.

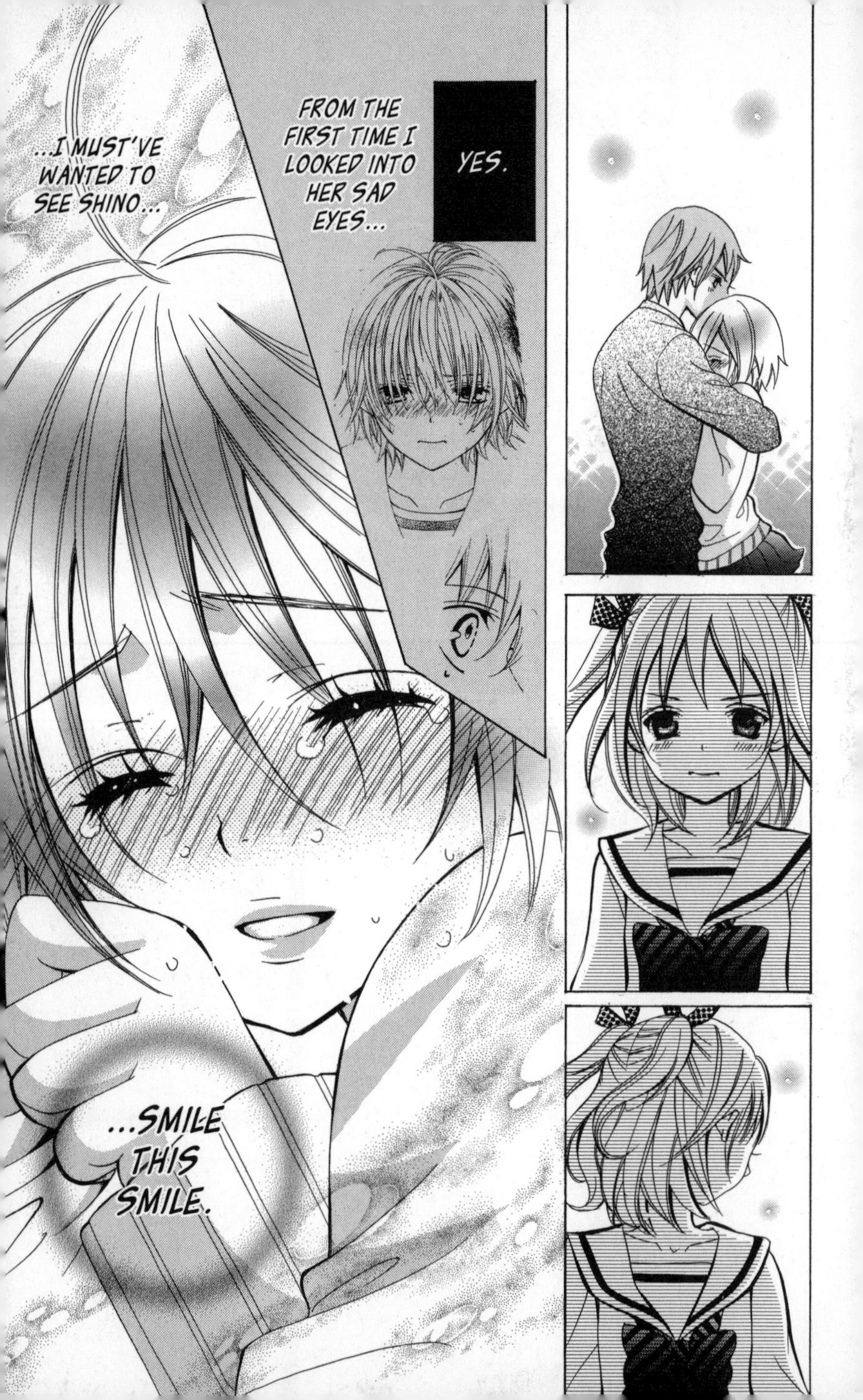
YES.
FROM THE FIRST TIME I LOOKED INTO HER SAD EYES...
...I MUST'VE WANTED TO SEE SHINO...
...SMILE THIS SMILE.

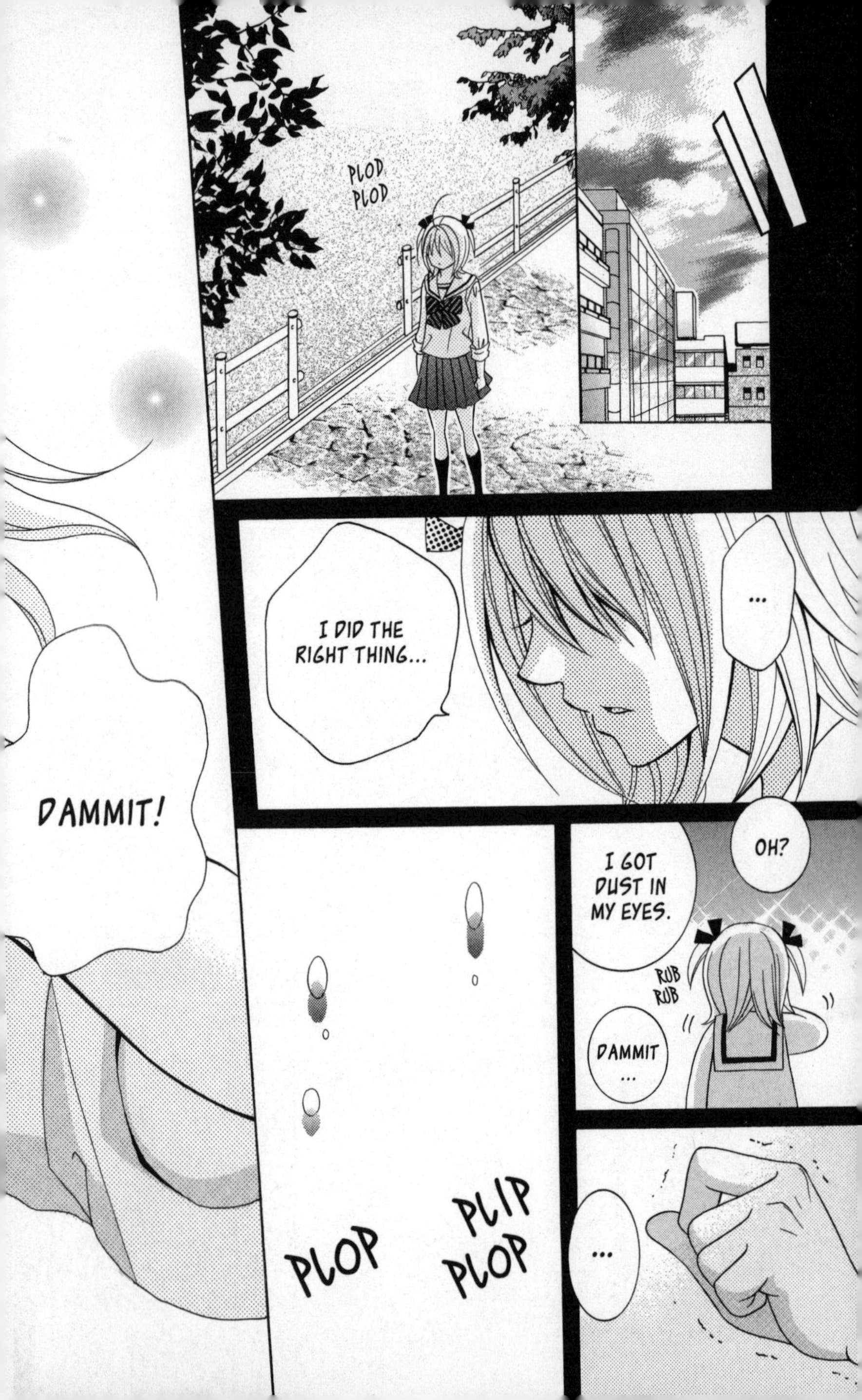
PLOD PLOD
...
I DID THE RIGHT THING...
OH?
I GOT DUST IN MY EYES.
RUB RUB
DAMMIT ...
...
PLIP PLOP
PLOP
DAMMIT!

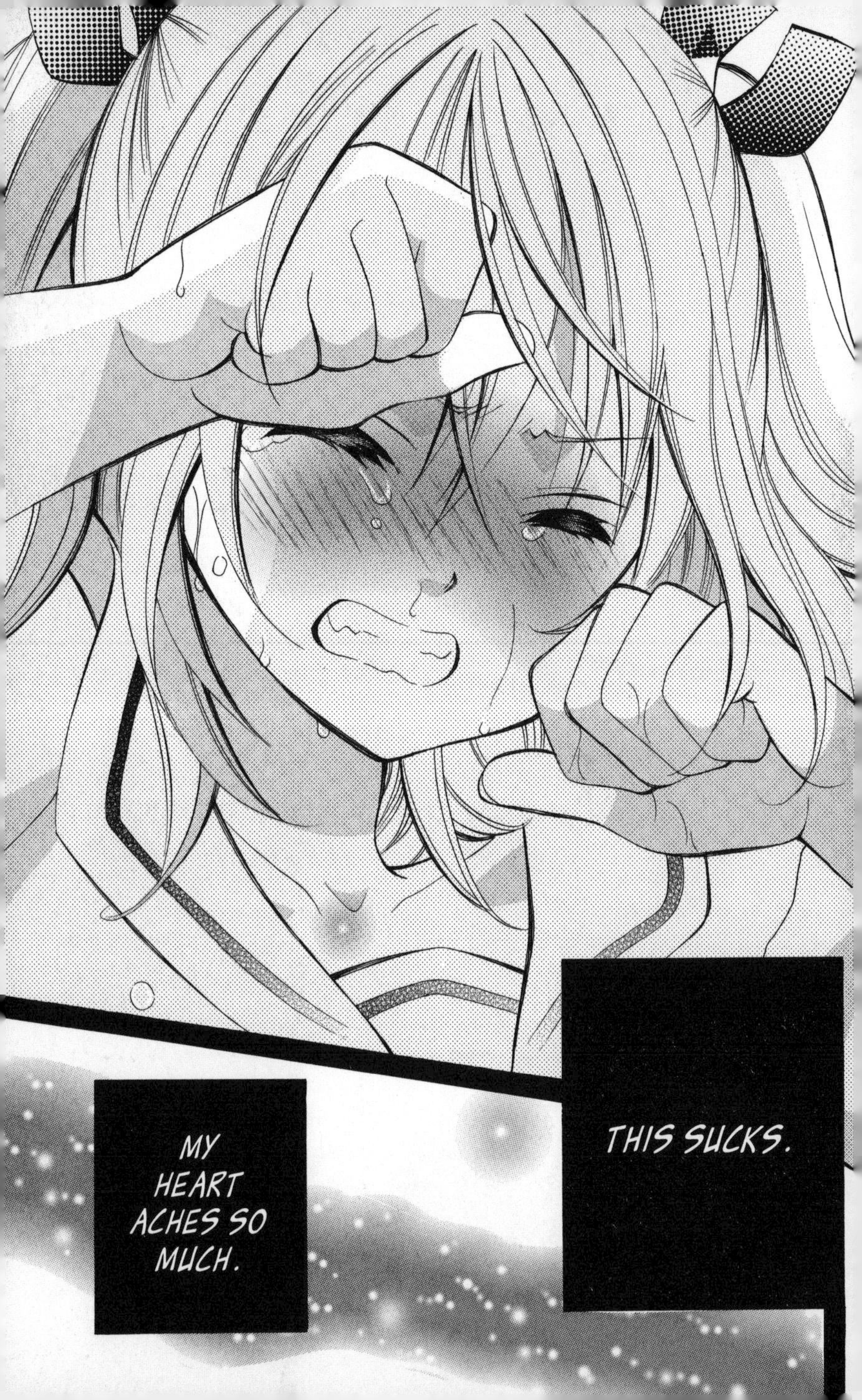
THIS SUCKS.
MY HEART ACHES SO MUCH.

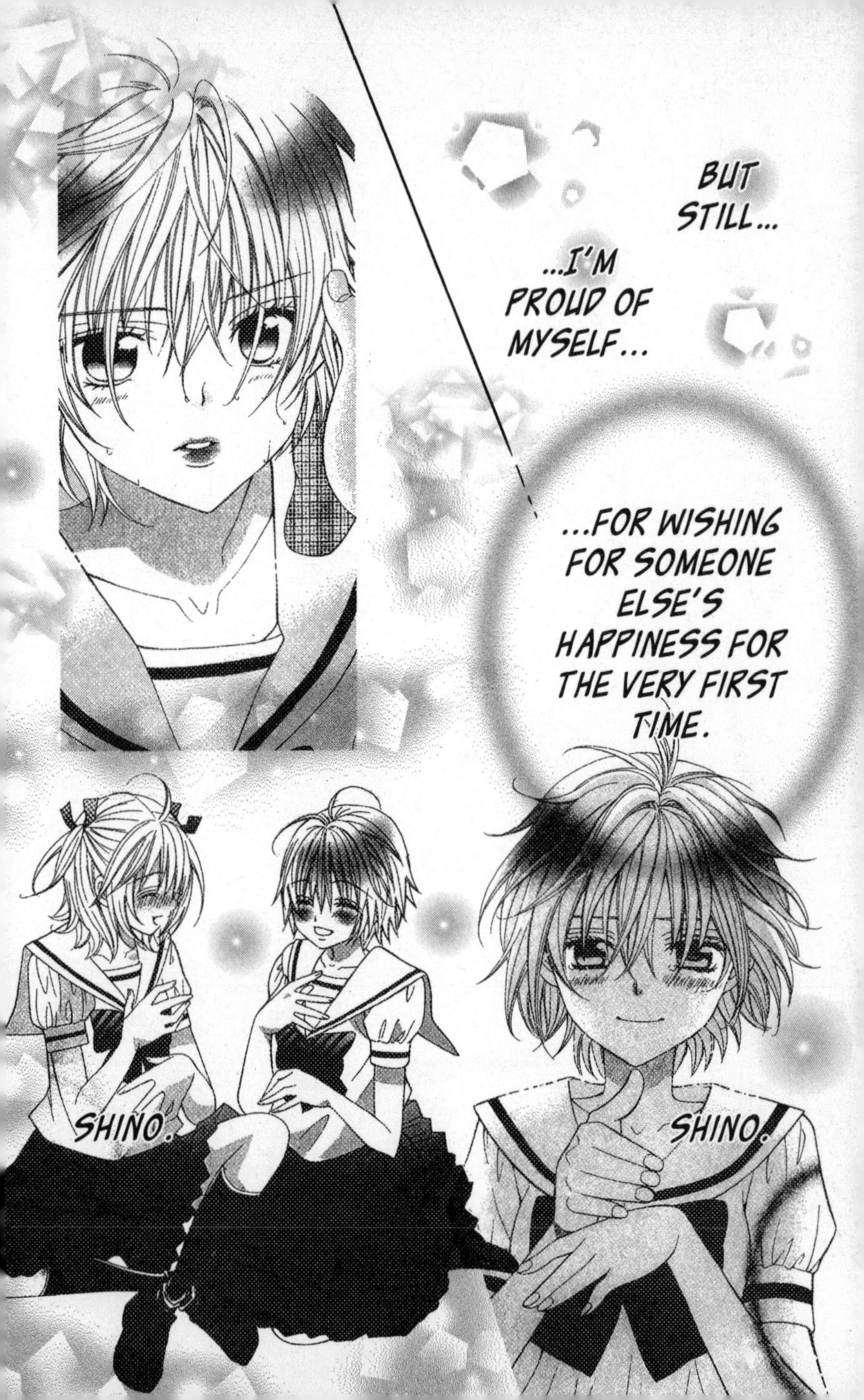
BUT STILL...
...I'M PROUD OF MYSELF...
...FOR WISHING FOR SOMEONE ELSE'S HAPPINESS FOR THE VERY FIRST TIME.
SHINO.
SHINO.

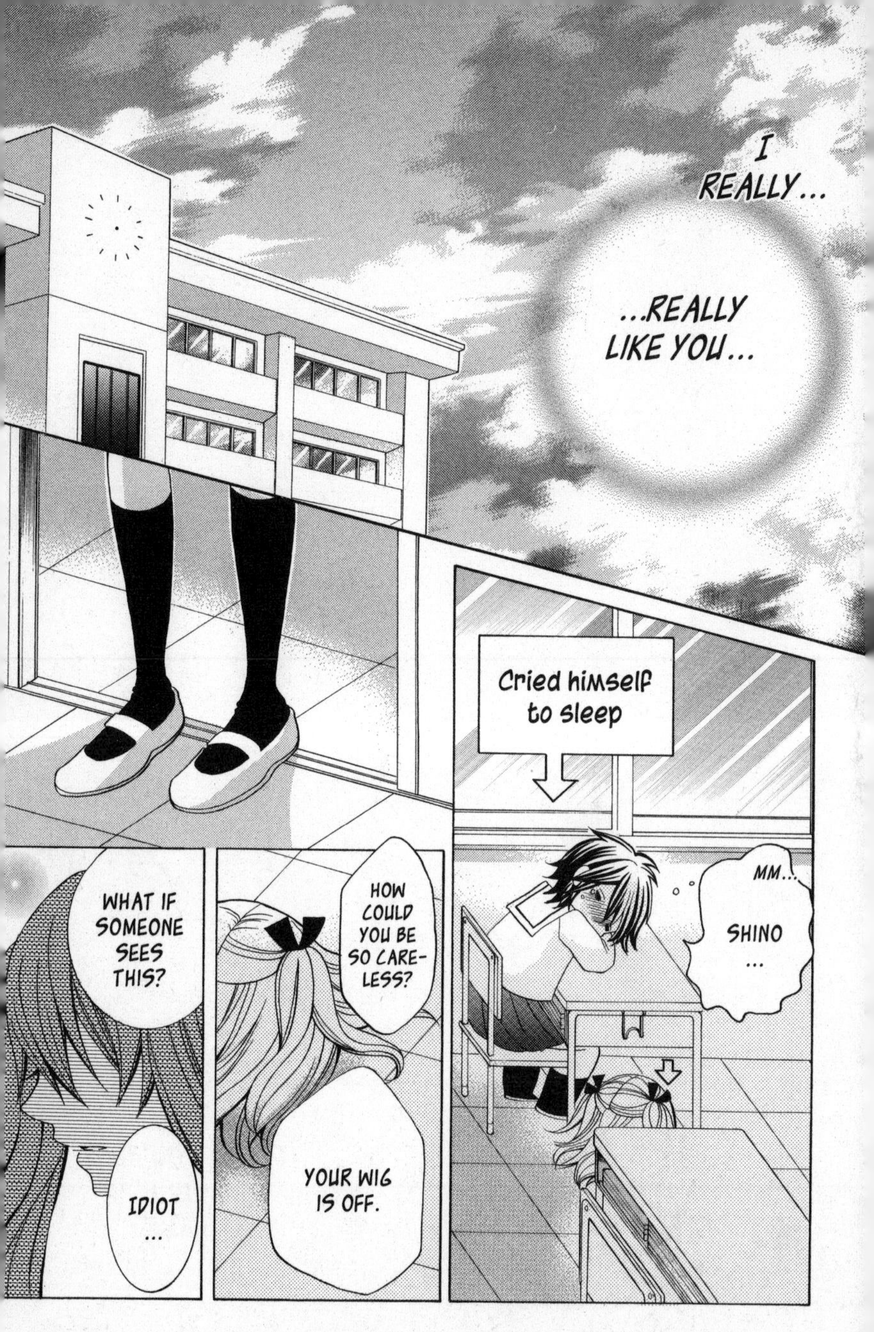
I REALLY...
...REALLY LIKE YOU...
Cried himself to sleep
MM... SHINO ...
HOW COULD YOU BE SO CARE-LESS?
YOUR WIG IS OFF.
WHAT IF SOMEONE SEES THIS?
IDIOT ...

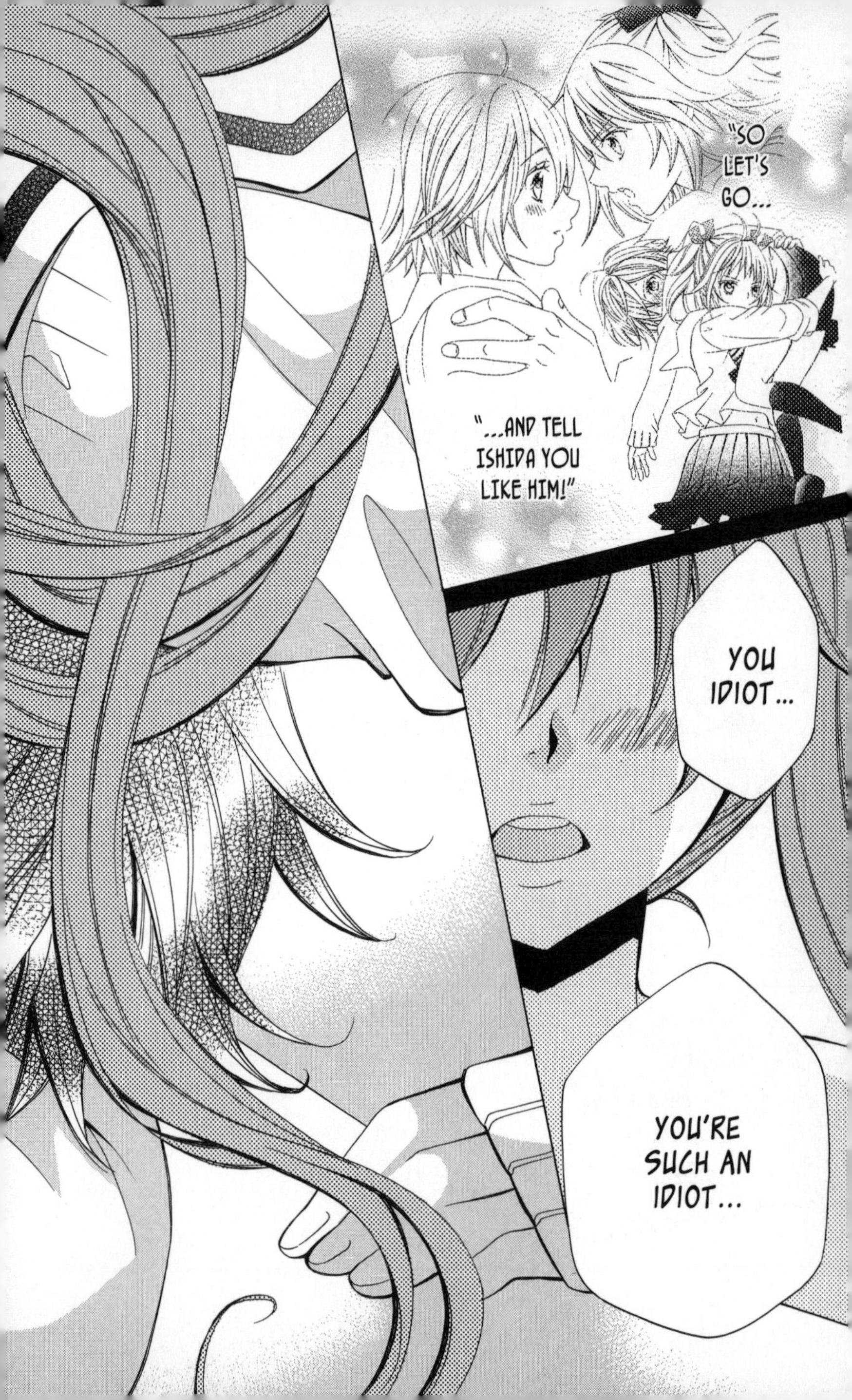
"SO LET'S GO...
"...AND TELL ISHIDA YOU LIKE HIM!"
YOU IDIOT...
YOU'RE SUCH AN IDIOT...

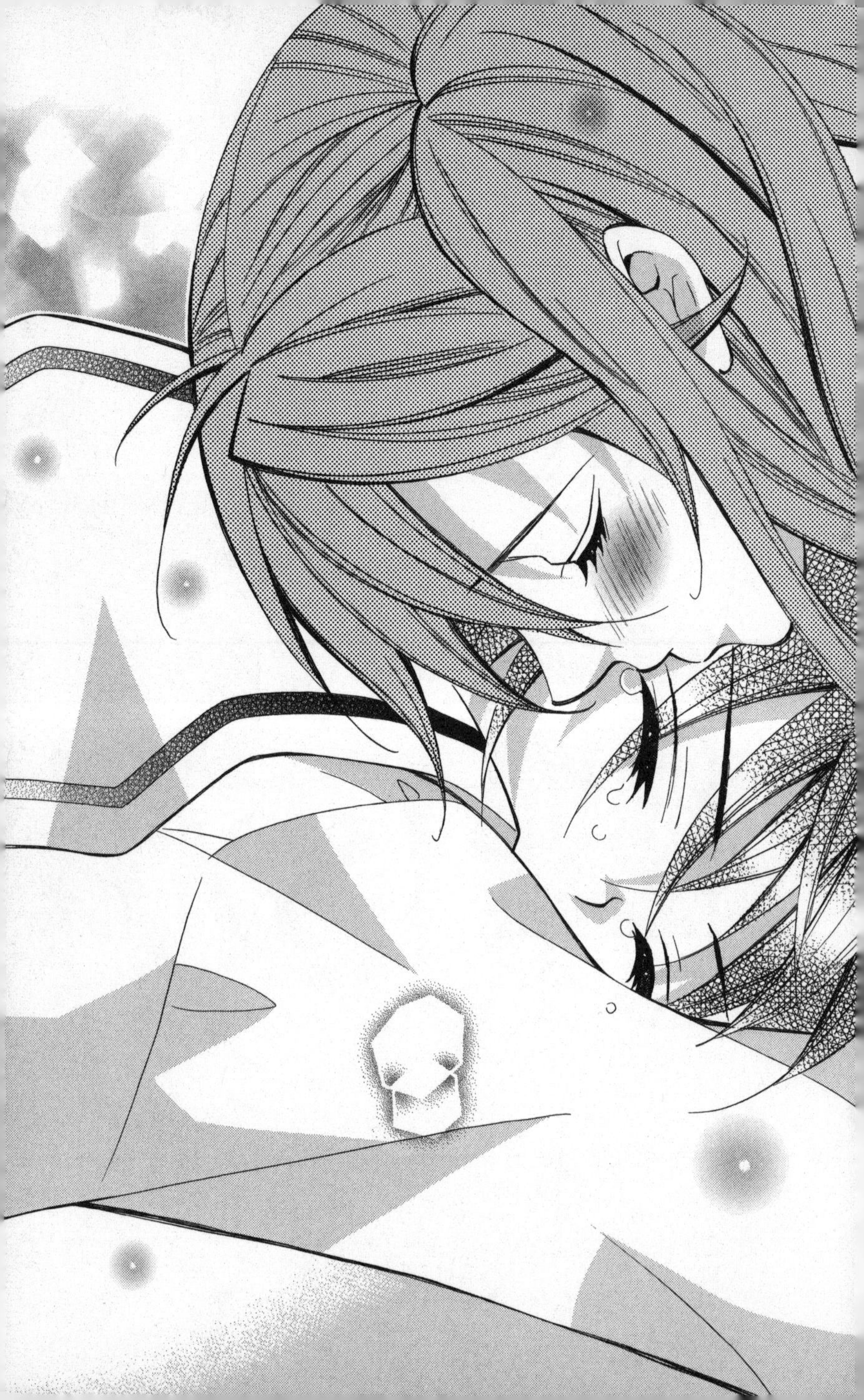

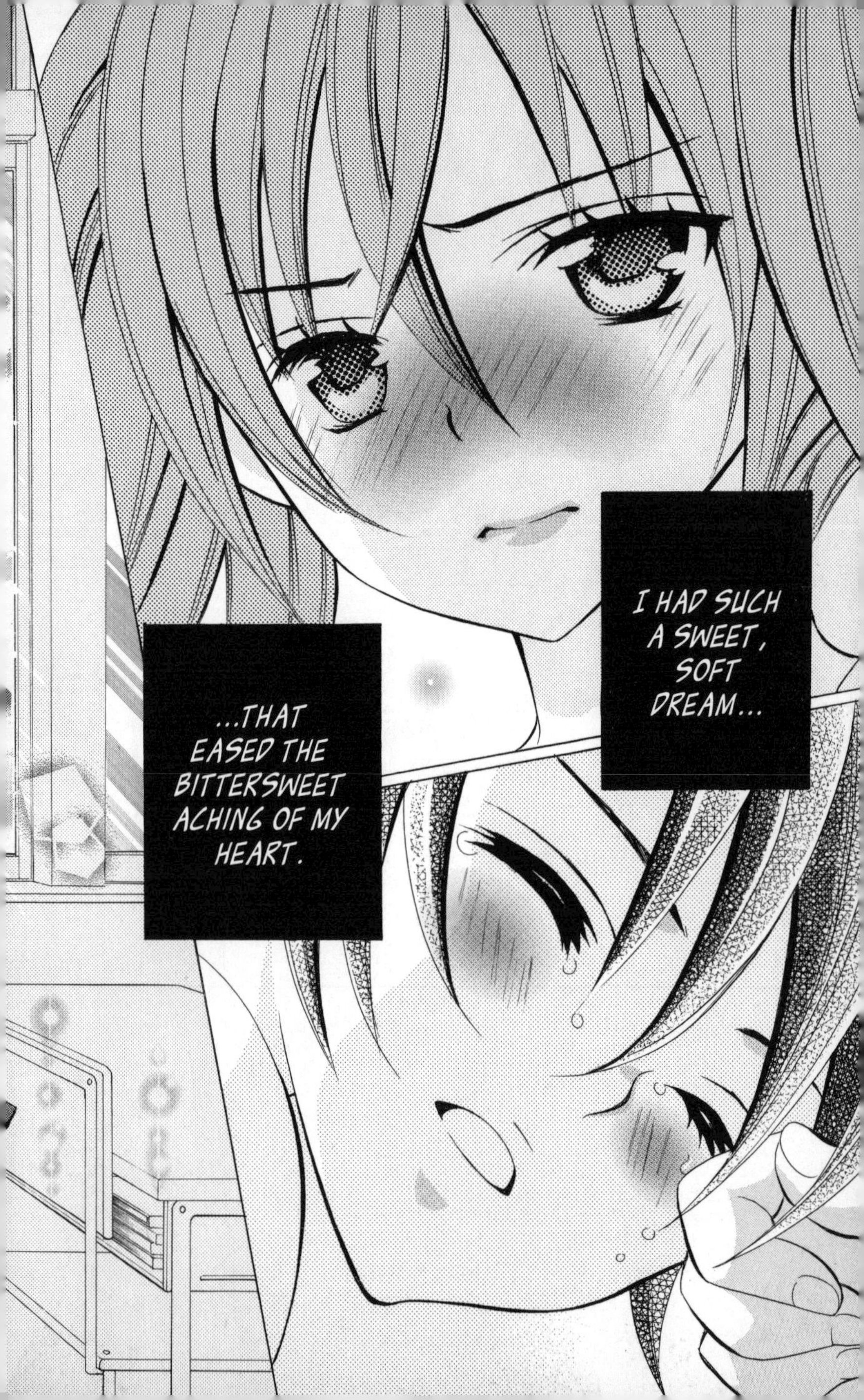
I HAD SUCH A SWEET, SOFT DREAM...
...THAT EASED THE BITTERSWEET ACHING OF MY HEART.

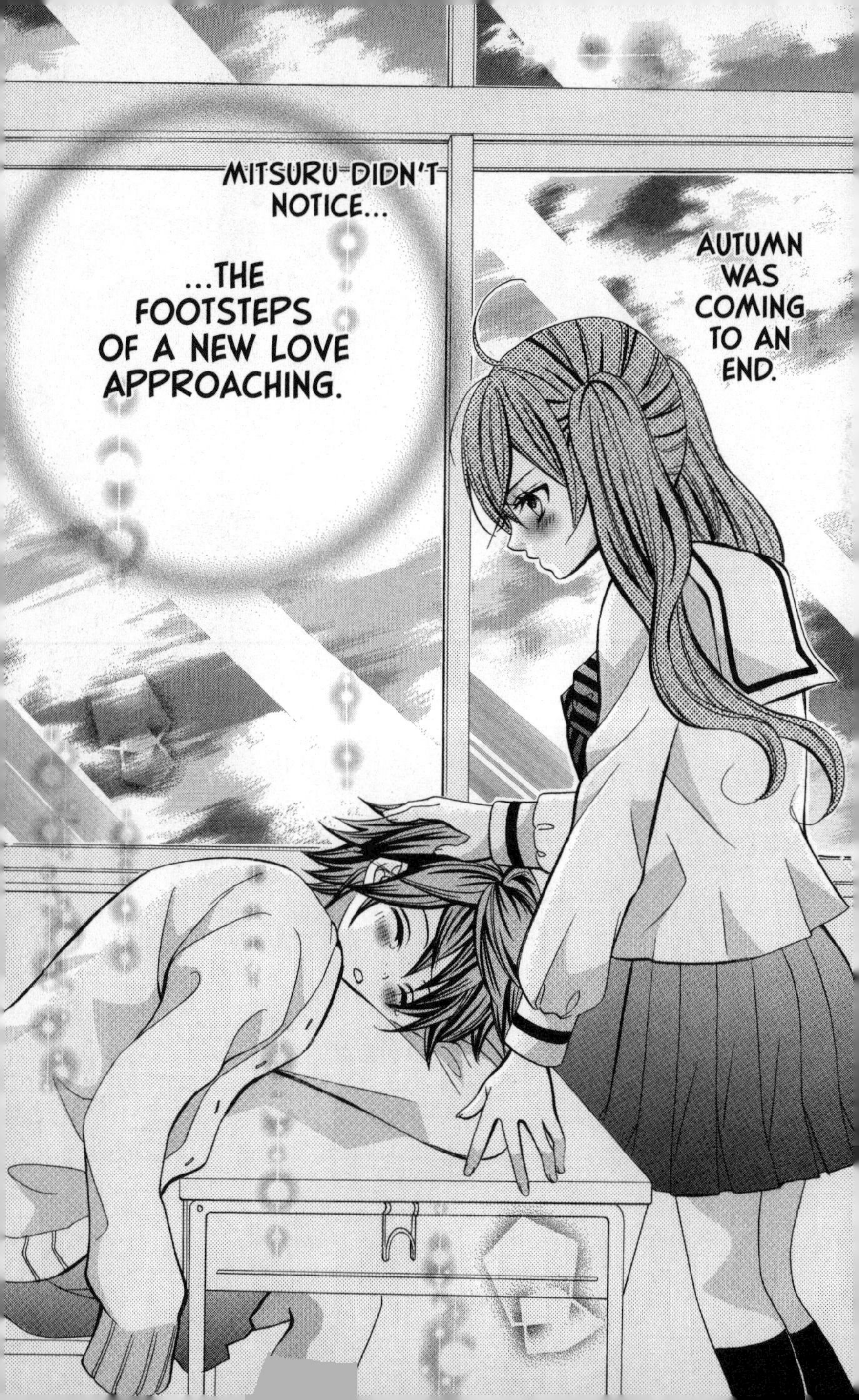
AUTUMN WAS COMING TO AN END.
MITSURU DIDN'T NOTICE...
...THE FOOTSTEPS OF A NEW LOVE APPROACHING.

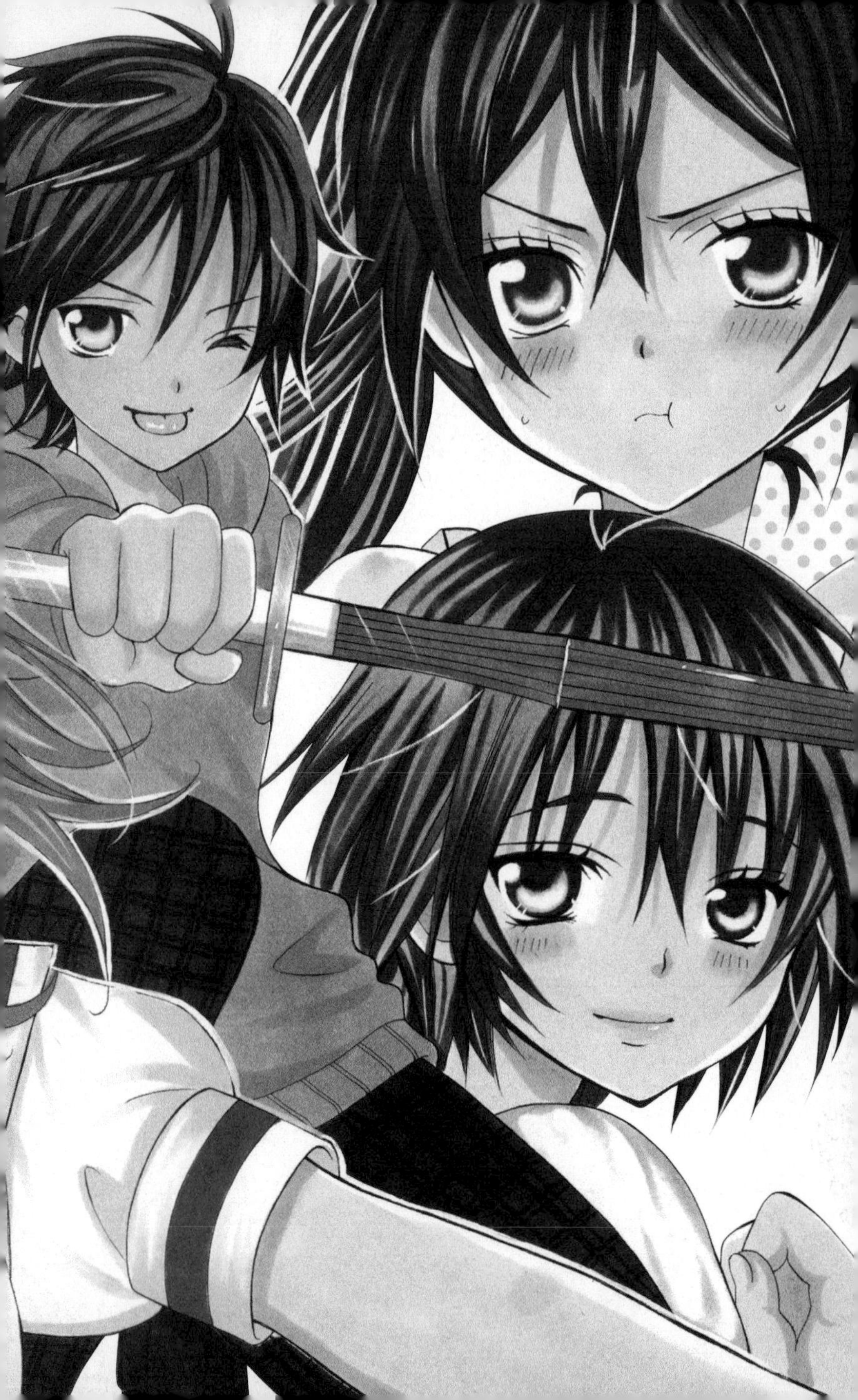

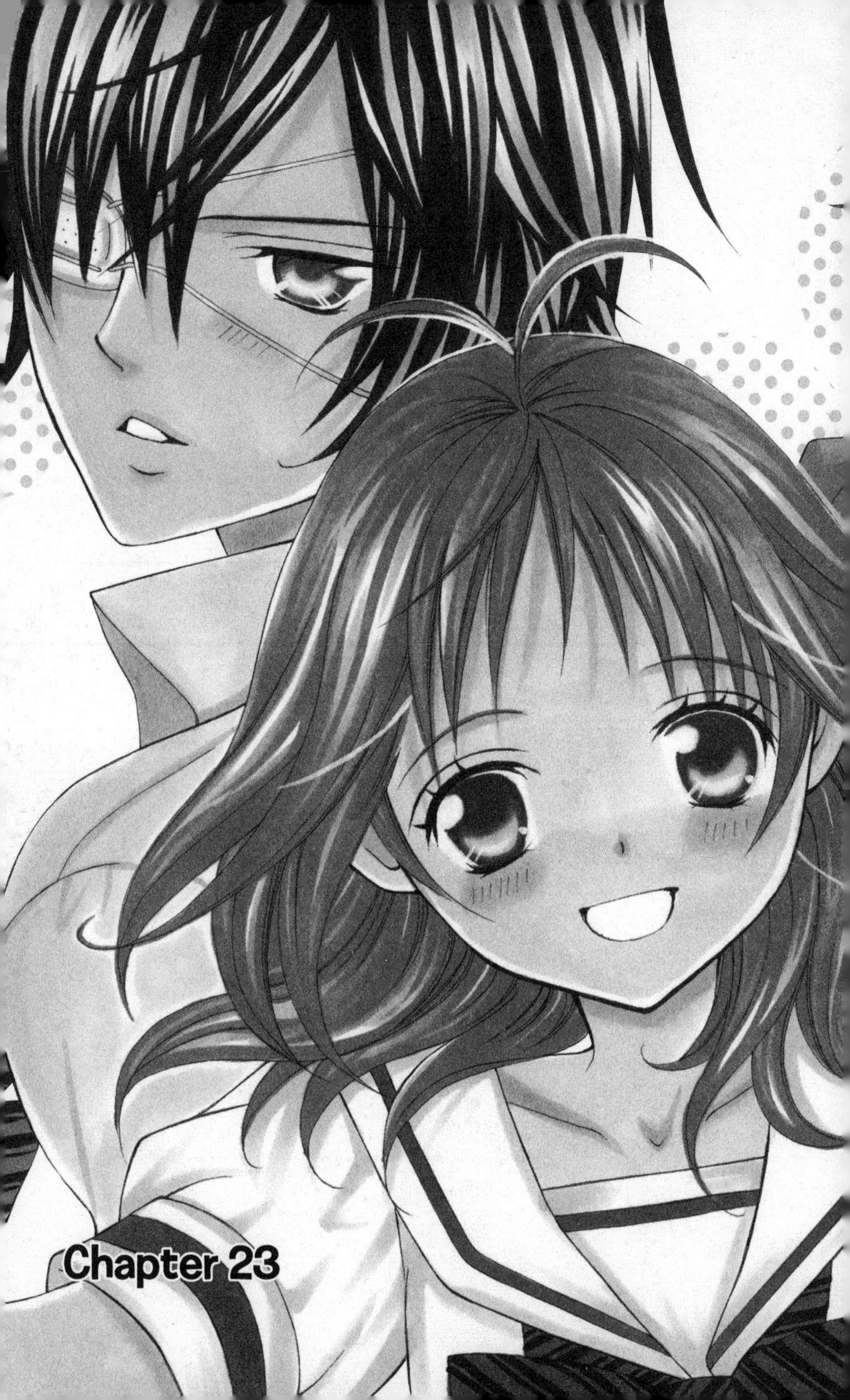
Chapter 23

EVERYONE'S DRAWINGS ARE SO CUTE, THEY HURT!!

SO CUTE! FAN ART FEATURE ♥

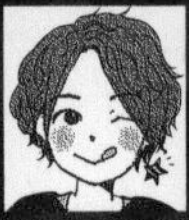

Editor Shoji

Here we show you everyone's fan art. ♪
Editor Shoji has commented on each one this time too!!

We've got lots of drawings this time.
The feature continues on page 116!!

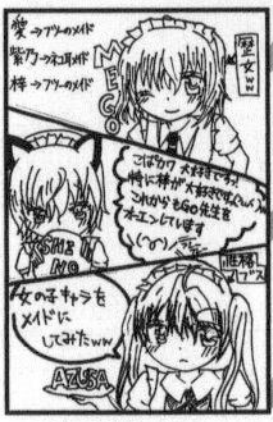
AZUSA

Editor: The three maids are just too cute!!

↑ Marisa (Osaka)

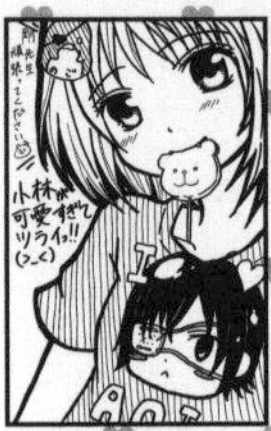

Editor: I want the Aoi T-shirt!!

↑ Kumanoko ☆ (Iwate)

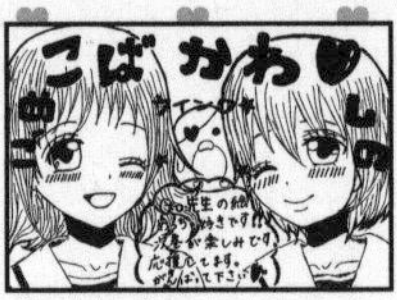
こばかわ♥

← Pyontaro (Osaka)

Editor: The eye-patch penguin sandwiched between the two heroines looks very odd. LOL.

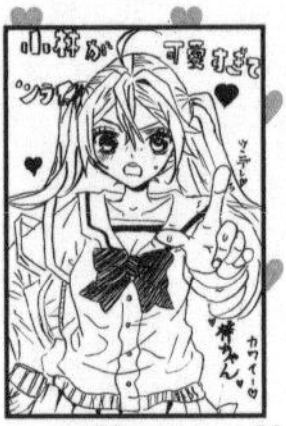

Editor: Everyone's drawing Azusa nowadays!

↑ Miyu Fukano (Kanagawa)

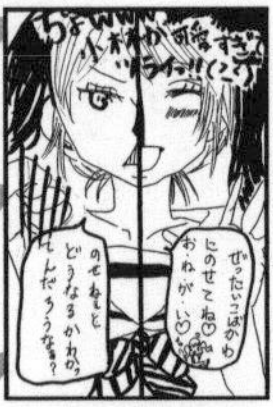

Editor: Y-yes, we'll publish it... (>_<)

↑ Ayaka Yokota (Fukuoka)

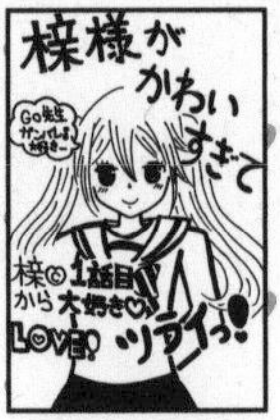
梓様がかわいすぎて
LOVE! ツライっ!!

Editor: Her popularity is soaring!! Azusa, Queen of tsundere! ♥

↑ Sakura Shishido (Tokushima)

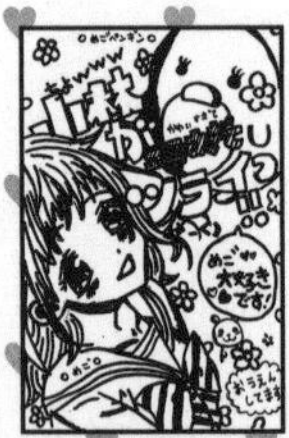

Editor: Mego the heroine is the most popular character!

↑ Tsubomi Honsa (Ishikawa)

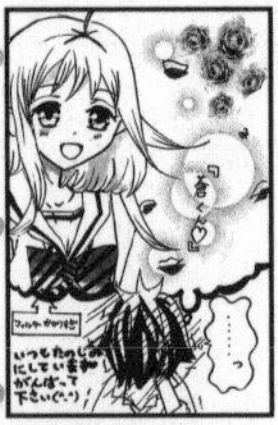

Editor: Aoi is always serious... ♥

↑ nyan-ko (Osaka)

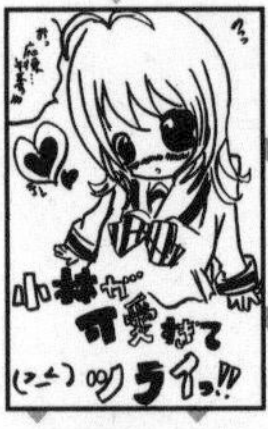
小林が可愛すぎてツライっ!!

Editor: This drawing is full of moe. ♥

↑ Juna Ooi (Tokyo)

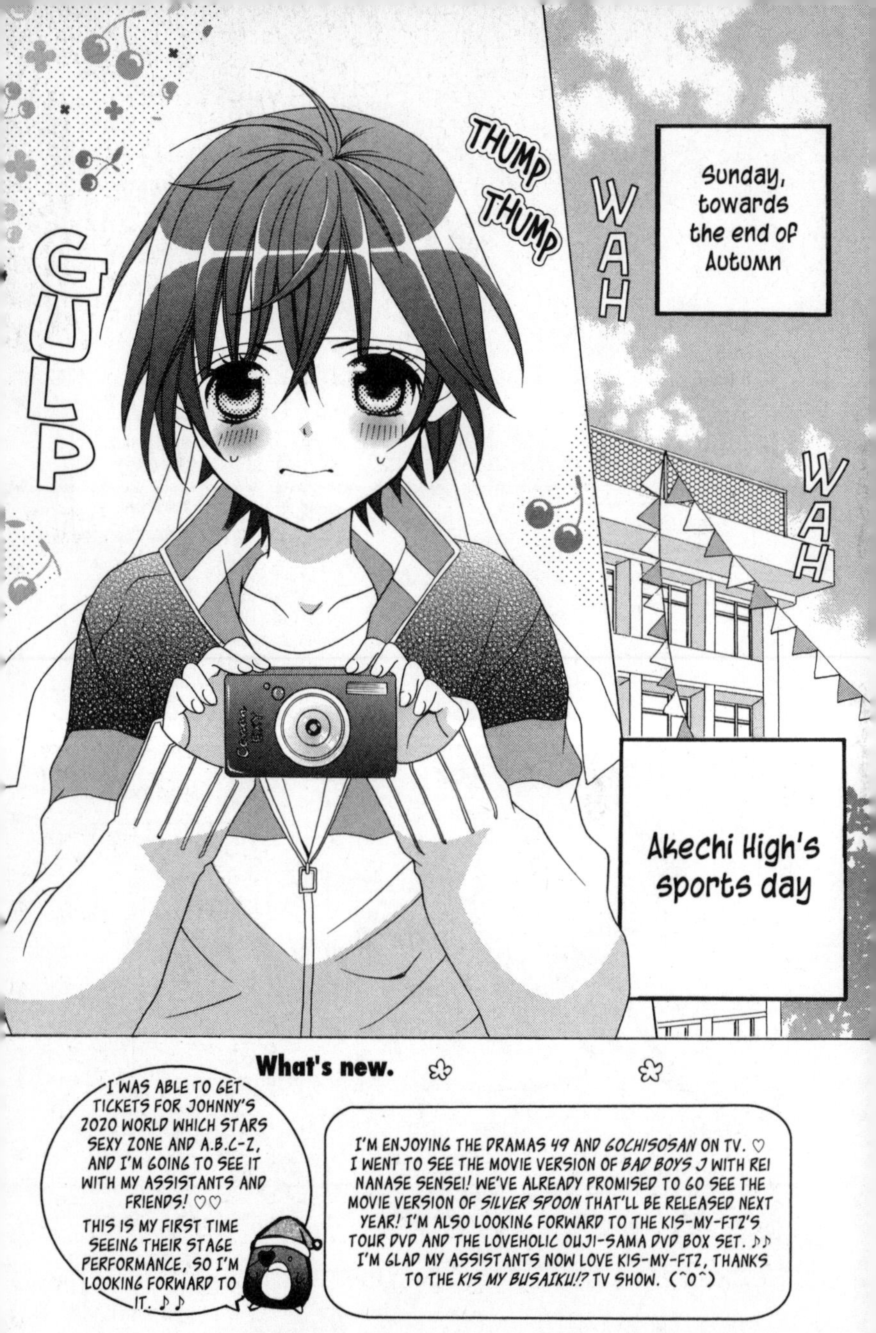
Sunday, towards the end of Autumn
WAH
THUMP THUMP
GULP
WAH
Akechi High's sports day

What's new.

I WAS ABLE TO GET TICKETS FOR JOHNNY'S 2020 WORLD WHICH STARS SEXY ZONE AND A.B.C-Z, AND I'M GOING TO SEE IT WITH MY ASSISTANTS AND FRIENDS! ♡♡
THIS IS MY FIRST TIME SEEING THEIR STAGE PERFORMANCE, SO I'M LOOKING FORWARD TO IT. ♪♪

I'M ENJOYING THE DRAMAS 49 AND *GOCHISOSAN* ON TV. ♡ I WENT TO SEE THE MOVIE VERSION OF *BAD BOYS J* WITH REI NANASE SENSEI! WE'VE ALREADY PROMISED TO GO SEE THE MOVIE VERSION OF *SILVER SPOON* THAT'LL BE RELEASED NEXT YEAR! I'M ALSO LOOKING FORWARD TO THE KIS-MY-FT2'S TOUR DVD AND THE LOVEHOLIC OUJI-SAMA DVD BOX SET. ♪♪ I'M GLAD MY ASSISTANTS NOW LOVE KIS-MY-FT2, THANKS TO THE *KIS MY BUSAIKU!?* TV SHOW. (^0^)

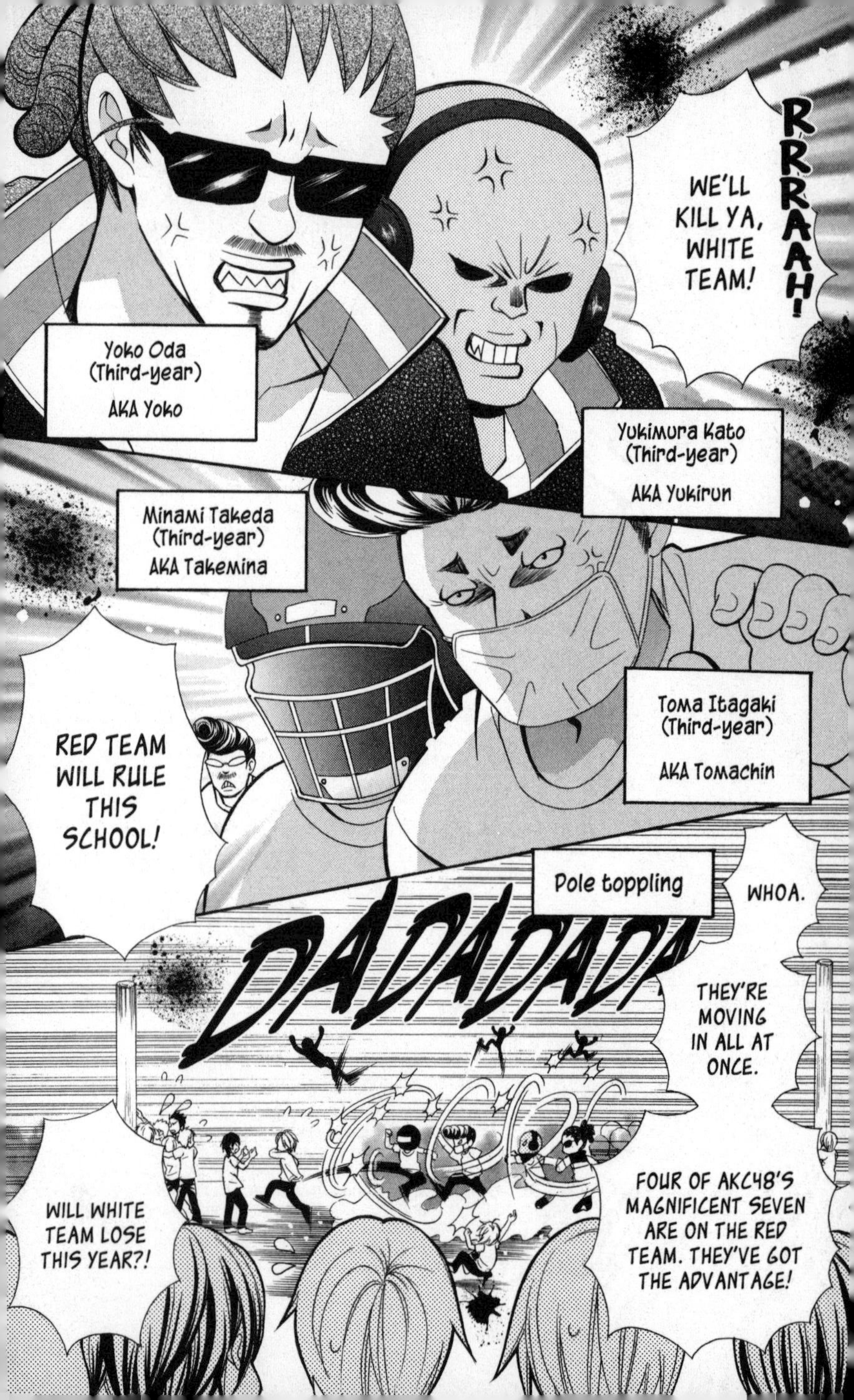
RRRAAH!
WE'LL KILL YA, WHITE TEAM!
Yukimura Kato (Third-year) AKA Yukirun
Yoko Oda (Third-year) AKA Yoko
Minami Takeda (Third-year) AKA Takemina
Toma Itagaki (Third-year) AKA Tomachin
RED TEAM WILL RULE THIS SCHOOL!
Pole toppling
WHOA.
DADADADA
THEY'RE MOVING IN ALL AT ONCE.
FOUR OF AKC48'S MAGNIFICENT SEVEN ARE ON THE RED TEAM. THEY'VE GOT THE ADVANTAGE!
WILL WHITE TEAM LOSE THIS YEAR?!

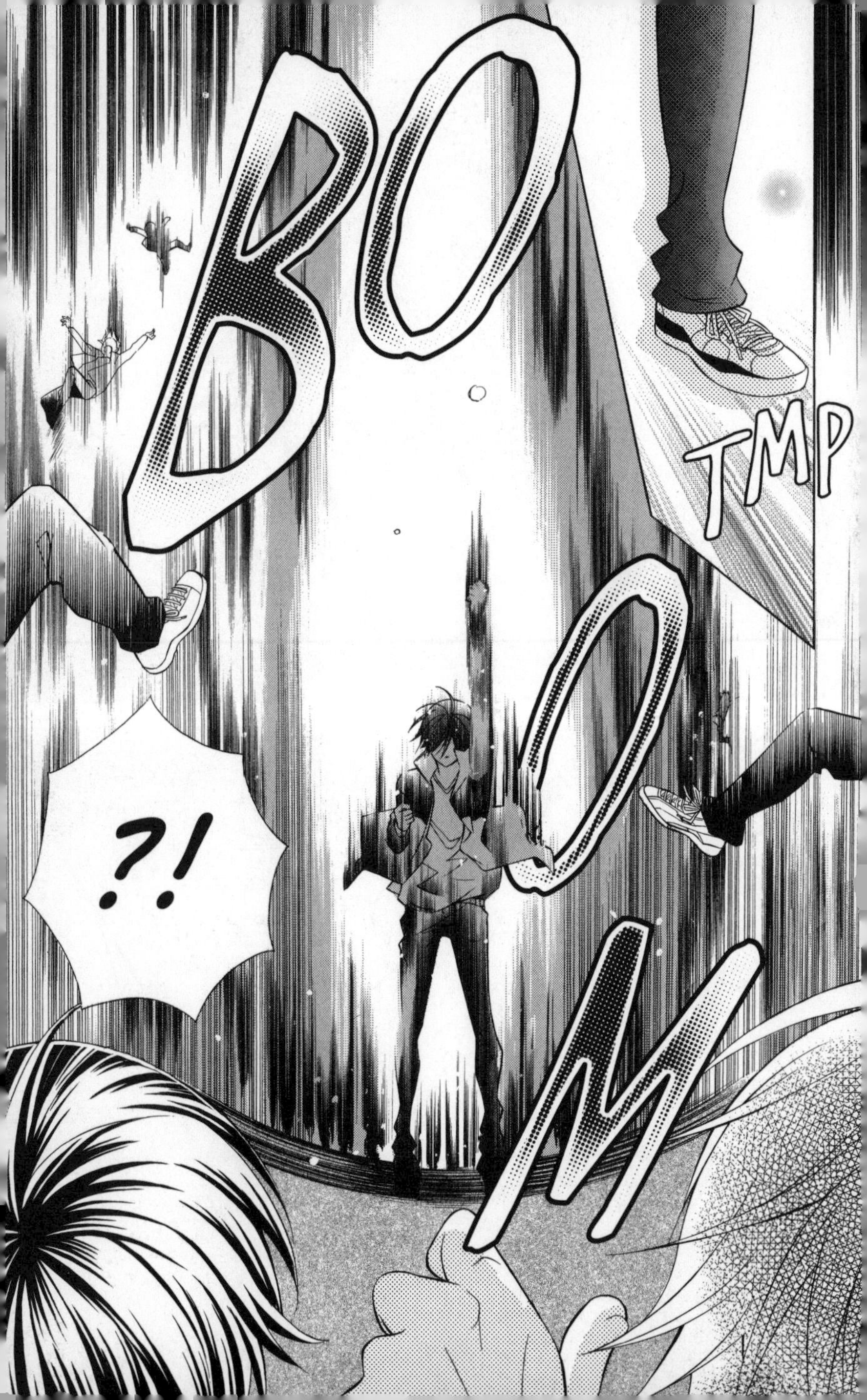
BOOM
TMP
?!

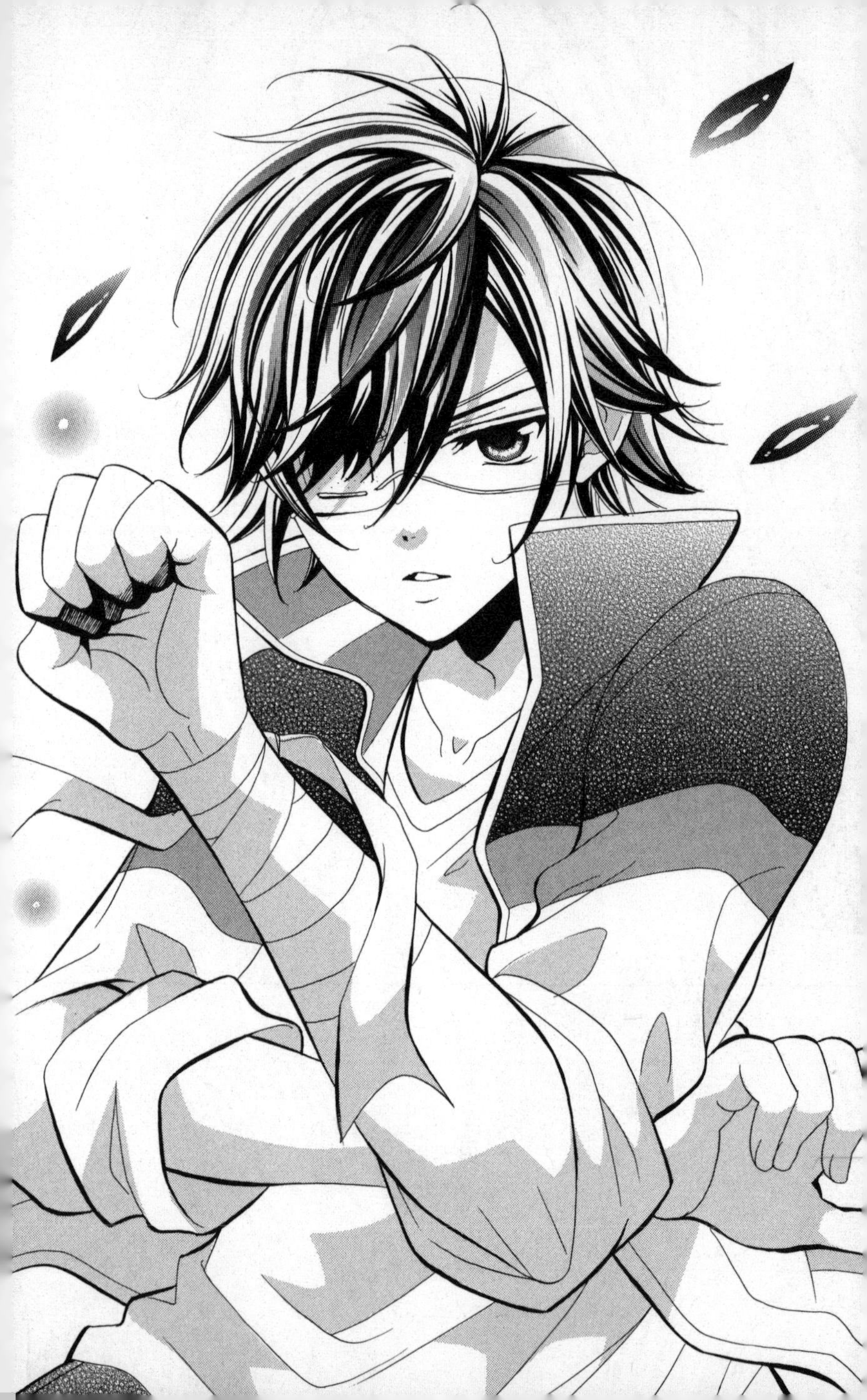

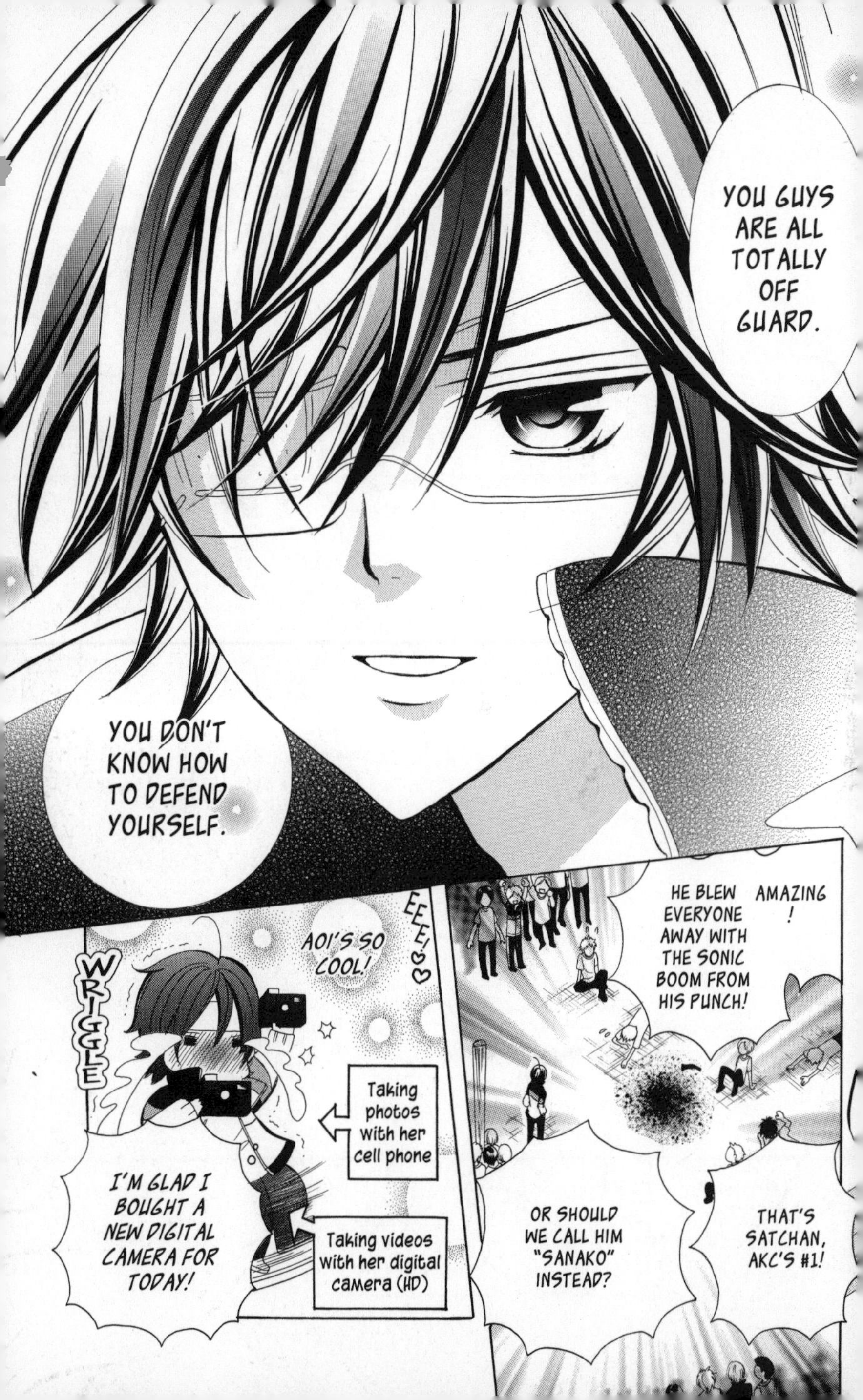
YOU GUYS ARE ALL TOTALLY OFF GUARD.
YOU DON'T KNOW HOW TO DEFEND YOURSELF.
AMAZING!
HE BLEW EVERYONE AWAY WITH THE SONIC BOOM FROM HIS PUNCH!
THAT'S SATCHAN, AKC'S #1!
OR SHOULD WE CALL HIM "SANAKO" INSTEAD?
EEE! ♡
AOI'S SO COOL!
WRIGGLE
Taking photos with her cell phone
Taking videos with her digital camera (HD)
I'M GLAD I BOUGHT A NEW DIGITAL CAMERA FOR TODAY!

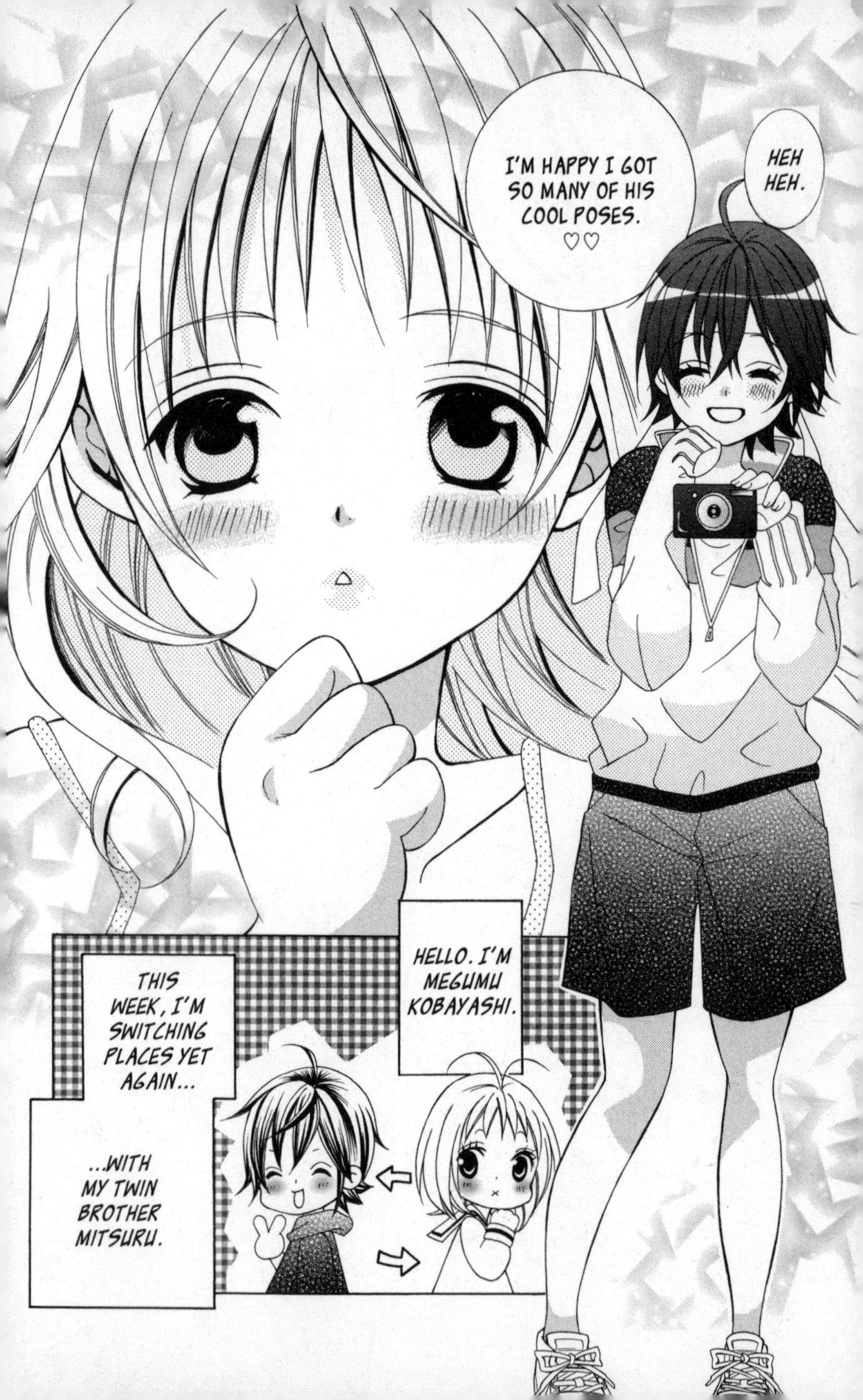
HEH HEH.
I'M HAPPY I GOT SO MANY OF HIS COOL POSES. ♡♡
HELLO. I'M MEGUMU KOBAYASHI.
THIS WEEK, I'M SWITCHING PLACES YET AGAIN...
...WITH MY TWIN BROTHER MITSURU.

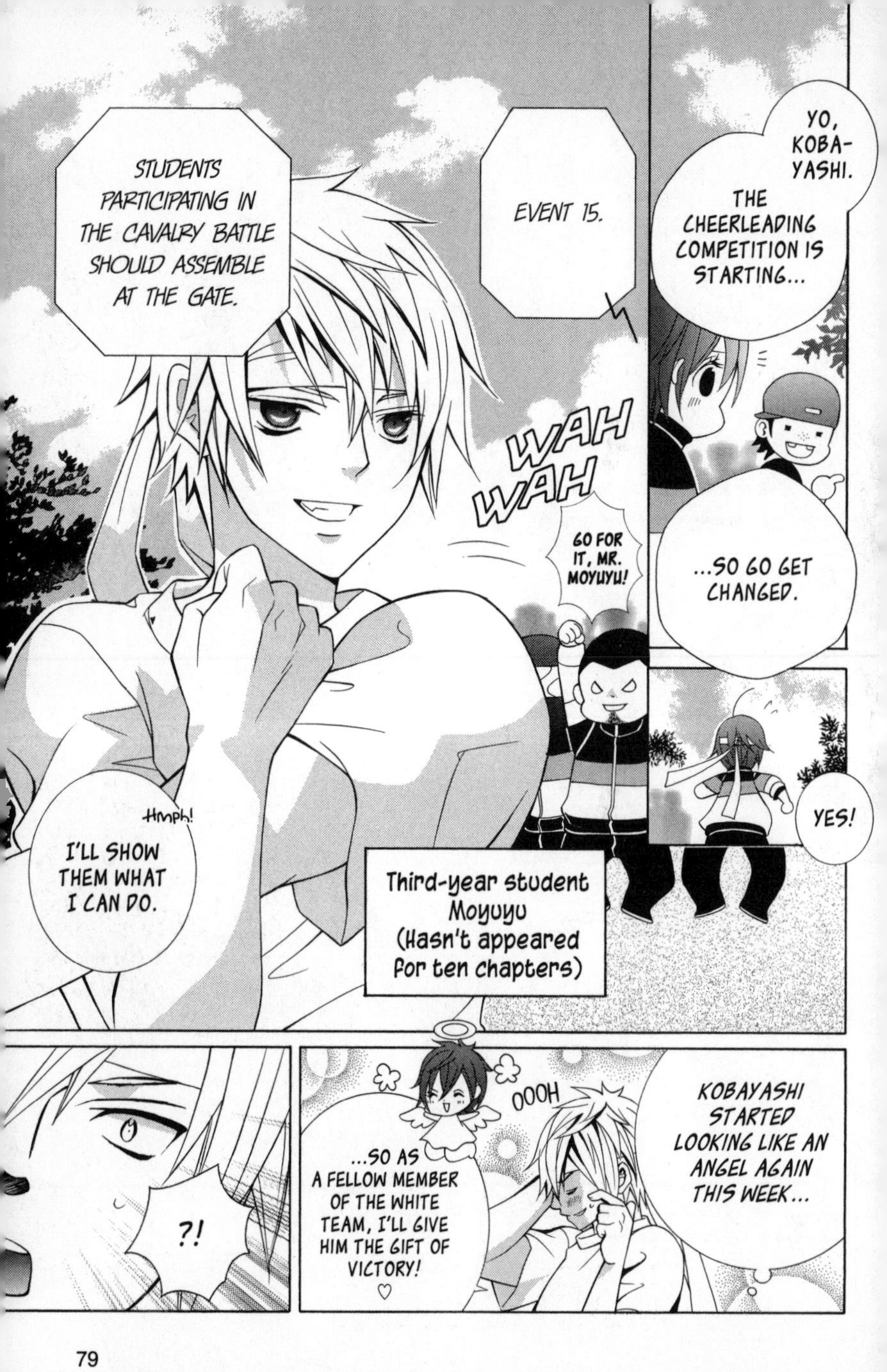
YO, KOBA-YASHI.
THE CHEERLEADING COMPETITION IS STARTING...
...SO GO GET CHANGED.
YES!
EVENT 15.
STUDENTS PARTICIPATING IN THE CAVALRY BATTLE SHOULD ASSEMBLE AT THE GATE.
WAH WAH
GO FOR IT, MR. MOYUYU!
Third-year student Moyuyu (Hasn't appeared for ten chapters)
Hmph!
I'LL SHOW THEM WHAT I CAN DO.
KOBAYASHI STARTED LOOKING LIKE AN ANGEL AGAIN THIS WEEK...
OOOH
...SO AS A FELLOW MEMBER OF THE WHITE TEAM, I'LL GIVE HIM THE GIFT OF VICTORY! ♡
?!

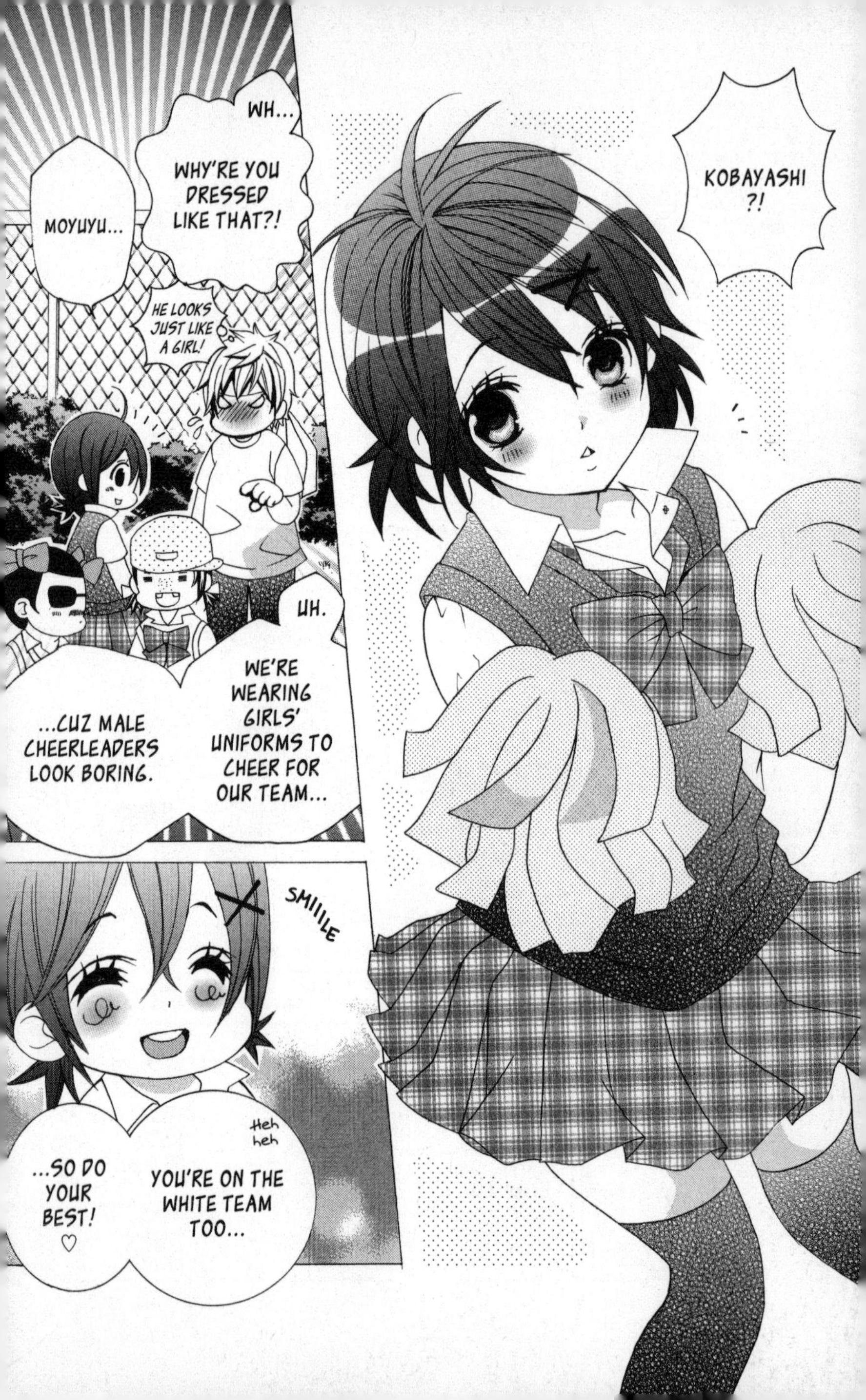
KOBAYASHI ?!
WH... WHY'RE YOU DRESSED LIKE THAT?!
MOYUYU...
HE LOOKS JUST LIKE A GIRL!
UH.
WE'RE WEARING GIRLS' UNIFORMS TO CHEER FOR OUR TEAM...
...CUZ MALE CHEERLEADERS LOOK BORING.
SMIIILE
Heh heh
YOU'RE ON THE WHITE TEAM TOO...
...SO DO YOUR BEST! ♡

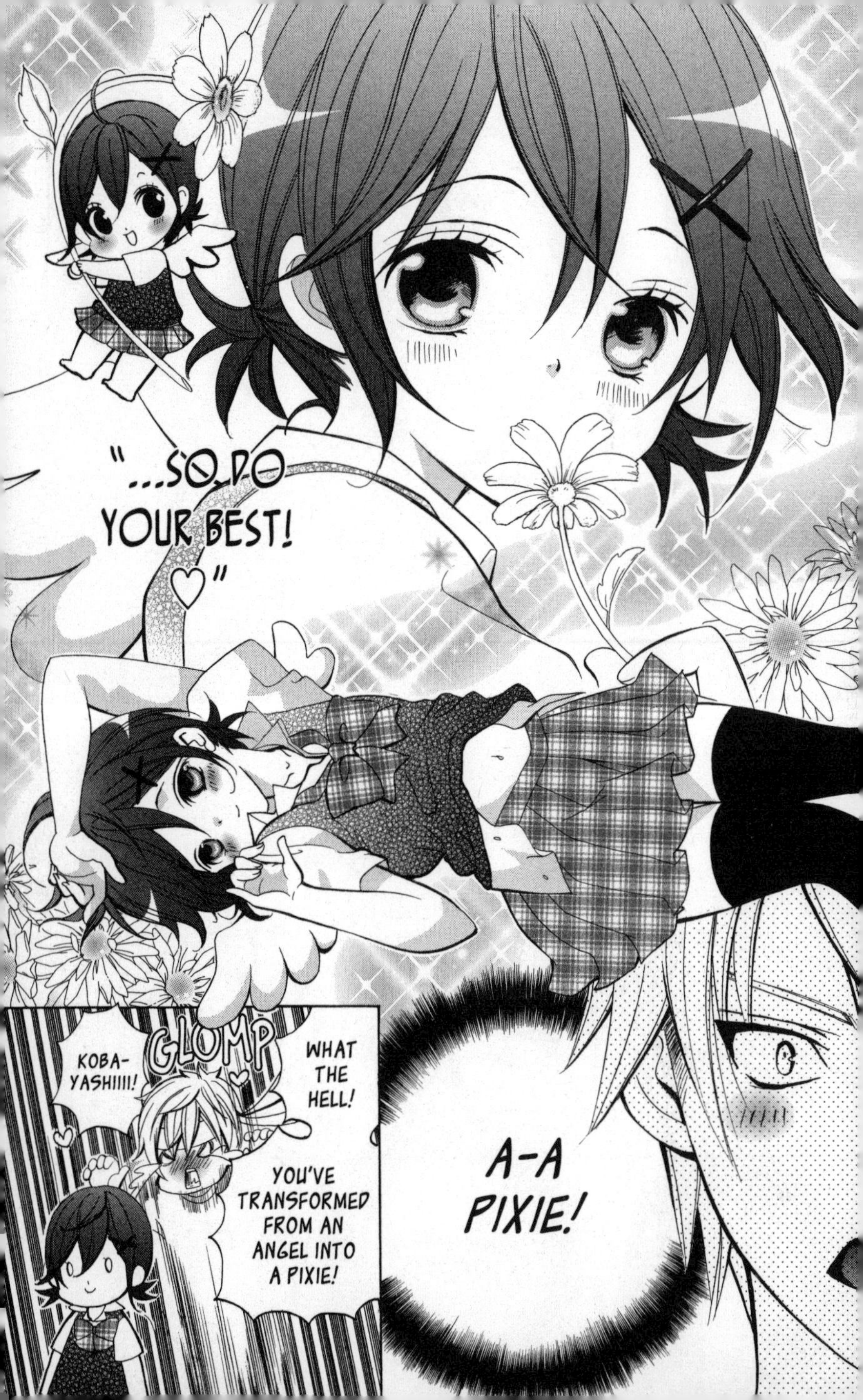
"...SO DO YOUR BEST! ♡"
A-A PIXIE!
WHAT THE HELL!
GLOMP
KOBA-YASHIIIII!
YOU'VE TRANSFORMED FROM AN ANGEL INTO A PIXIE!

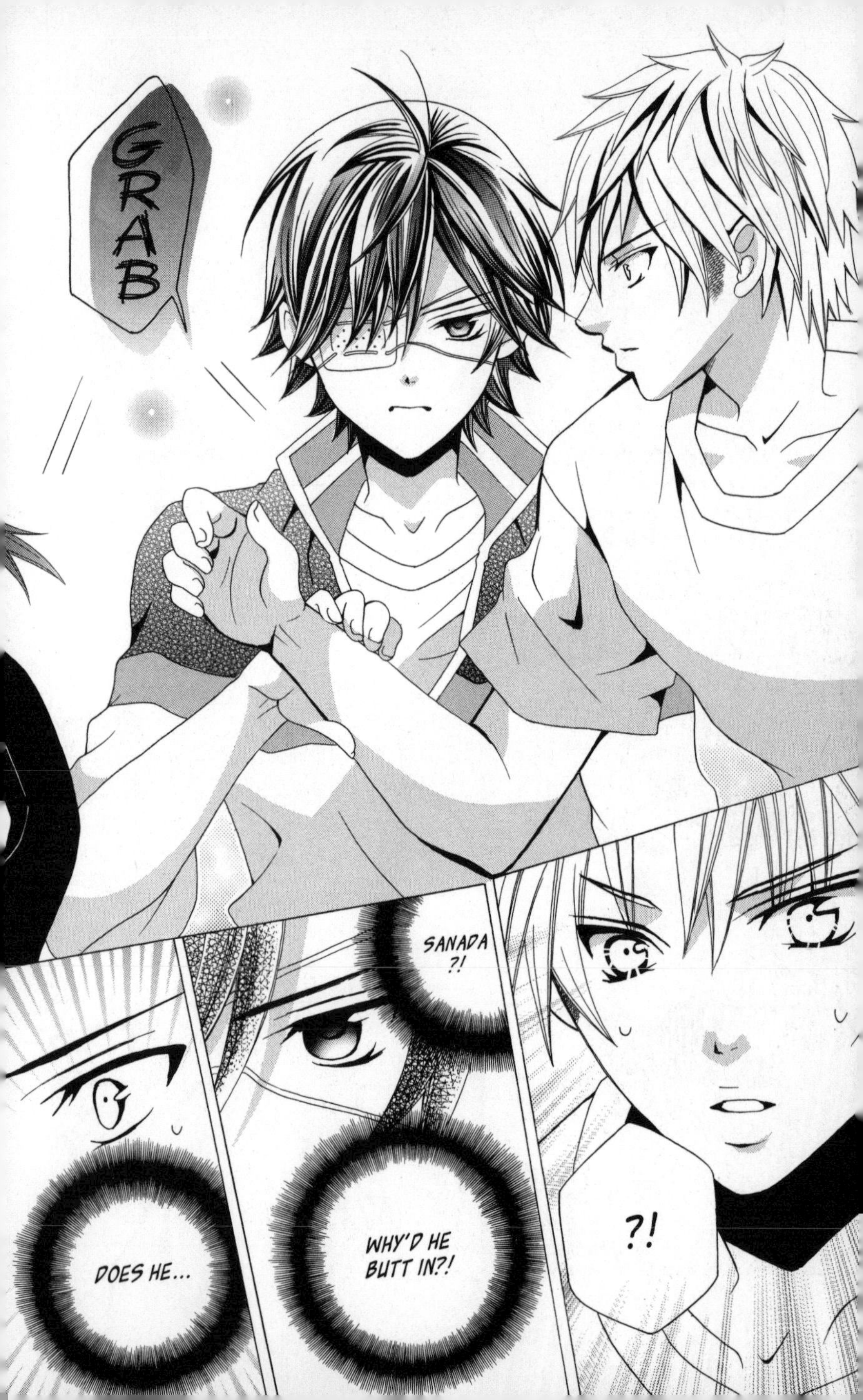
GRAB
?!
SANADA ?!
WHY'D HE BUTT IN?!
DOES HE...

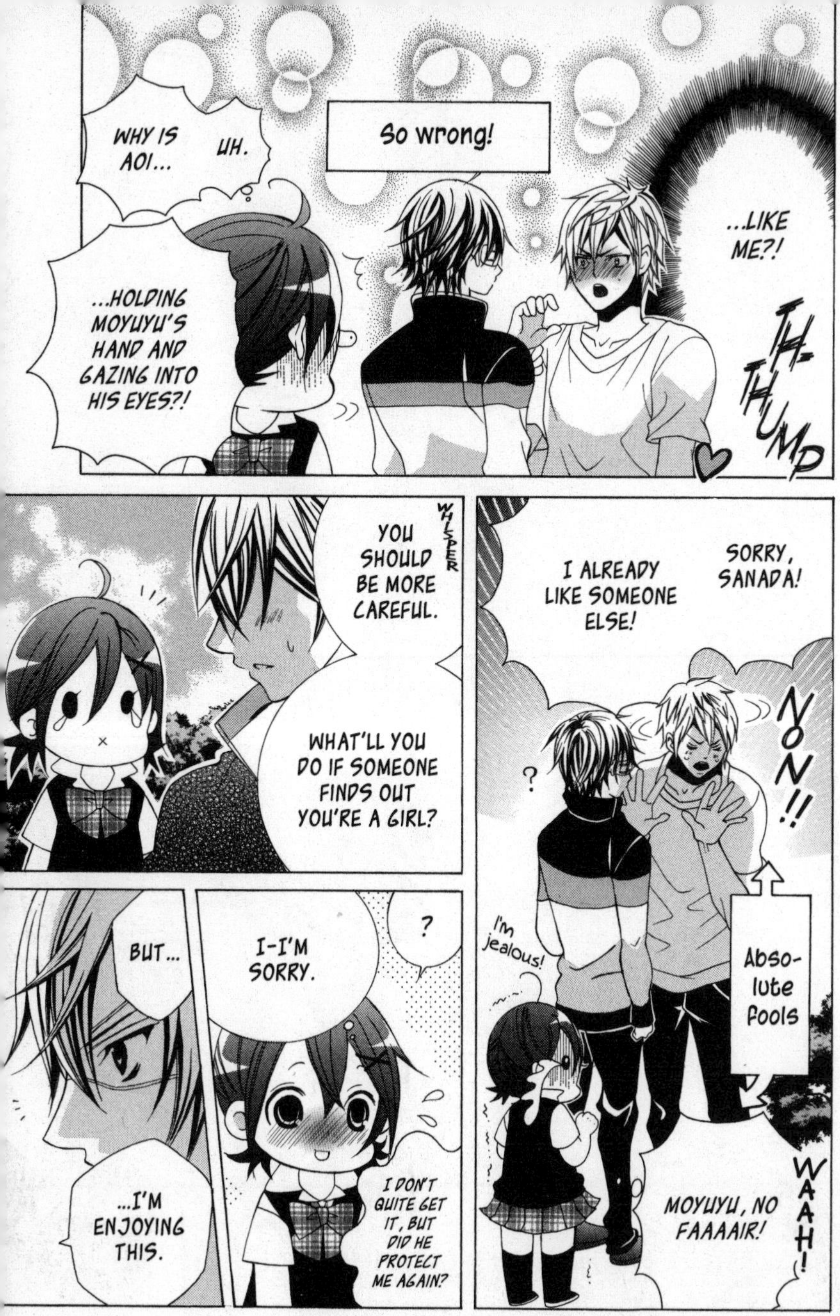
So wrong!
...LIKE ME?!
TH-THUMP
WHY IS AOI...
UH.
...HOLDING MOYUYU'S HAND AND GAZING INTO HIS EYES?!
SORRY, SANADA!
I ALREADY LIKE SOMEONE ELSE!
NON!!
Abso-lute fools
I'm jealous!
WAAH!
MOYUYU, NO FAAAAIR!
WHISPER
YOU SHOULD BE MORE CAREFUL.
WHAT'LL YOU DO IF SOMEONE FINDS OUT YOU'RE A GIRL?
?
I-I'M SORRY.
I DON'T QUITE GET IT, BUT DID HE PROTECT ME AGAIN?
BUT...
...I'M ENJOYING THIS.

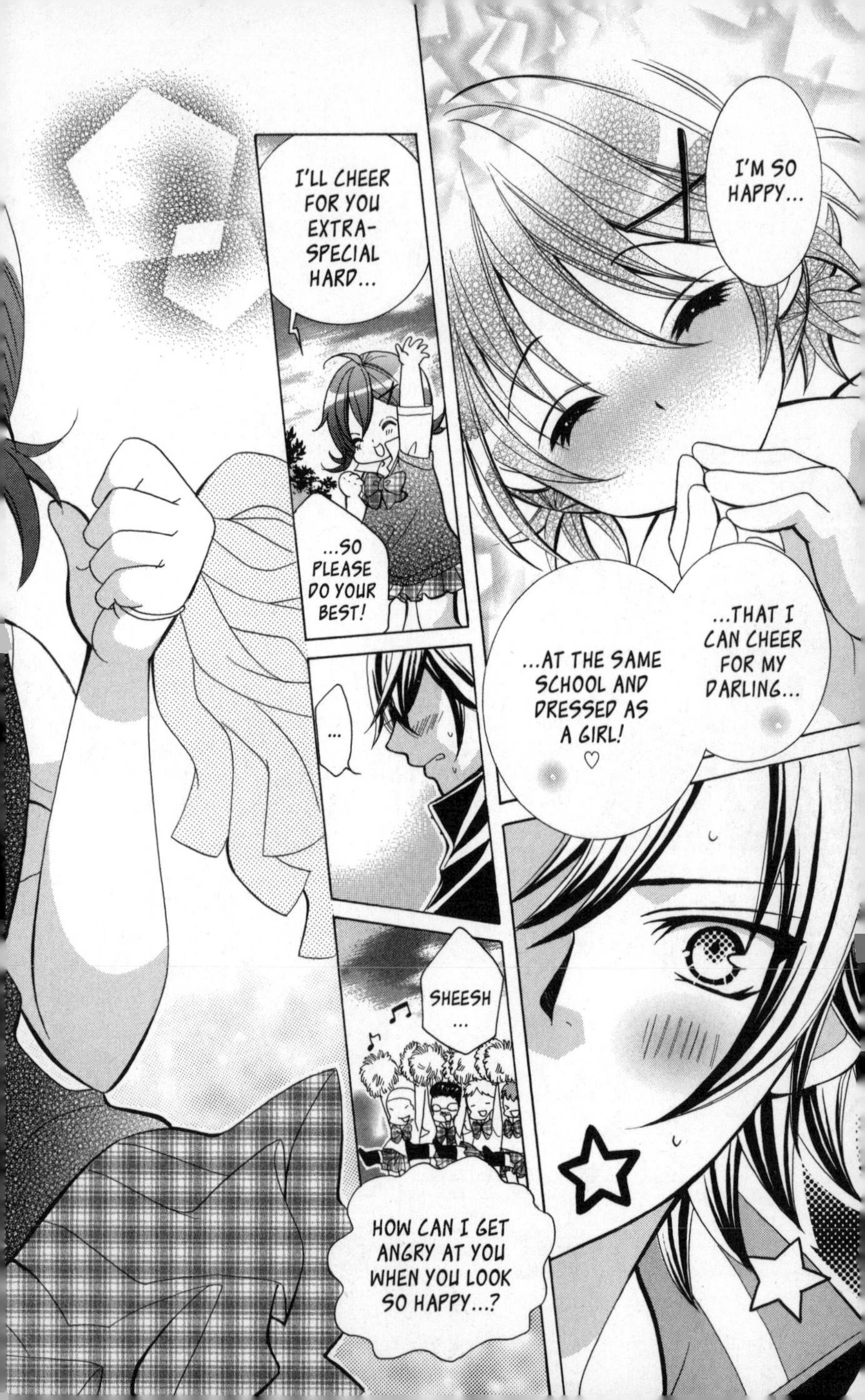
I'M SO HAPPY...
...THAT I CAN CHEER FOR MY DARLING...
...AT THE SAME SCHOOL AND DRESSED AS A GIRL! ♡
I'LL CHEER FOR YOU EXTRA-SPECIAL HARD...
...SO PLEASE DO YOUR BEST!
...
SHEESH...
HOW CAN I GET ANGRY AT YOU WHEN YOU LOOK SO HAPPY...?

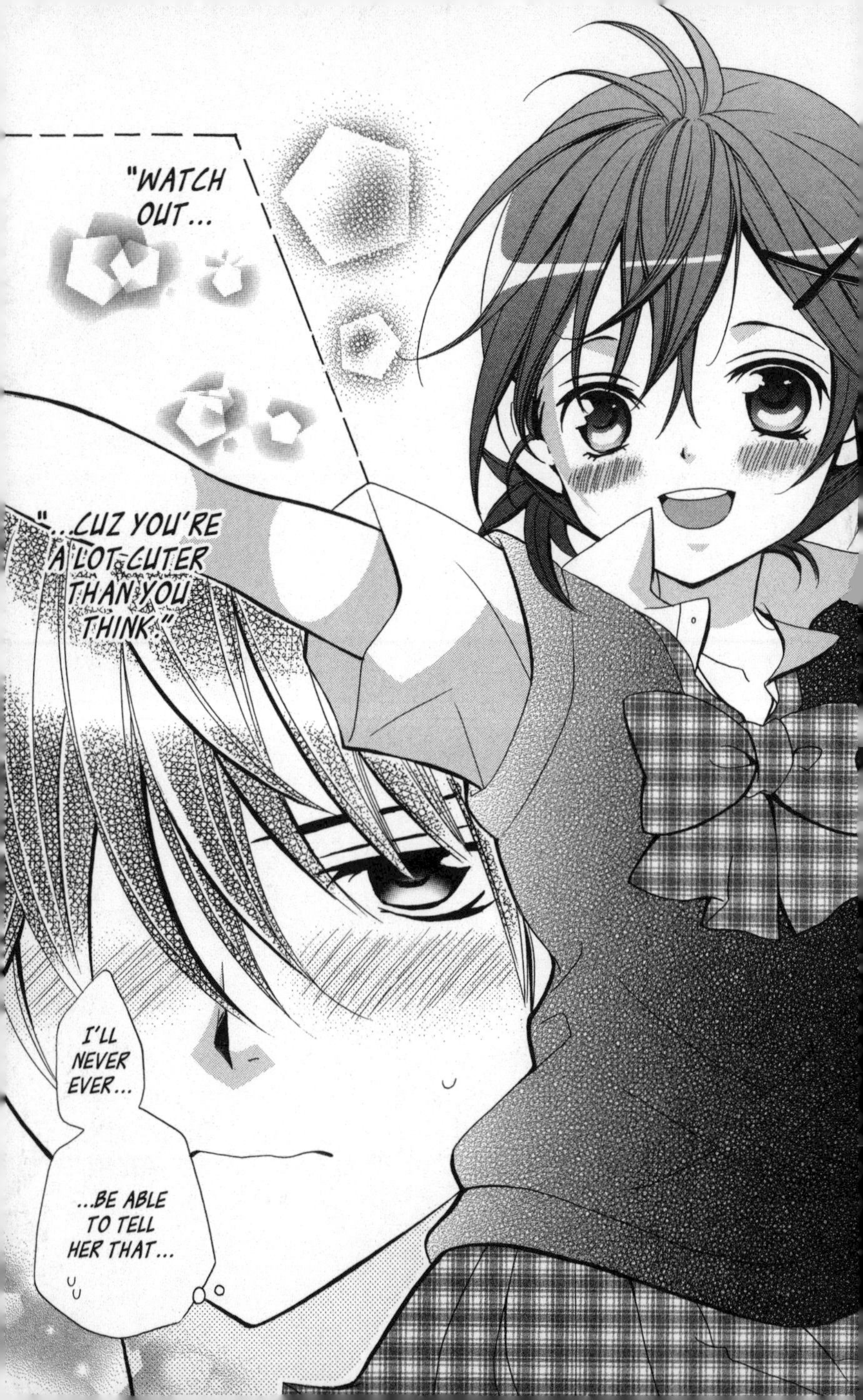
"WATCH OUT...
"...CUZ YOU'RE A LOT CUTER THAN YOU THINK."
I'LL NEVER EVER...
...BE ABLE TO TELL HER THAT...

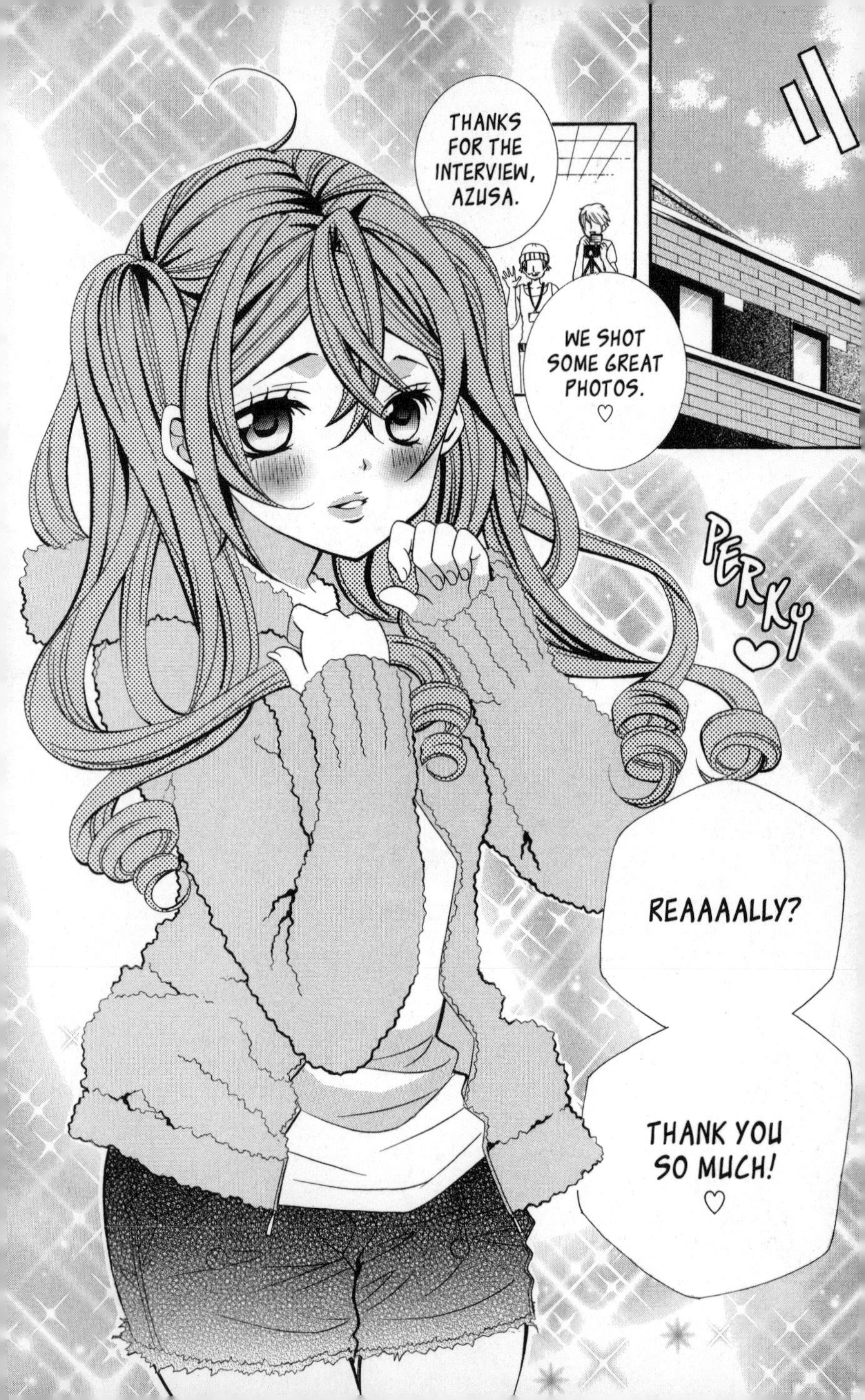
THANKS FOR THE INTERVIEW, AZUSA.
WE SHOT SOME GREAT PHOTOS. ♡
PERKY ♡
REAAAALLY?
THANK YOU SO MUCH! ♡

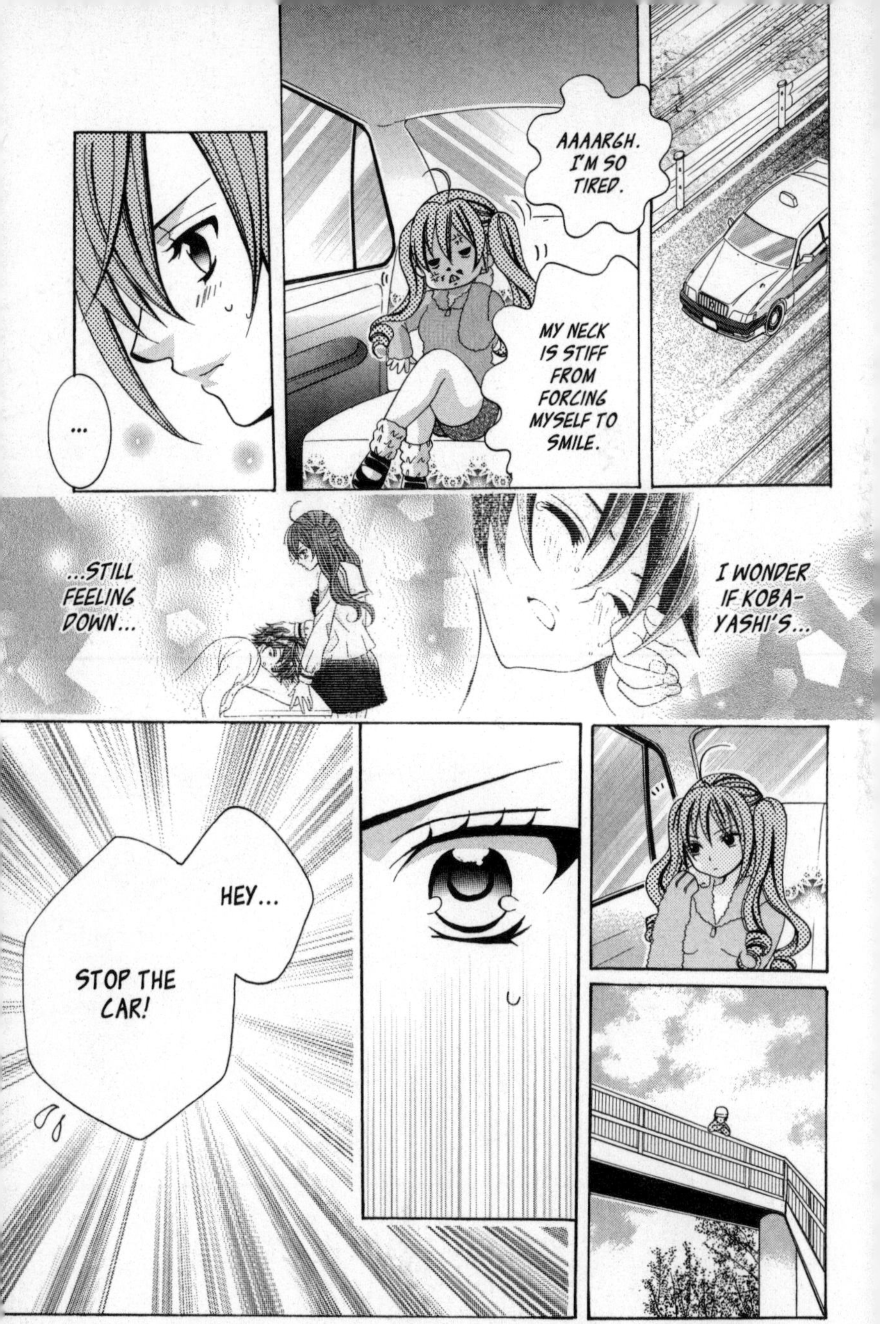
AAAARGH. I'M SO TIRED.
MY NECK IS STIFF FROM FORCING MYSELF TO SMILE.
...
I WONDER IF KOBA-YASHI'S...
...STILL FEELING DOWN...
HEY...
STOP THE CAR!

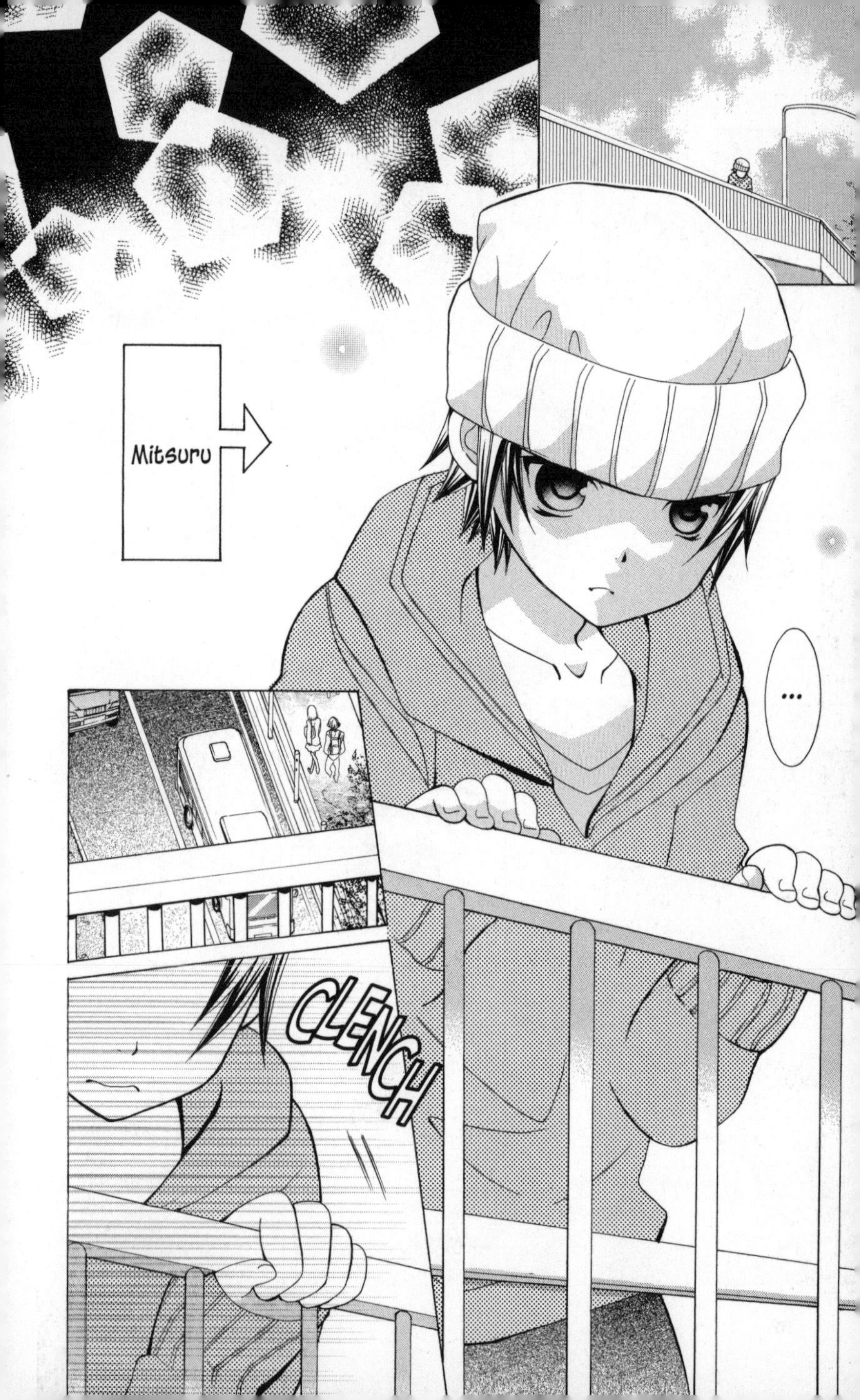
...
Mitsuru
CLENCH

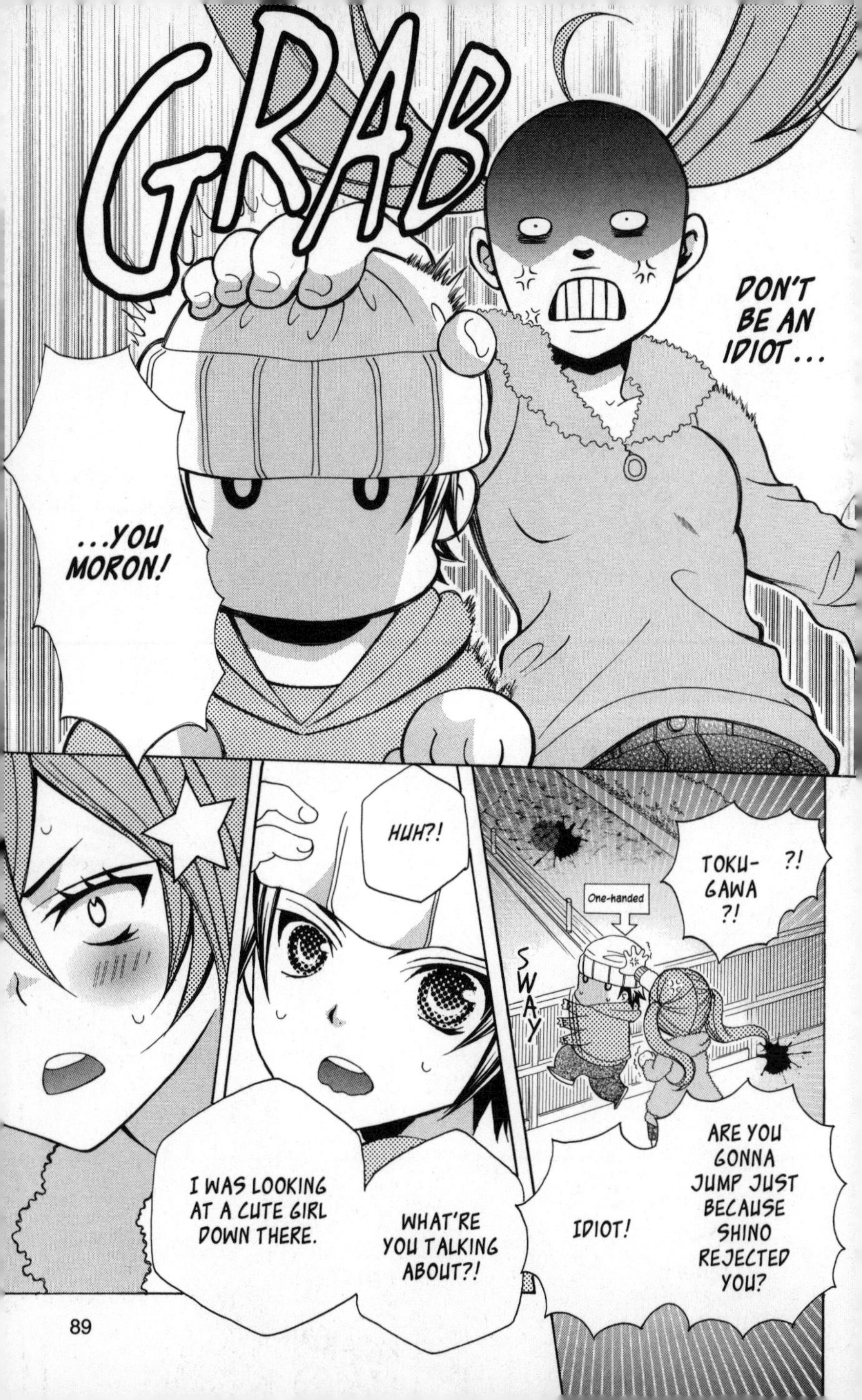
GRAB
DON'T BE AN IDIOT...
...YOU MORON!
TOKU-GAWA?!
?!
One-handed
SWAY
ARE YOU GONNA JUMP JUST BECAUSE SHINO REJECTED YOU?
IDIOT!
HUH?!
WHAT'RE YOU TALKING ABOUT?!
I WAS LOOKING AT A CUTE GIRL DOWN THERE.

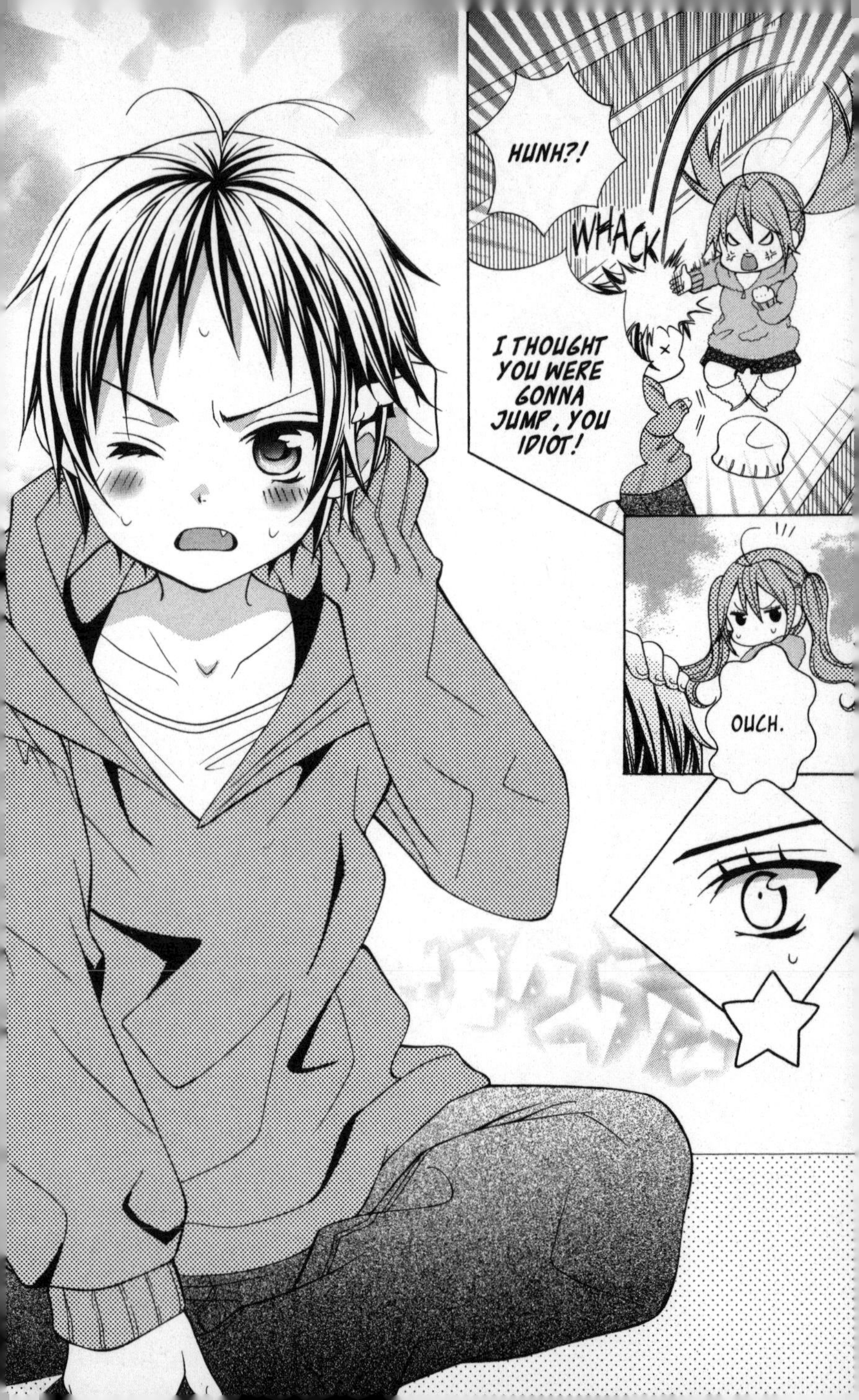
HUNH?!
WHACK
I THOUGHT YOU WERE GONNA JUMP, YOU IDIOT!
OUCH.

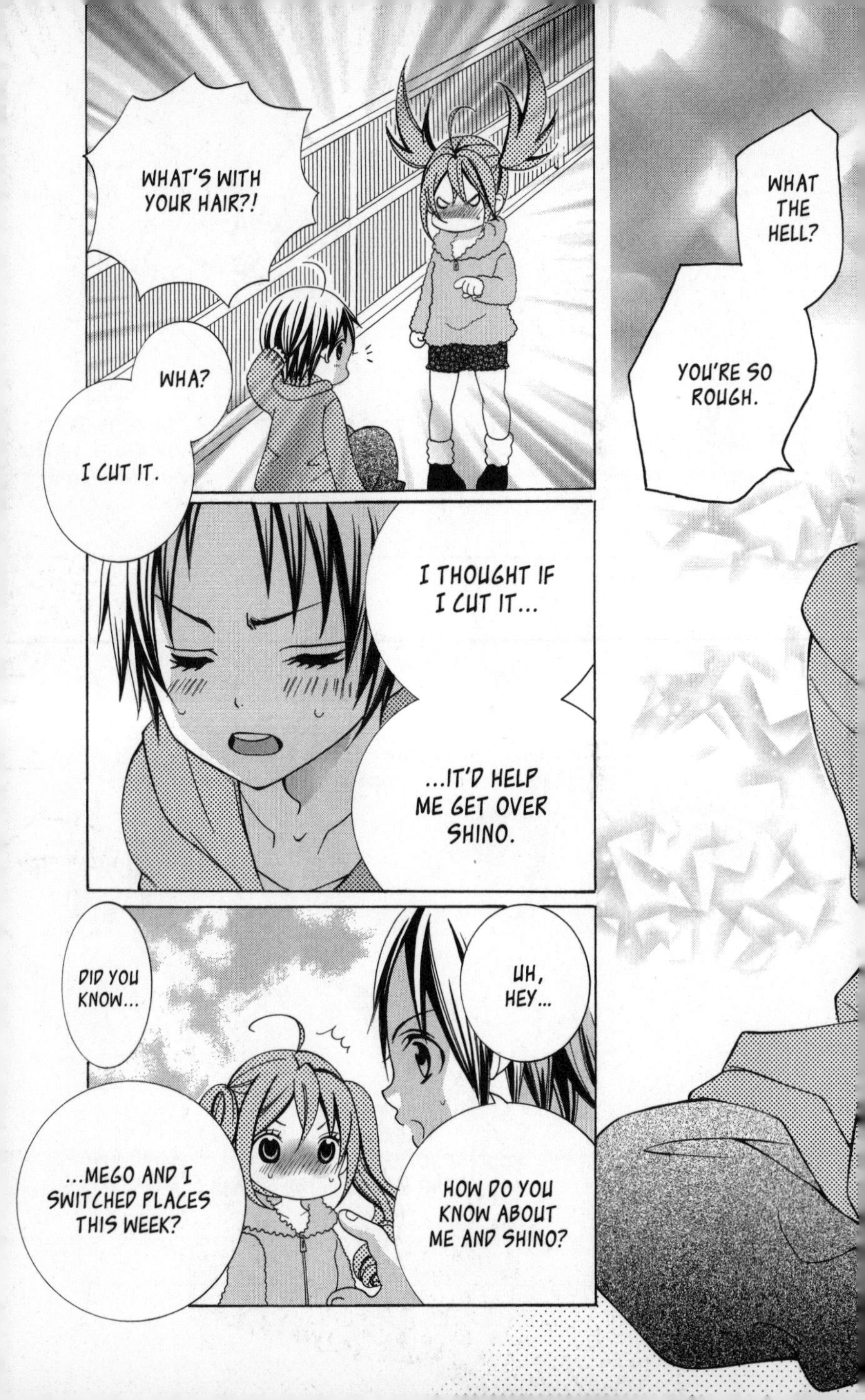
WHAT THE HELL?
YOU'RE SO ROUGH.
WHAT'S WITH YOUR HAIR?!
WHA?
I CUT IT.
I THOUGHT IF I CUT IT...
...IT'D HELP ME GET OVER SHINO.
UH, HEY...
HOW DO YOU KNOW ABOUT ME AND SHINO?
DID YOU KNOW...
...MEGO AND I SWITCHED PLACES THIS WEEK?

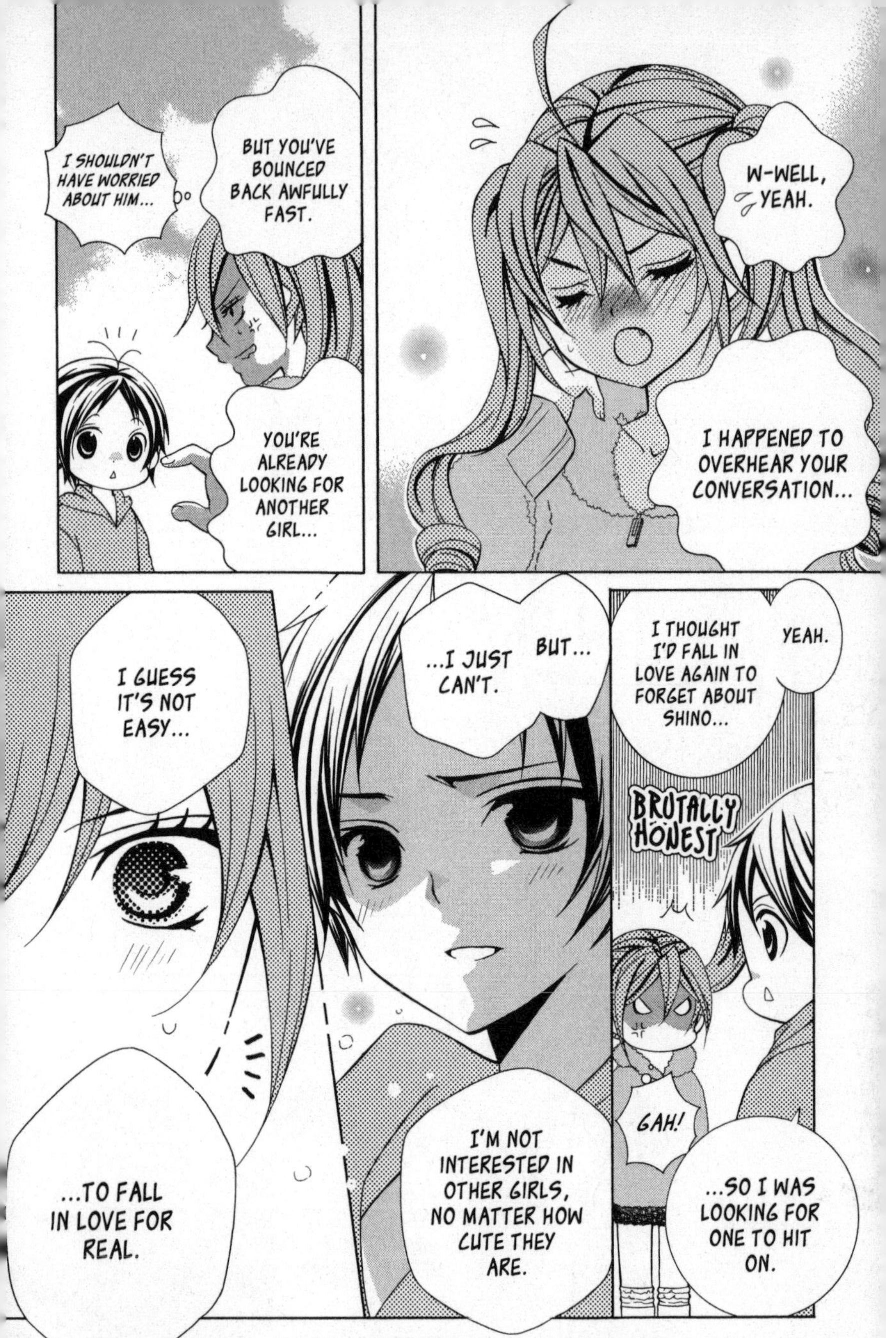
W-WELL, YEAH.
I HAPPENED TO OVERHEAR YOUR CONVERSATION...
BUT YOU'VE BOUNCED BACK AWFULLY FAST.
I SHOULDN'T HAVE WORRIED ABOUT HIM...
YOU'RE ALREADY LOOKING FOR ANOTHER GIRL...
YEAH.
I THOUGHT I'D FALL IN LOVE AGAIN TO FORGET ABOUT SHINO...
BRUTALLY HONEST
GAH!
...SO I WAS LOOKING FOR ONE TO HIT ON.
BUT...
...I JUST CAN'T.
I'M NOT INTERESTED IN OTHER GIRLS, NO MATTER HOW CUTE THEY ARE.
I GUESS IT'S NOT EASY...
...TO FALL IN LOVE FOR REAL.

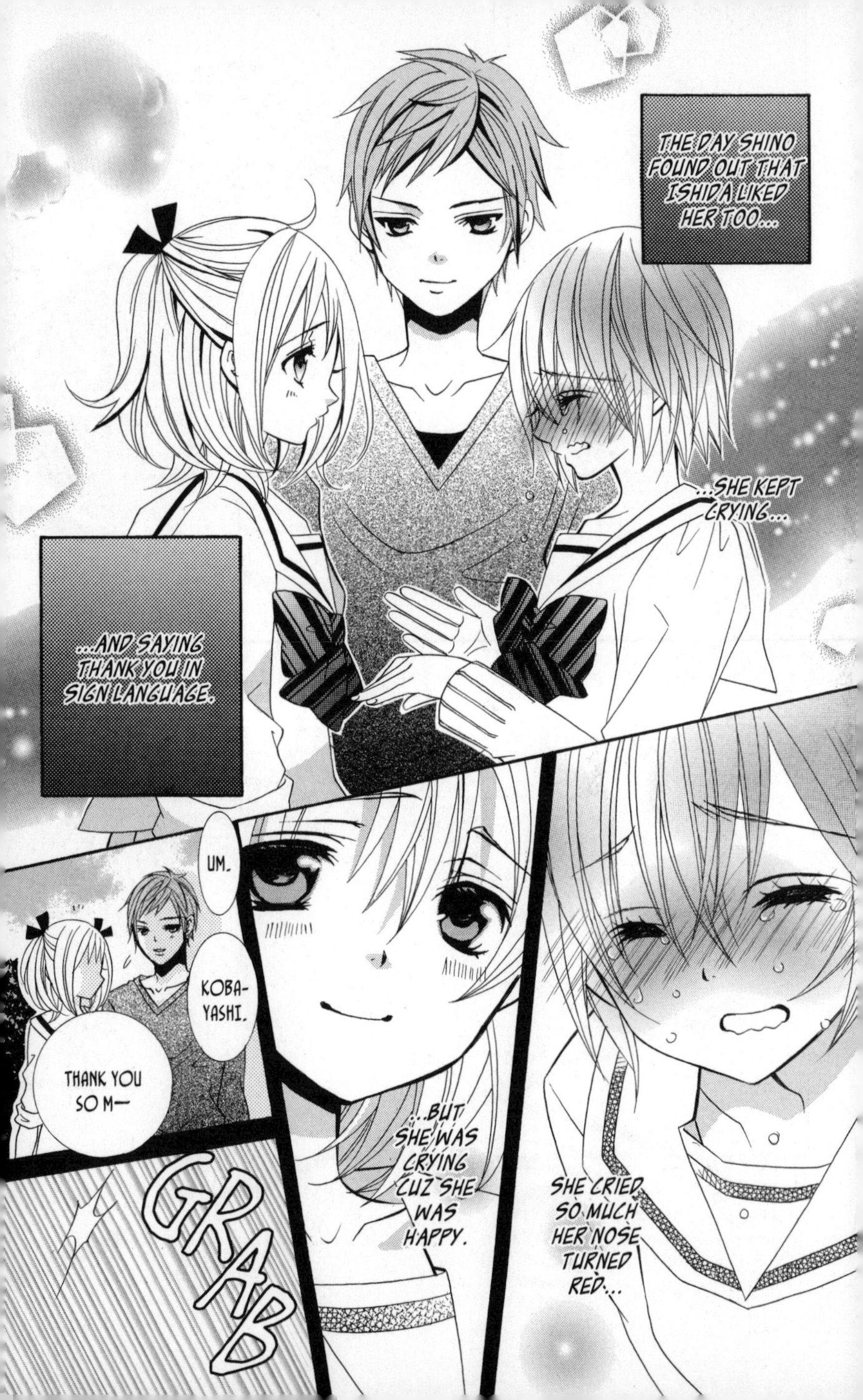
THE DAY SHINO FOUND OUT THAT ISHIDA LIKED HER TOO...
...SHE KEPT CRYING...
...AND SAYING THANK YOU IN SIGN LANGUAGE.
SHE CRIED SO MUCH HER NOSE TURNED RED...
...BUT SHE WAS CRYING CUZ SHE WAS HAPPY.
UM...
KOBA-YASHI.
THANK YOU SO M—
GRAB

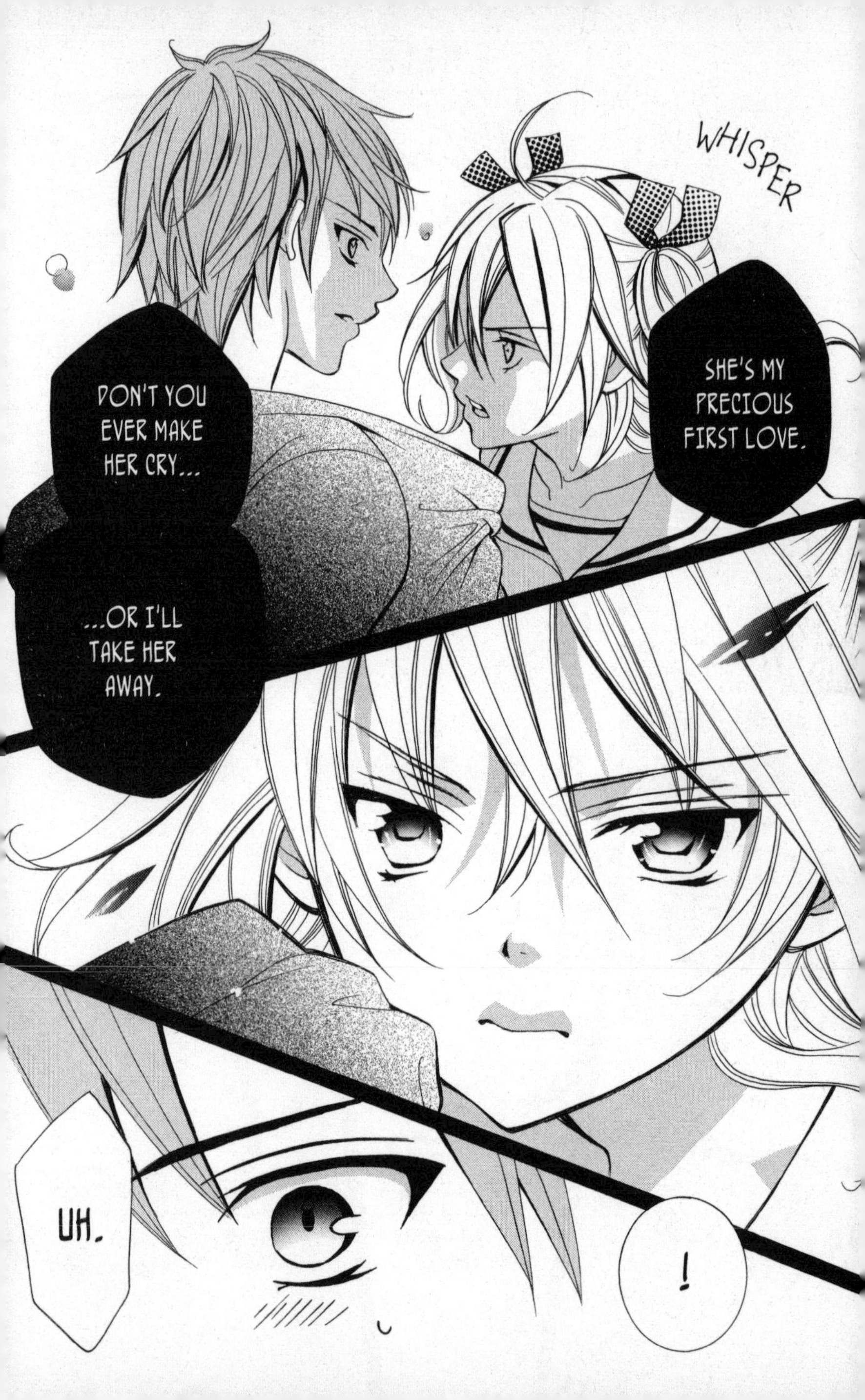
WHISPER
SHE'S MY PRECIOUS FIRST LOVE.
DON'T YOU EVER MAKE HER CRY...
...OR I'LL TAKE HER AWAY.
!
UH.

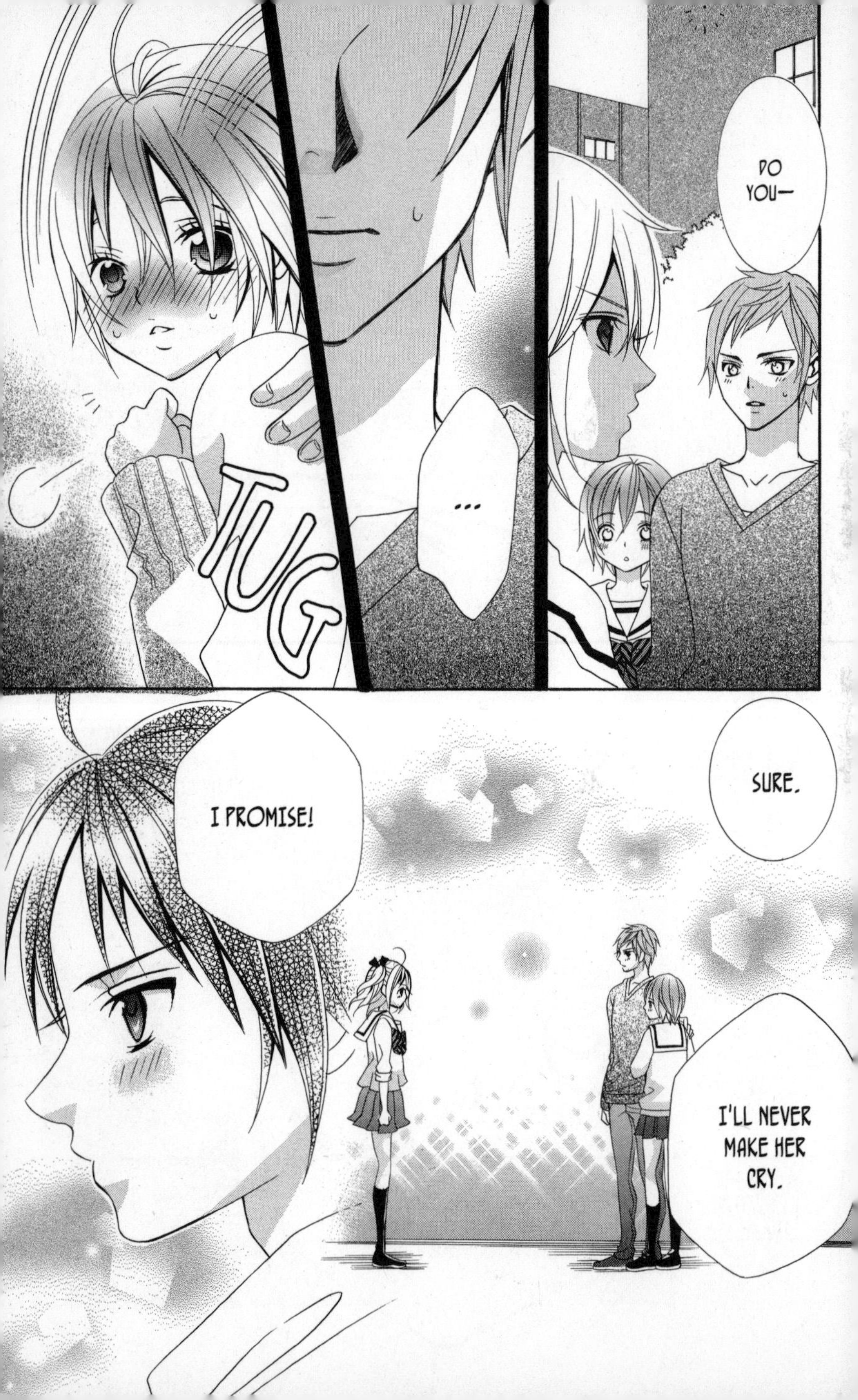
DO YOU—
...
TUG
SURE.
I'LL NEVER MAKE HER CRY.
I PROMISE!

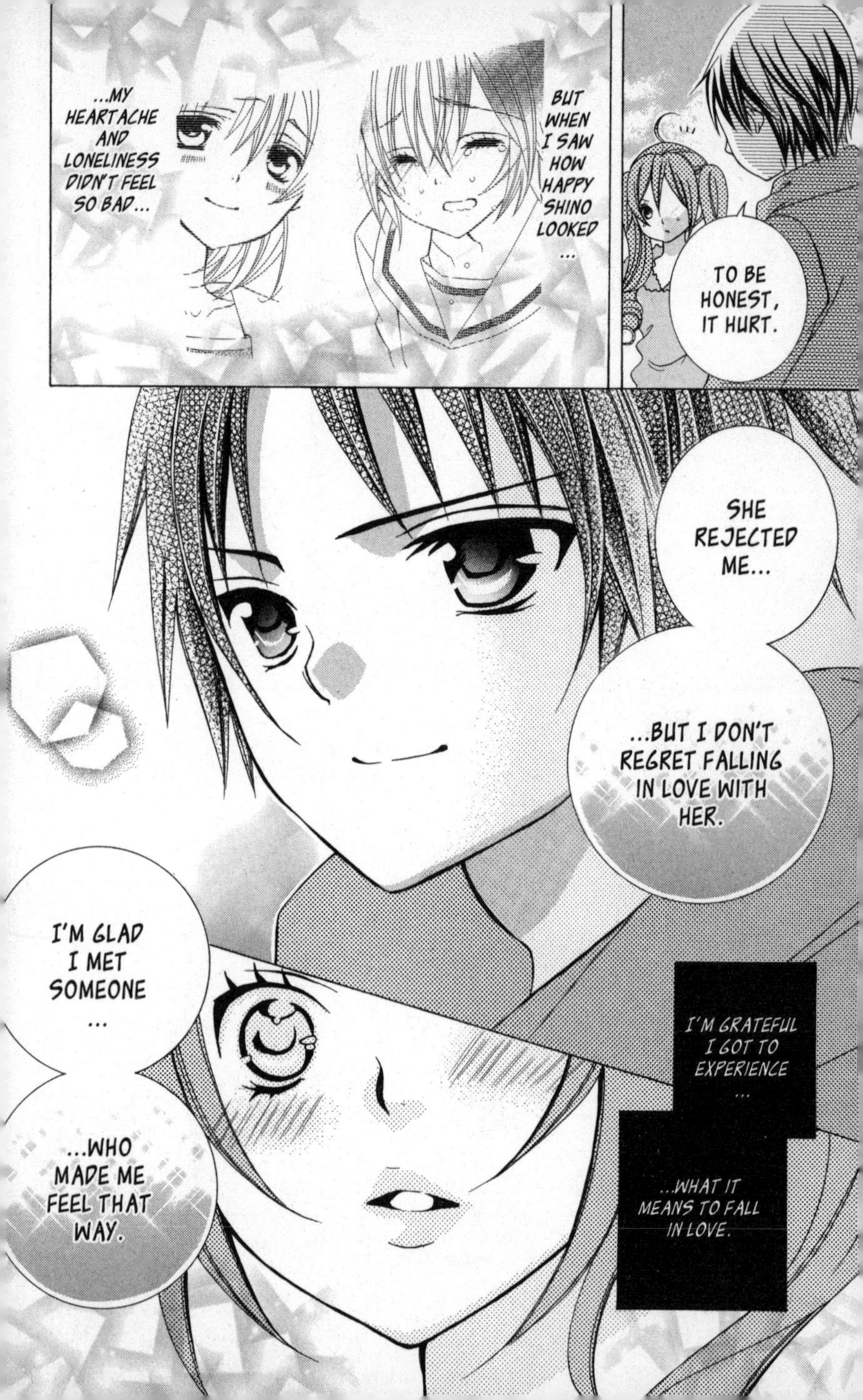
TO BE HONEST, IT HURT.
BUT WHEN I SAW HOW HAPPY SHINO LOOKED...
...MY HEARTACHE AND LONELINESS DIDN'T FEEL SO BAD...
SHE REJECTED ME...
...BUT I DON'T REGRET FALLING IN LOVE WITH HER.
I'M GLAD I MET SOMEONE...
...WHO MADE ME FEEL THAT WAY.
I'M GRATEFUL I GOT TO EXPERIENCE...
...WHAT IT MEANS TO FALL IN LOVE.

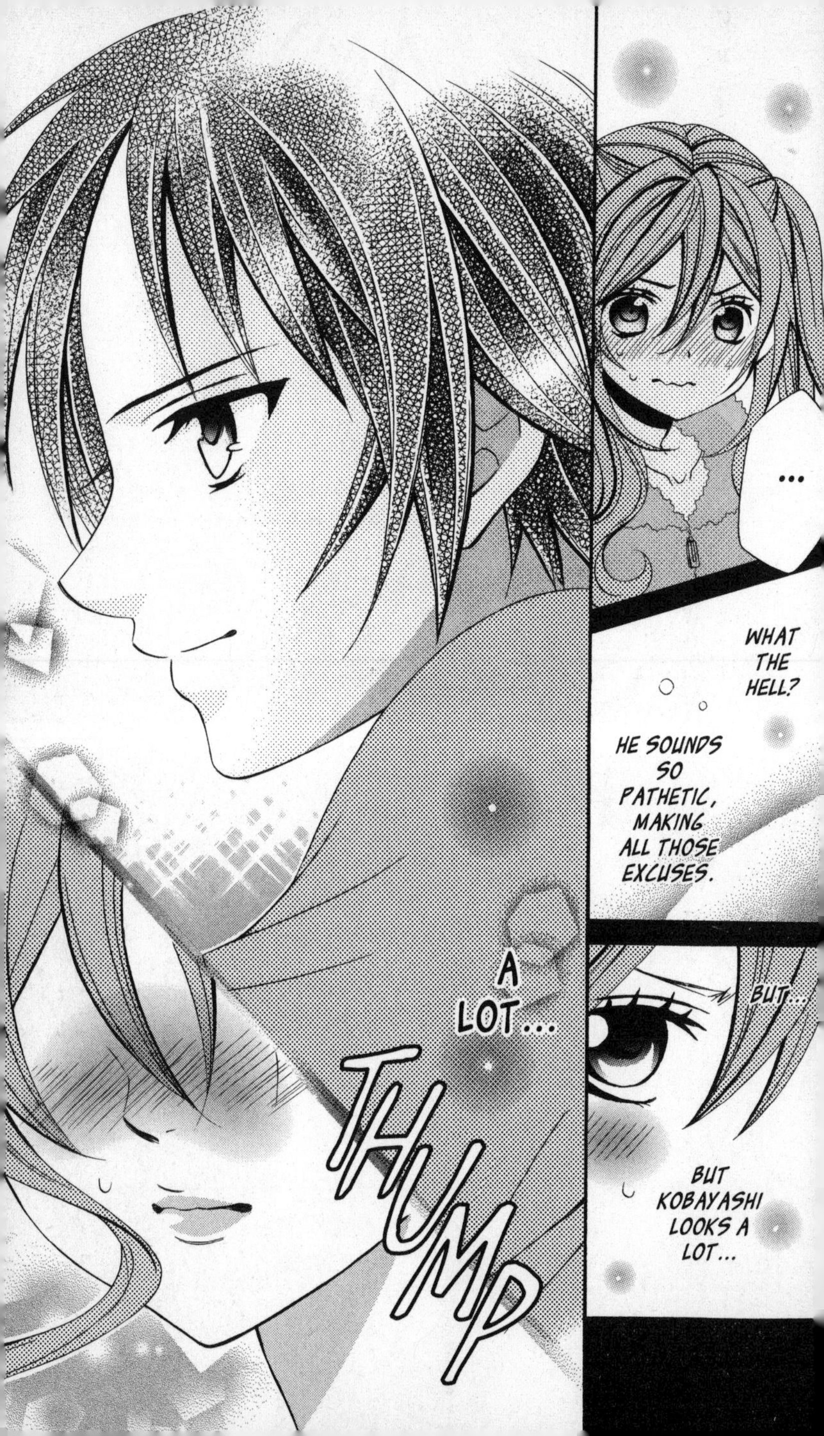
...
WHAT THE HELL?
HE SOUNDS SO PATHETIC, MAKING ALL THOSE EXCUSES.
BUT...
BUT KOBAYASHI LOOKS A LOT...
A LOT...
THUMP

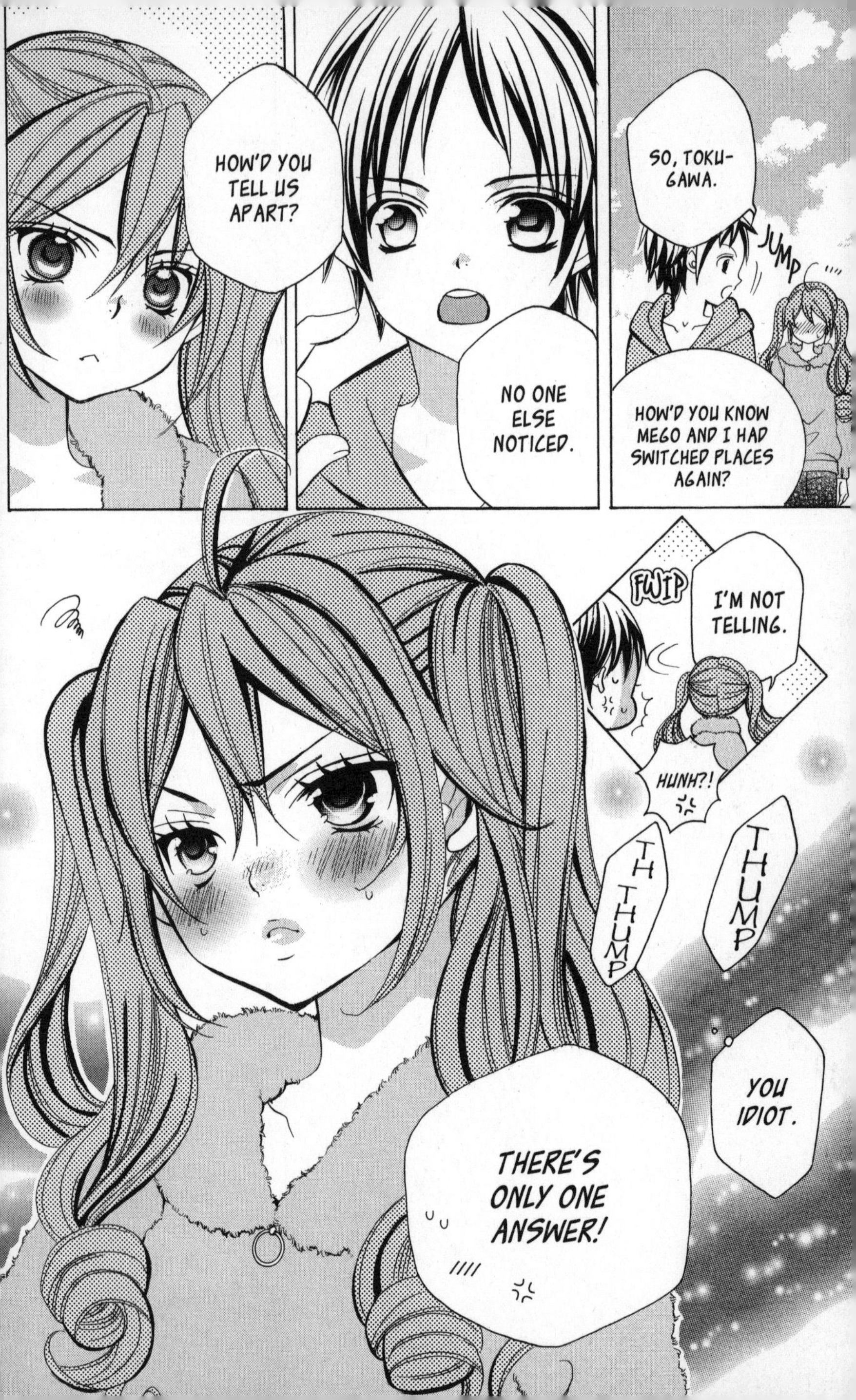

SO, TOKU-GAWA.
JUMP
HOW'D YOU KNOW MEGO AND I HAD SWITCHED PLACES AGAIN?
NO ONE ELSE NOTICED.
HOW'D YOU TELL US APART?
FWIP
I'M NOT TELLING.
HUNH?!
THUMP
TH THUMP
YOU IDIOT.
THERE'S ONLY ONE ANSWER!

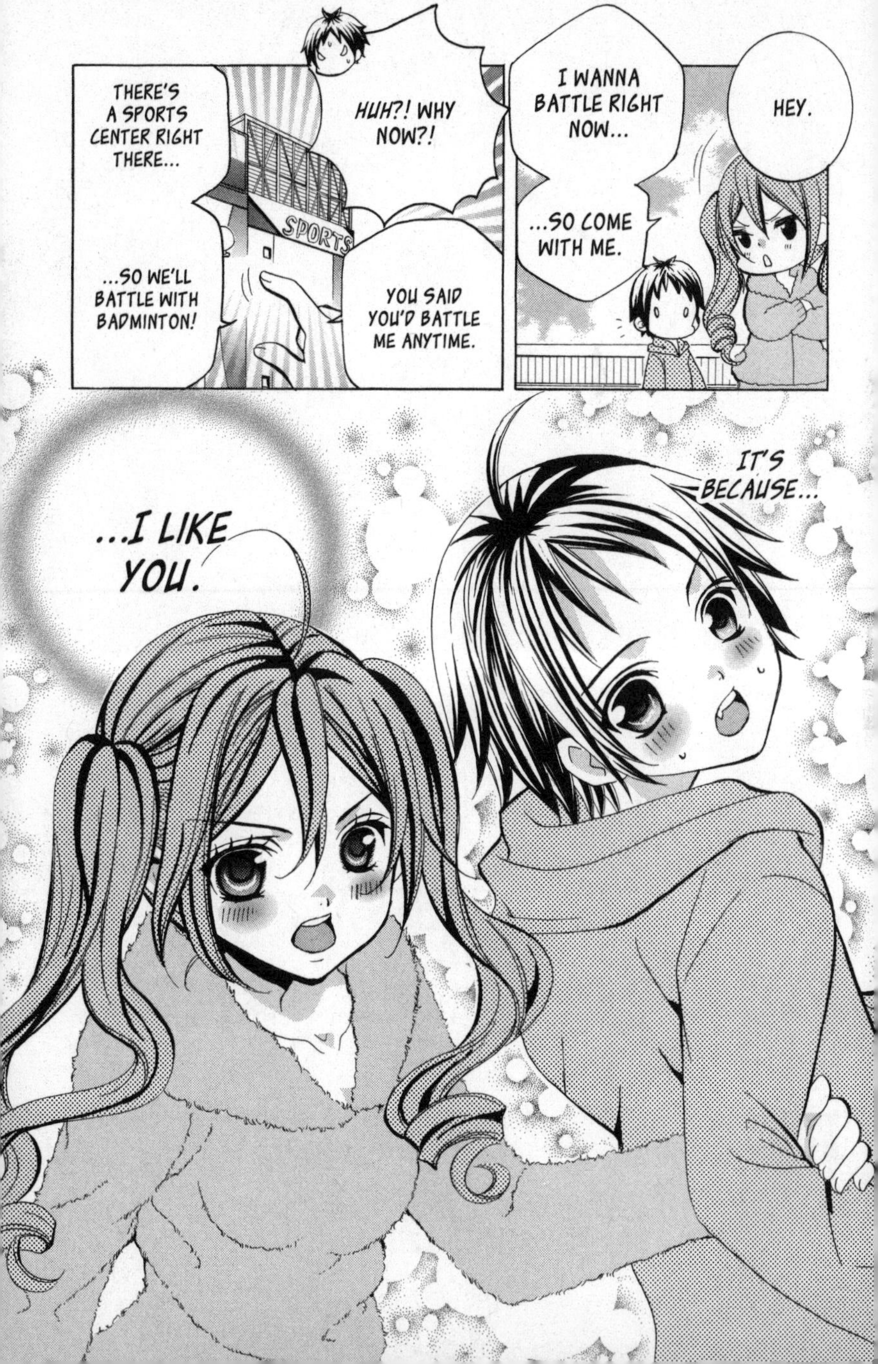
HEY.
I WANNA BATTLE RIGHT NOW...
...SO COME WITH ME.
HUH?! WHY NOW?!
YOU SAID YOU'D BATTLE ME ANYTIME.
THERE'S A SPORTS CENTER RIGHT THERE...
SPORTS
...SO WE'LL BATTLE WITH BADMINTON!
IT'S BECAUSE...
...I LIKE YOU.

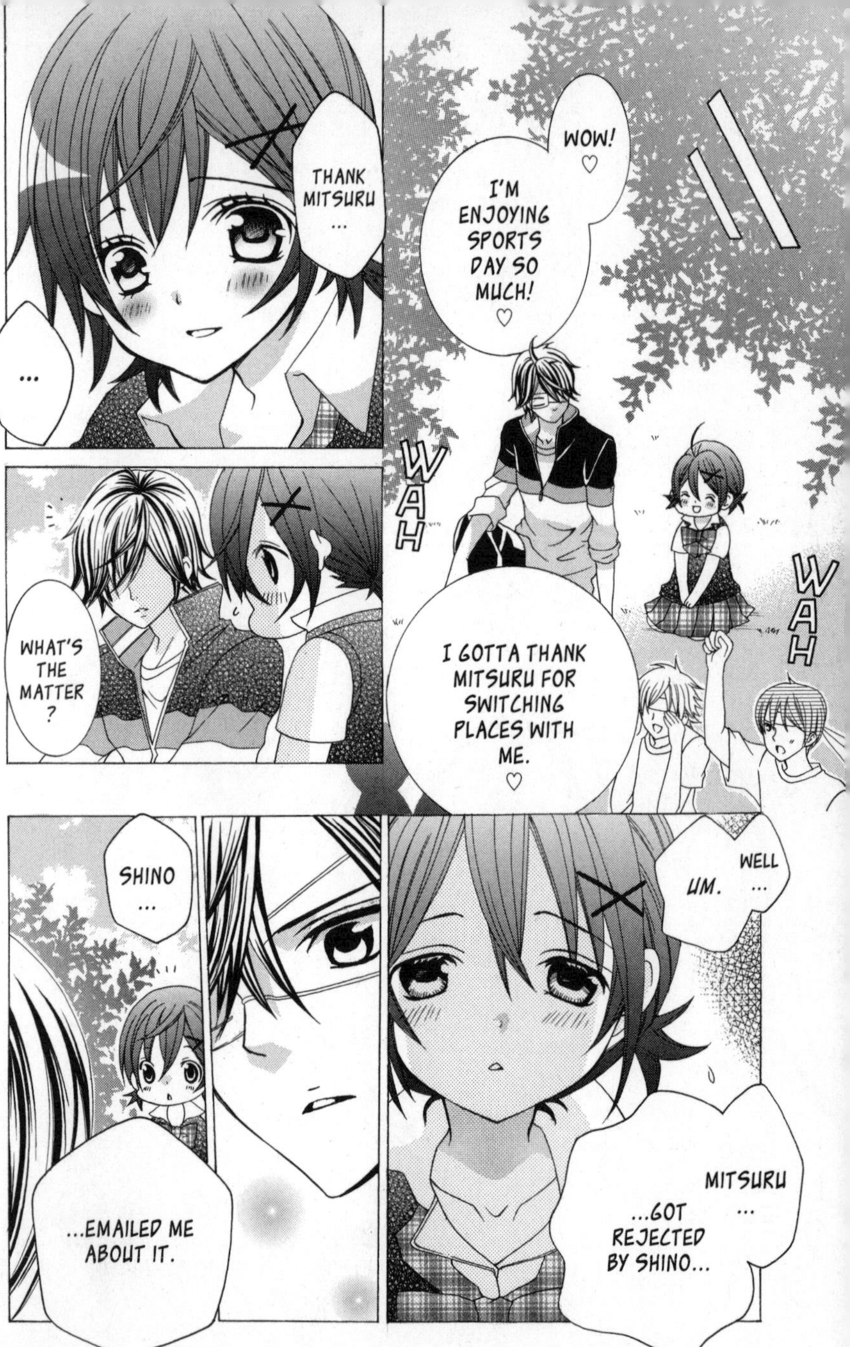

WOW! ♡
I'M ENJOYING SPORTS DAY SO MUCH! ♡
WAH
WAH
I GOTTA THANK MITSURU FOR SWITCHING PLACES WITH ME. ♡
THANK MITSURU ...
...
WHAT'S THE MATTER?
WELL ... UM.
MITSURU ... ...GOT REJECTED BY SHINO...
SHINO ...
...EMAILED ME ABOUT IT.

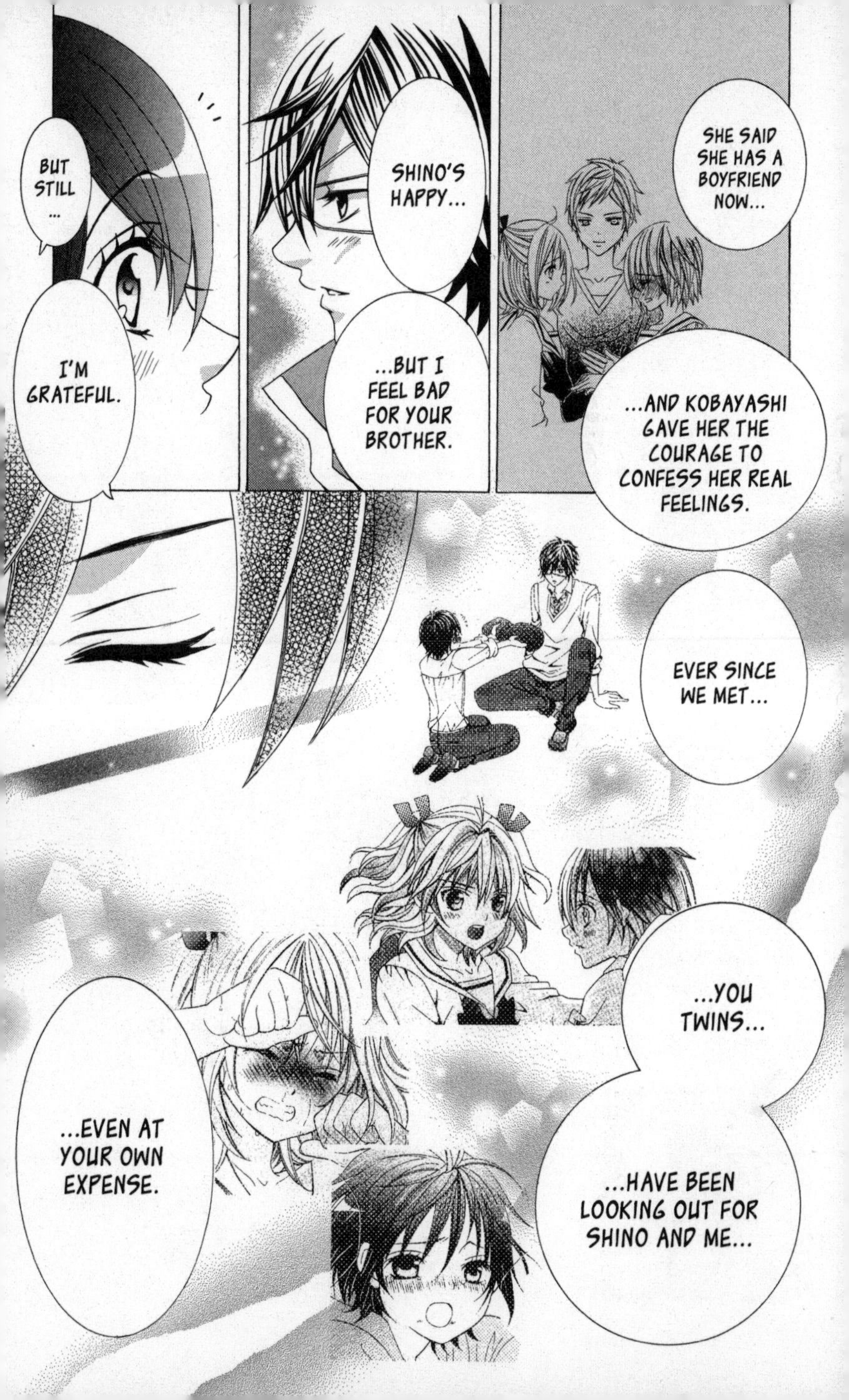
SHE SAID SHE HAS A BOYFRIEND NOW...
...AND KOBAYASHI GAVE HER THE COURAGE TO CONFESS HER REAL FEELINGS.
SHINO'S HAPPY...
...BUT I FEEL BAD FOR YOUR BROTHER.
BUT STILL...
I'M GRATEFUL.
EVER SINCE WE MET...
...YOU TWINS...
...HAVE BEEN LOOKING OUT FOR SHINO AND ME...
...EVEN AT YOUR OWN EXPENSE.

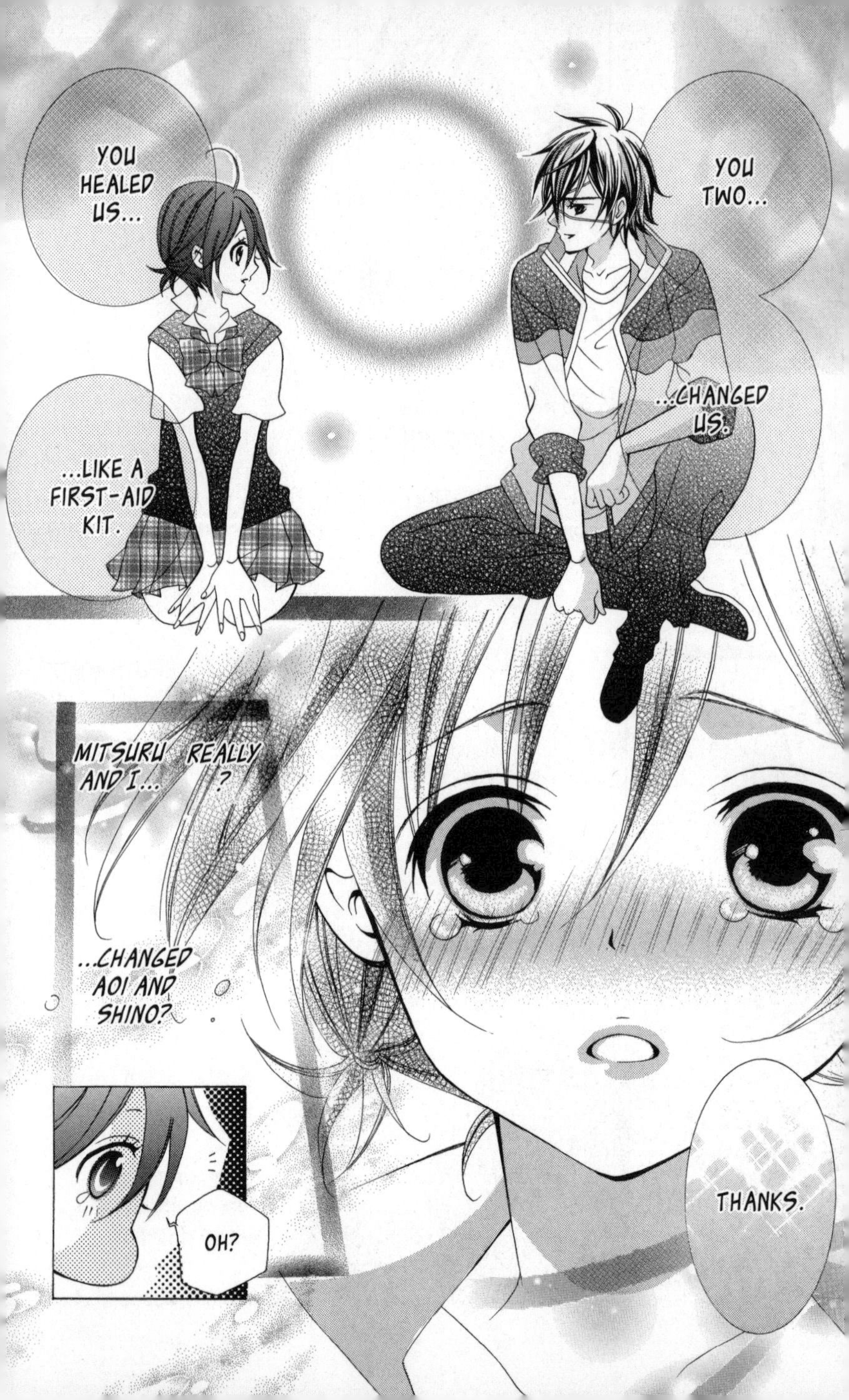

YOU TWO...
...CHANGED US.
YOU HEALED US...
...LIKE A FIRST-AID KIT.
REALLY?
MITSURU AND I...
...CHANGED AOI AND SHINO?
THANKS.
OH?

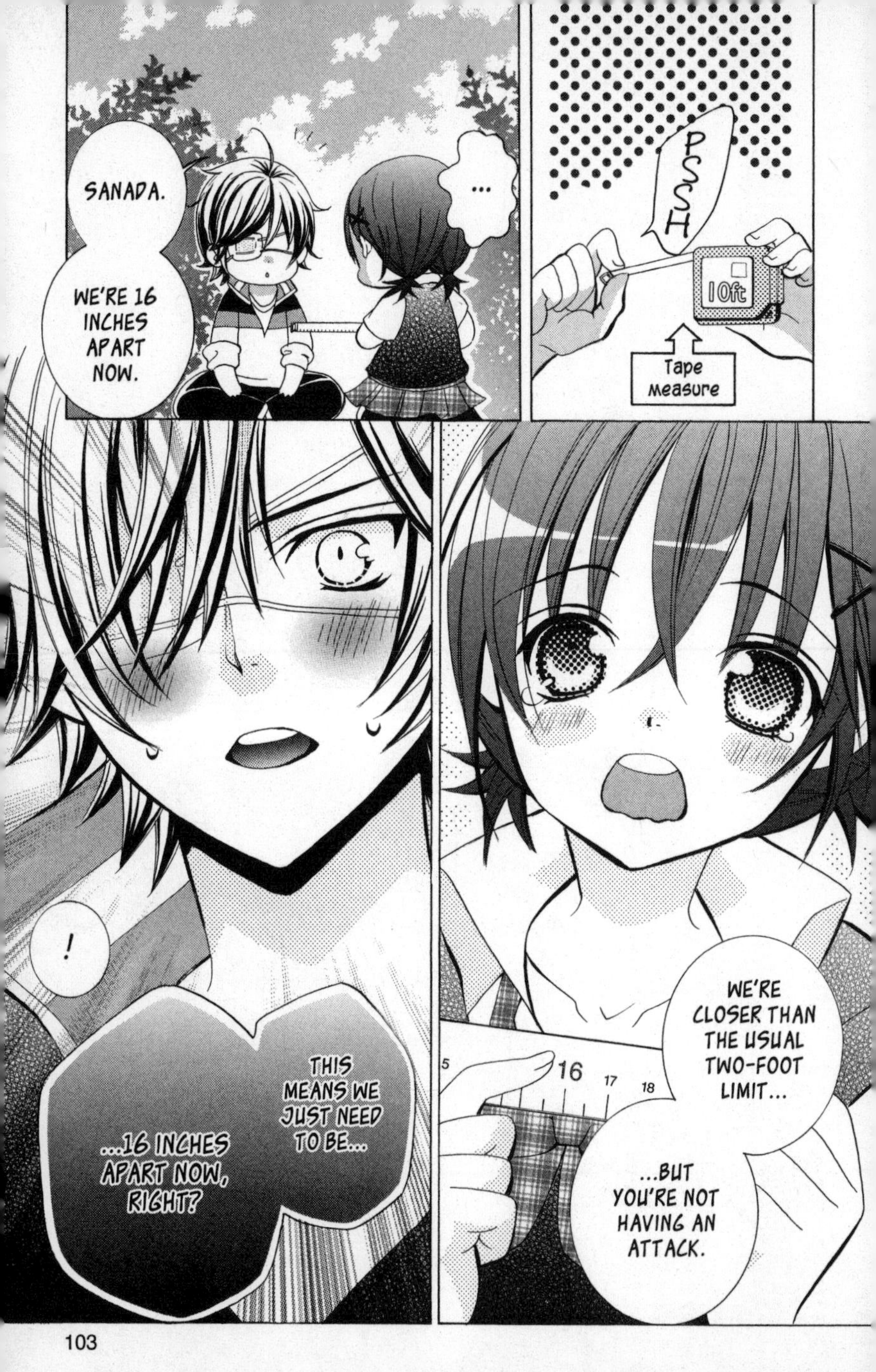
PSSH
10ft
Tape Measure
...
SANADA.
WE'RE 16 INCHES APART NOW.
WE'RE CLOSER THAN THE USUAL TWO-FOOT LIMIT...
...BUT YOU'RE NOT HAVING AN ATTACK.
5
16
17
18
!
THIS MEANS WE JUST NEED TO BE...
...16 INCHES APART NOW, RIGHT?

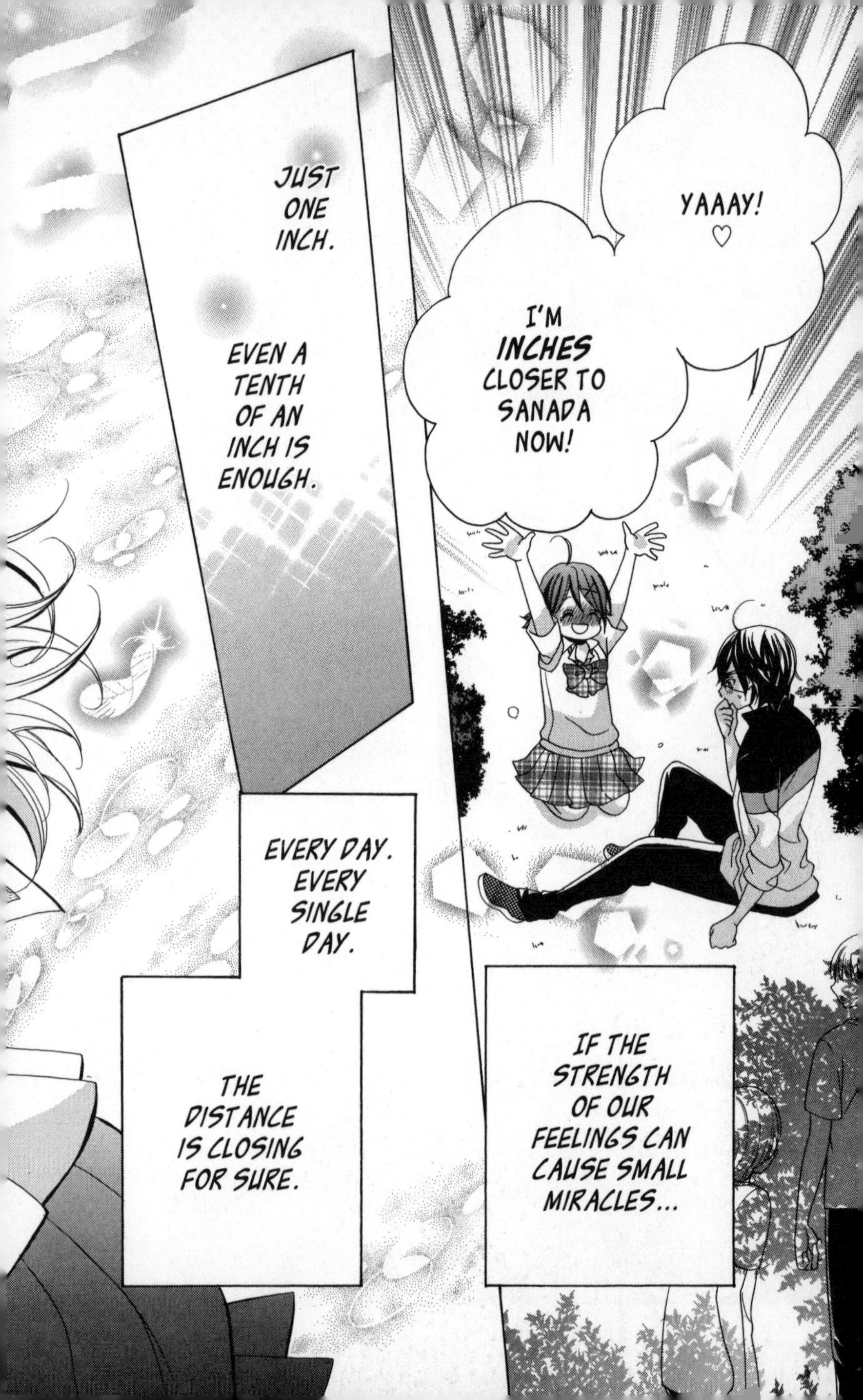
YAAAY! ♡
I'M INCHES CLOSER TO SANADA NOW!
IF THE STRENGTH OF OUR FEELINGS CAN CAUSE SMALL MIRACLES...
JUST ONE INCH.
EVEN A TENTH OF AN INCH IS ENOUGH.
EVERY DAY. EVERY SINGLE DAY.
THE DISTANCE IS CLOSING FOR SURE.

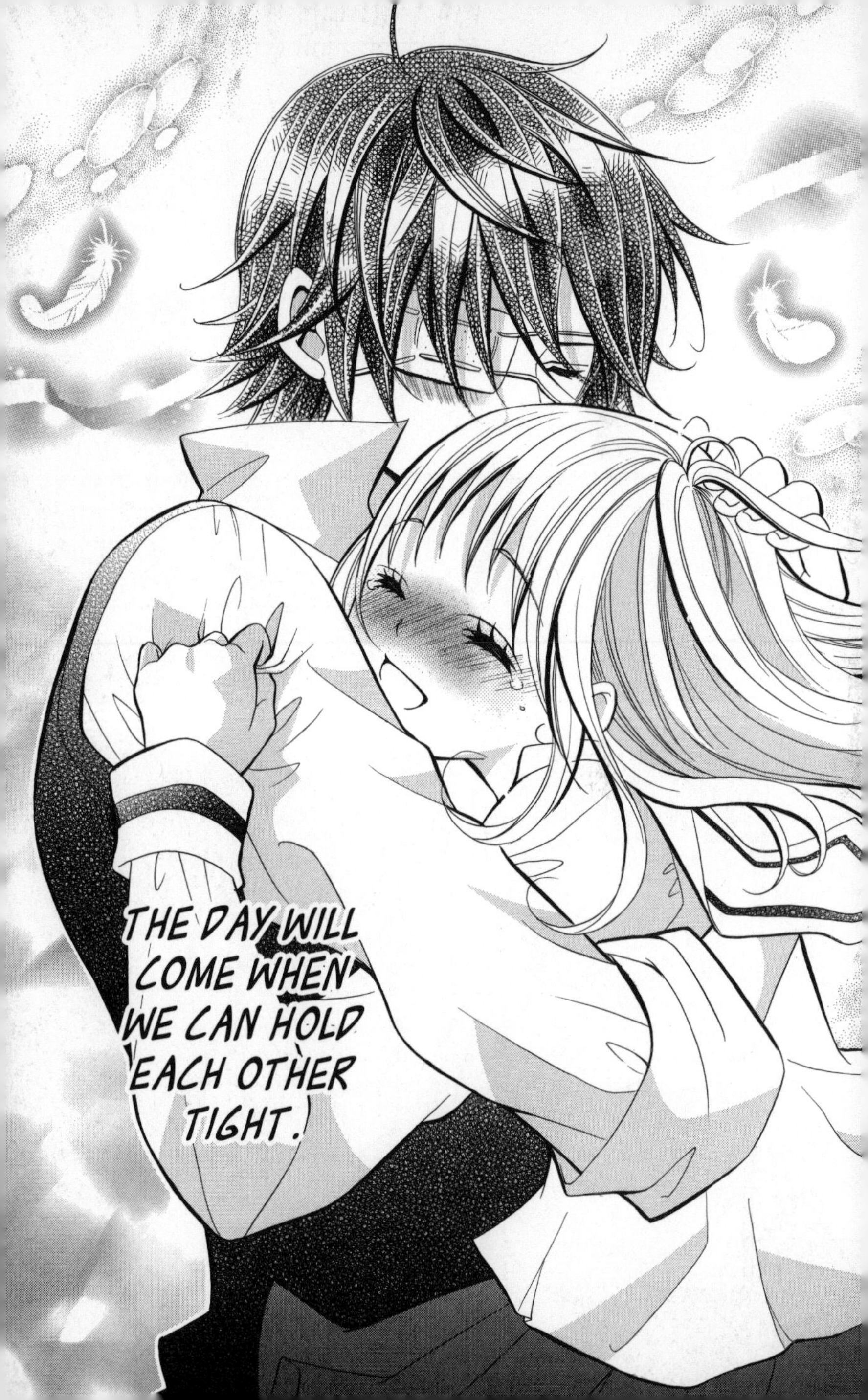
THE DAY WILL COME WHEN WE CAN HOLD EACH OTHER TIGHT.

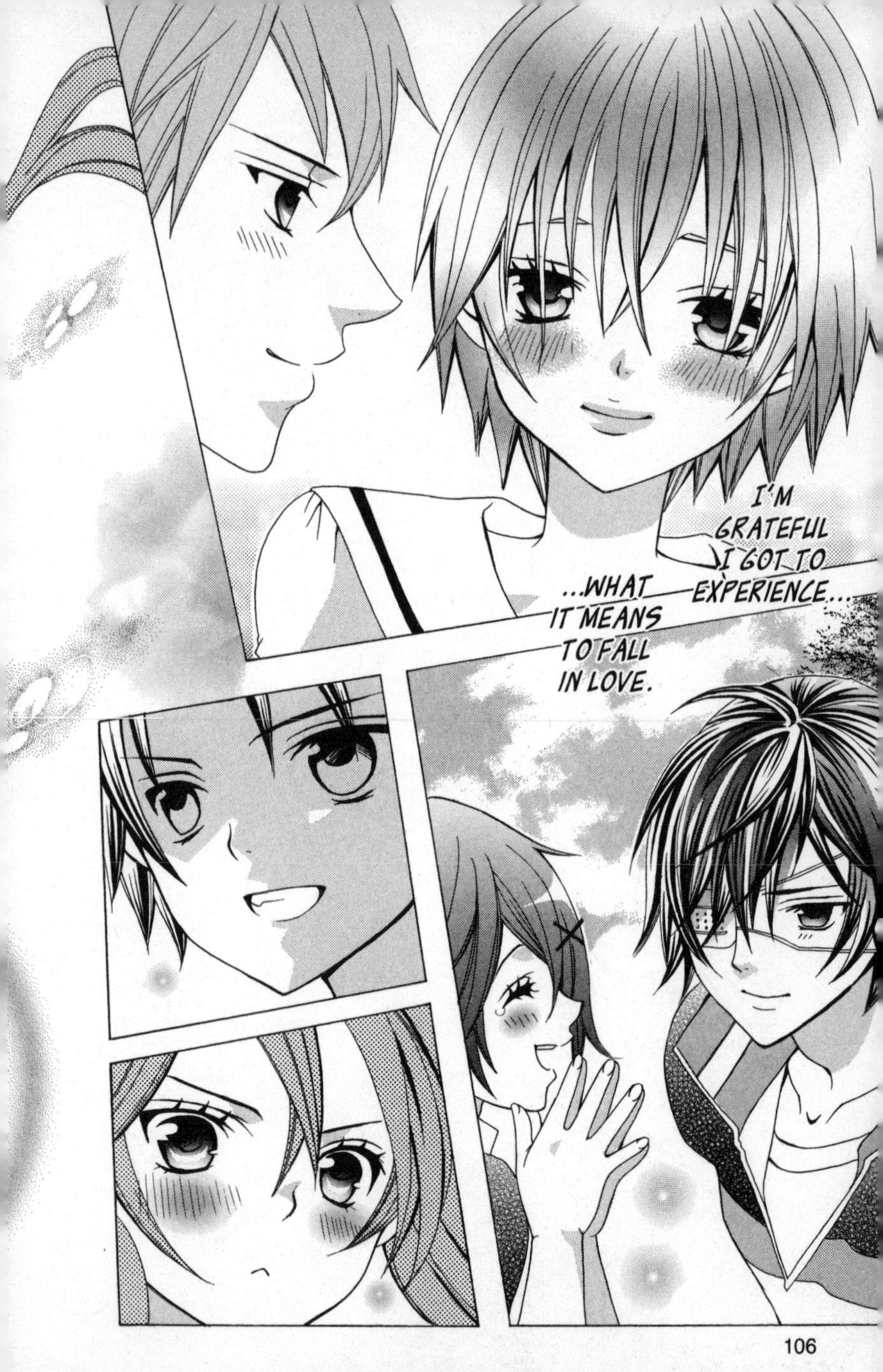
I'M GRATEFUL I GOT TO EXPERIENCE...
...WHAT IT MEANS TO FALL IN LOVE.

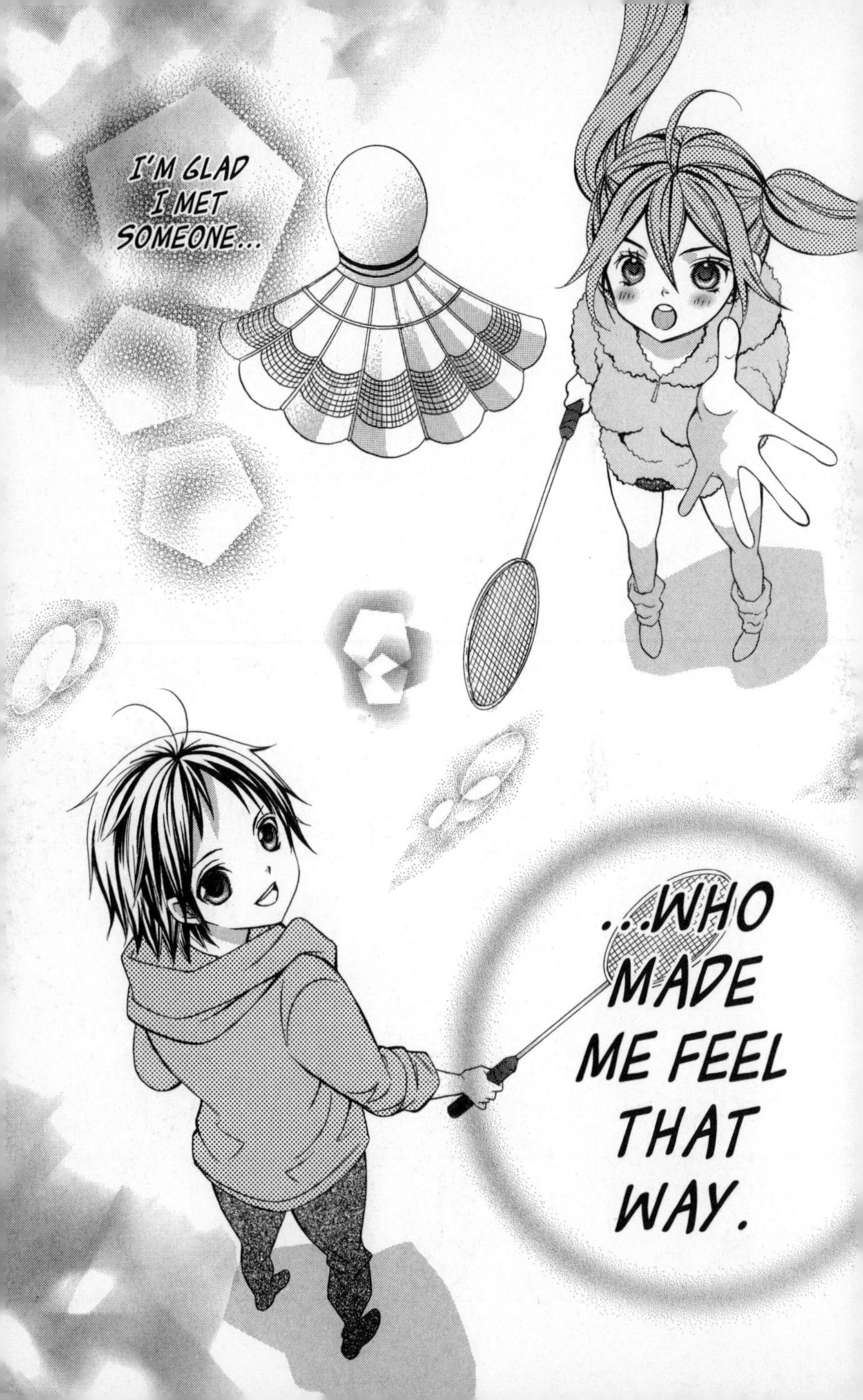
I'M GLAD I MET SOMEONE...
...WHO MADE ME FEEL THAT WAY.

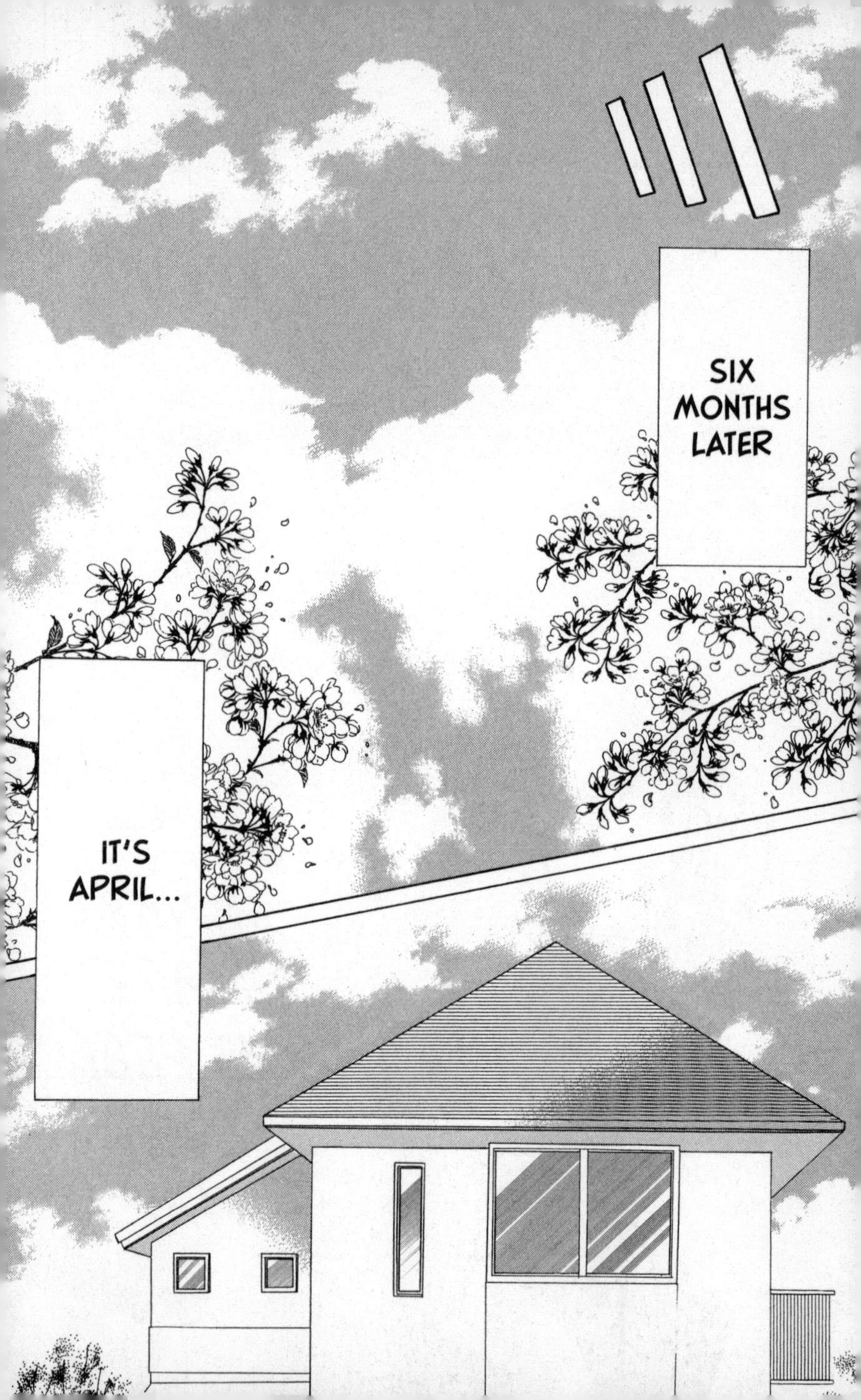
SIX MONTHS LATER
IT'S APRIL...

HEEEY.
MEGO!
YOU'LL BE LATE FOR THE FIRST DAY IF YOU DON'T HURRY!
Mitsuru Kobayashi
(second-year high school student)

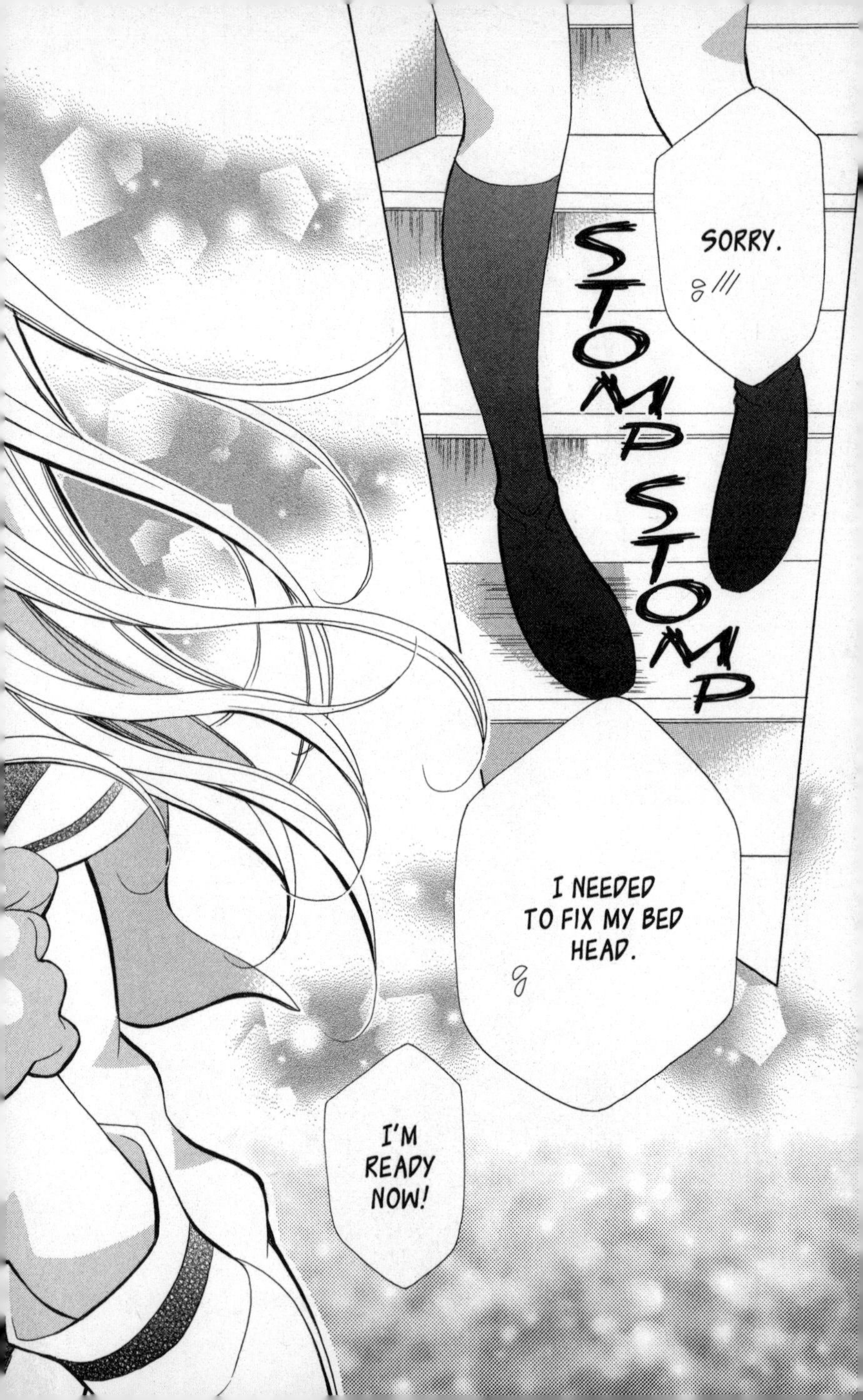
SORRY.
STOMP STOMP
I NEEDED TO FIX MY BED HEAD.
I'M READY NOW!

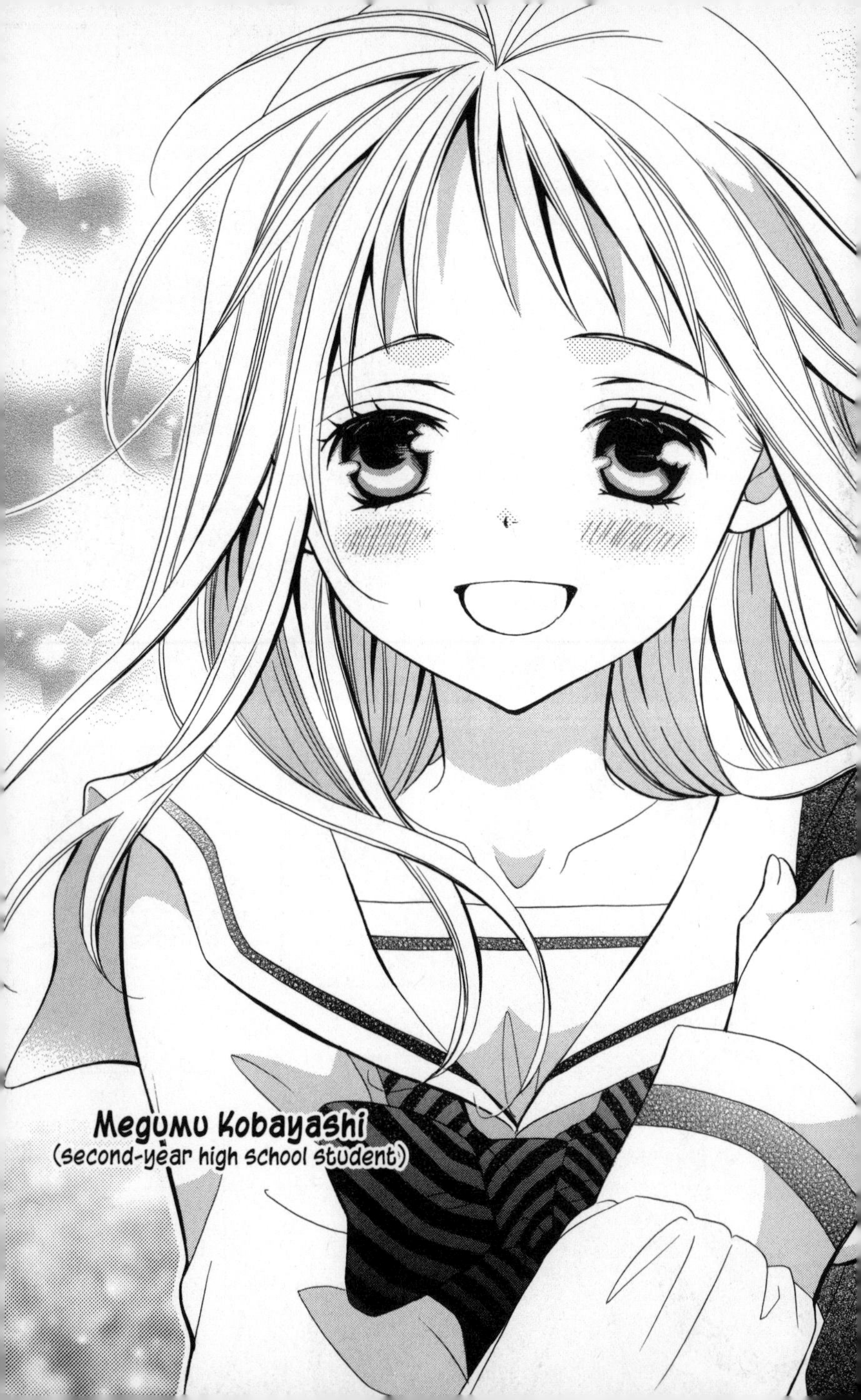
Megumu Kobayashi
(second-year high school student)

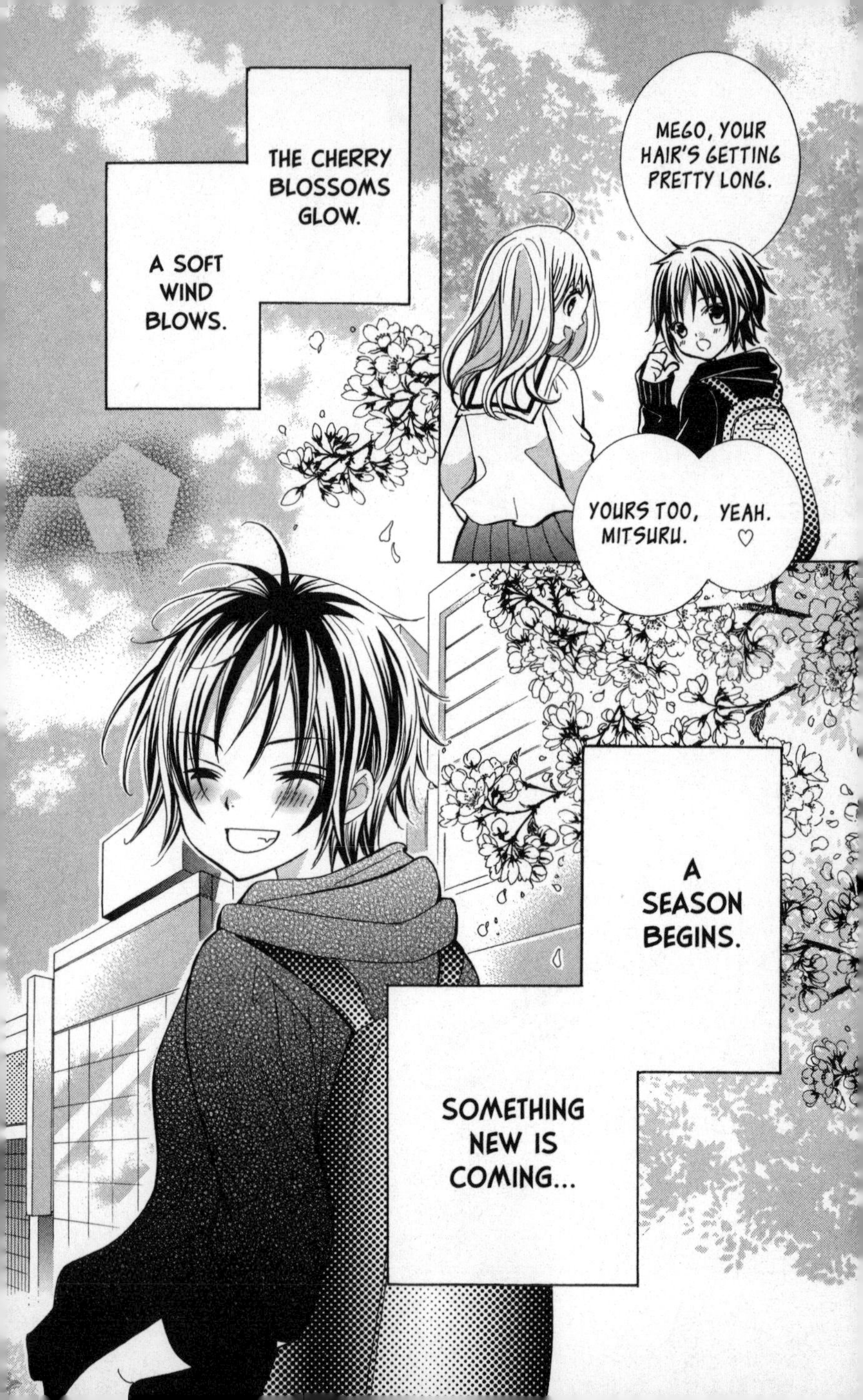
MEGO, YOUR HAIR'S GETTING PRETTY LONG.
YEAH. ♡
YOURS TOO, MITSURU.
THE CHERRY BLOSSOMS GLOW.
A SOFT WIND BLOWS.
A SEASON BEGINS.
SOMETHING NEW IS COMING...

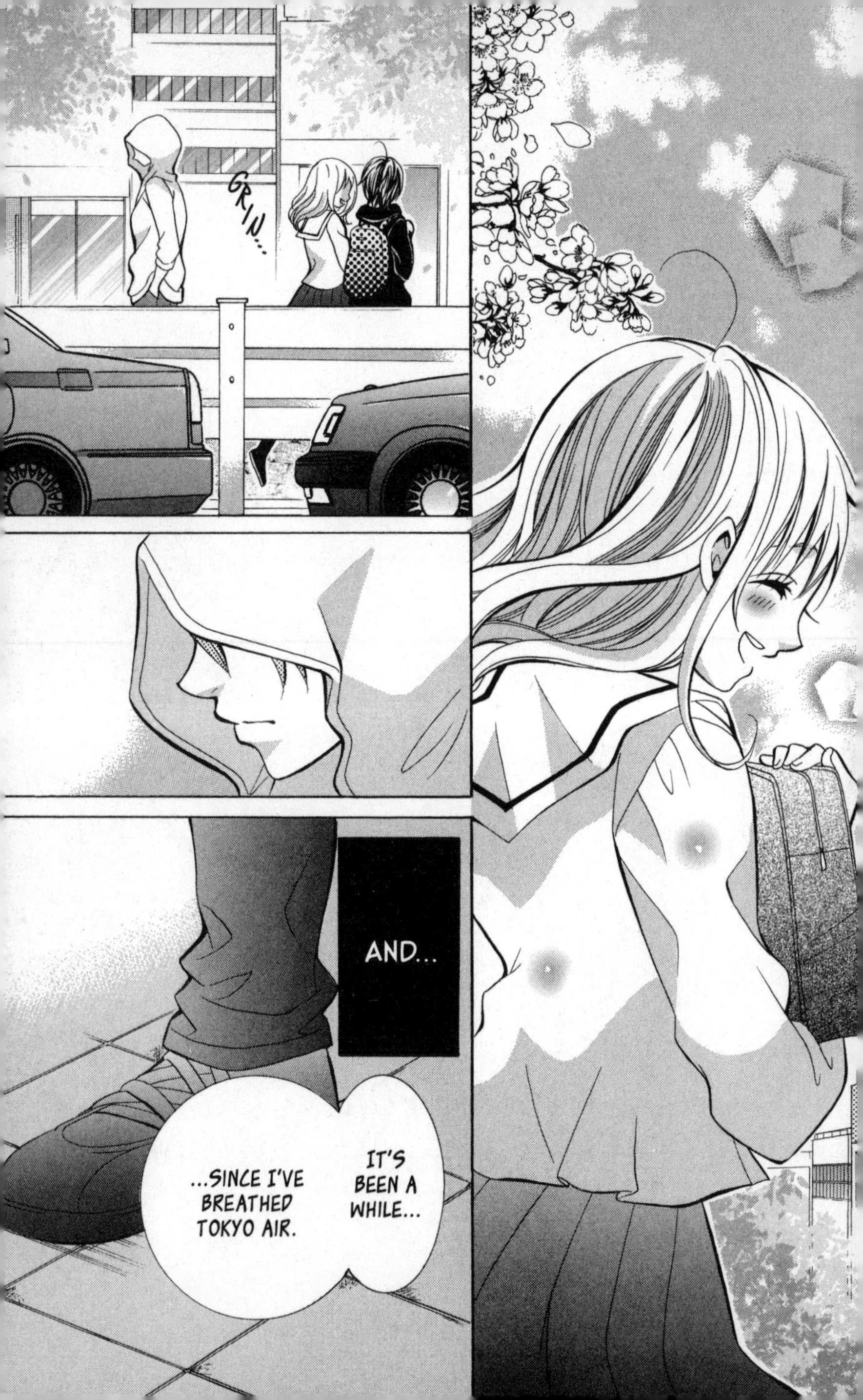
GRIN...
AND...
IT'S BEEN A WHILE...
...SINCE I'VE BREATHED TOKYO AIR.

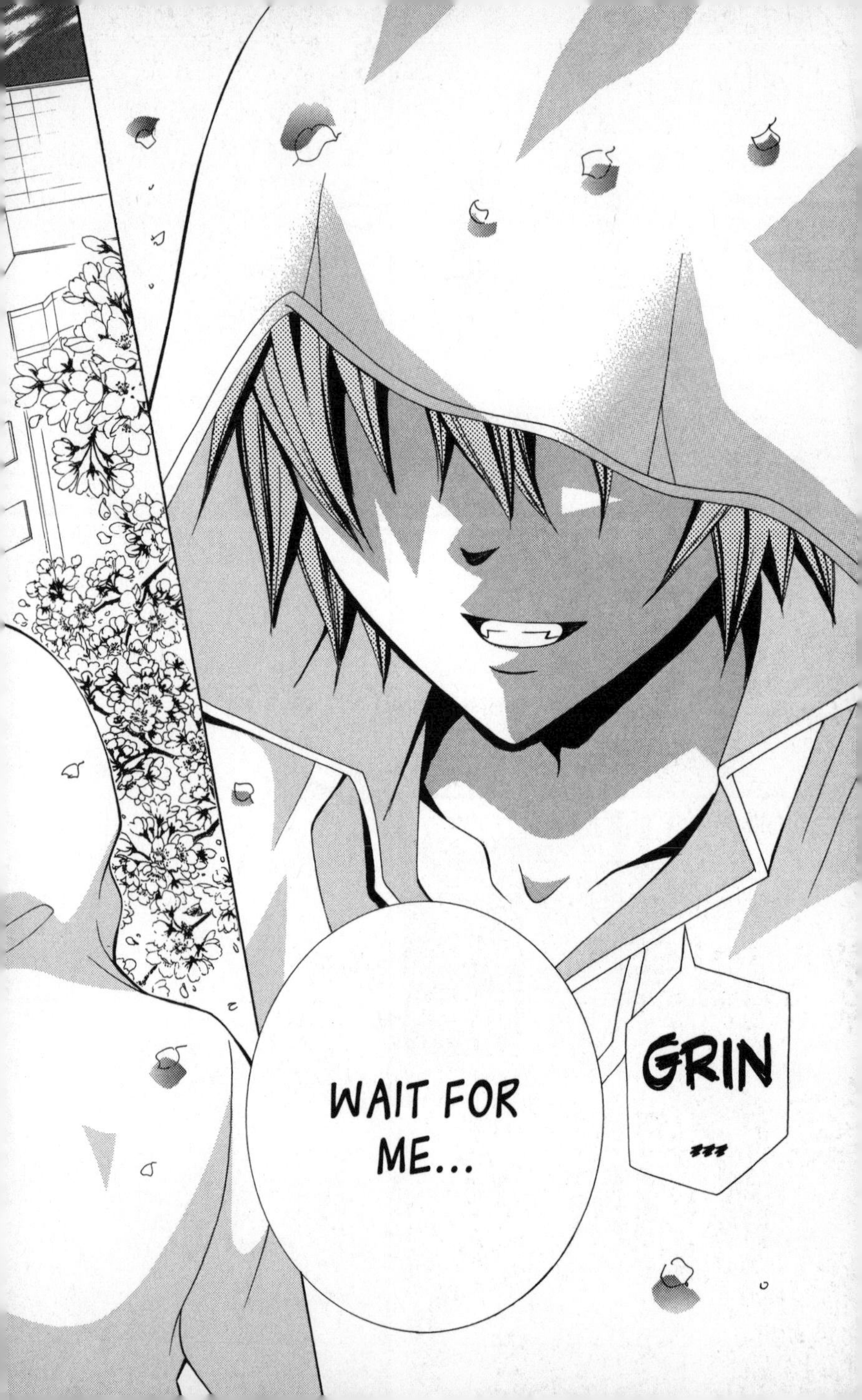
GRIN
WAIT FOR ME...

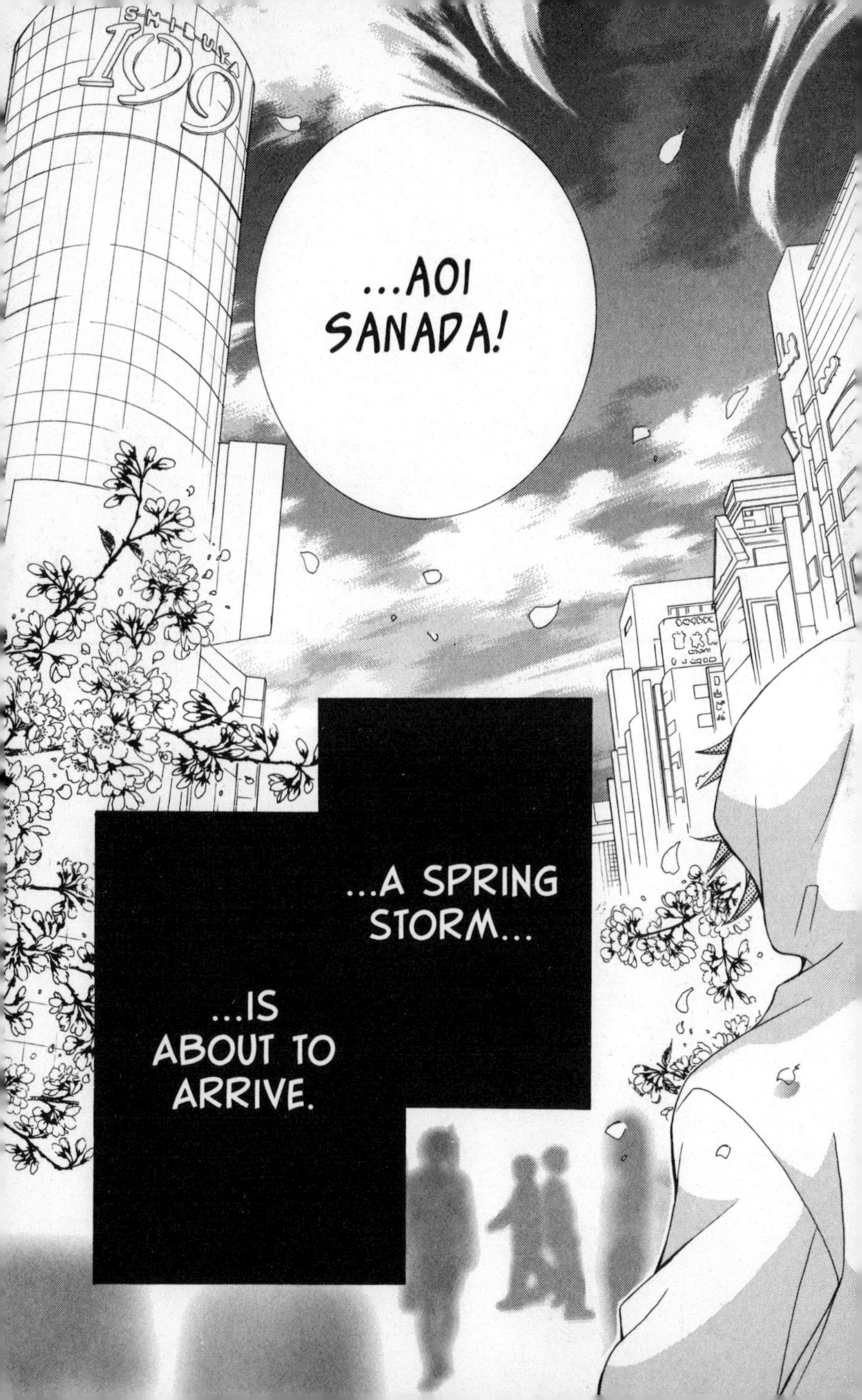
SHIBUYA 109
...AOI SANADA!
...A SPRING STORM...
...IS ABOUT TO ARRIVE.

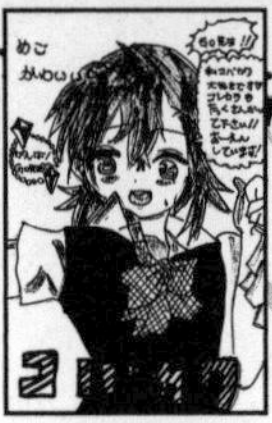

Editor: Cross-dressed... then not! Mego's cute either way!

↑ M-D Nanoda☆ (Hiroshima)

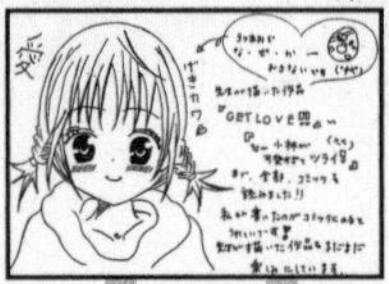

← Mioko (Yamanashi)

Editor: Second-year Mego has longer hair, but she looks cute in braids too. ♥

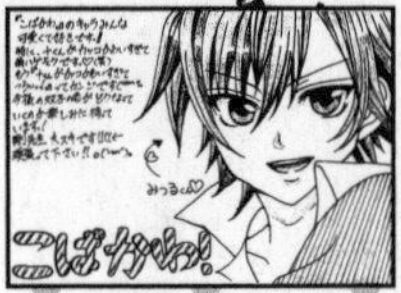

← Arisa Yoshida (Shizuoka)

Editor: I wonder who Mitsuru'll end up with?!

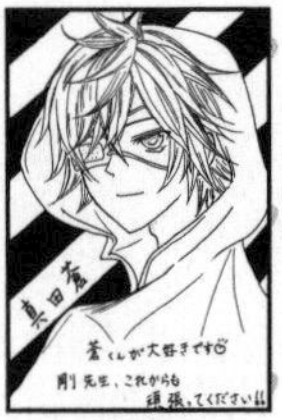

Editor: Lots of people draw Aoi wearing a hoodie. ♪

↑ Mukkun (Saitama)

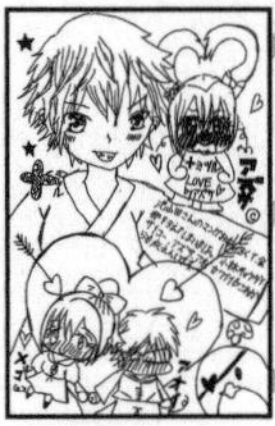

Editor: Will Azusa be able to shoot her arrow through Mitsuru's heart?!

↑ Hana Suzuki (Tochigi)

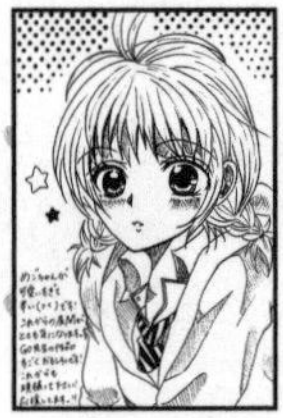

Editor: Braids again! People secretly like it...

↑ Kuro usagi (Saitama)

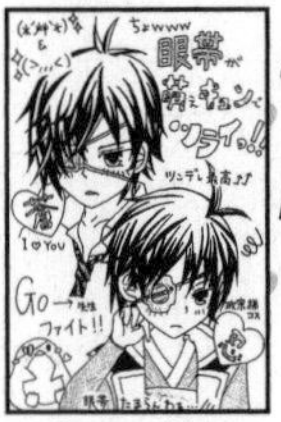

Editor: An eye-patch collab with Lord Masamune !!

↑ Magic Rin ☆ (Gifu)

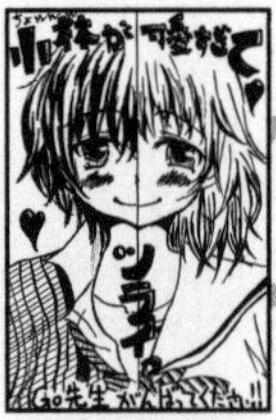

Editor: Both of them are so, so cute it hurts!!

↑ Harusame (Hokkaido)

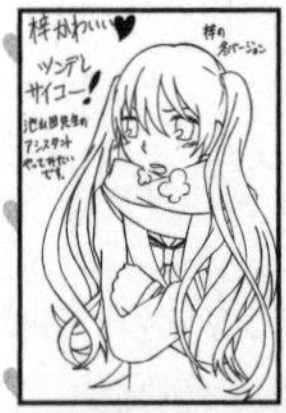

Editor: I want him to keep me warm during the cold winter... (>_<)

↑ Hiroka Oosawa (Chiba)

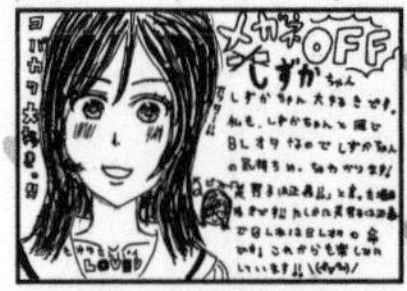

← Yukine Kataoka (Hokkaido)

Editor: First time I've seen Shizuka without glasses!!

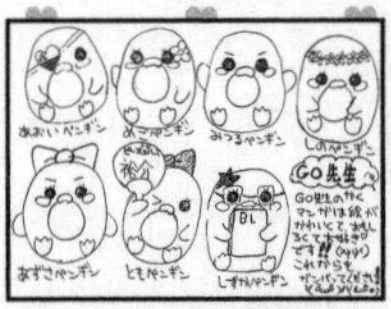

← Haruka Kato (Ibaraki)

Editor: F-Festival of Penguins!!!!

Send your fan mail to:

Go Ikeyamada
c/o Shojo Beat
VIZ Media, LLC
P.O. Box 77010
San Francisco, CA
94107

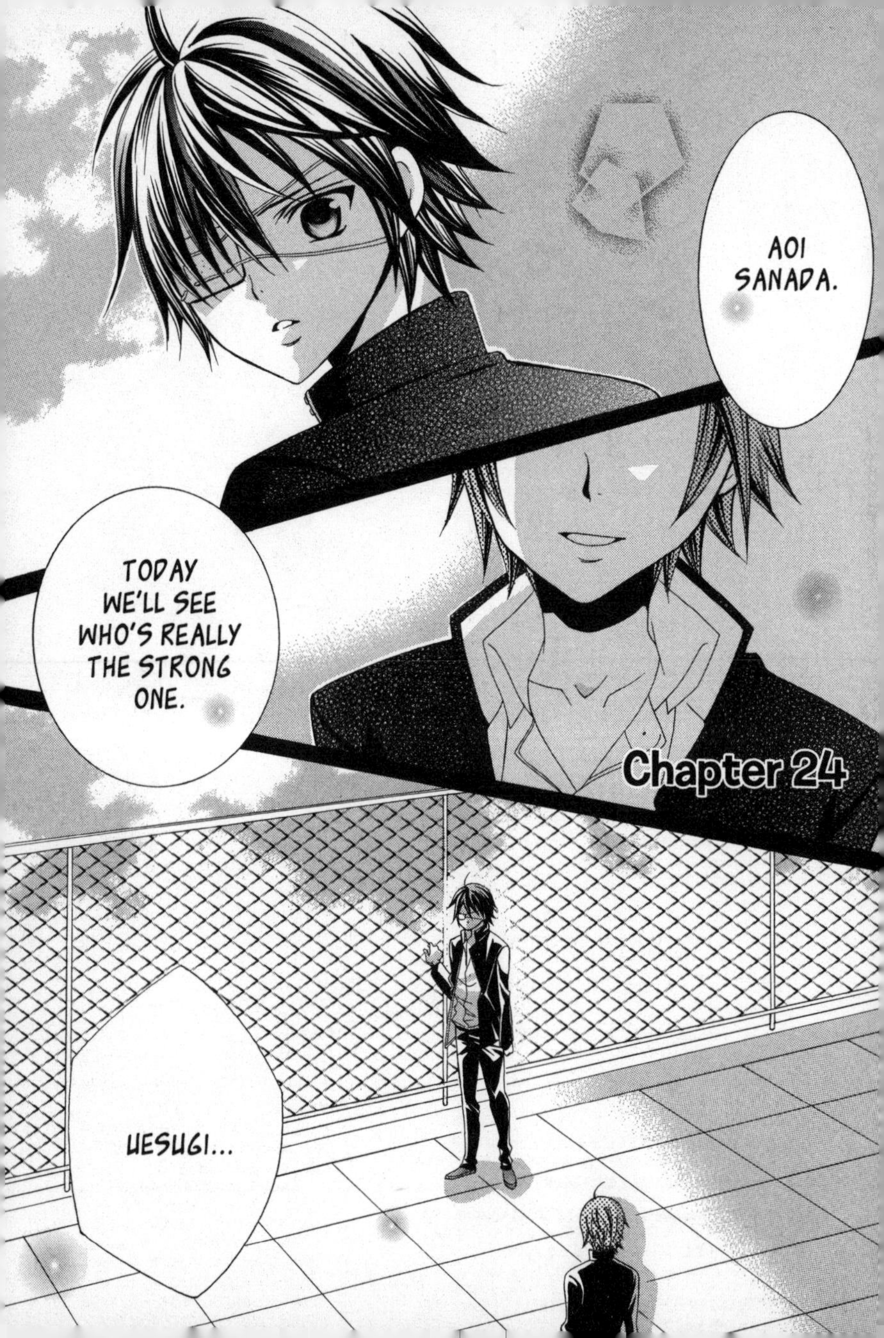
AOI SANADA.
TODAY WE'LL SEE WHO'S REALLY THE STRONG ONE.
Chapter 24
UESUGI...

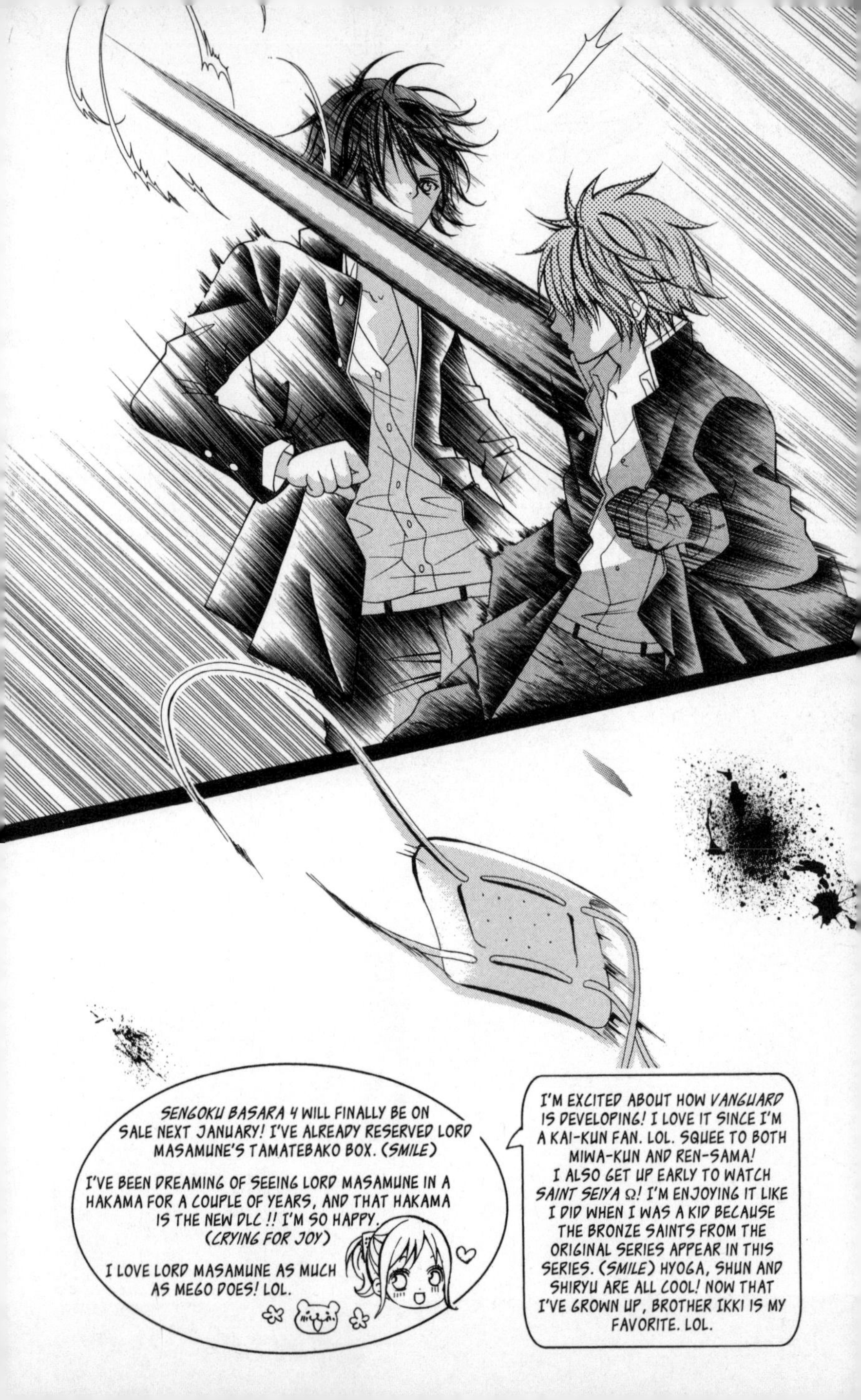

I'M EXCITED ABOUT HOW *VANGUARD* IS DEVELOPING! I LOVE IT SINCE I'M A KAI-KUN FAN. LOL. SQUEE TO BOTH MIWA-KUN AND REN-SAMA!
I ALSO GET UP EARLY TO WATCH *SAINT SEIYA Ω*! I'M ENJOYING IT LIKE I DID WHEN I WAS A KID BECAUSE THE BRONZE SAINTS FROM THE ORIGINAL SERIES APPEAR IN THIS SERIES. (*SMILE*) HYOGA, SHUN AND SHIRYU ARE ALL COOL! NOW THAT I'VE GROWN UP, BROTHER IKKI IS MY FAVORITE. LOL.
SENGOKU BASARA 4 WILL FINALLY BE ON SALE NEXT JANUARY! I'VE ALREADY RESERVED LORD MASAMUNE'S TAMATEBAKO BOX. (*SMILE*)
I'VE BEEN DREAMING OF SEEING LORD MASAMUNE IN A HAKAMA FOR A COUPLE OF YEARS, AND THAT HAKAMA IS THE NEW DLC !! I'M SO HAPPY. (*CRYING FOR JOY*)
I LOVE LORD MASAMUNE AS MUCH AS MEGO DOES! LOL.

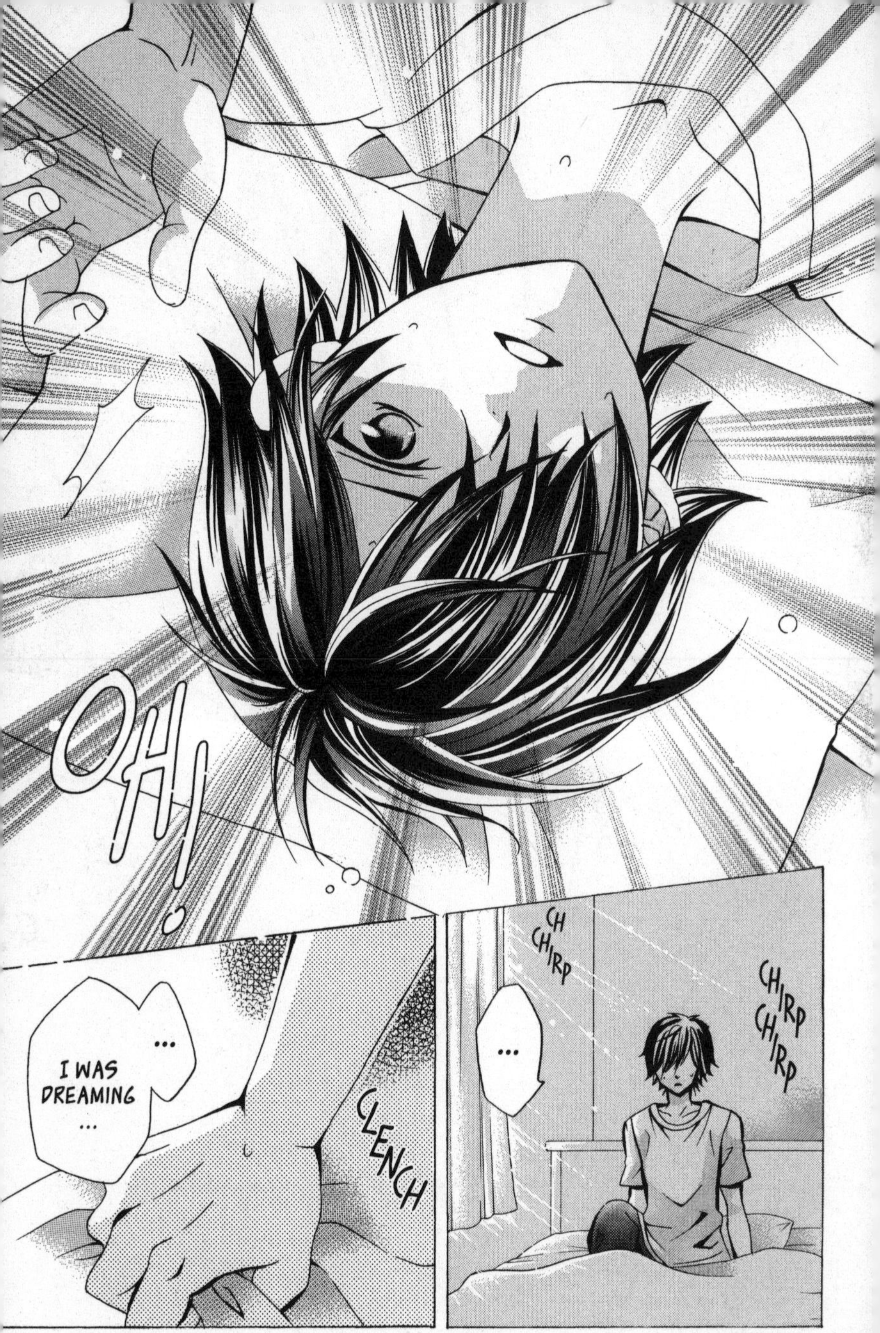
OH!
CH CHIRP
CHIRP CHIRP
...
...
I WAS DREAMING ...
CLENCH

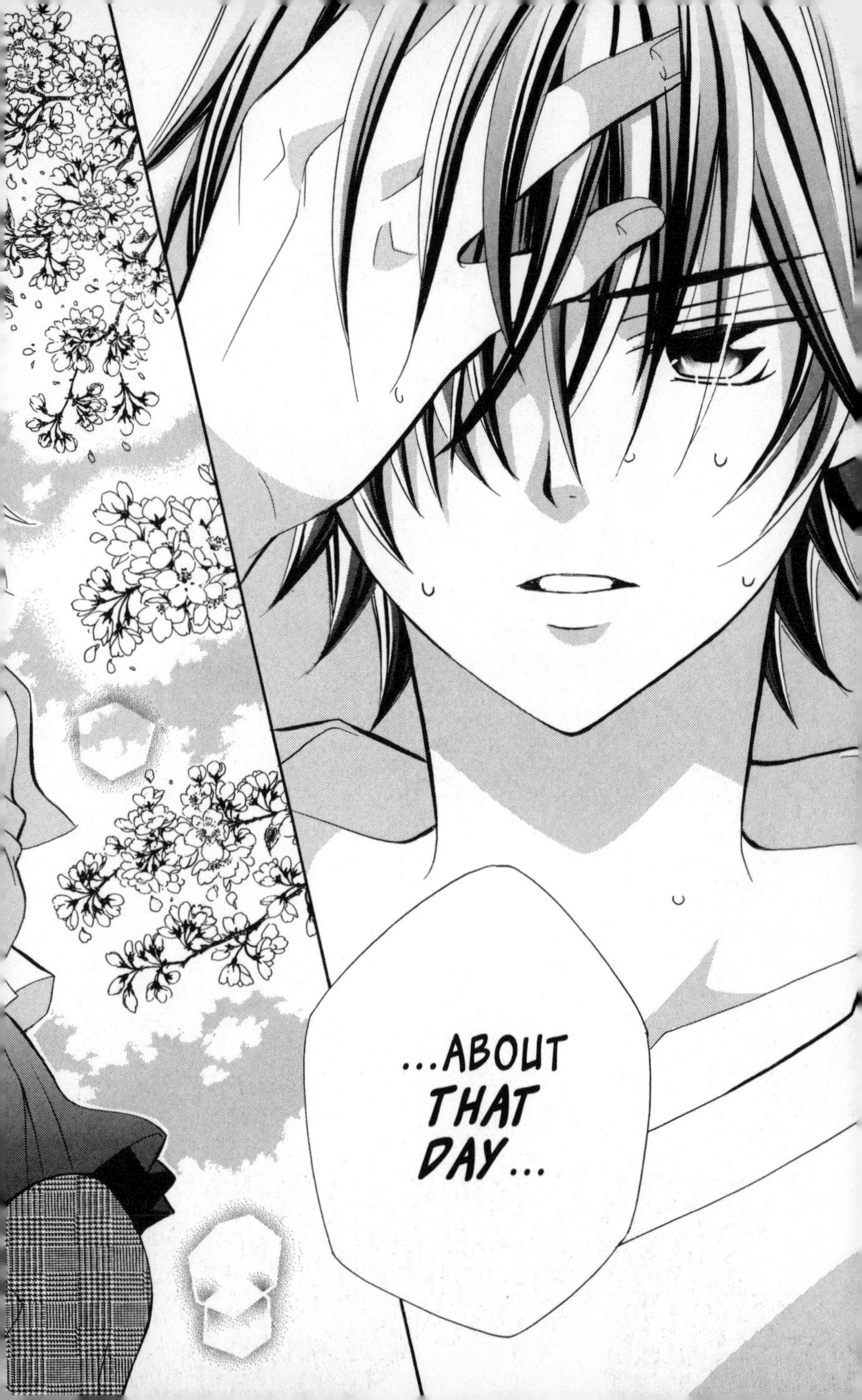
...ABOUT THAT DAY...

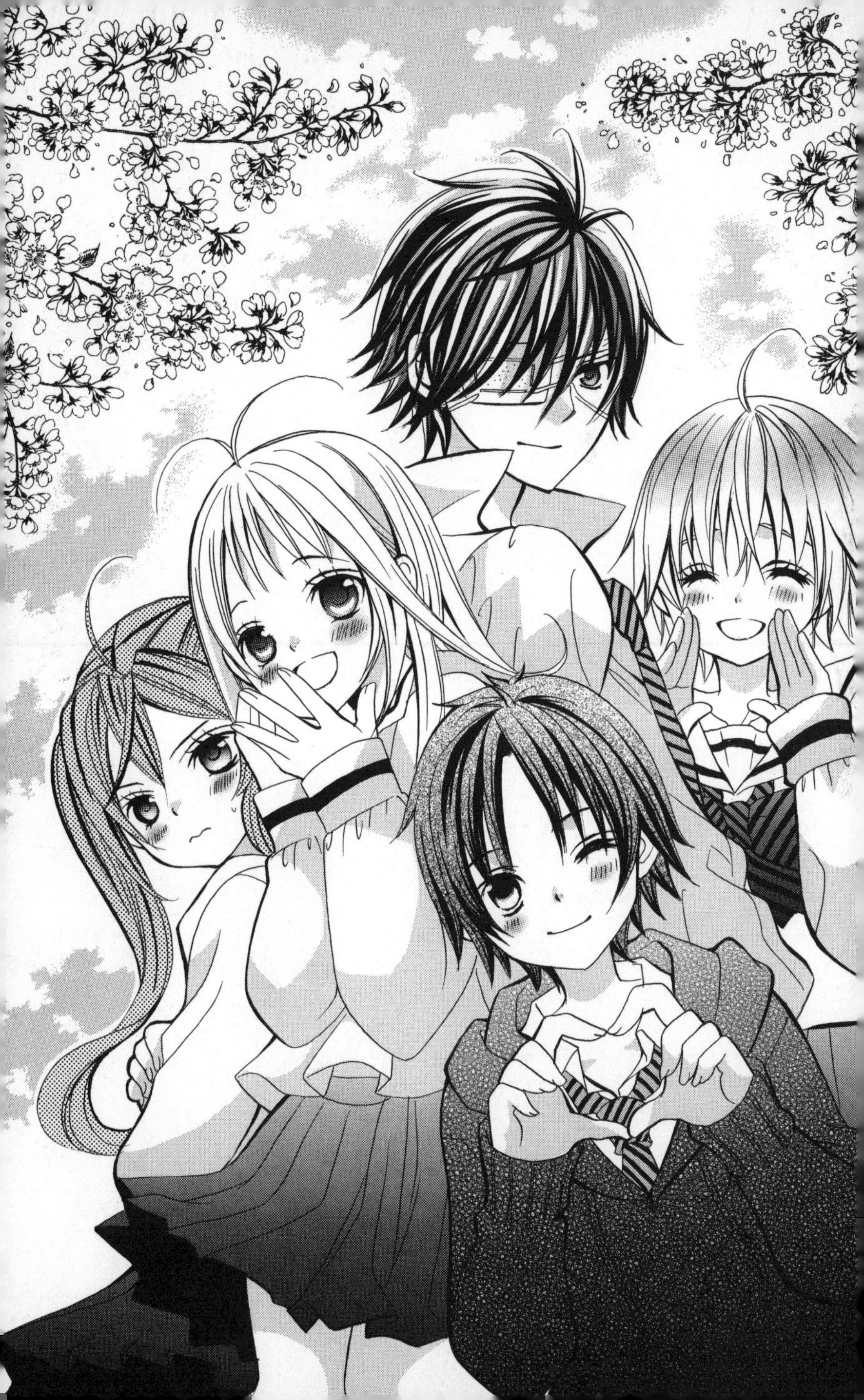

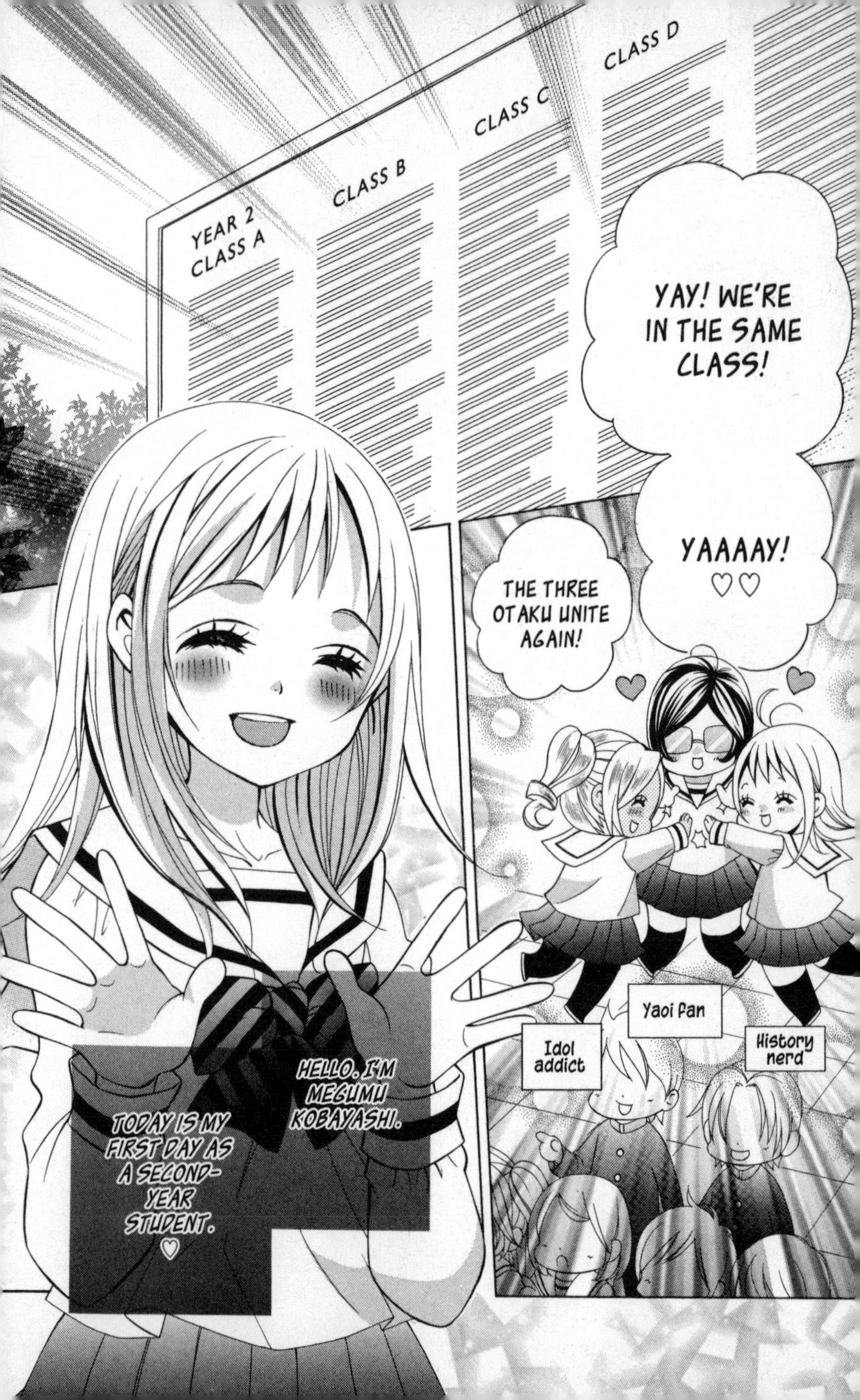
YEAR 2 CLASS A
CLASS B
CLASS C
CLASS D
YAY! WE'RE IN THE SAME CLASS!
YAAAAY! ♡♡
THE THREE OTAKU UNITE AGAIN!
Yaoi fan
History nerd
Idol addict
HELLO. I'M MEGUMU KOBAYASHI.
TODAY IS MY FIRST DAY AS A SECOND-YEAR STUDENT. ♡

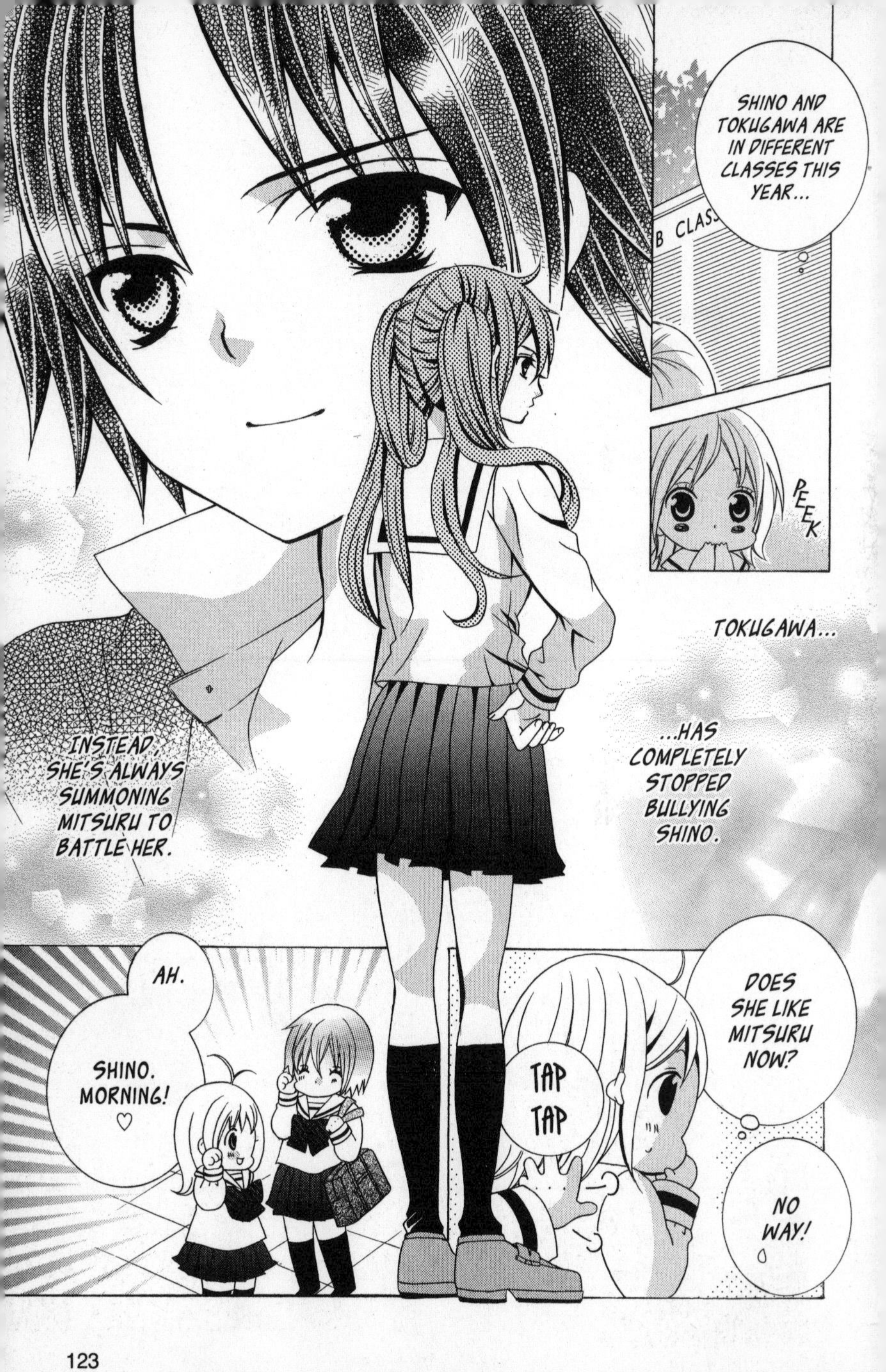
SHINO AND TOKUGAWA ARE IN DIFFERENT CLASSES THIS YEAR...
B CLASS
PEEK
TOKUGAWA...
...HAS COMPLETELY STOPPED BULLYING SHINO.
INSTEAD, SHE'S ALWAYS SUMMONING MITSURU TO BATTLE HER.
DOES SHE LIKE MITSURU NOW?
NO WAY!
TAP TAP
AH.
SHINO. MORNING! ♡

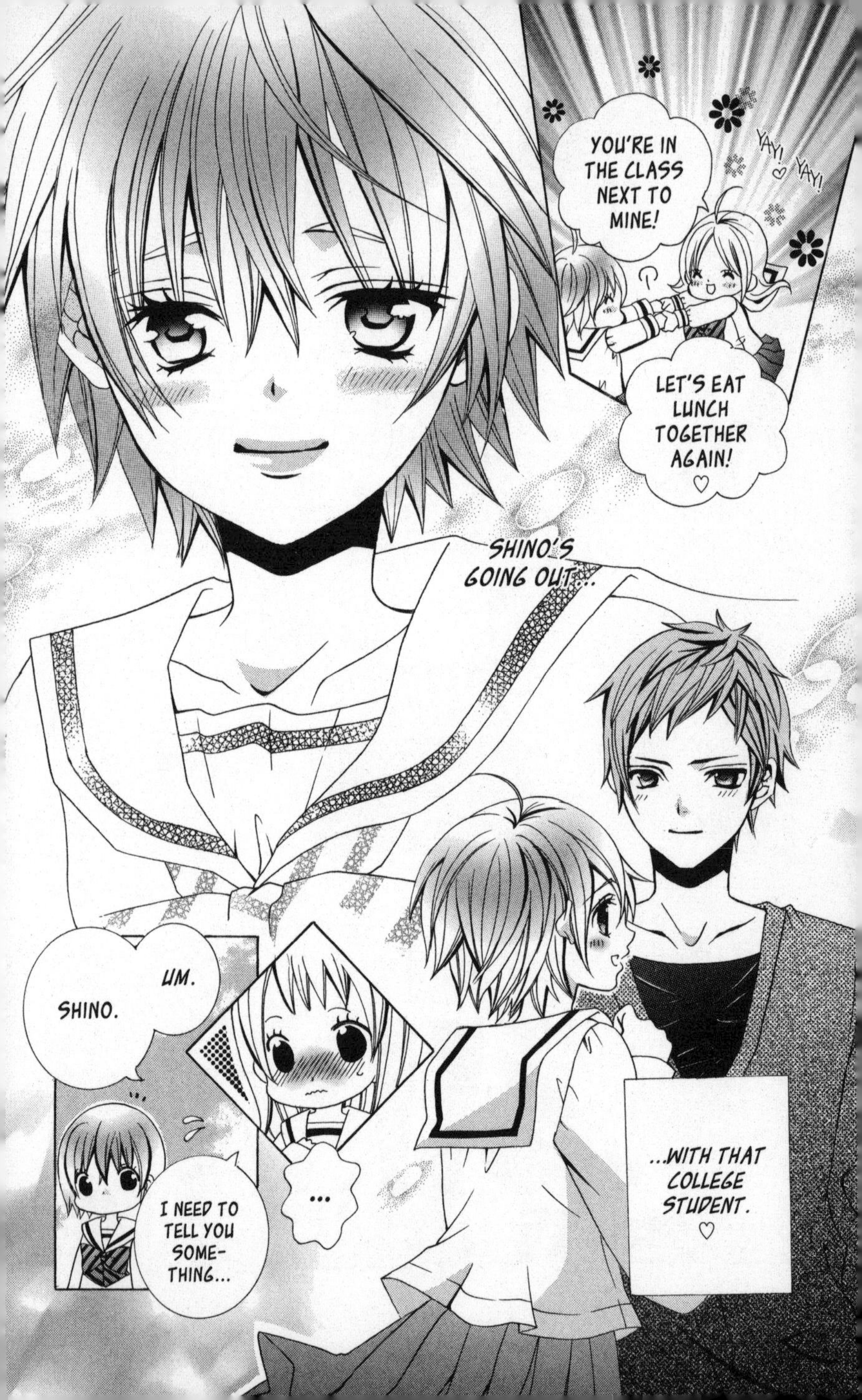
YOU'RE IN THE CLASS NEXT TO MINE!
YAY! ♡ YAY!
LET'S EAT LUNCH TOGETHER AGAIN! ♡
SHINO'S GOING OUT...
...WITH THAT COLLEGE STUDENT. ♡
...
UM. SHINO.
I NEED TO TELL YOU SOME-THING...

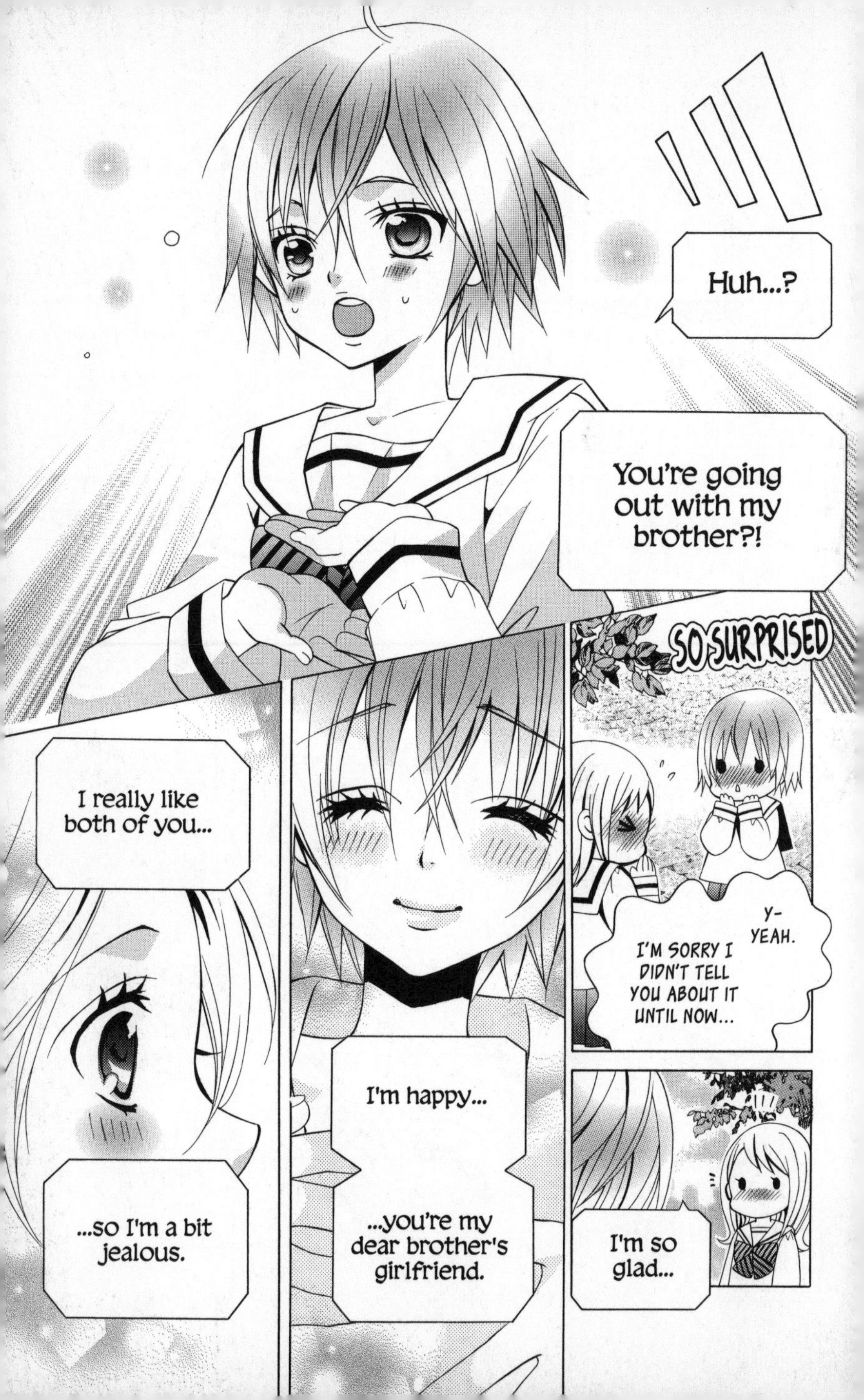
Huh...?
You're going out with my brother?!
SO SURPRISED
Y- YEAH.
I'M SORRY I DIDN'T TELL YOU ABOUT IT UNTIL NOW...
I'm so glad...
I'm happy...
...you're my dear brother's girlfriend.
I really like both of you...
...so I'm a bit jealous.

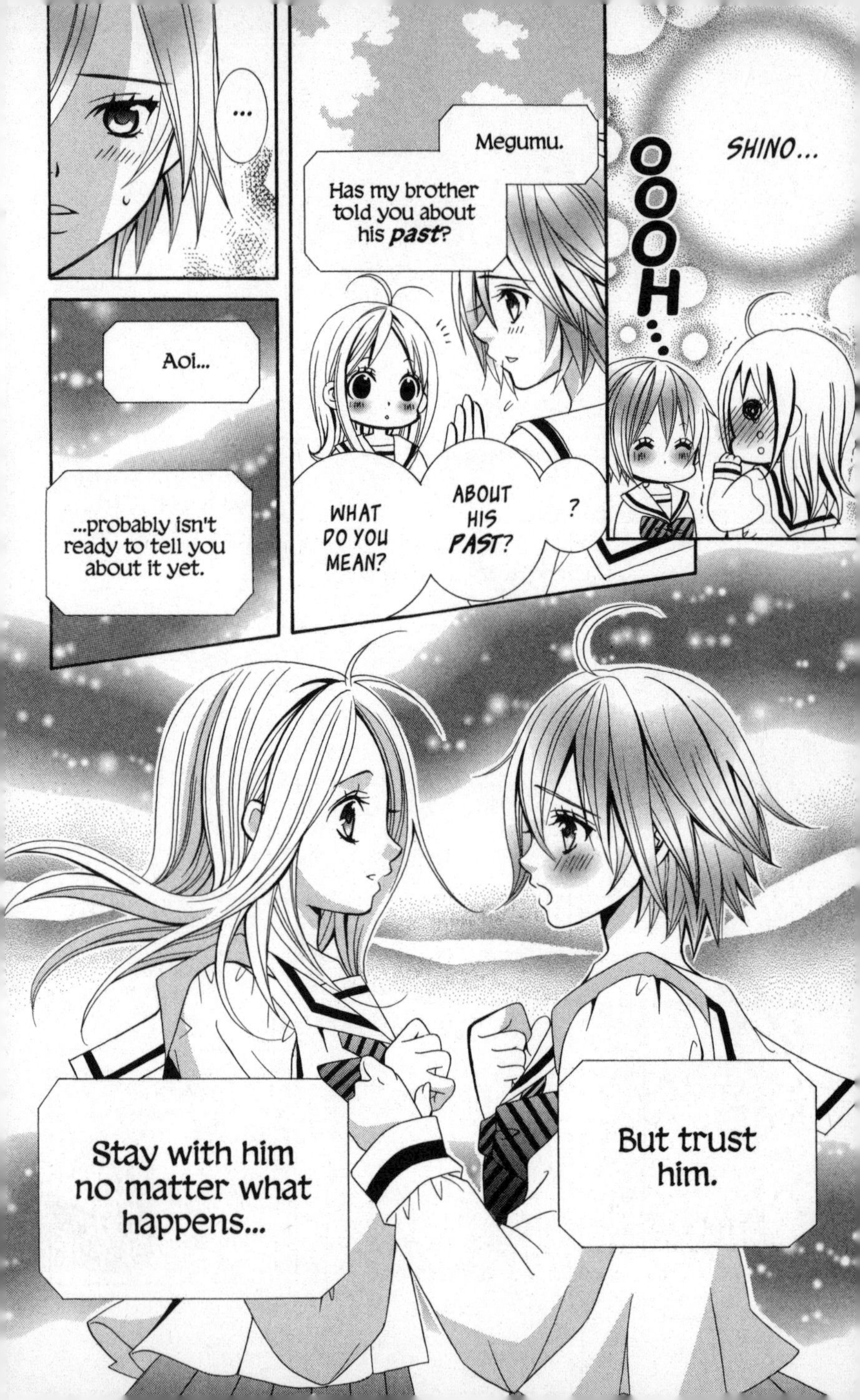
SHINO...
OOOH...
Megumu.
Has my brother told you about his *past*?
WHAT DO YOU MEAN? ABOUT HIS *PAST*? ?
...
Aoi...
...probably isn't ready to tell you about it yet.
But trust him.
Stay with him no matter what happens...

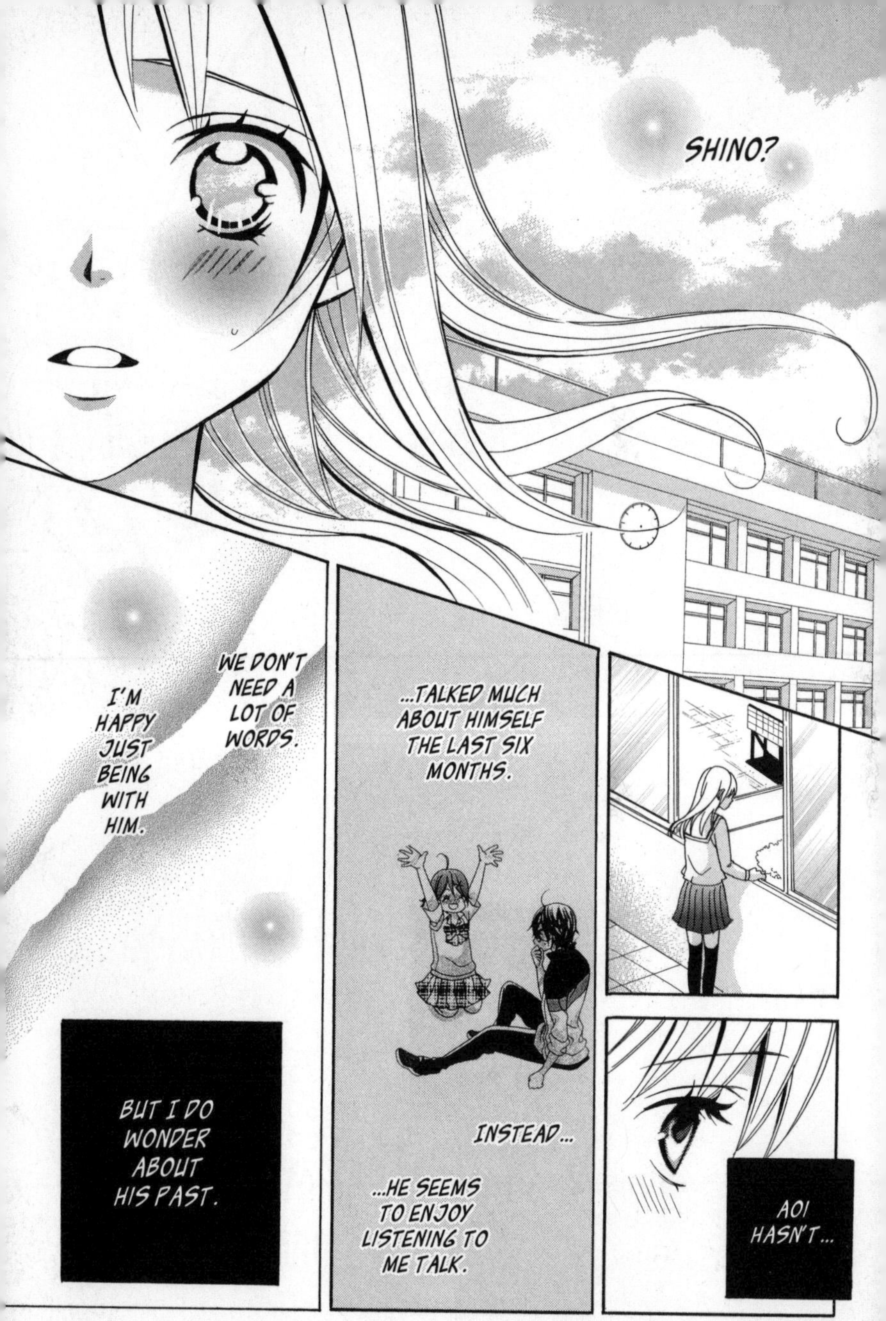
SHINO?
AOI HASN'T...
...TALKED MUCH ABOUT HIMSELF THE LAST SIX MONTHS.
INSTEAD...
...HE SEEMS TO ENJOY LISTENING TO ME TALK.
WE DON'T NEED A LOT OF WORDS.
I'M HAPPY JUST BEING WITH HIM.
BUT I DO WONDER ABOUT HIS PAST.

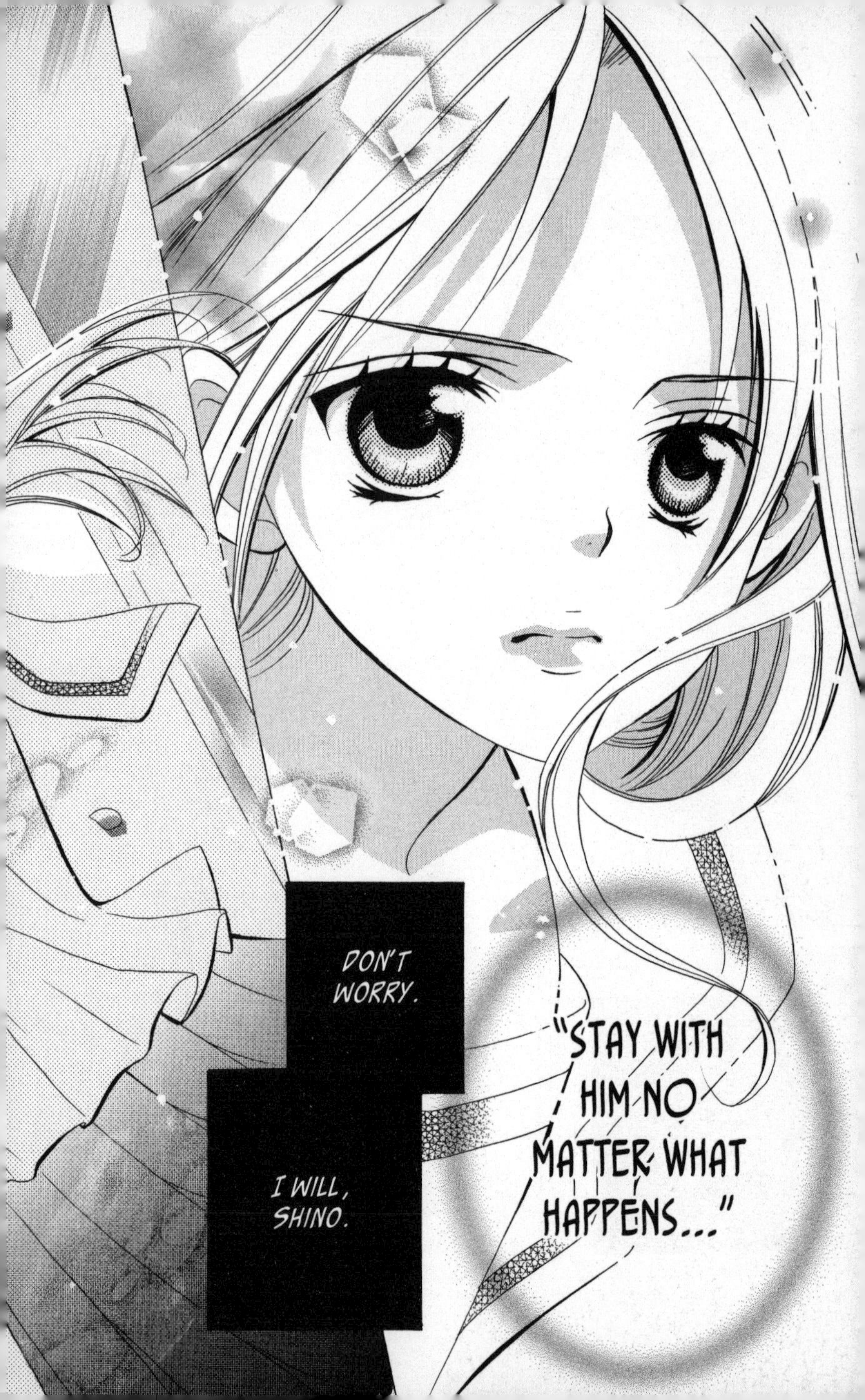
"STAY WITH HIM NO MATTER WHAT HAPPENS..."
DON'T WORRY.
I WILL, SHINO.

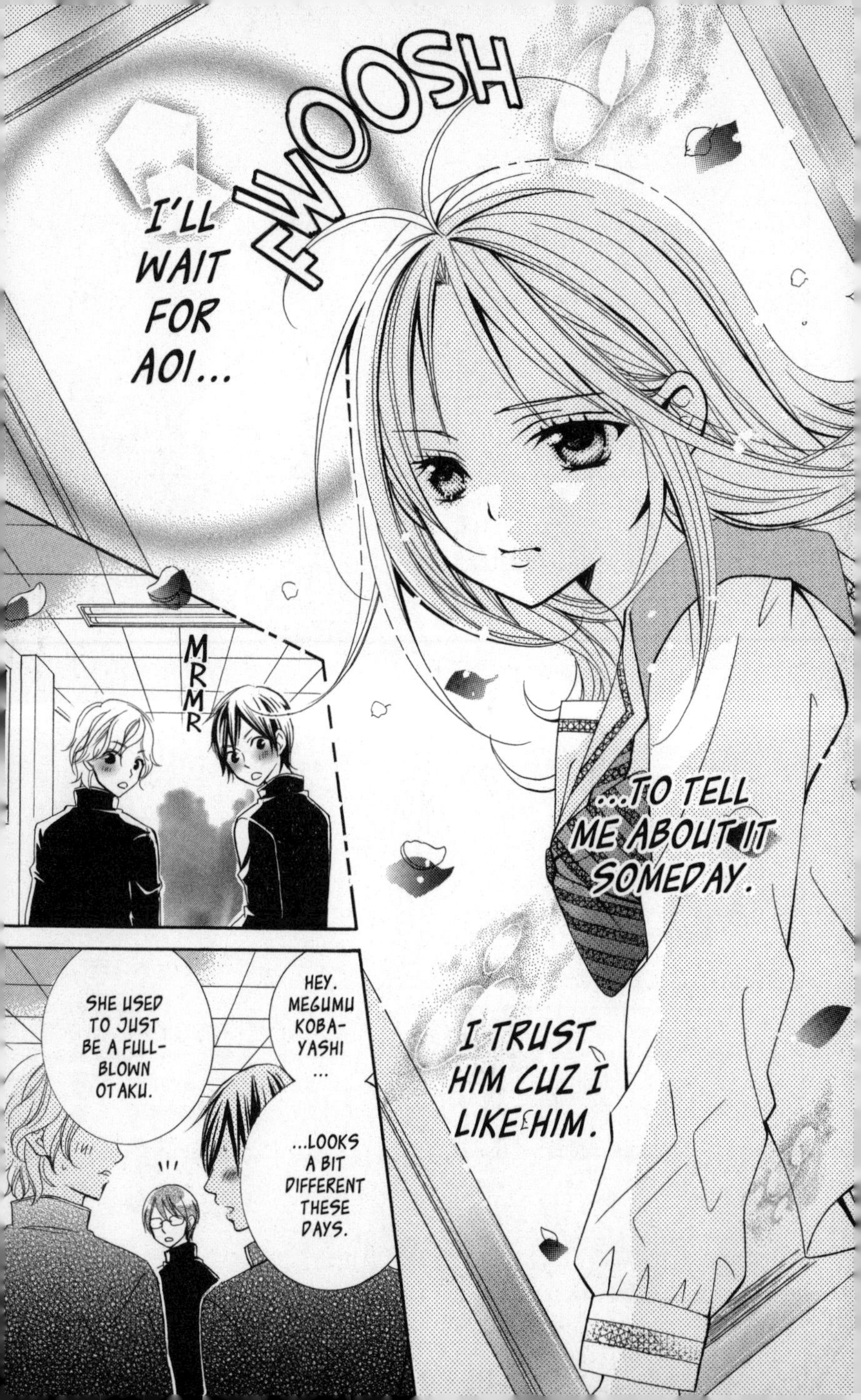

WOOSH
I'LL WAIT FOR AOI...
...TO TELL ME ABOUT IT SOMEDAY.
I TRUST HIM CUZ I LIKE HIM.
MRMR
HEY. MEGUMU KOBA-YASHI...
...LOOKS A BIT DIFFERENT THESE DAYS.
SHE USED TO JUST BE A FULL-BLOWN OTAKU.

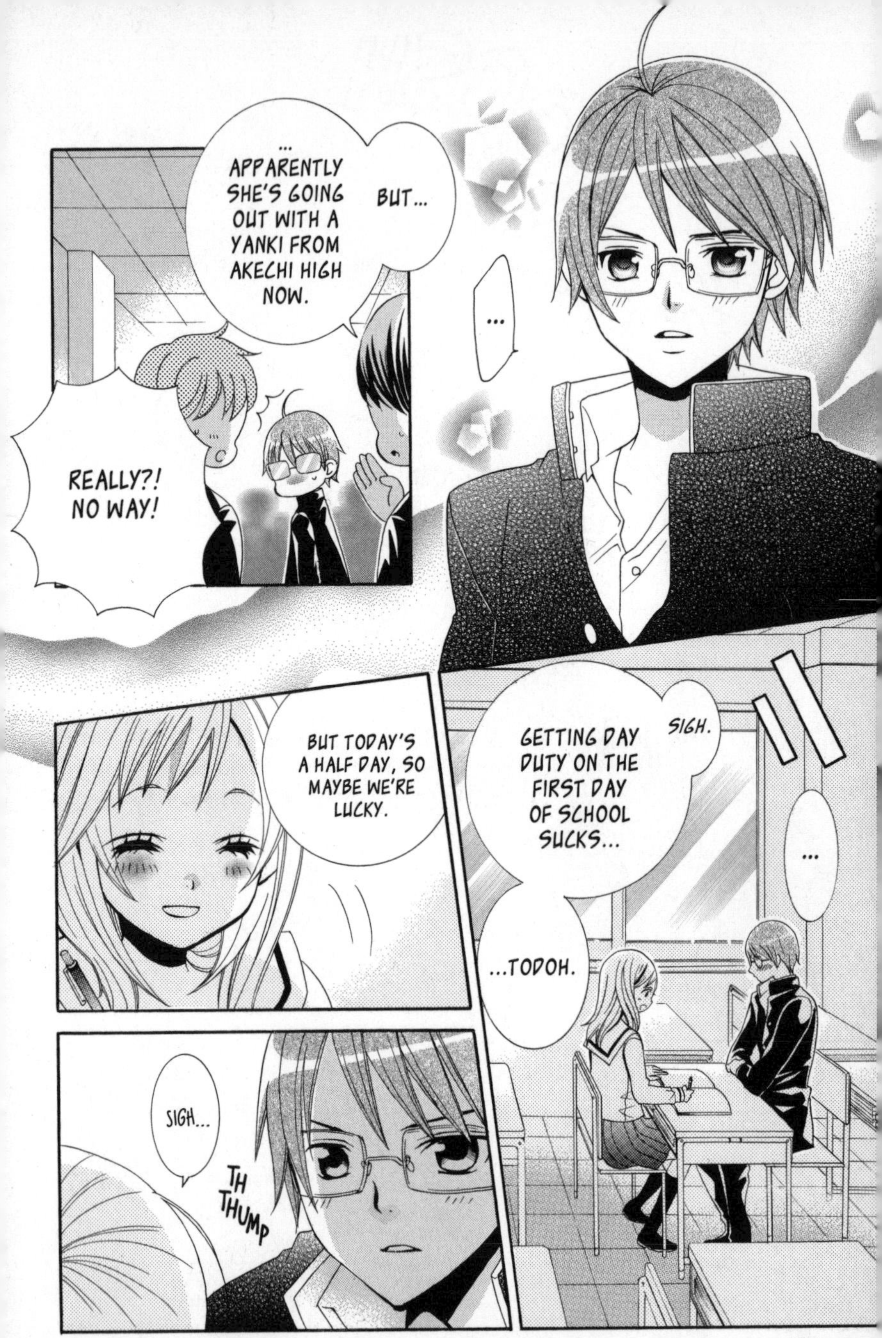
...
BUT...
...APPARENTLY SHE'S GOING OUT WITH A YANKI FROM AKECHI HIGH NOW.
REALLY?! NO WAY!
SIGH.
GETTING DAY DUTY ON THE FIRST DAY OF SCHOOL SUCKS...
...
...TODOH.
BUT TODAY'S A HALF DAY, SO MAYBE WE'RE LUCKY.
SIGH...
TH THUMP

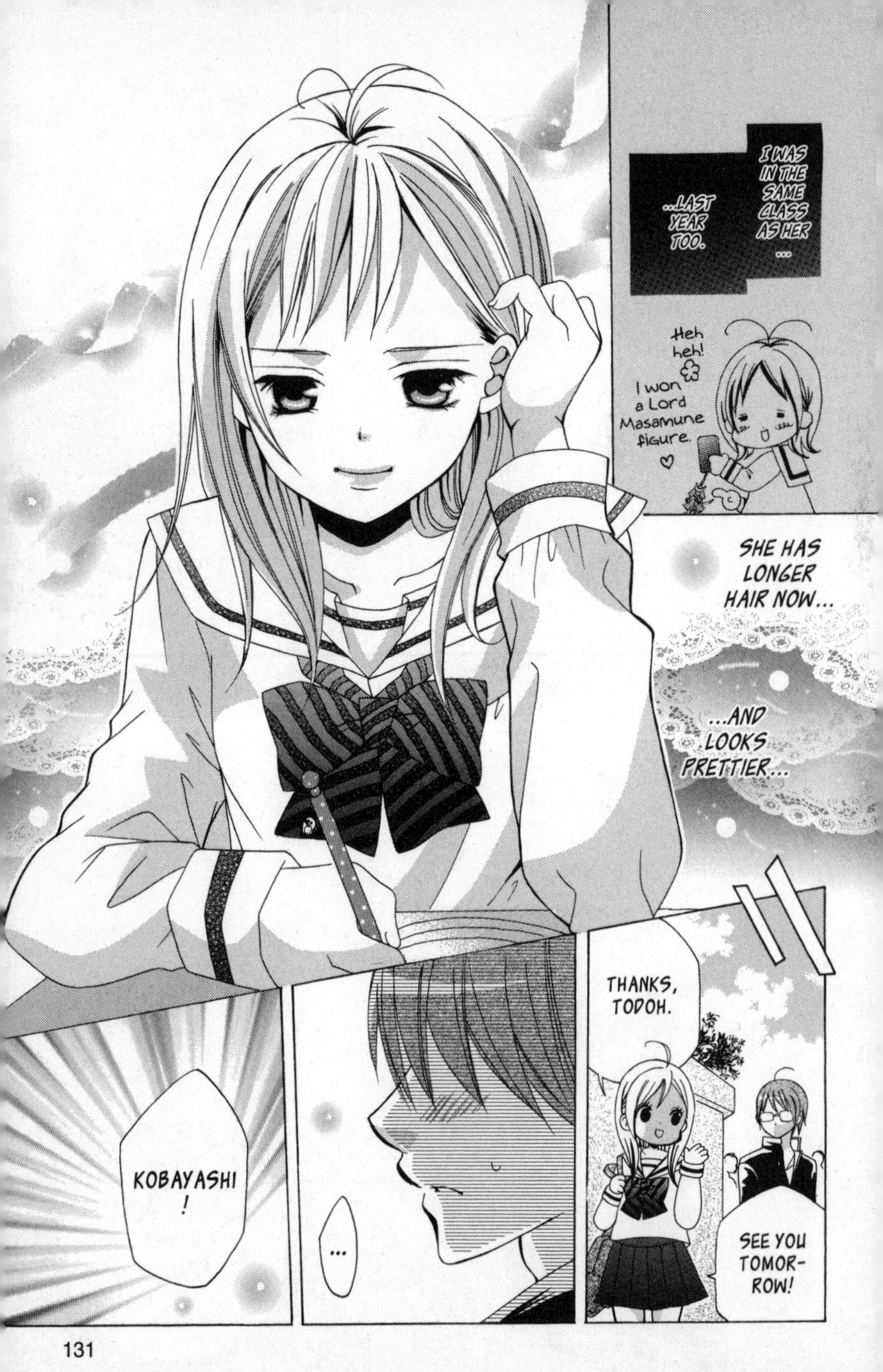
I WAS IN THE SAME CLASS AS HER ...
...LAST YEAR TOO.
Heh heh! I won a Lord Masamune figure.
SHE HAS LONGER HAIR NOW...
...AND LOOKS PRETTIER...
THANKS, TODOH.
SEE YOU TOMOR-ROW!
...
KOBAYASHI!

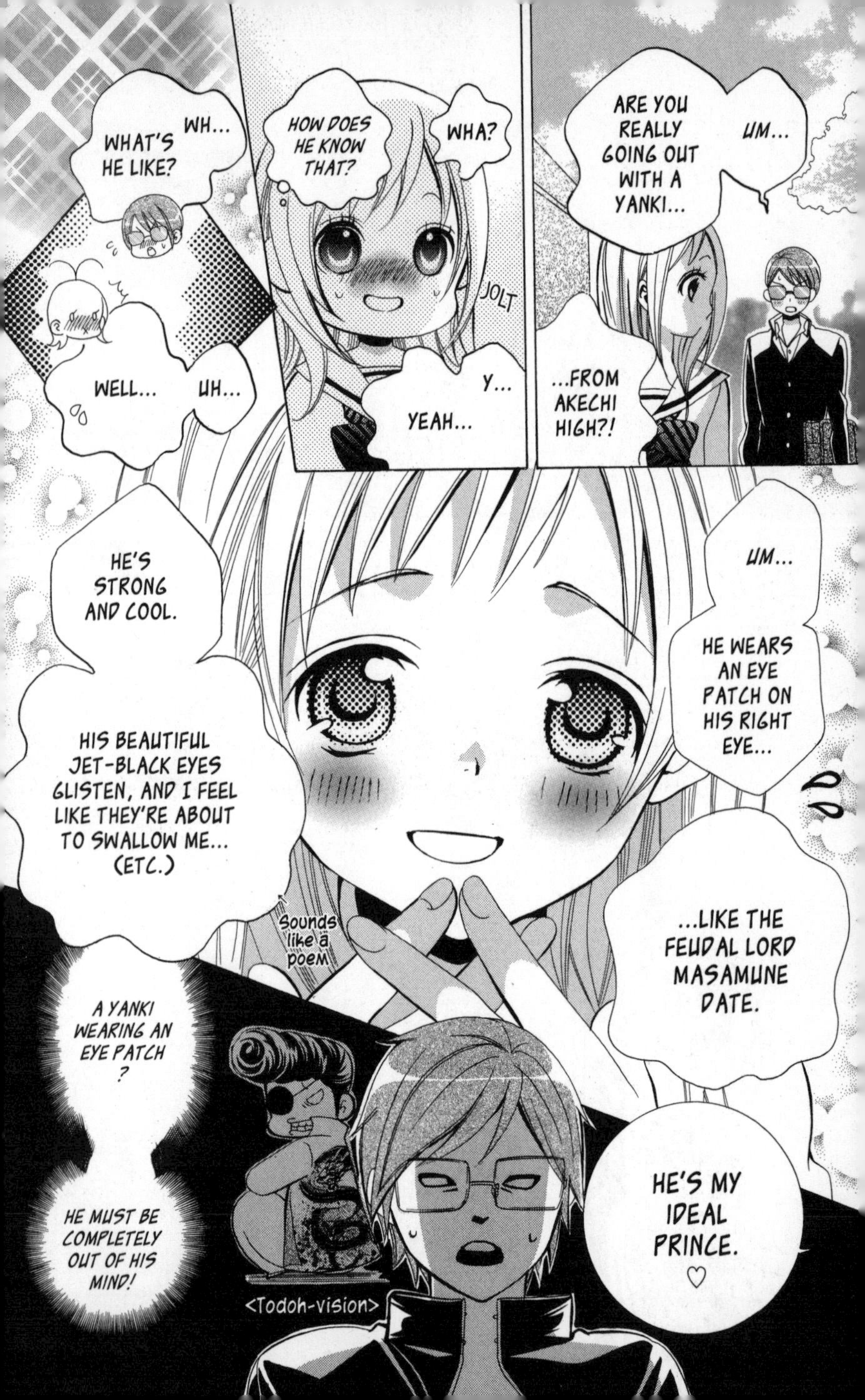
UM...
ARE YOU REALLY GOING OUT WITH A YANKI...
...FROM AKECHI HIGH?!
WHA?
HOW DOES HE KNOW THAT?
JOLT
Y... YEAH...
WH... WHAT'S HE LIKE?
UH... WELL...
UM...
HE WEARS AN EYE PATCH ON HIS RIGHT EYE...
HE'S STRONG AND COOL.
...LIKE THE FEUDAL LORD MASAMUNE DATE.
HIS BEAUTIFUL JET-BLACK EYES GLISTEN, AND I FEEL LIKE THEY'RE ABOUT TO SWALLOW ME... (ETC.)
Sounds like a poem
HE'S MY IDEAL PRINCE. ♡
A YANKI WEARING AN EYE PATCH ?
HE MUST BE COMPLETELY OUT OF HIS MIND!
<Todoh-vision>

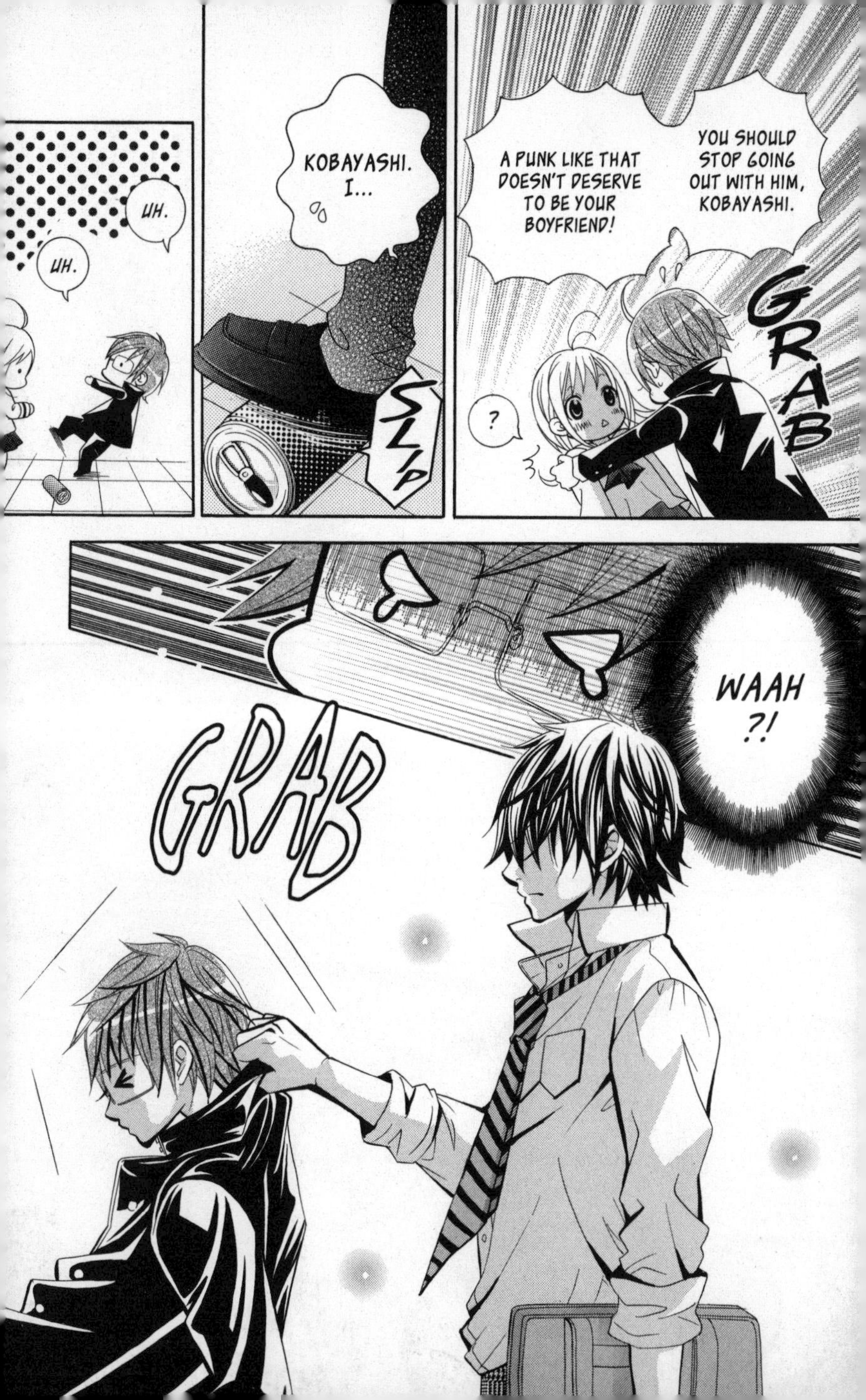

YOU SHOULD STOP GOING OUT WITH HIM, KOBAYASHI.
A PUNK LIKE THAT DOESN'T DESERVE TO BE YOUR BOYFRIEND!
?
GRAB
KOBAYASHI. I...
SLIP
UH.
UH.
WAAH ?!
GRAB

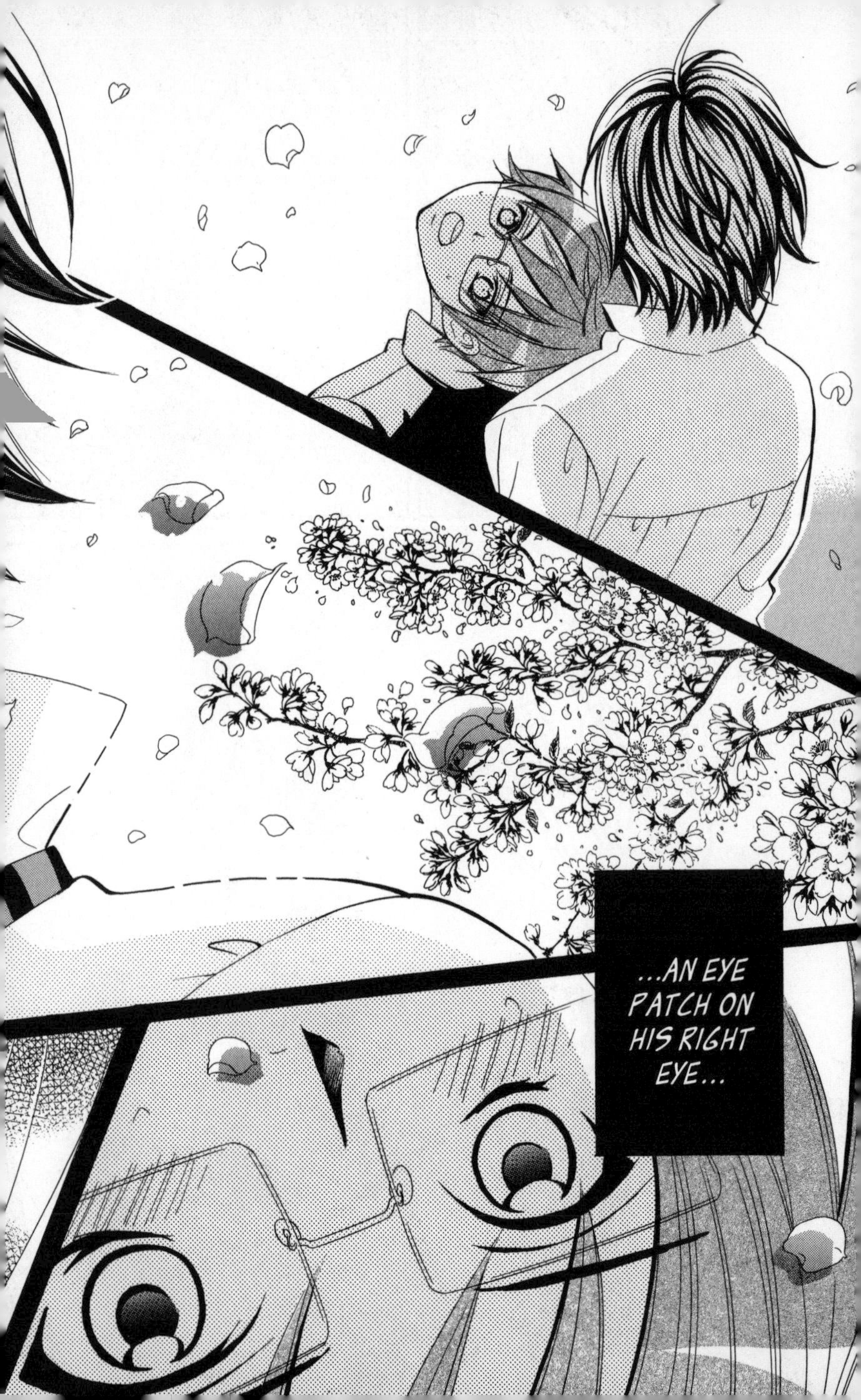
...AN EYE PATCH ON HIS RIGHT EYE...

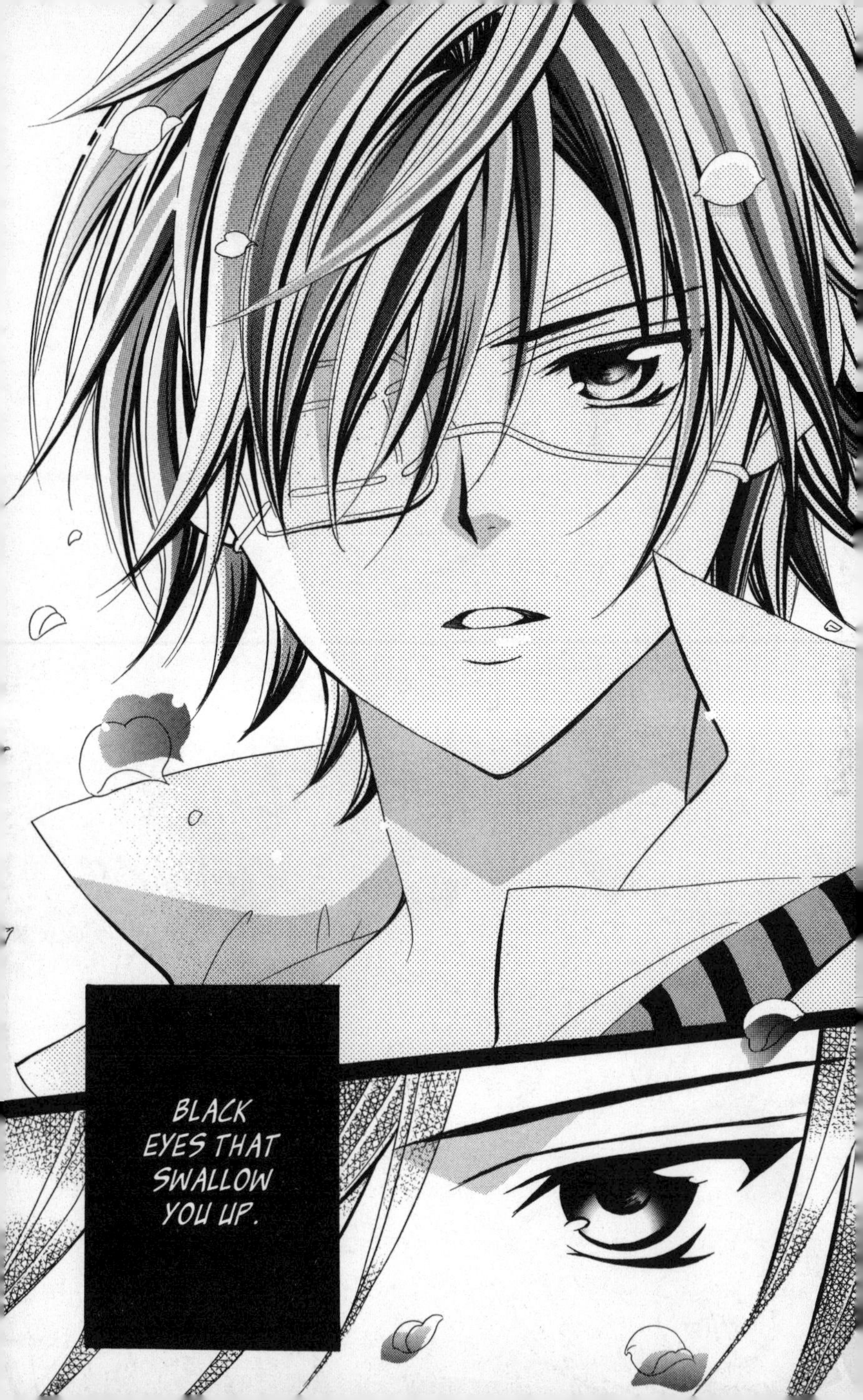
BLACK EYES THAT SWALLOW YOU UP.

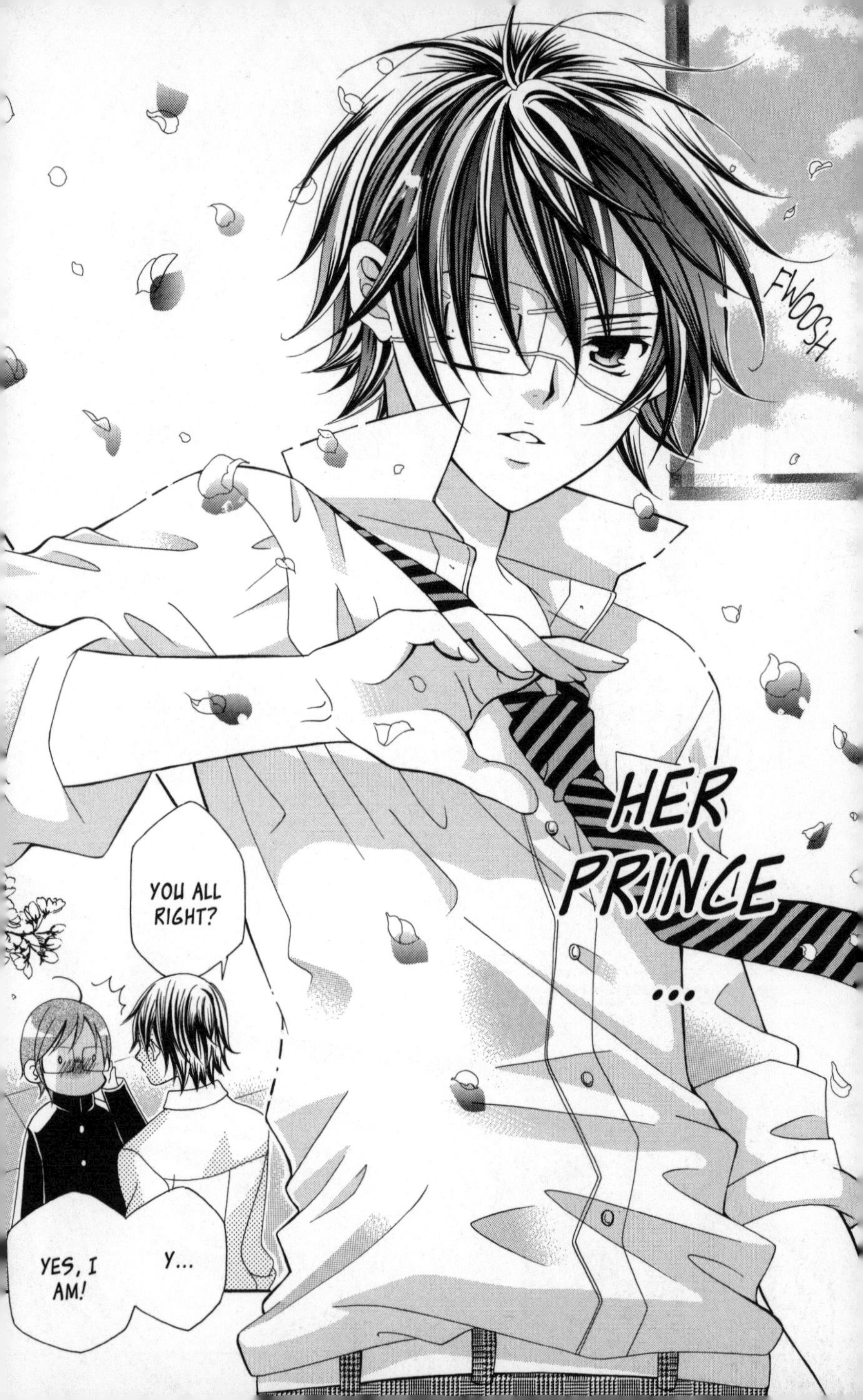
FWOOSH
HER PRINCE ...
YOU ALL RIGHT?
Y...
YES, I AM!

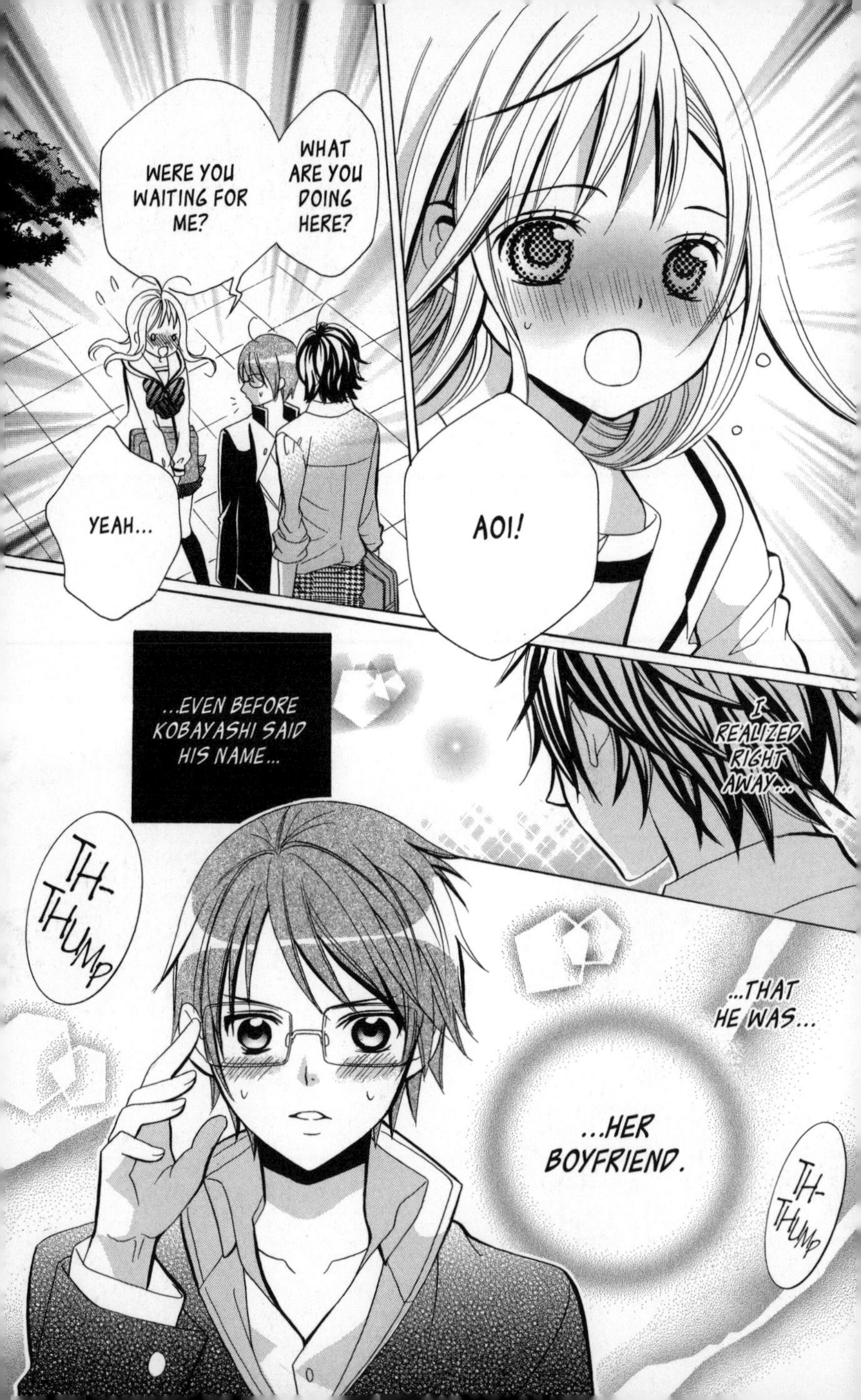
AOI!
WHAT ARE YOU DOING HERE?
WERE YOU WAITING FOR ME?
YEAH...
I REALIZED RIGHT AWAY...
...EVEN BEFORE KOBAYASHI SAID HIS NAME...
...THAT HE WAS...
...HER BOYFRIEND.
TH-THUMP
TH-THUMP

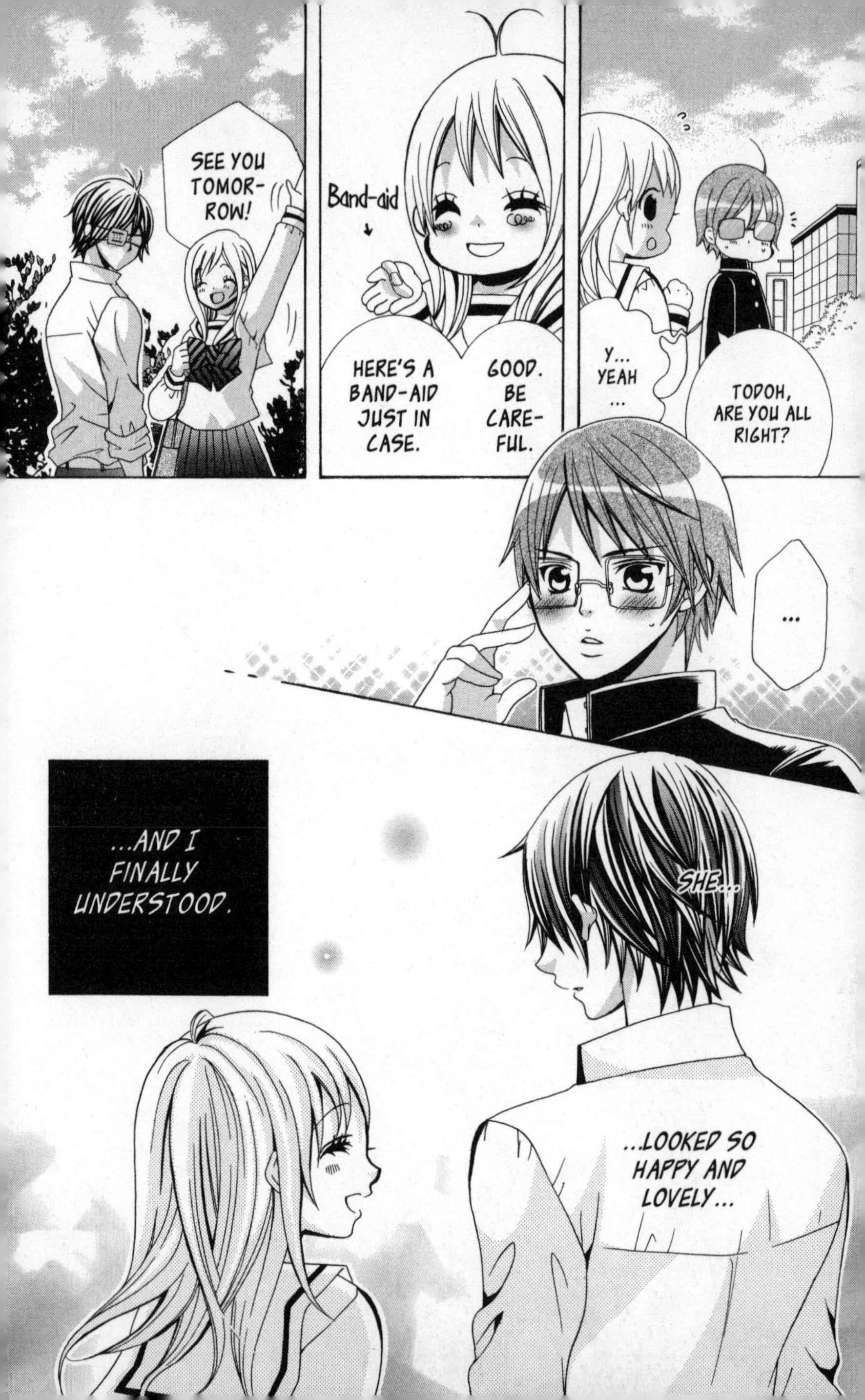
TODOH, ARE YOU ALL RIGHT?
Y... YEAH ...
Band-aid
GOOD. BE CARE-FUL.
HERE'S A BAND-AID JUST IN CASE.
SEE YOU TOMOR-ROW!
...
SHE...
...LOOKED SO HAPPY AND LOVELY...
...AND I FINALLY UNDERSTOOD.

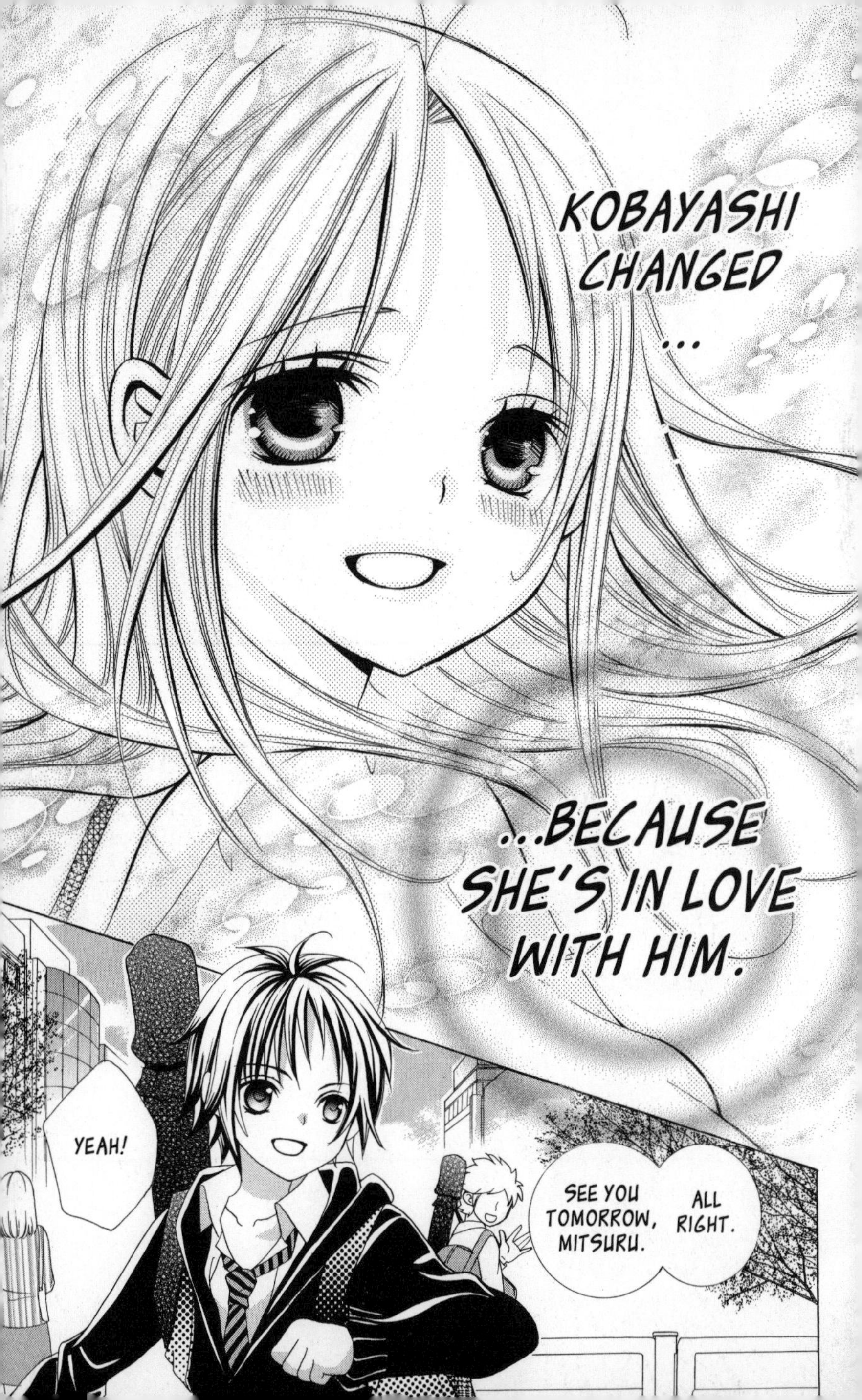
KOBAYASHI CHANGED ...
...BECAUSE SHE'S IN LOVE WITH HIM.
ALL RIGHT.
SEE YOU TOMORROW, MITSURU.
YEAH!

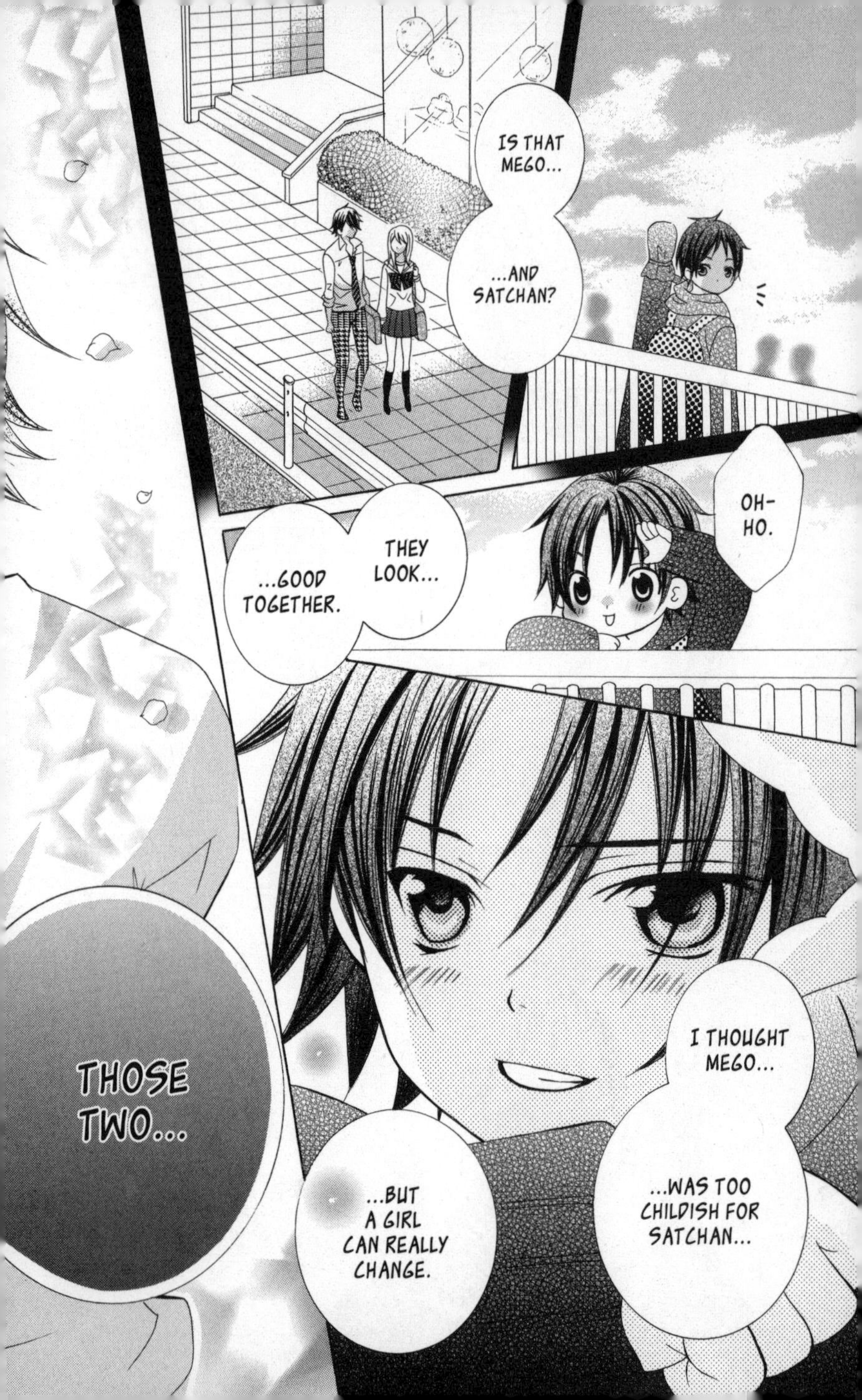
IS THAT MEGO...
...AND SATCHAN?
OH-HO.
THEY LOOK...
...GOOD TOGETHER.
I THOUGHT MEGO...
...WAS TOO CHILDISH FOR SATCHAN...
...BUT A GIRL CAN REALLY CHANGE.
THOSE TWO...

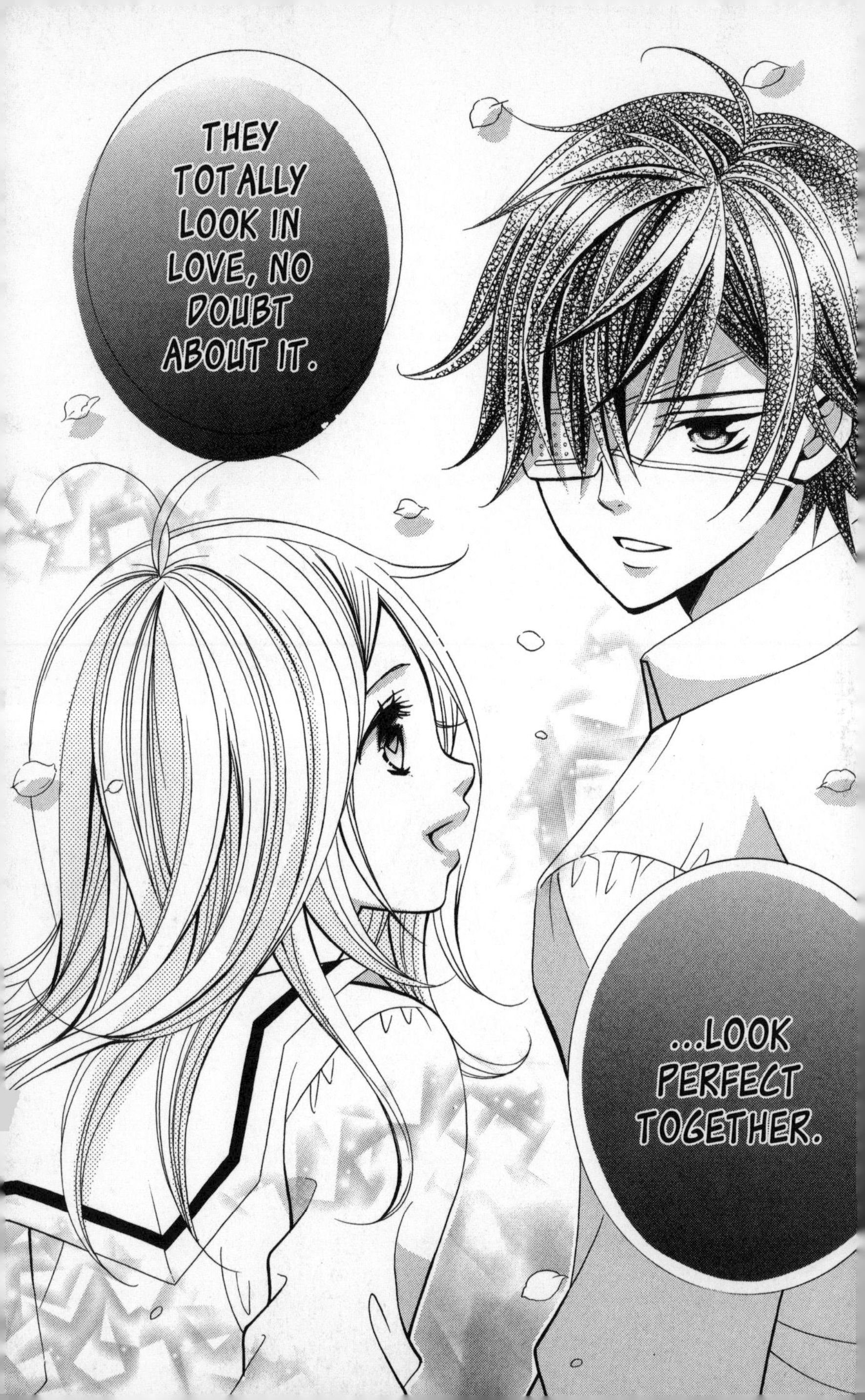
THEY TOTALLY LOOK IN LOVE, NO DOUBT ABOUT IT.
...LOOK PERFECT TOGETHER.

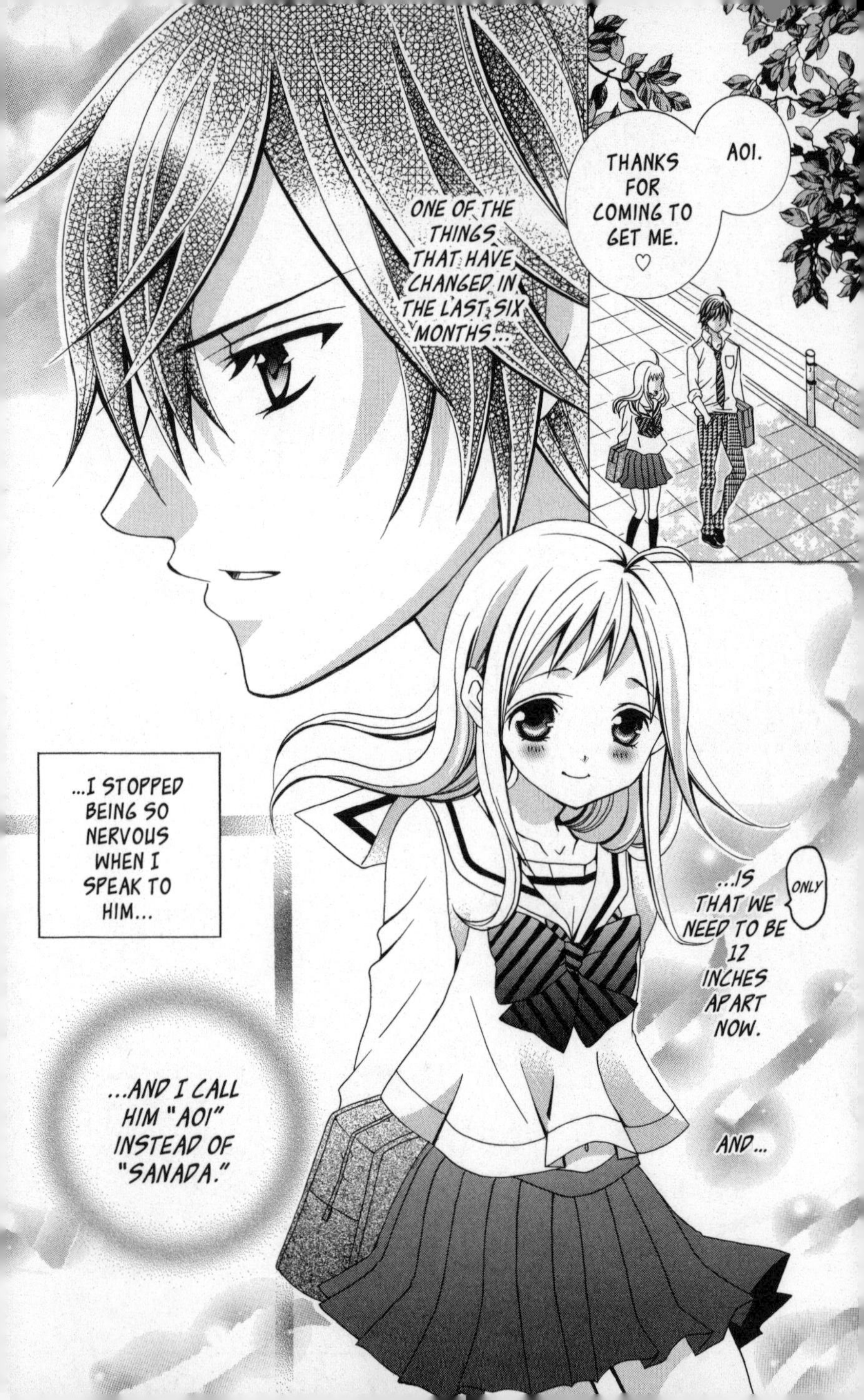
AOI.
THANKS FOR COMING TO GET ME. ♡
ONE OF THE THINGS THAT HAVE CHANGED IN THE LAST SIX MONTHS...
...IS THAT WE NEED TO BE 12 INCHES APART NOW.
ONLY
AND...
...I STOPPED BEING SO NERVOUS WHEN I SPEAK TO HIM...
...AND I CALL HIM "AOI" INSTEAD OF "SANADA."

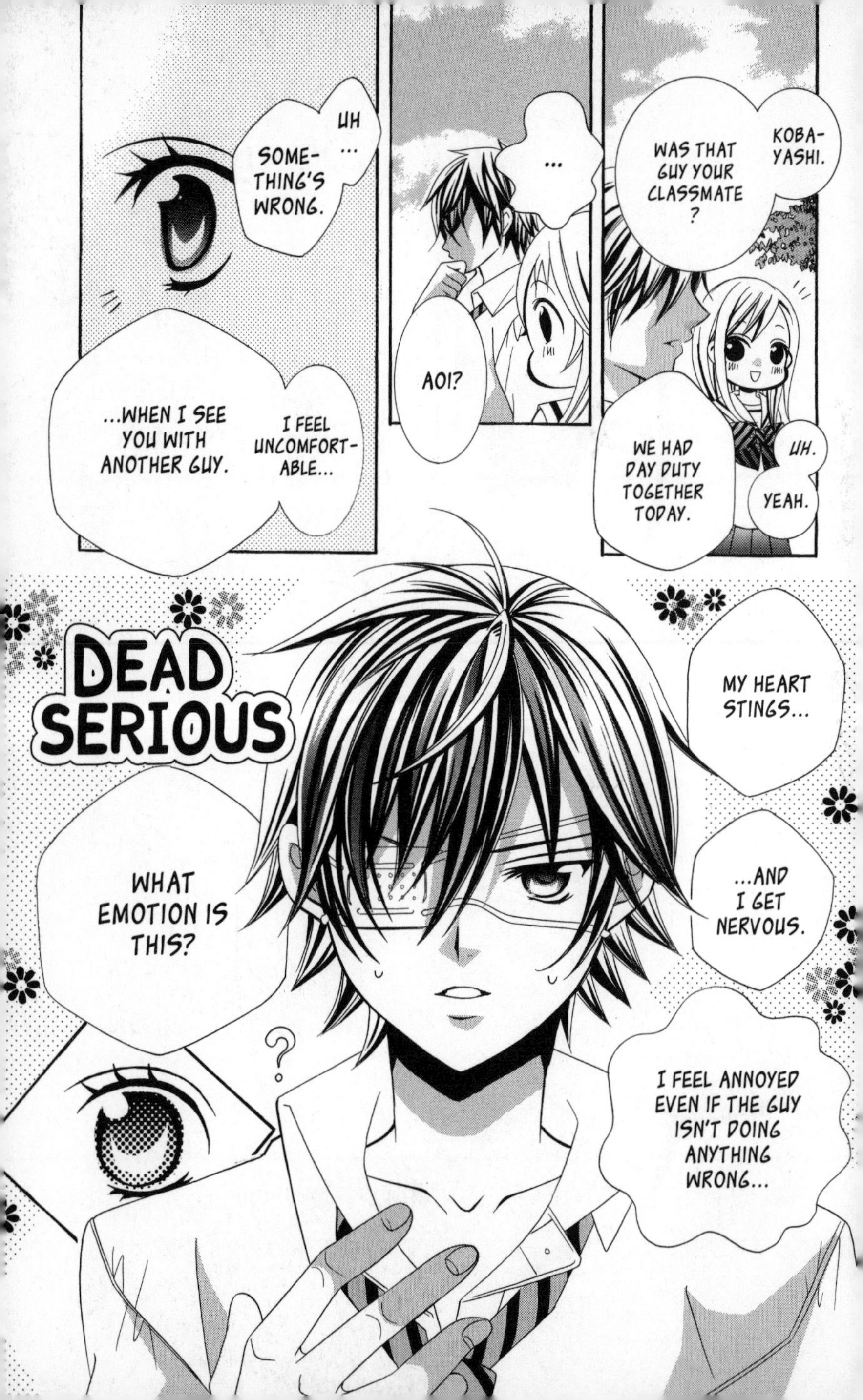
KOBA-YASHI.
WAS THAT GUY YOUR CLASSMATE ?
UH.
YEAH.
WE HAD DAY DUTY TOGETHER TODAY.
...
AOI!?
UH ...
SOME-THING'S WRONG.
I FEEL UNCOMFORT-ABLE...
...WHEN I SEE YOU WITH ANOTHER GUY.
MY HEART STINGS...
...AND I GET NERVOUS.
I FEEL ANNOYED EVEN IF THE GUY ISN'T DOING ANYTHING WRONG...
DEAD SERIOUS
WHAT EMOTION IS THIS?

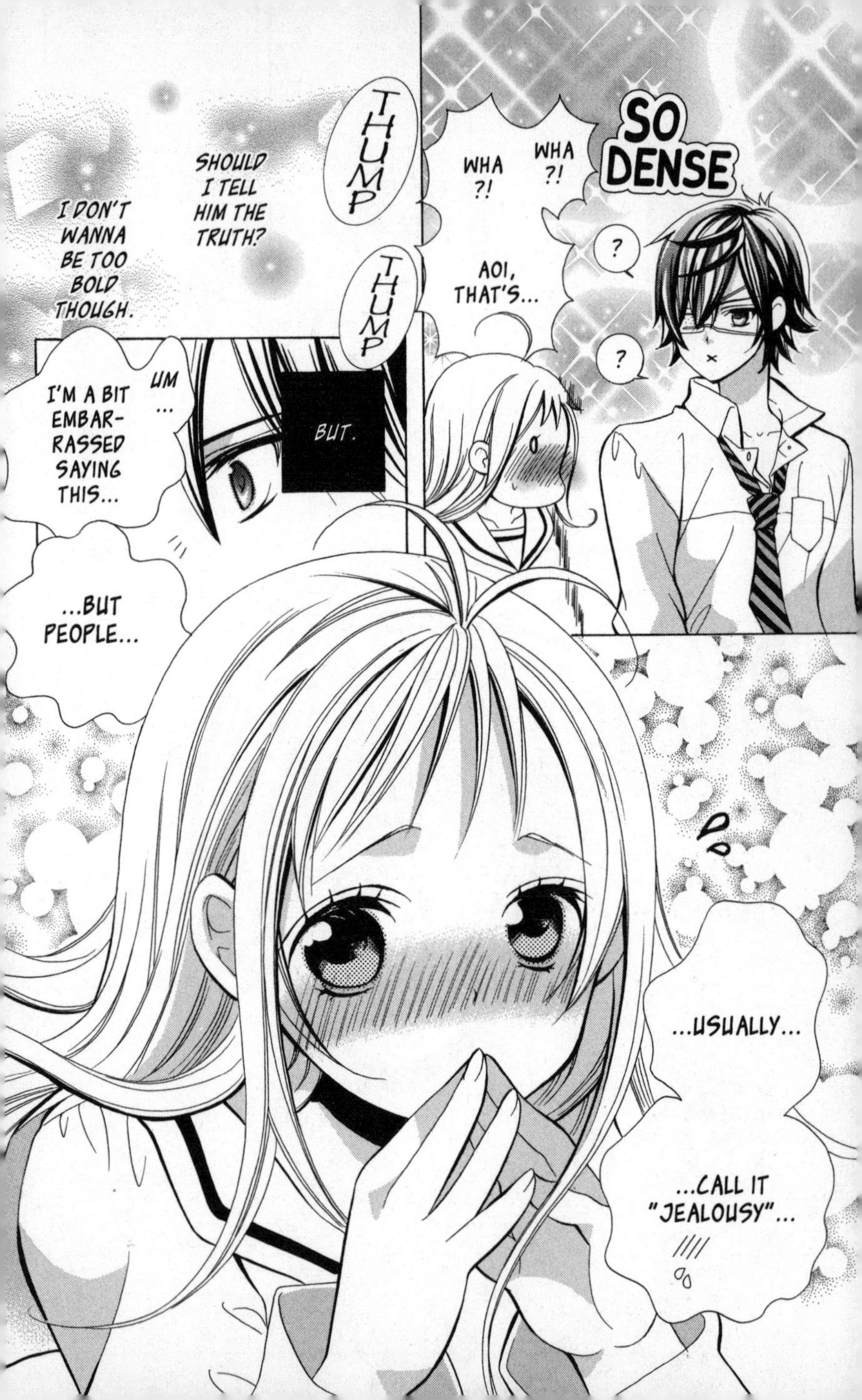
SO DENSE
WHA ?!
WHA ?!
AOI, THAT'S...
?
?
THUMP
THUMP
SHOULD I TELL HIM THE TRUTH?
I DON'T WANNA BE TOO BOLD THOUGH.
BUT.
UM ...
I'M A BIT EMBAR-RASSED SAYING THIS...
...BUT PEOPLE...
...USUALLY...
...CALL IT "JEALOUSY"...

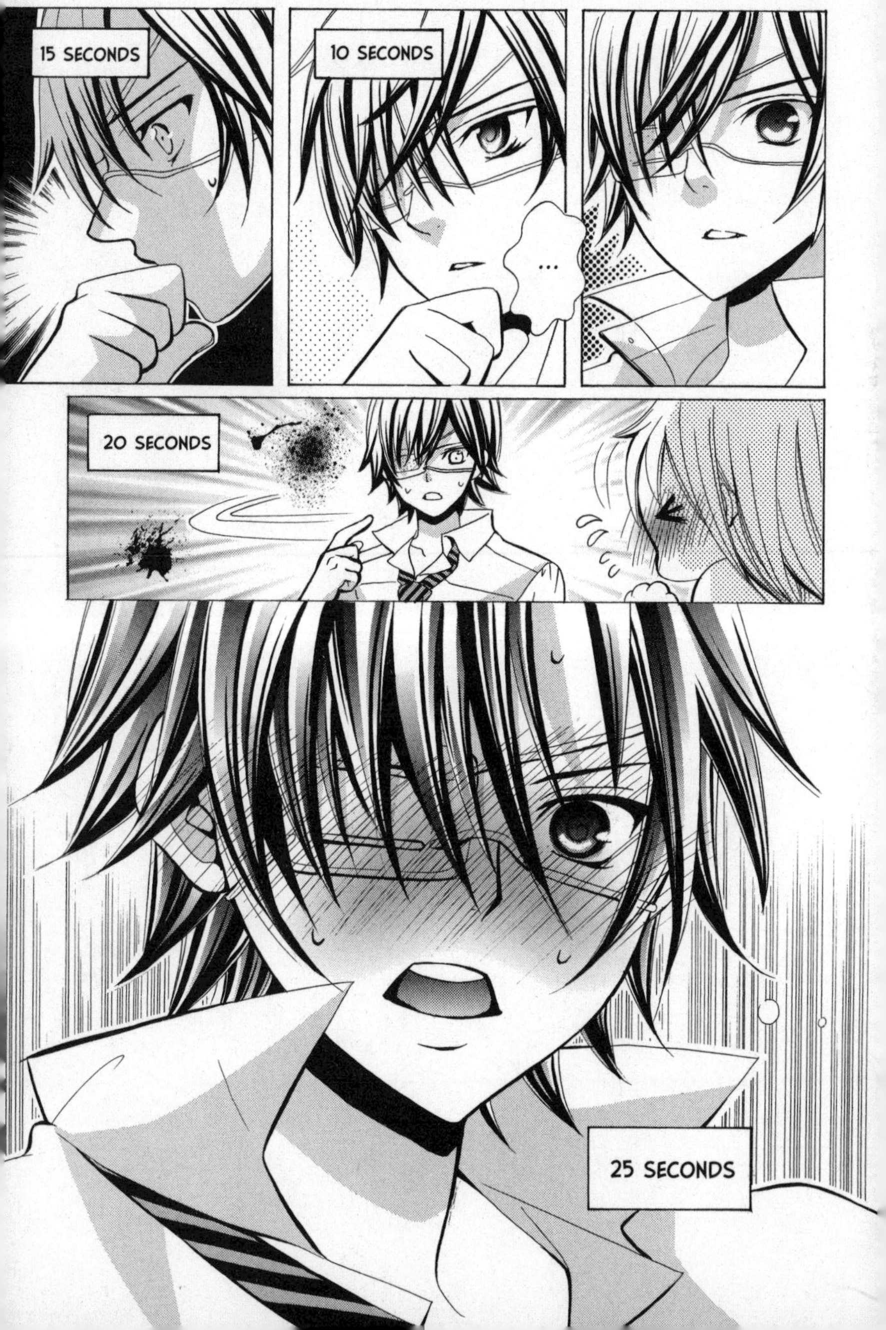
10 SECONDS
...
15 SECONDS
20 SECONDS
25 SECONDS

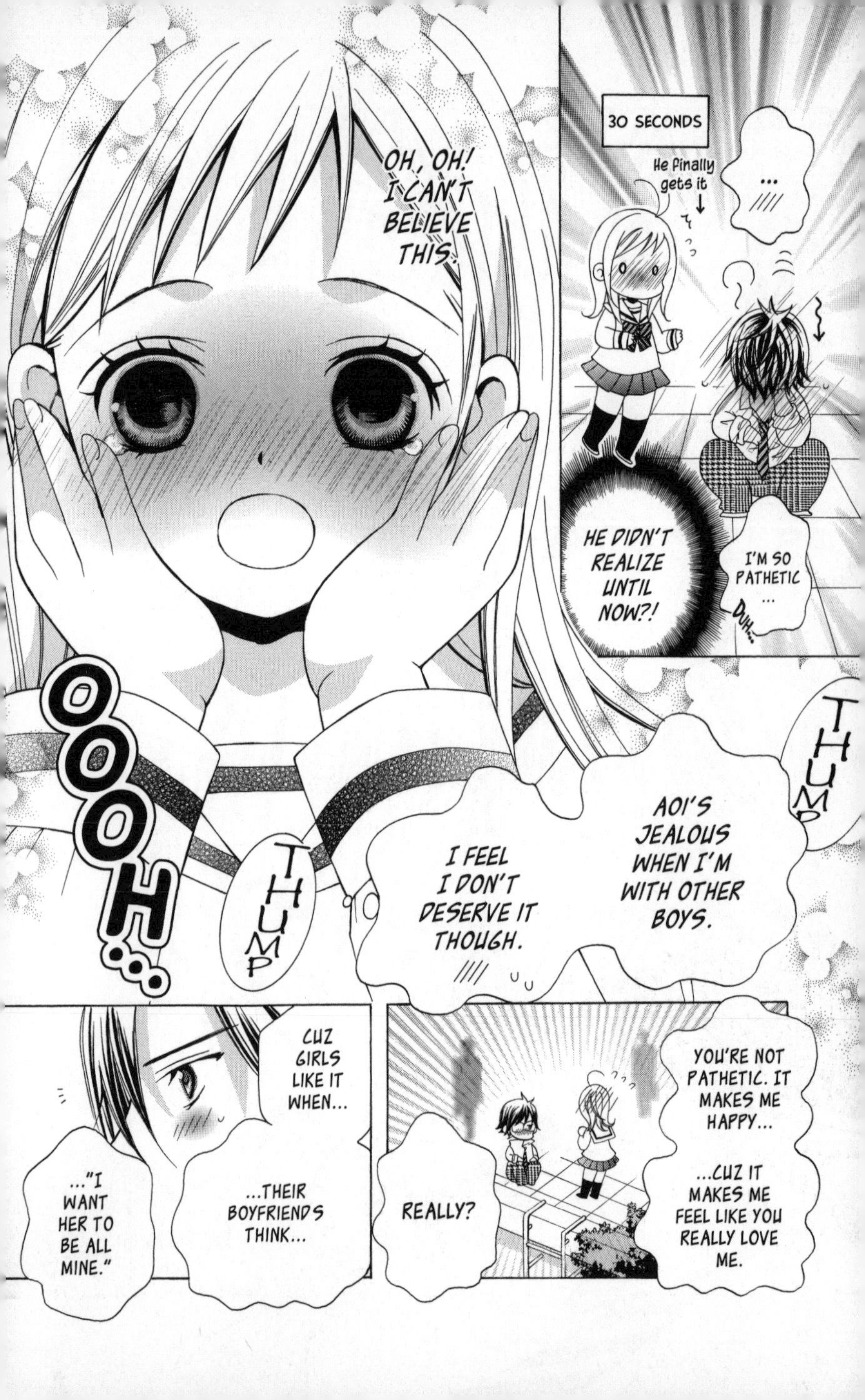

30 SECONDS
He finally gets it
...
HE DIDN'T REALIZE UNTIL NOW?!
I'M SO PATHETIC...
DUH...
OH, OH! I CAN'T BELIEVE THIS.
THUMP
AOI'S JEALOUS WHEN I'M WITH OTHER BOYS.
I FEEL I DON'T DESERVE IT THOUGH.
THUMP
OOOH...
YOU'RE NOT PATHETIC. IT MAKES ME HAPPY...
...CUZ IT MAKES ME FEEL LIKE YOU REALLY LOVE ME.
REALLY?
CUZ GIRLS LIKE IT WHEN...
...THEIR BOYFRIENDS THINK...
..."I WANT HER TO BE ALL MINE."

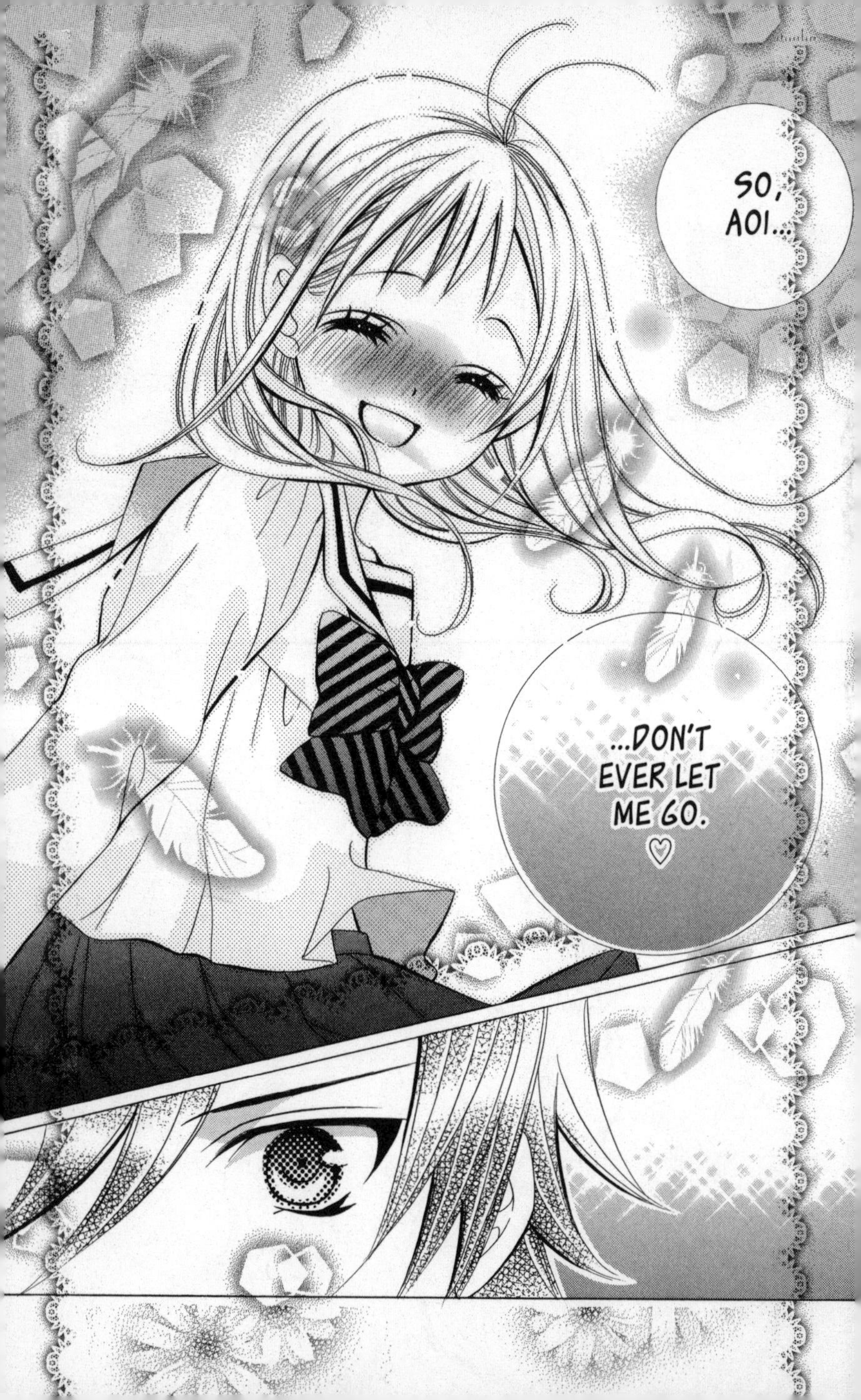
SO, AOI...
...DON'T EVER LET ME GO. ♡

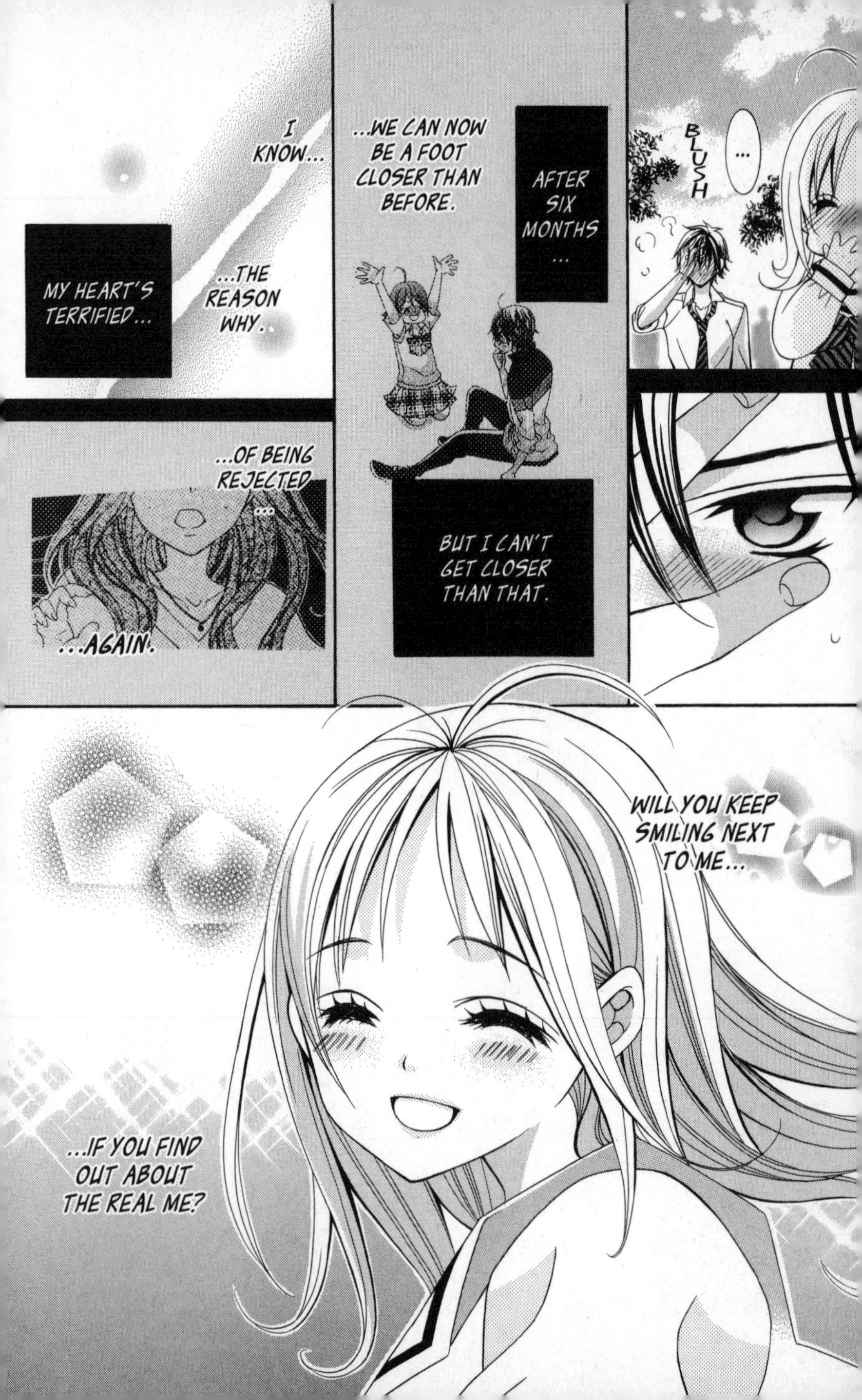
...
BLUSH
AFTER SIX MONTHS...
...WE CAN NOW BE A FOOT CLOSER THAN BEFORE.
BUT I CAN'T GET CLOSER THAN THAT.
I KNOW...
...THE REASON WHY...
MY HEART'S TERRIFIED...
...OF BEING REJECTED...
...AGAIN.
WILL YOU KEEP SMILING NEXT TO ME...
...IF YOU FIND OUT ABOUT THE REAL ME?

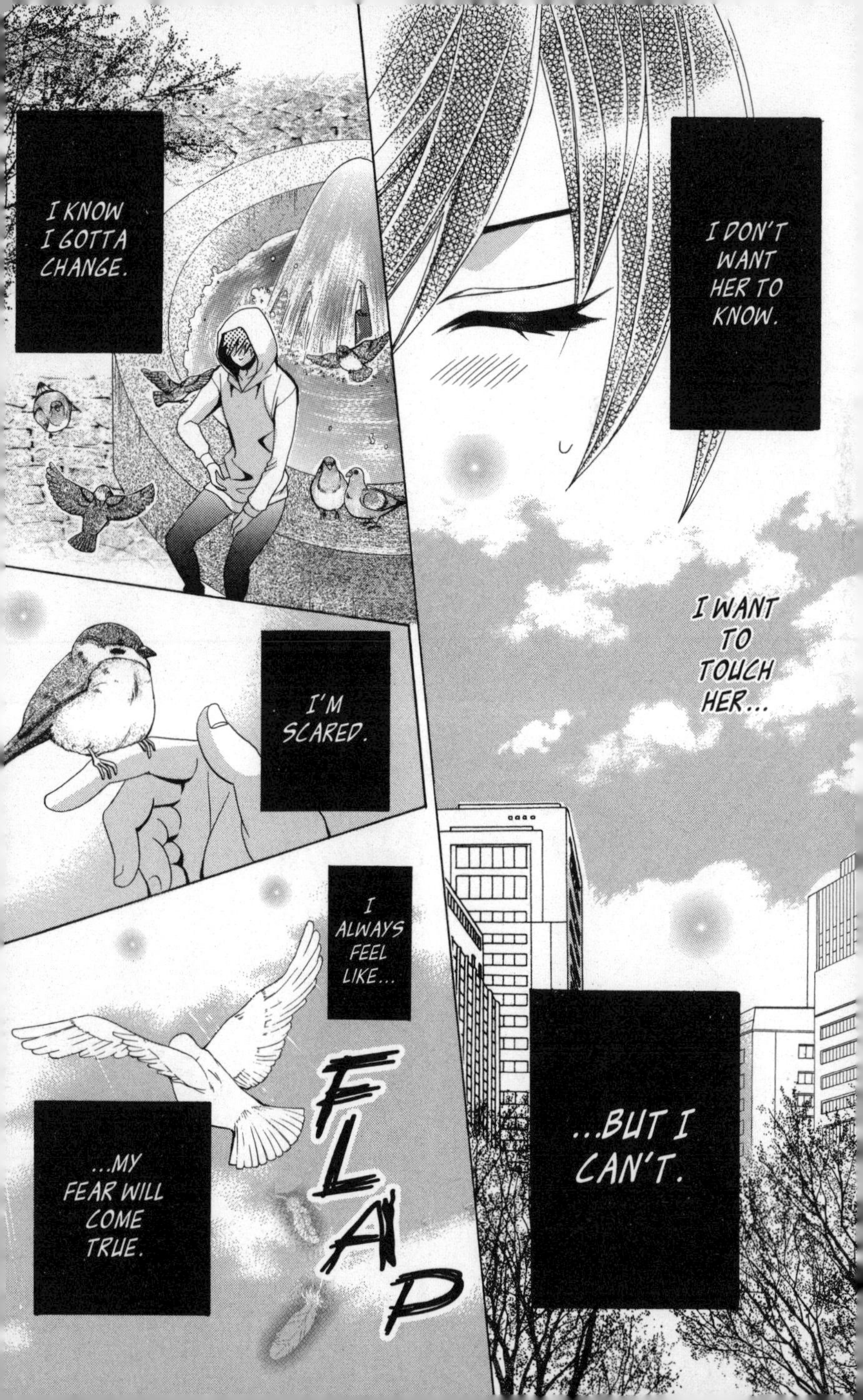
I DON'T WANT HER TO KNOW.
I WANT TO TOUCH HER...
...BUT I CAN'T.
I KNOW I GOTTA CHANGE.
I'M SCARED.
I ALWAYS FEEL LIKE...
FLAP
...MY FEAR WILL COME TRUE.

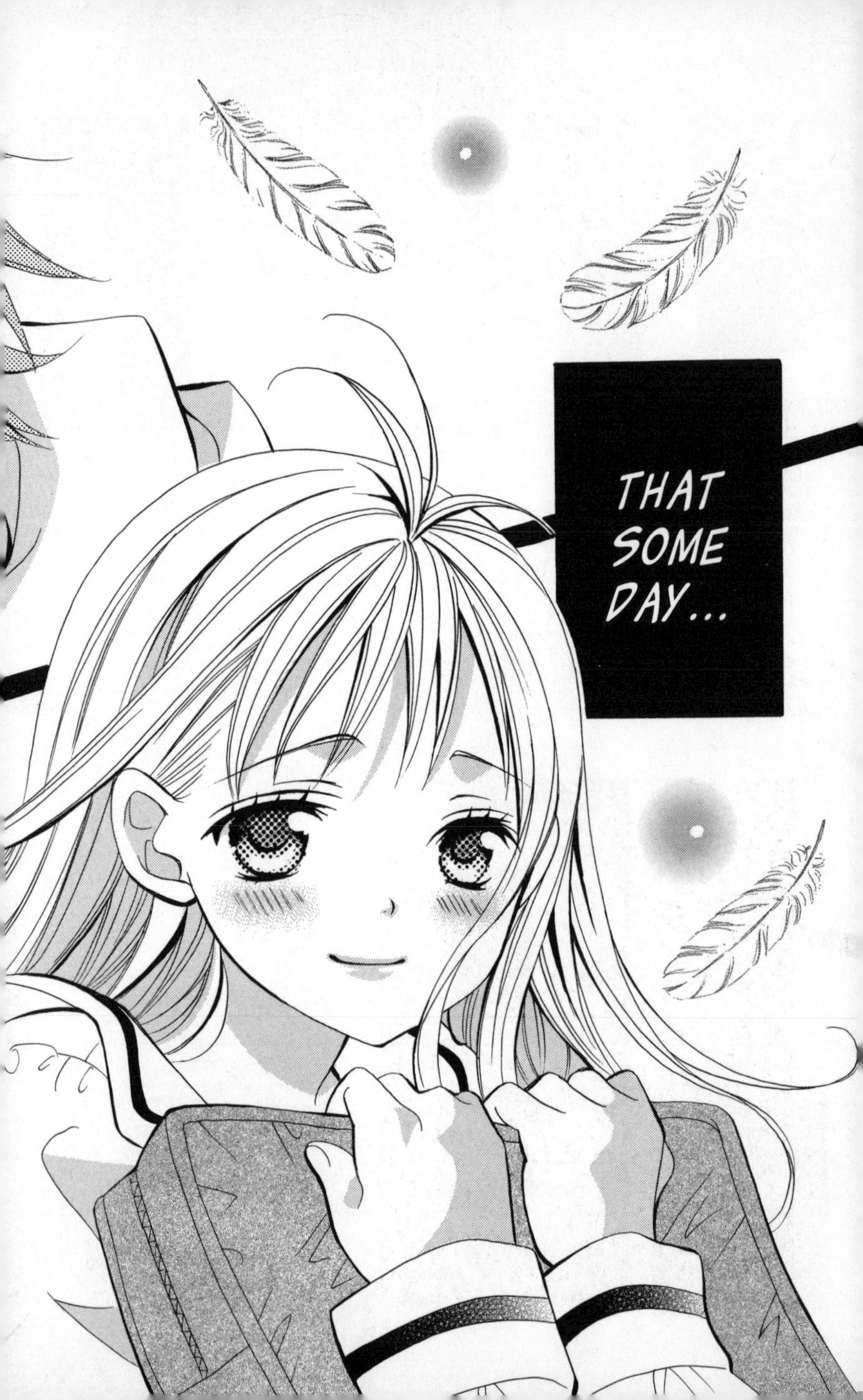
THAT SOME DAY...

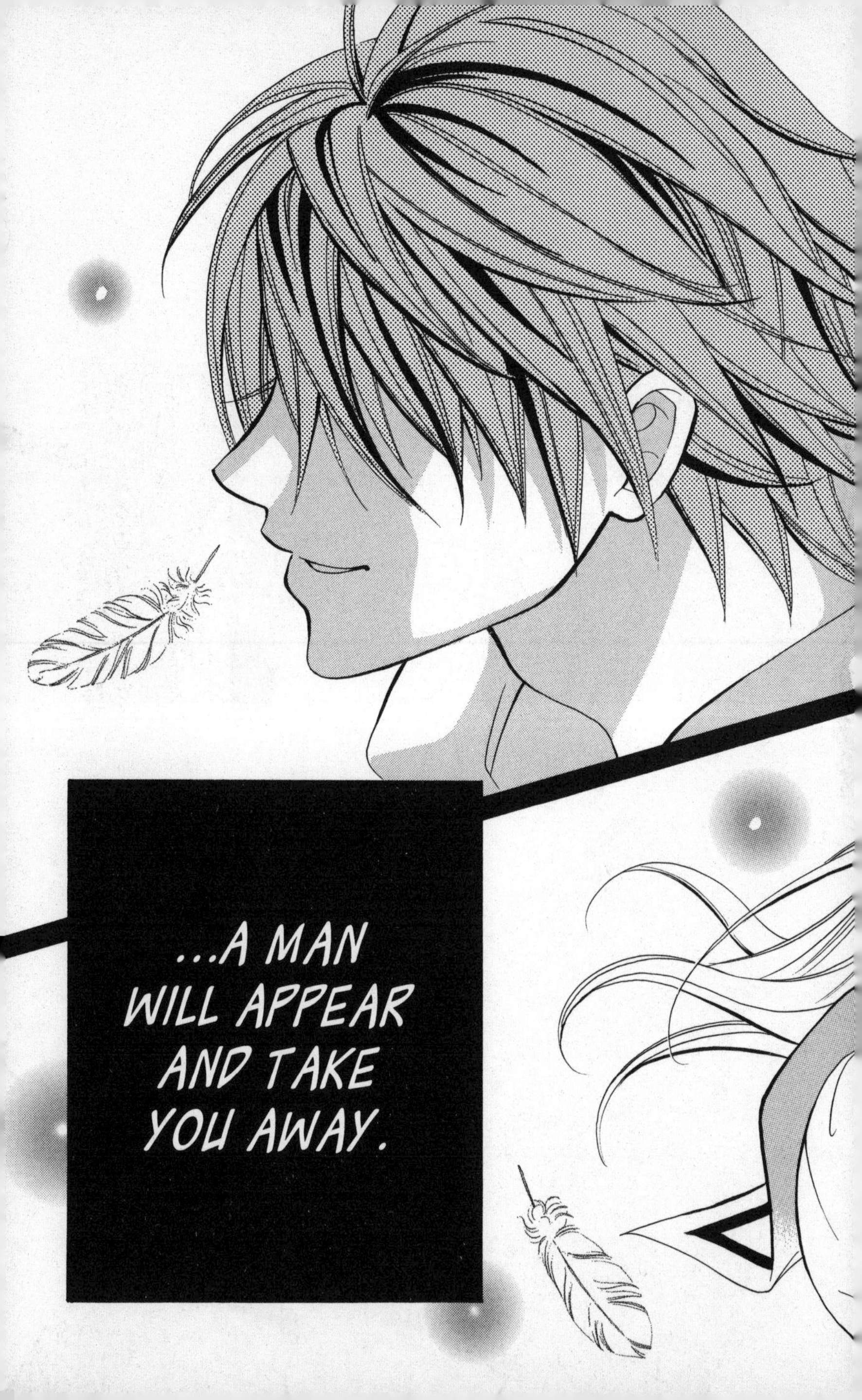
...A MAN WILL APPEAR AND TAKE YOU AWAY.

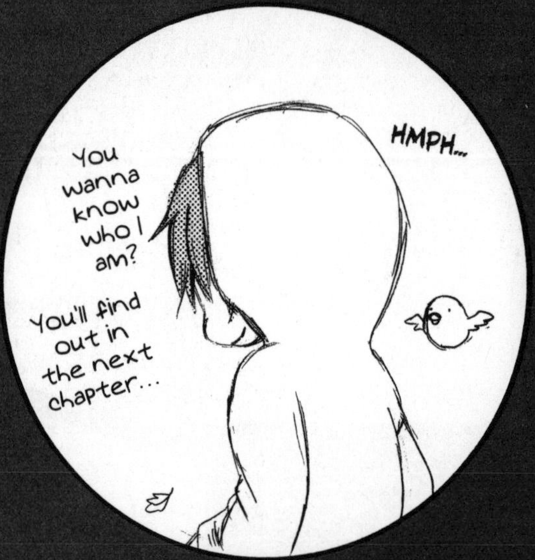
HMPH...
You wanna know who I am?
You'll find out in the next chapter...

Chapter 25

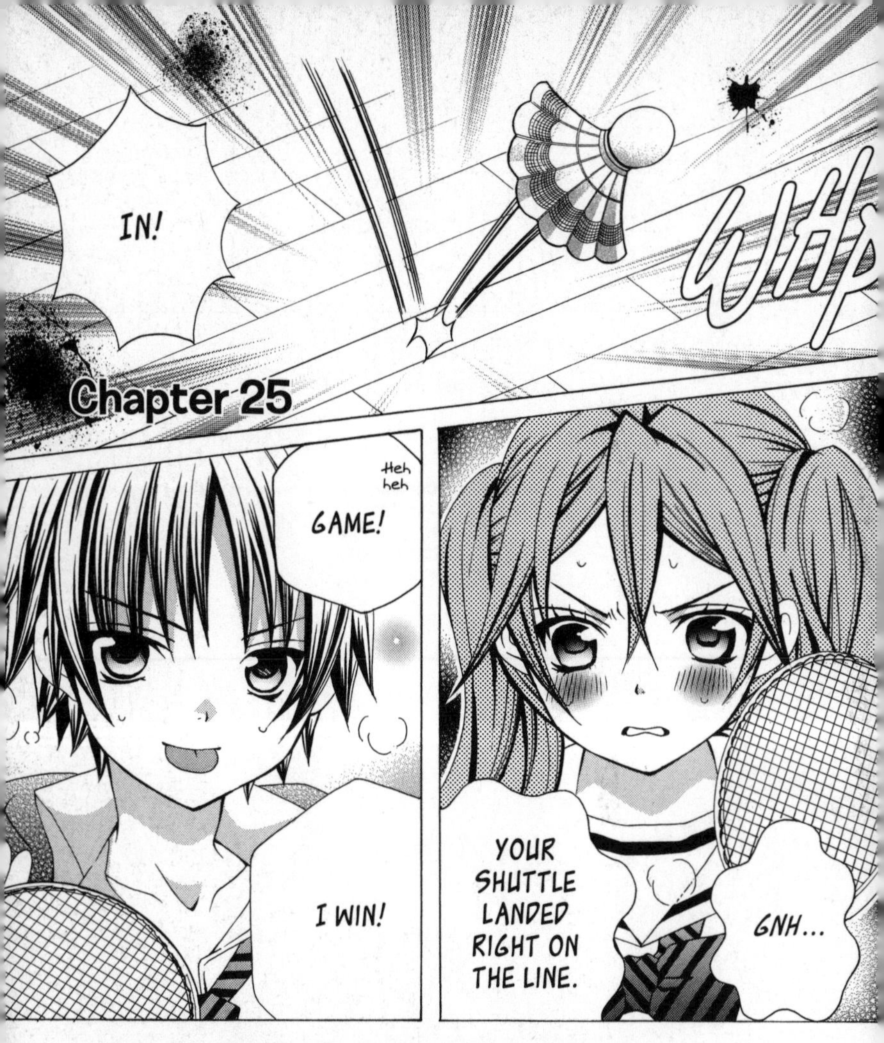
IN!
YOUR SHUTTLE LANDED RIGHT ON THE LINE.
GNH...
Heh heh
GAME!
I WIN!

IT'S A BIT EARLY, BUT THIS IS THE AFTERWORD. THANK YOU FOR READING VOLUME 5 OF *SO CUTE!* ♡ WHEN I WAS DRAWING THE CONCLUSION OF MITSURU'S FIRST LOVE, I KEPT GETTING NERVOUS ABOUT HOW SHINO'S AND AZUSA'S FANS WOULD REACT. I LIKE BOTH SHINO AND AZUSA, BUT I WANTED MITSURU TO MATURE AND BECOME EVEN GENTLER BY EXPERIENCING THE PAIN OF A BROKEN HEART. I HOPE YOU KEEP READING TO SEE WHETHER AZUSA MANAGES TO WIN MITSURU OVER (*SMILE*) OR WHETHER SHINO COMES BACK. THE SECOND ARC OF THE SERIES BEGINS IN THIS VOLUME WHEN MEGO AND MITSURU BECOME SECOND-YEAR STUDENTS. I'M GLAD READERS LIKE MEGO WITH LONGER HAIR. (^o^)! I HOPE YOU'RE LOOKING FORWARD TO WHAT HAPPENS TO MEGO'S LOVE NOW THAT THE MYSTERIOUS BOY FROM AOI'S PAST HAS APPEARED!!

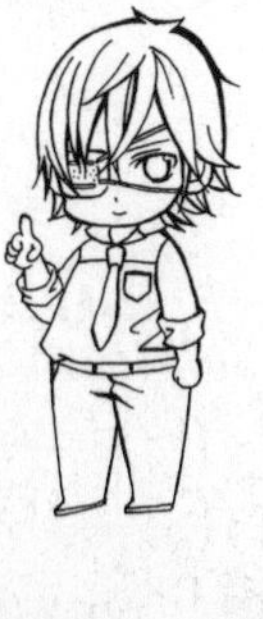

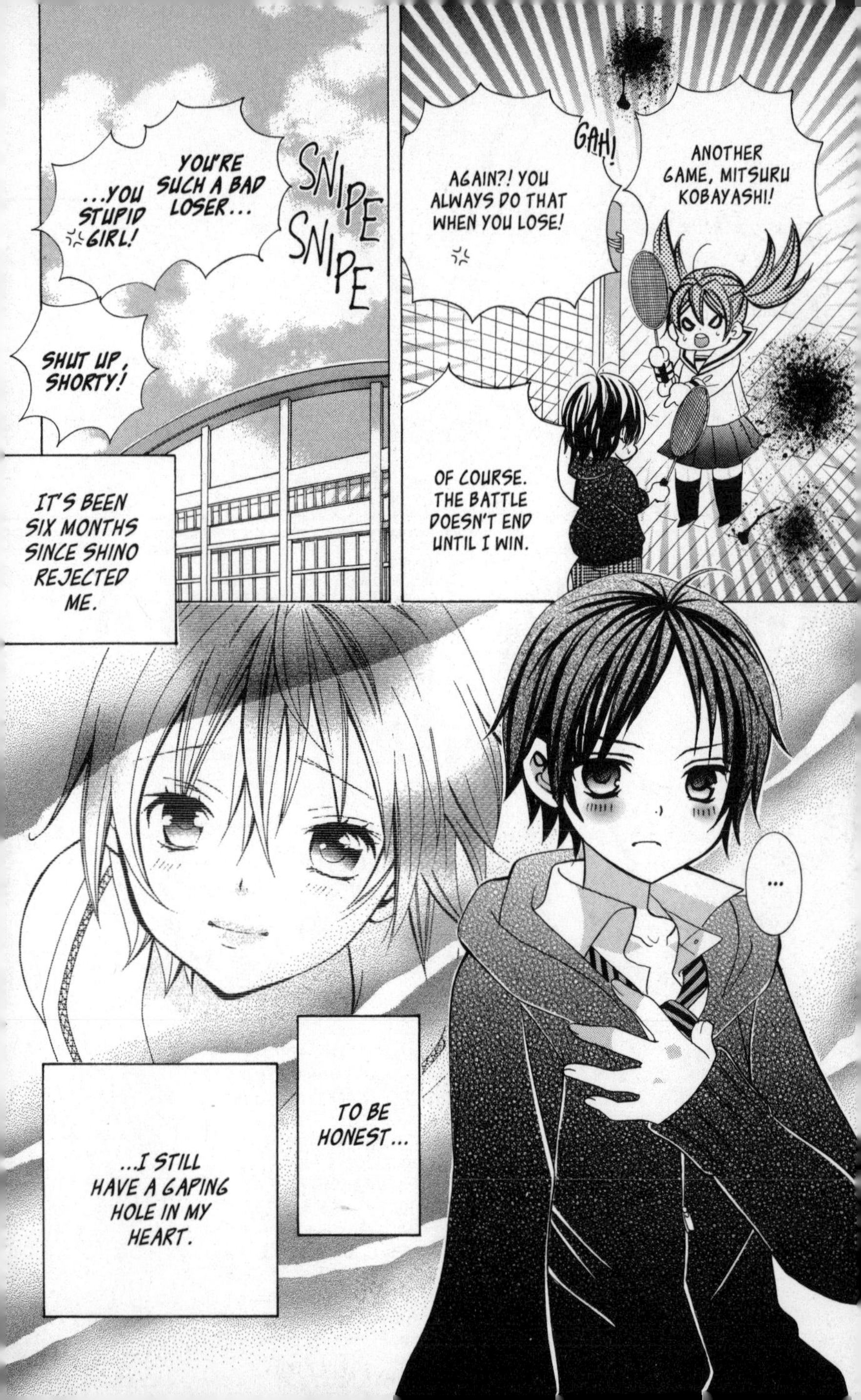
ANOTHER GAME, MITSURU KOBAYASHI!
GAH!
AGAIN?! YOU ALWAYS DO THAT WHEN YOU LOSE!
OF COURSE. THE BATTLE DOESN'T END UNTIL I WIN.
SNIPE SNIPE
YOU'RE SUCH A BAD LOSER...
...YOU STUPID GIRL!
SHUT UP, SHORTY!
IT'S BEEN SIX MONTHS SINCE SHINO REJECTED ME.
...
TO BE HONEST...
...I STILL HAVE A GAPING HOLE IN MY HEART.

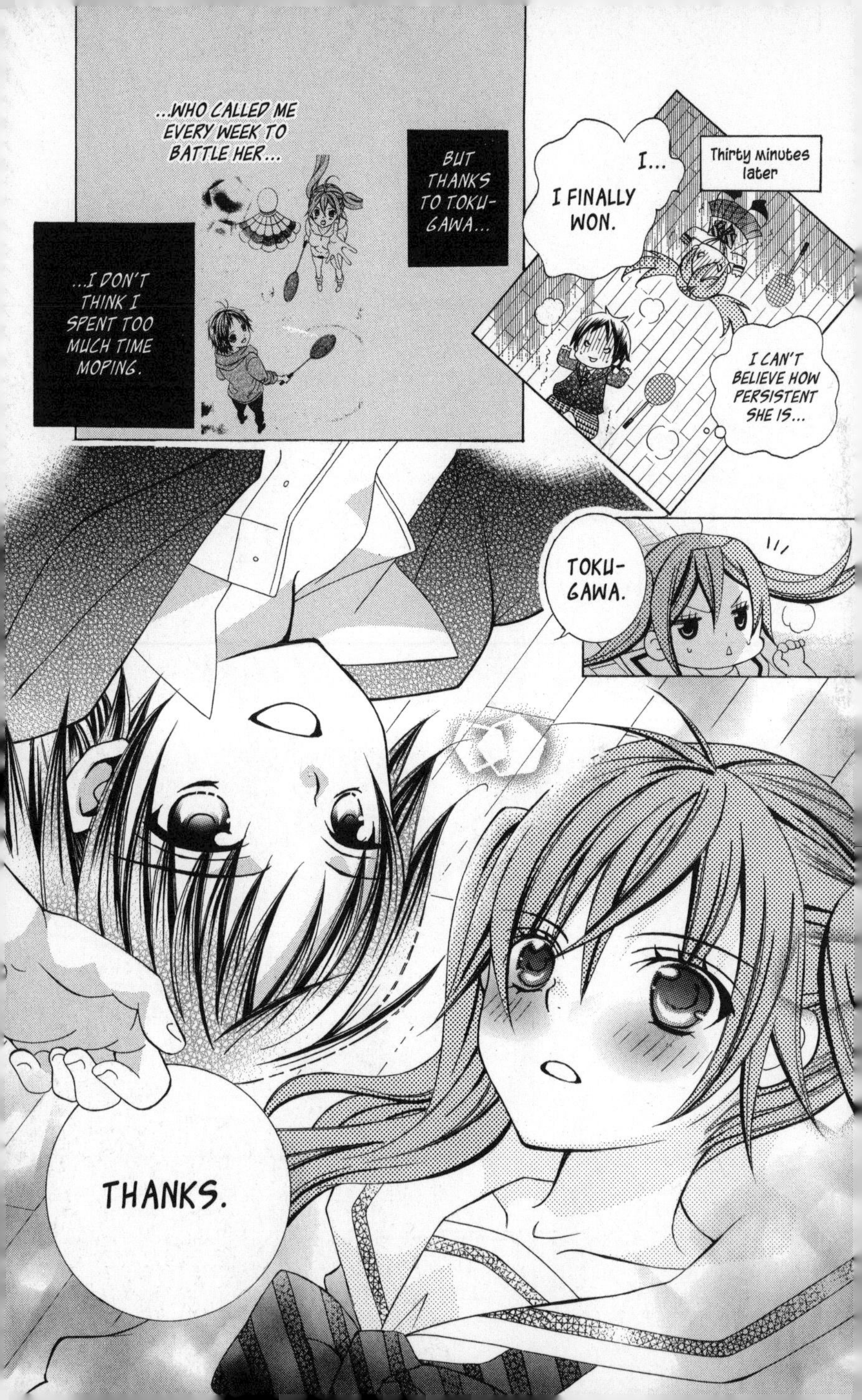
Thirty minutes later
I...
I FINALLY WON.
I CAN'T BELIEVE HOW PERSISTENT SHE IS...
BUT THANKS TO TOKU-GAWA...
...WHO CALLED ME EVERY WEEK TO BATTLE HER...
...I DON'T THINK I SPENT TOO MUCH TIME MOPING.
TOKU-GAWA.
THANKS.

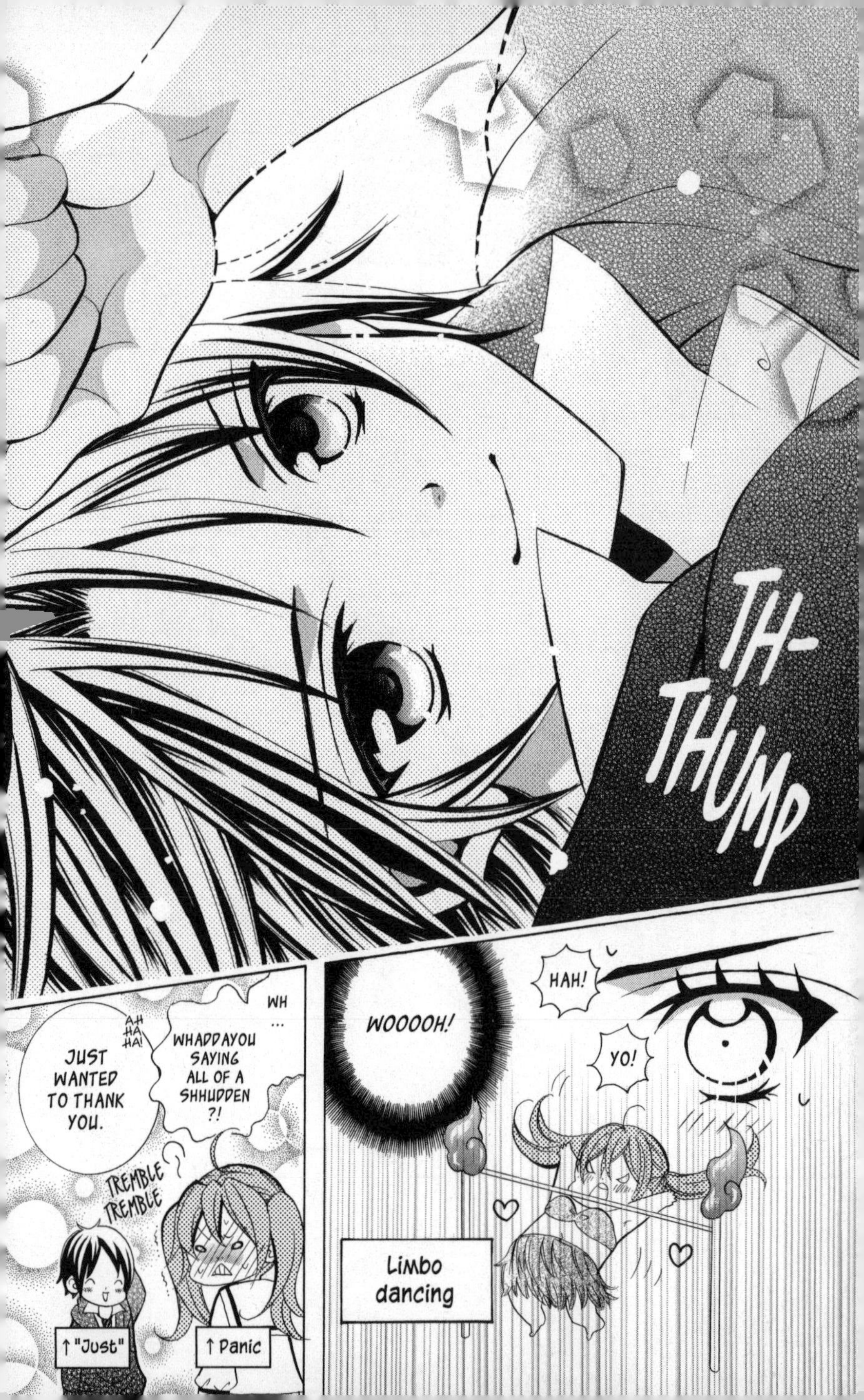
TH-THUMP
HAH!
YO!
WOOOOH!
Limbo dancing
WH...
WHADDAYOU SAYING ALL OF A SHHUDDEN?!
AH HA HA!
JUST WANTED TO THANK YOU.
TREMBLE TREMBLE
↑ Panic
↑ "Just"

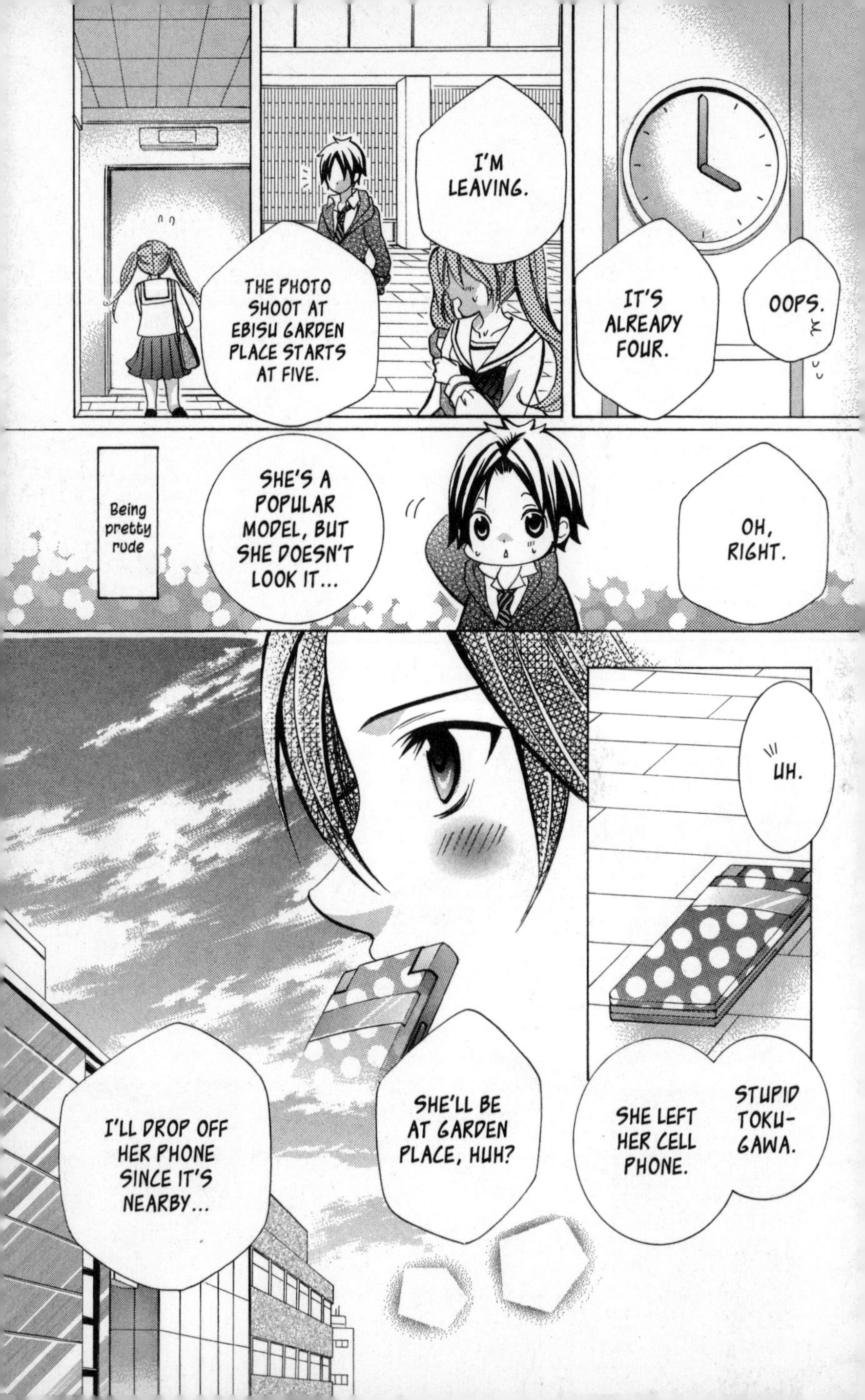
OOPS.
IT'S ALREADY FOUR.
I'M LEAVING.
THE PHOTO SHOOT AT EBISU GARDEN PLACE STARTS AT FIVE.
OH, RIGHT.
SHE'S A POPULAR MODEL, BUT SHE DOESN'T LOOK IT...
Being pretty rude
UH.
STUPID TOKUGAWA.
SHE LEFT HER CELL PHONE.
SHE'LL BE AT GARDEN PLACE, HUH?
I'LL DROP OFF HER PHONE SINCE IT'S NEARBY...

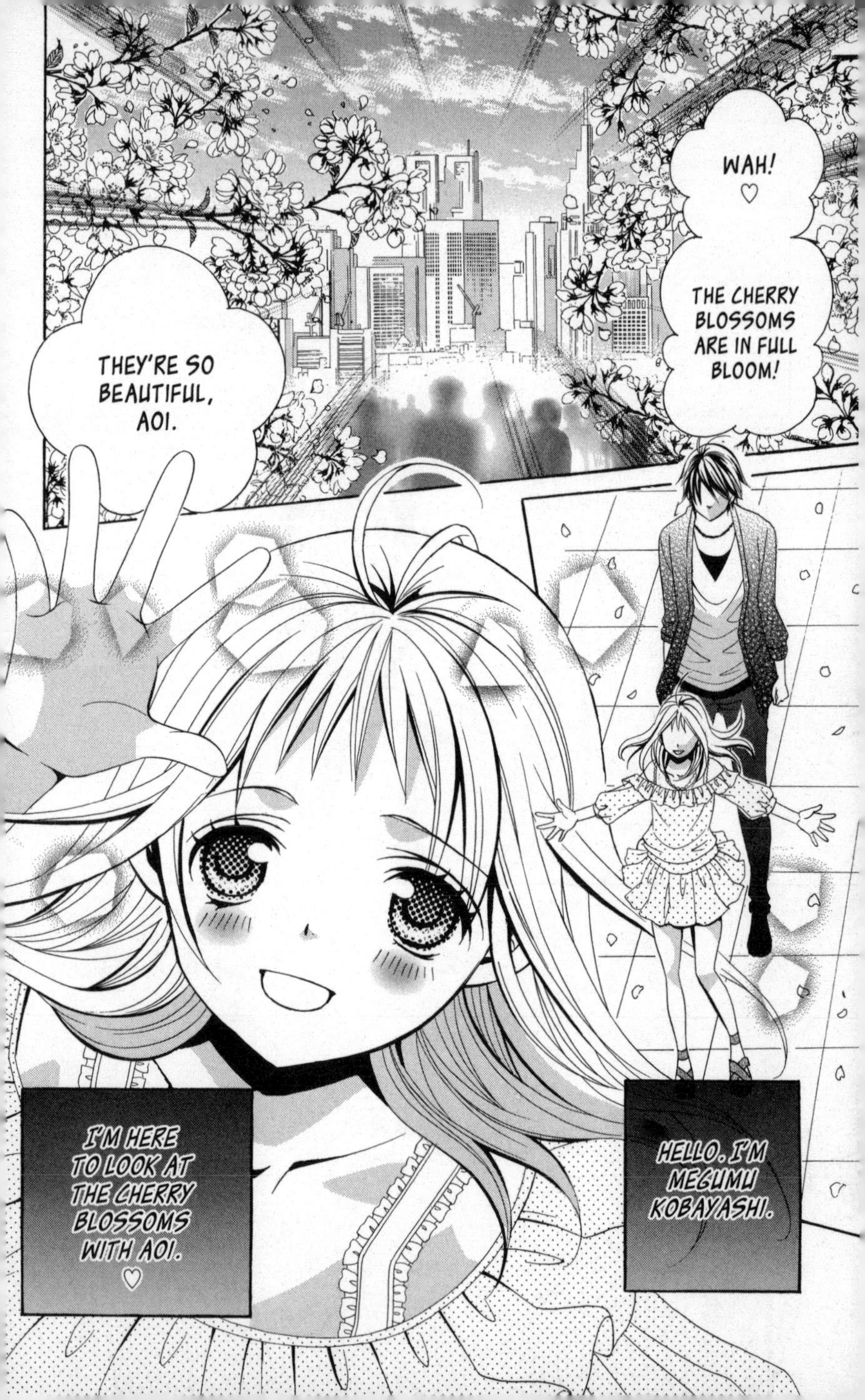
WAH! ♡
THE CHERRY BLOSSOMS ARE IN FULL BLOOM!
THEY'RE SO BEAUTIFUL, AOI.
HELLO. I'M MEGUMU KOBAYASHI.
I'M HERE TO LOOK AT THE CHERRY BLOSSOMS WITH AOI. ♡

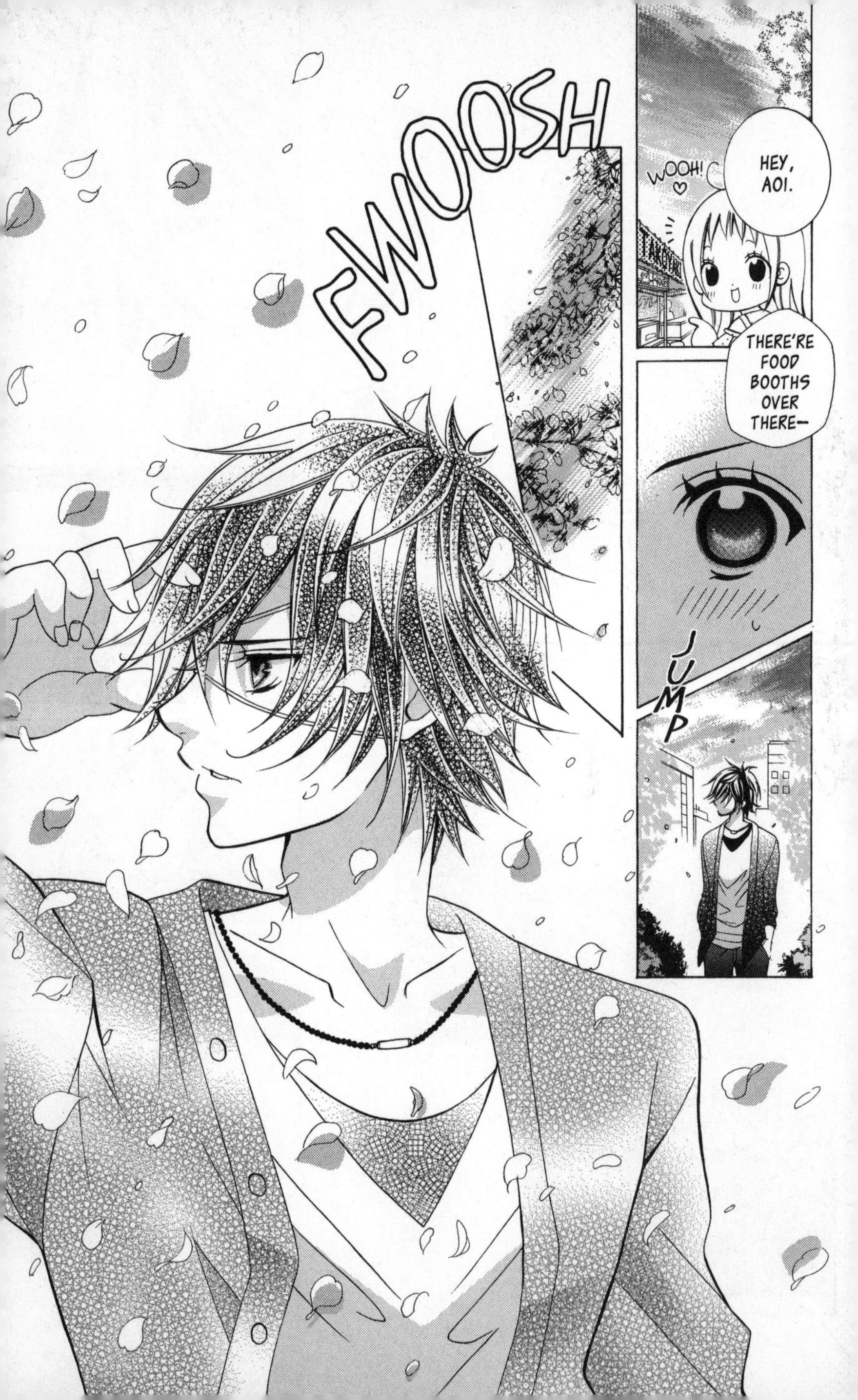
HEY, AOI.
WOOH!
THERE'RE FOOD BOOTHS OVER THERE—
JUMP
FWOOSH

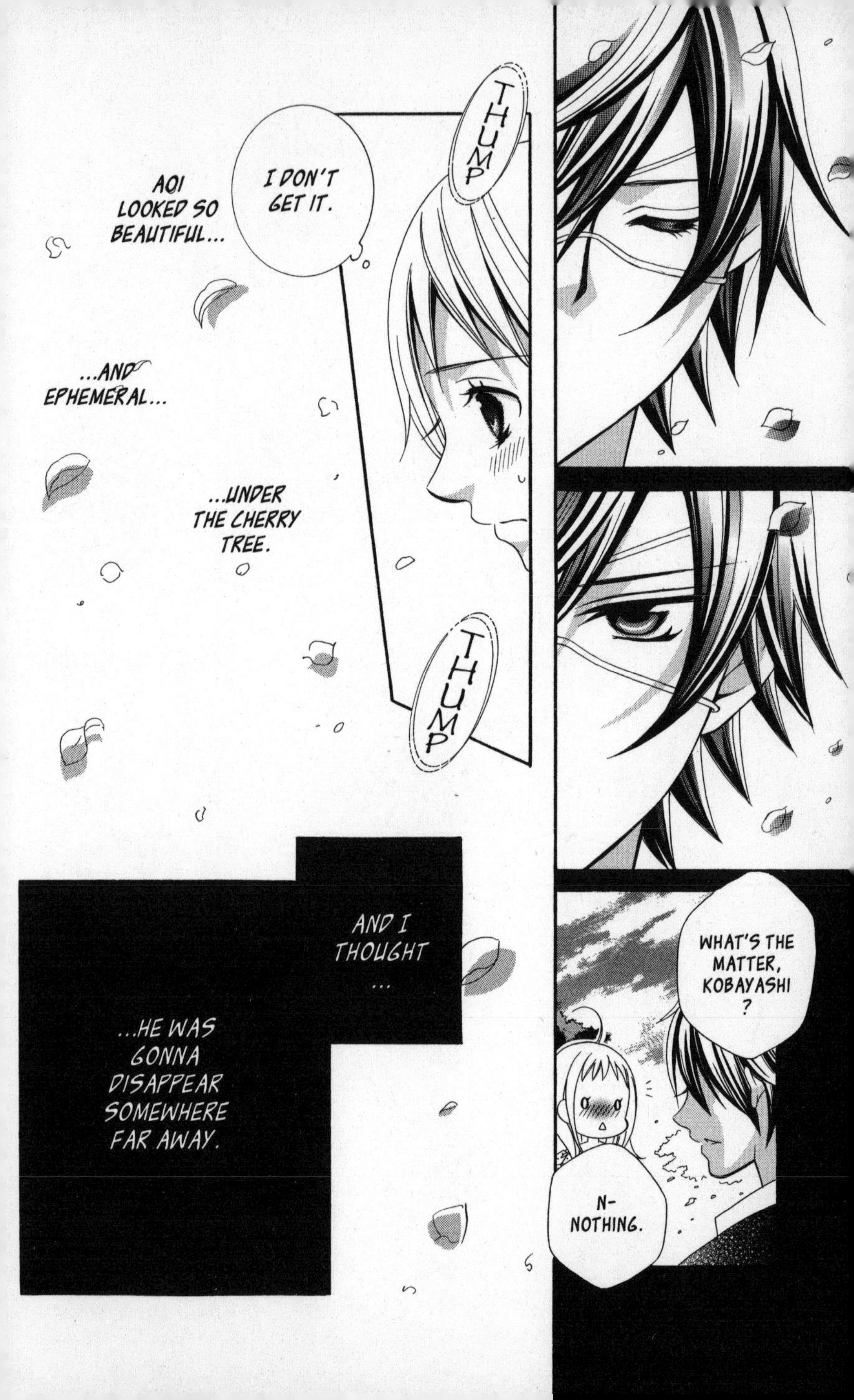
THUMP
I DON'T GET IT.
AOI LOOKED SO BEAUTIFUL...
...AND EPHEMERAL...
...UNDER THE CHERRY TREE.
THUMP
WHAT'S THE MATTER, KOBAYASHI?
N-NOTHING.
AND I THOUGHT...
...HE WAS GONNA DISAPPEAR SOMEWHERE FAR AWAY.

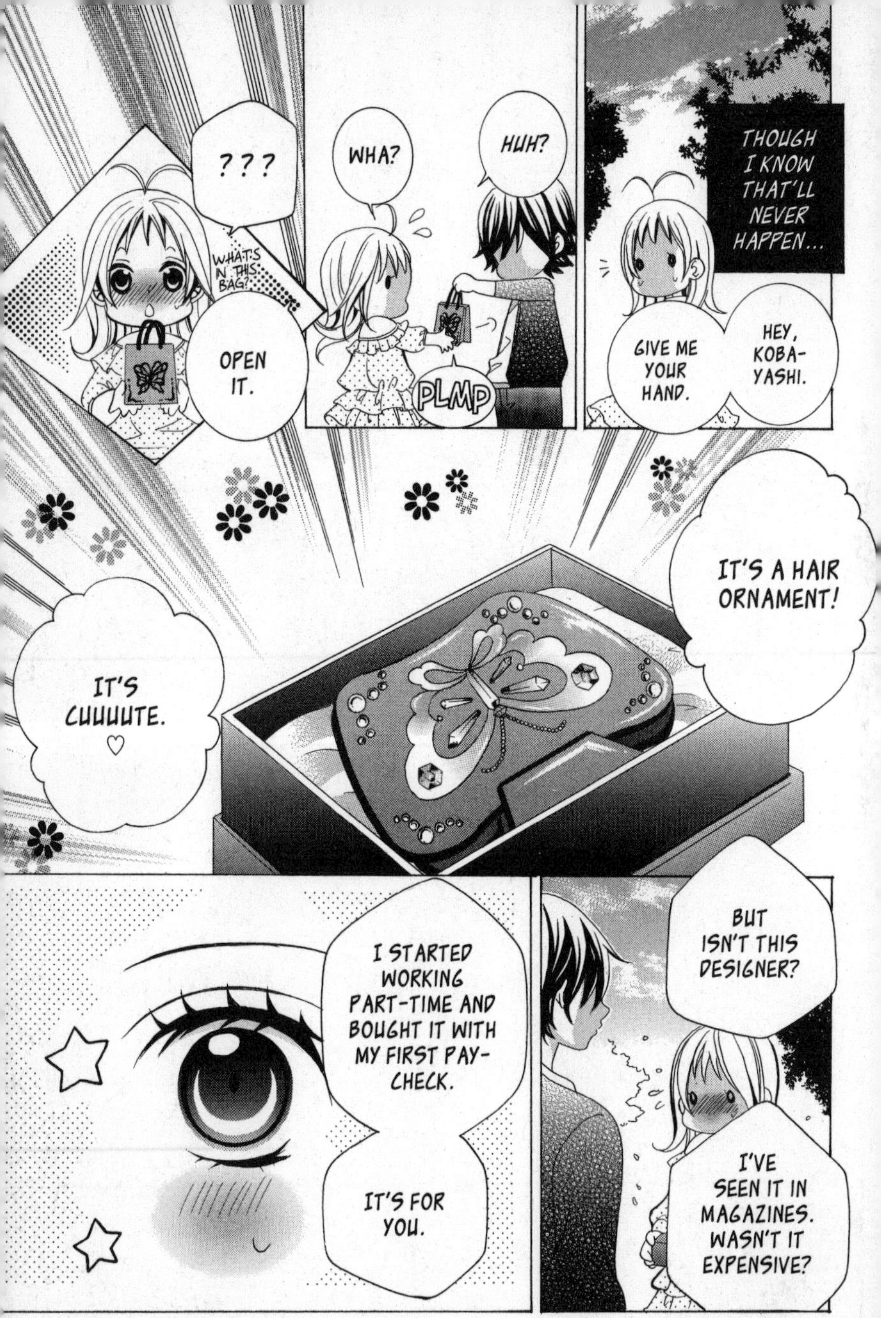
THOUGH I KNOW THAT'LL NEVER HAPPEN...
HEY, KOBA-YASHI.
GIVE ME YOUR HAND.
HUH?
WHA?
PLMP
???
WHAT'S IN THIS BAG?
OPEN IT.
IT'S A HAIR ORNAMENT!
IT'S CUUUUTE. ♡
BUT ISN'T THIS DESIGNER?
I'VE SEEN IT IN MAGAZINES. WASN'T IT EXPENSIVE?
I STARTED WORKING PART-TIME AND BOUGHT IT WITH MY FIRST PAY-CHECK.
IT'S FOR YOU.

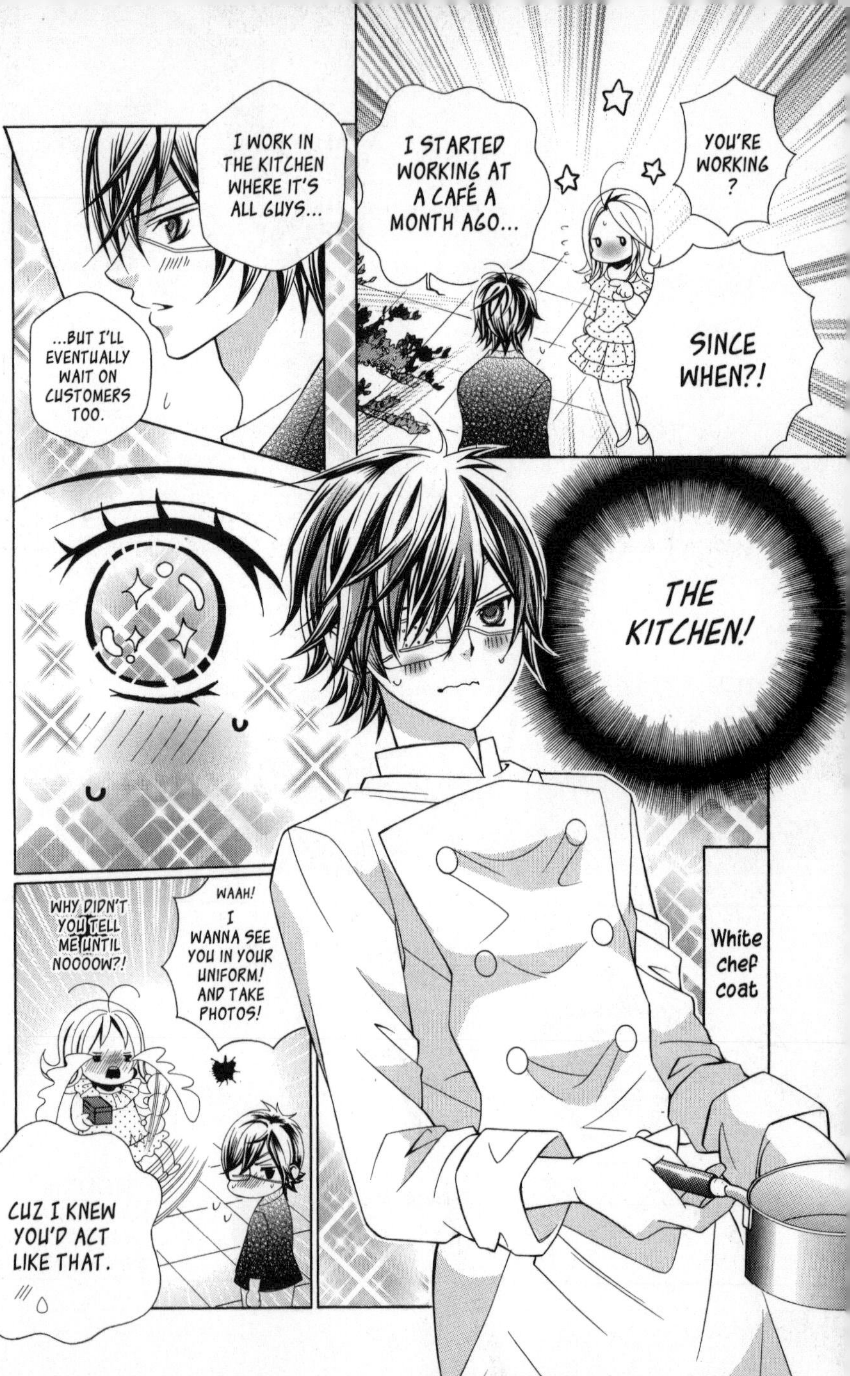
YOU'RE WORKING?
I STARTED WORKING AT A CAFÉ A MONTH AGO...
SINCE WHEN?!
I WORK IN THE KITCHEN WHERE IT'S ALL GUYS...
...BUT I'LL EVENTUALLY WAIT ON CUSTOMERS TOO.
THE KITCHEN!
White chef coat
WAAH! I WANNA SEE YOU IN YOUR UNIFORM! AND TAKE PHOTOS!
WHY DIDN'T YOU TELL ME UNTIL NOOOOW?!
CUZ I KNEW YOU'D ACT LIKE THAT.

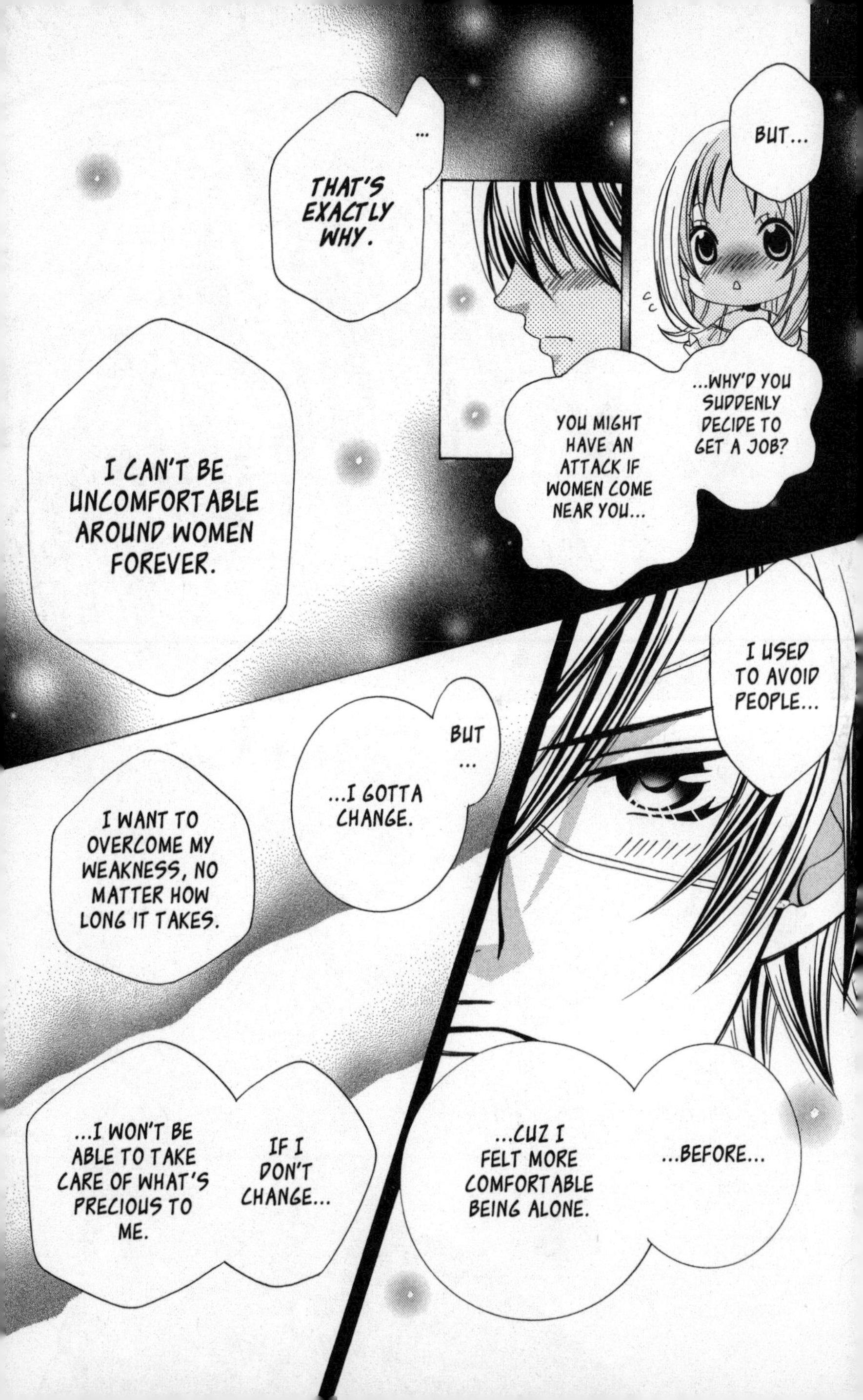
BUT...
...WHY'D YOU SUDDENLY DECIDE TO GET A JOB?
YOU MIGHT HAVE AN ATTACK IF WOMEN COME NEAR YOU...
...
THAT'S EXACTLY WHY.
I CAN'T BE UNCOMFORTABLE AROUND WOMEN FOREVER.
I USED TO AVOID PEOPLE...
...BEFORE...
...CUZ I FELT MORE COMFORTABLE BEING ALONE.
BUT ...
...I GOTTA CHANGE.
I WANT TO OVERCOME MY WEAKNESS, NO MATTER HOW LONG IT TAKES.
IF I DON'T CHANGE...
...I WON'T BE ABLE TO TAKE CARE OF WHAT'S PRECIOUS TO ME.

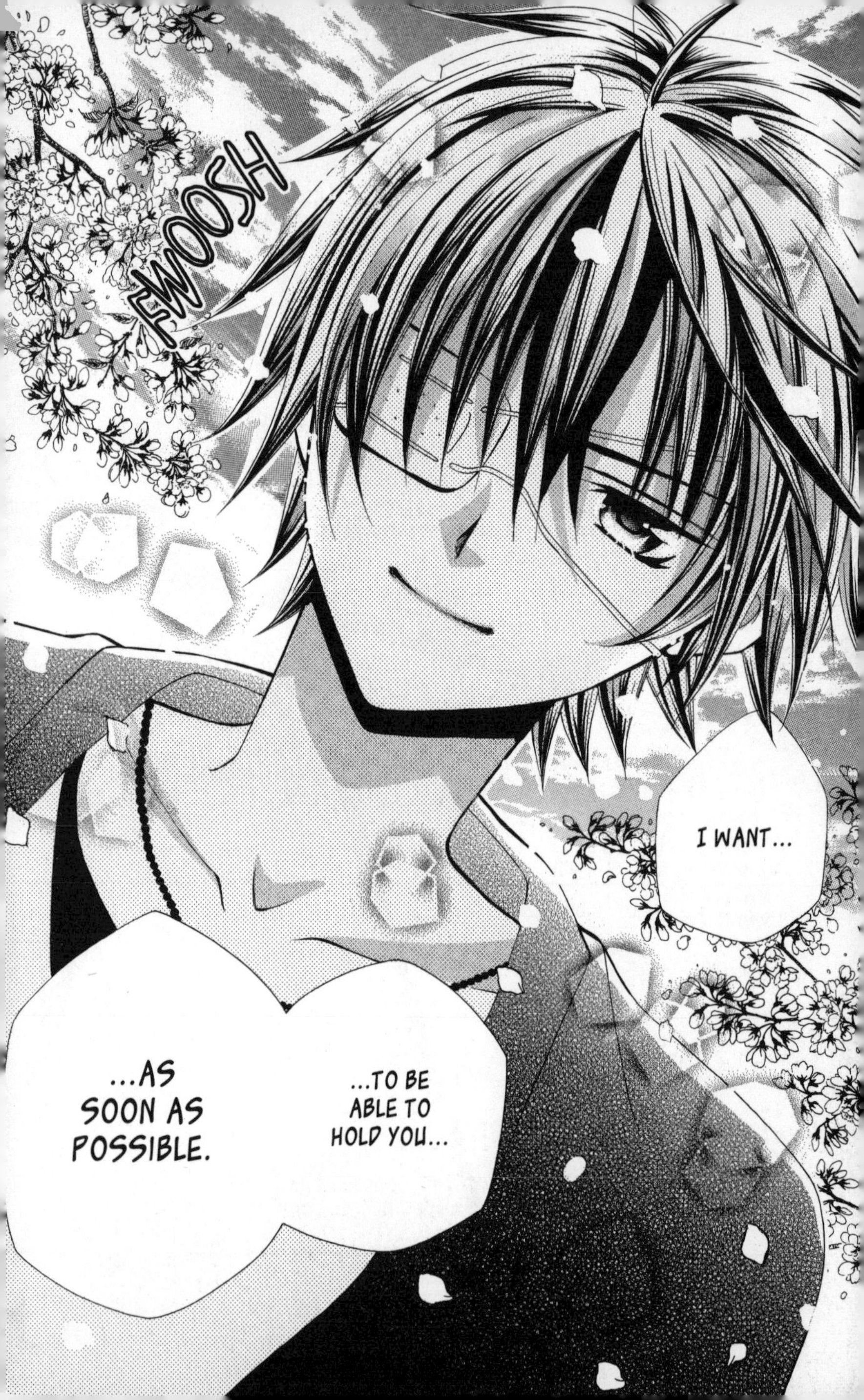
WHOOSH
I WANT...
...TO BE ABLE TO HOLD YOU...
...AS SOON AS POSSIBLE.

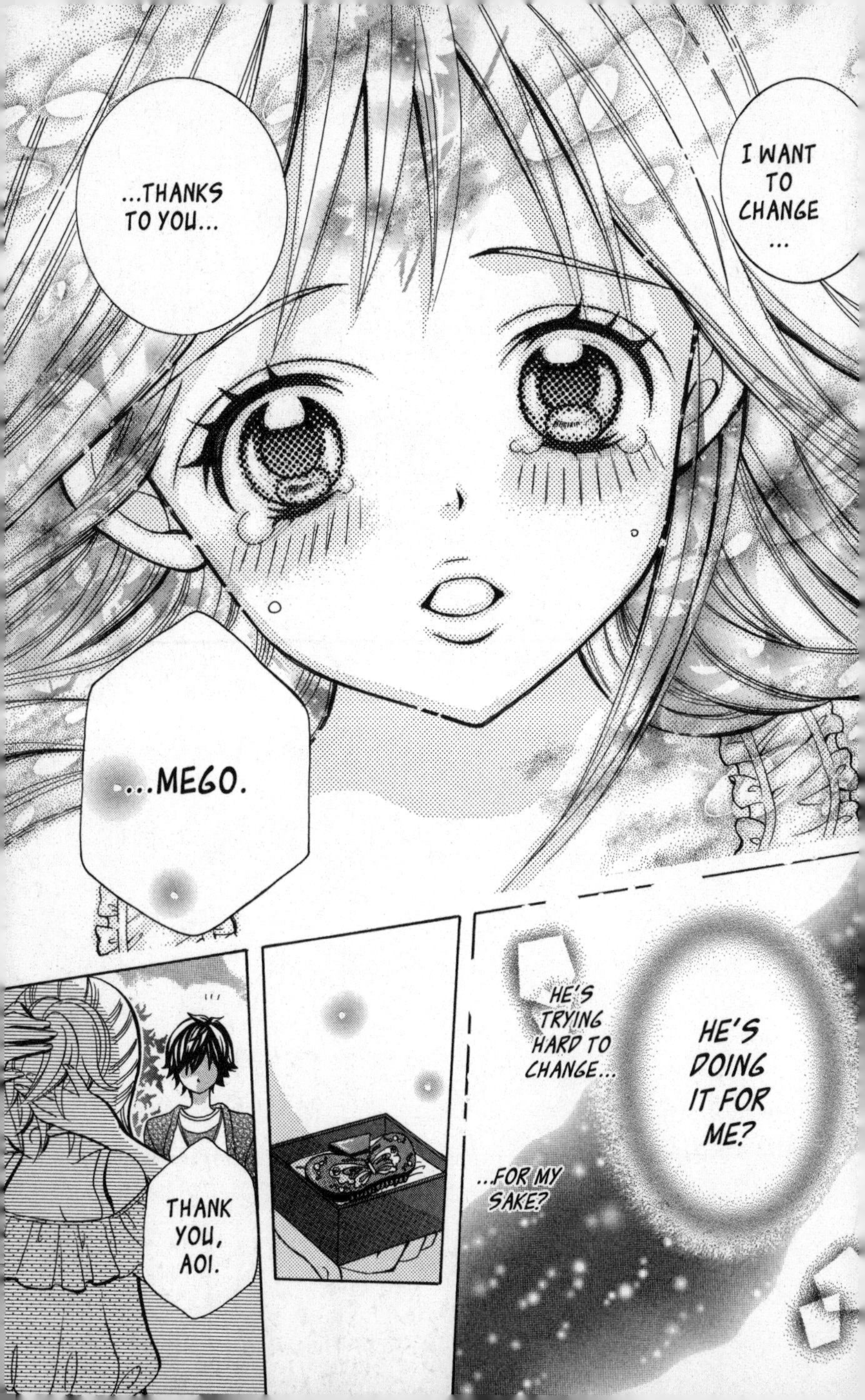
I WANT TO CHANGE ...
...THANKS TO YOU...
...MEGO.
HE'S DOING IT FOR ME?
HE'S TRYING HARD TO CHANGE...
...FOR MY SAKE?
THANK YOU, AOI.

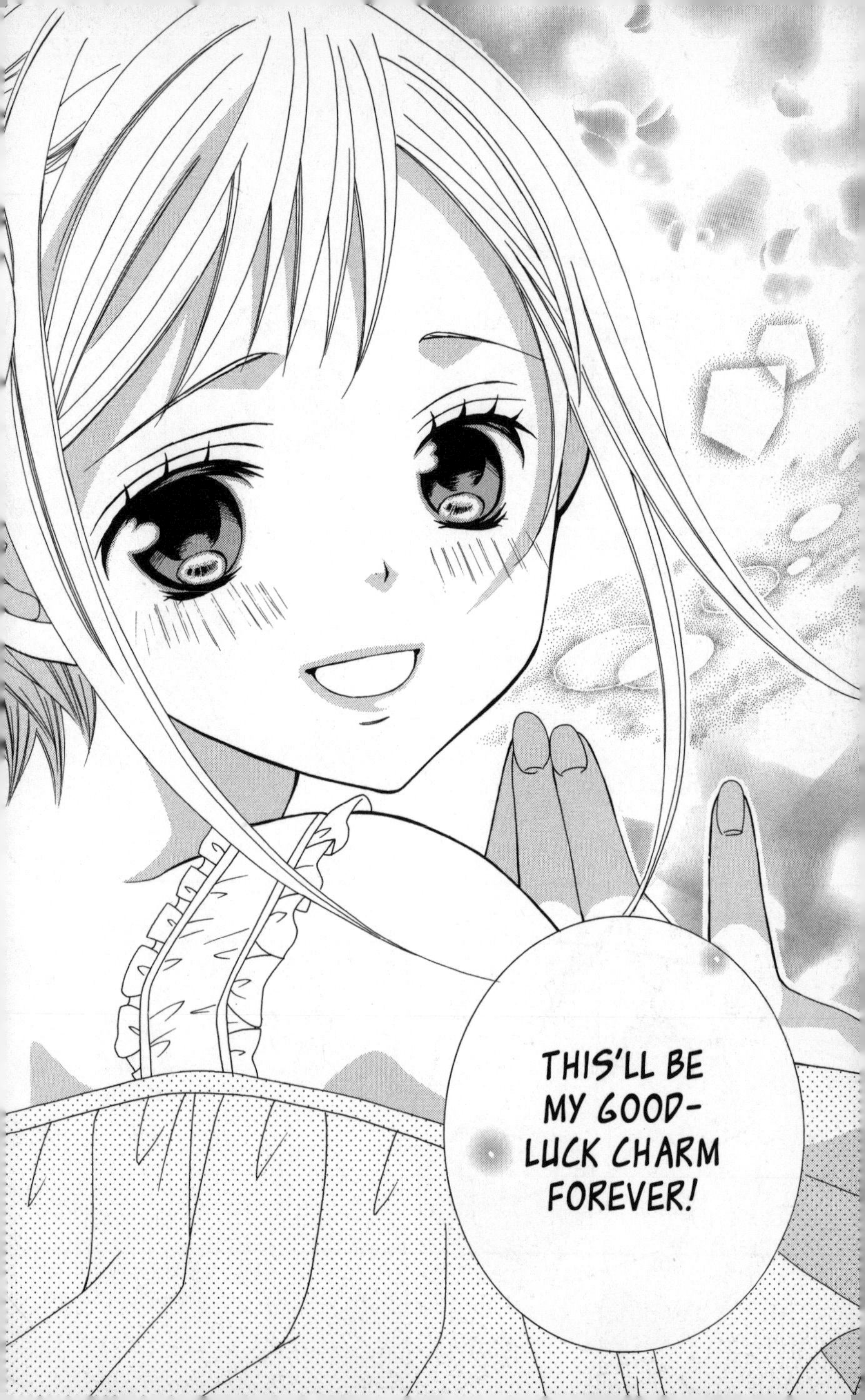
THIS'LL BE MY GOOD-LUCK CHARM FOREVER!

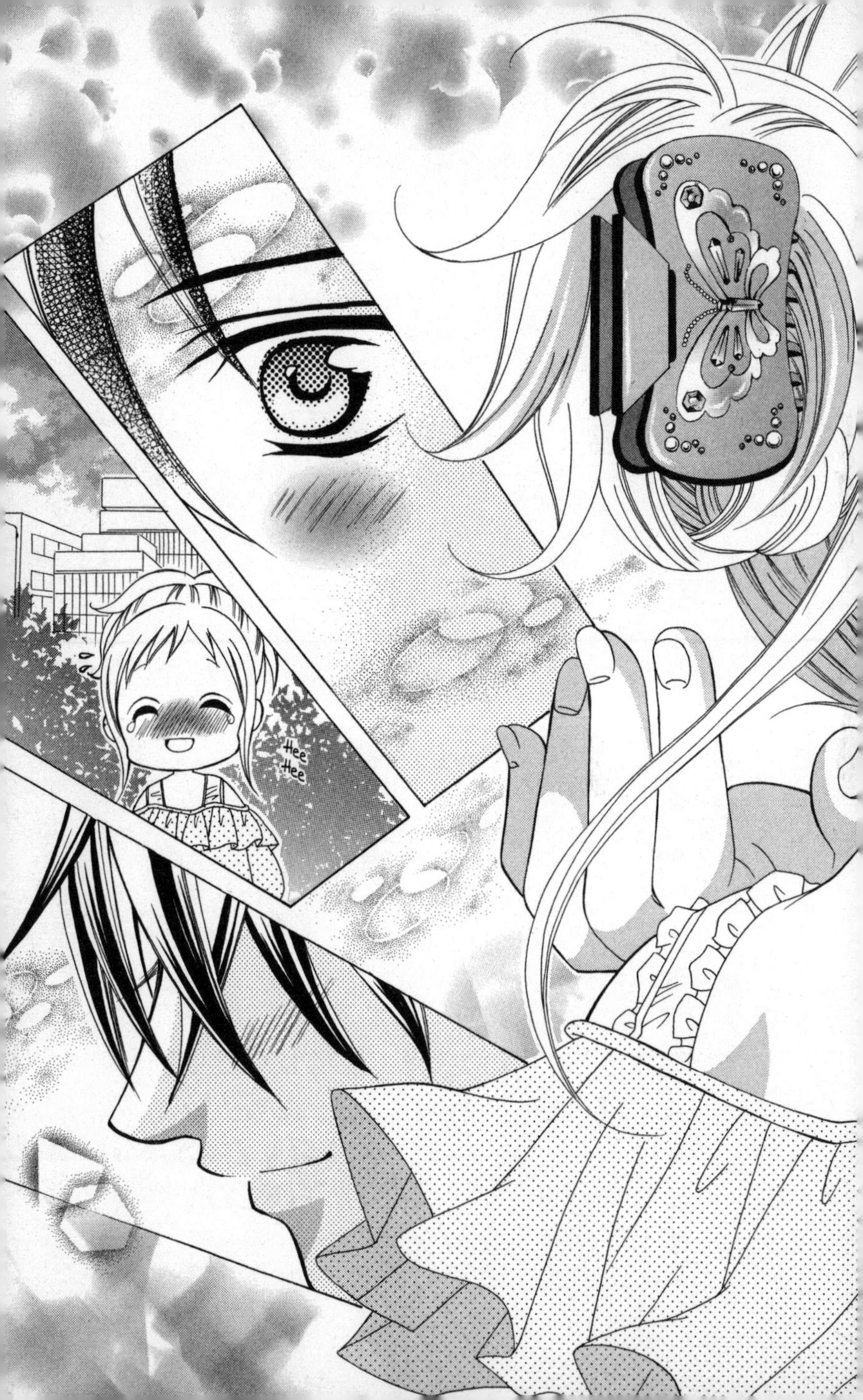
Hee Hee

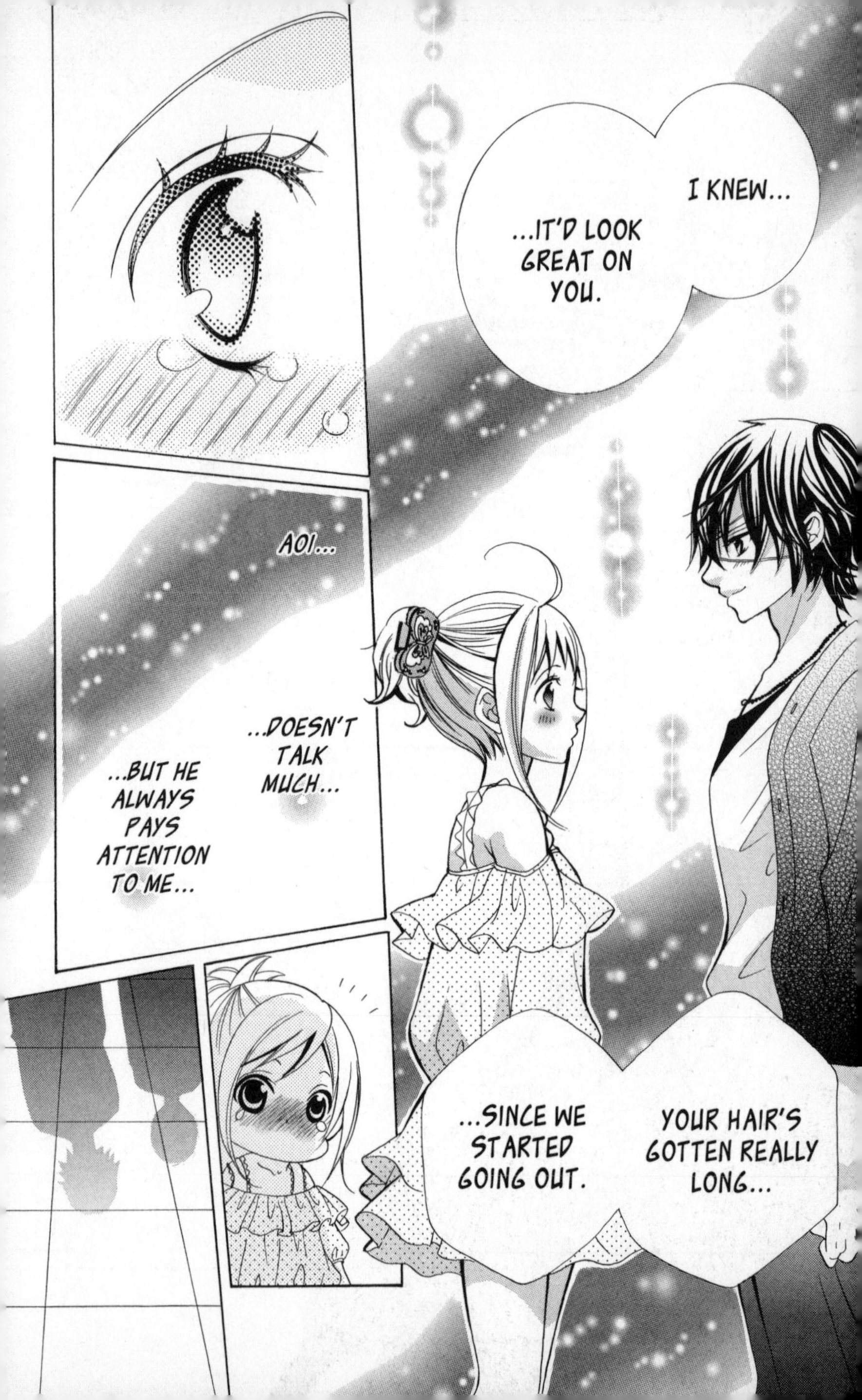
I KNEW...
...IT'D LOOK GREAT ON YOU.
YOUR HAIR'S GOTTEN REALLY LONG...
...SINCE WE STARTED GOING OUT.
AOI...
...DOESN'T TALK MUCH...
...BUT HE ALWAYS PAYS ATTENTION TO ME...

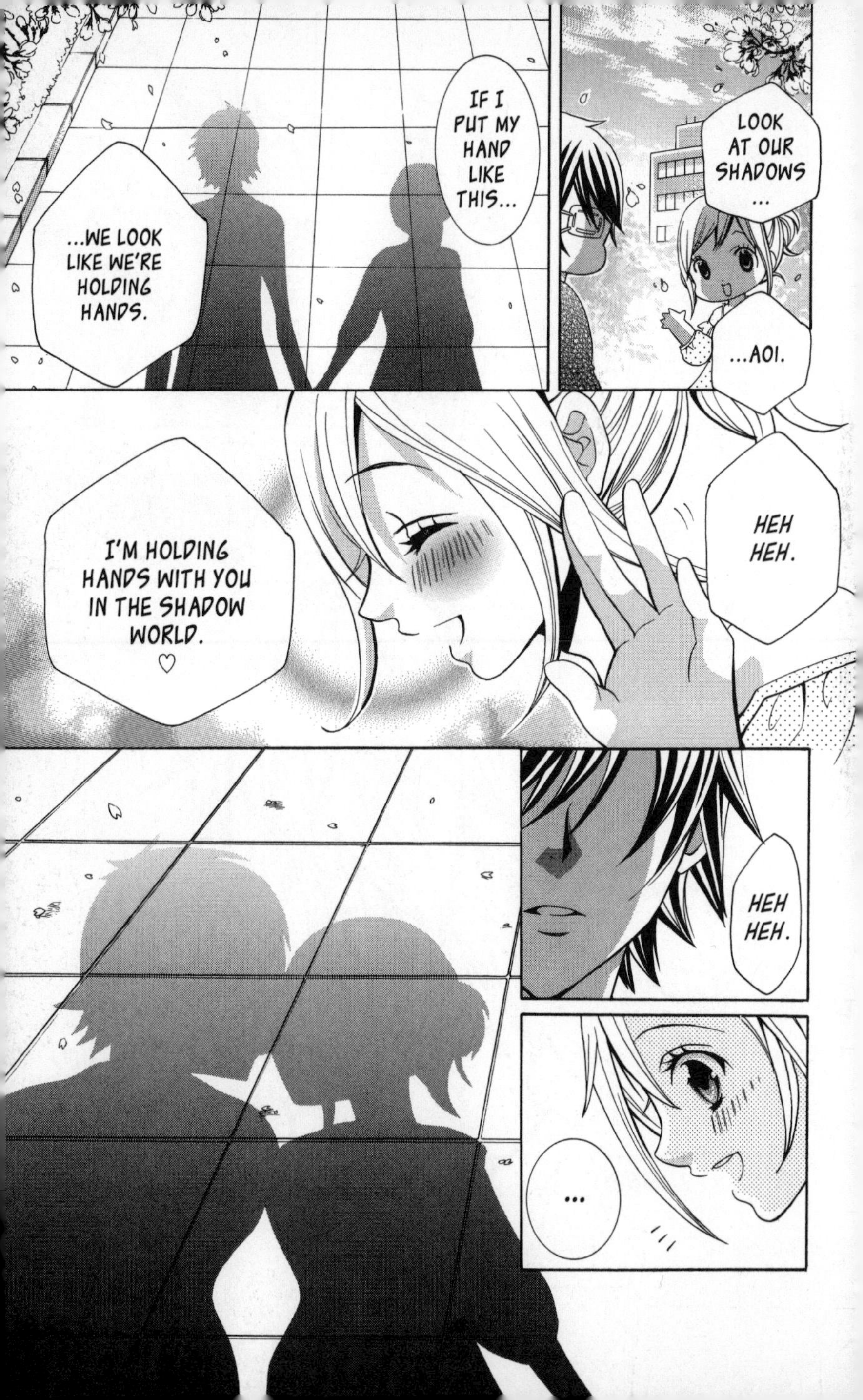
LOOK AT OUR SHADOWS ...
...AOI.
IF I PUT MY HAND LIKE THIS...
...WE LOOK LIKE WE'RE HOLDING HANDS.
HEH HEH.
I'M HOLDING HANDS WITH YOU IN THE SHADOW WORLD. ♡
HEH HEH.
...

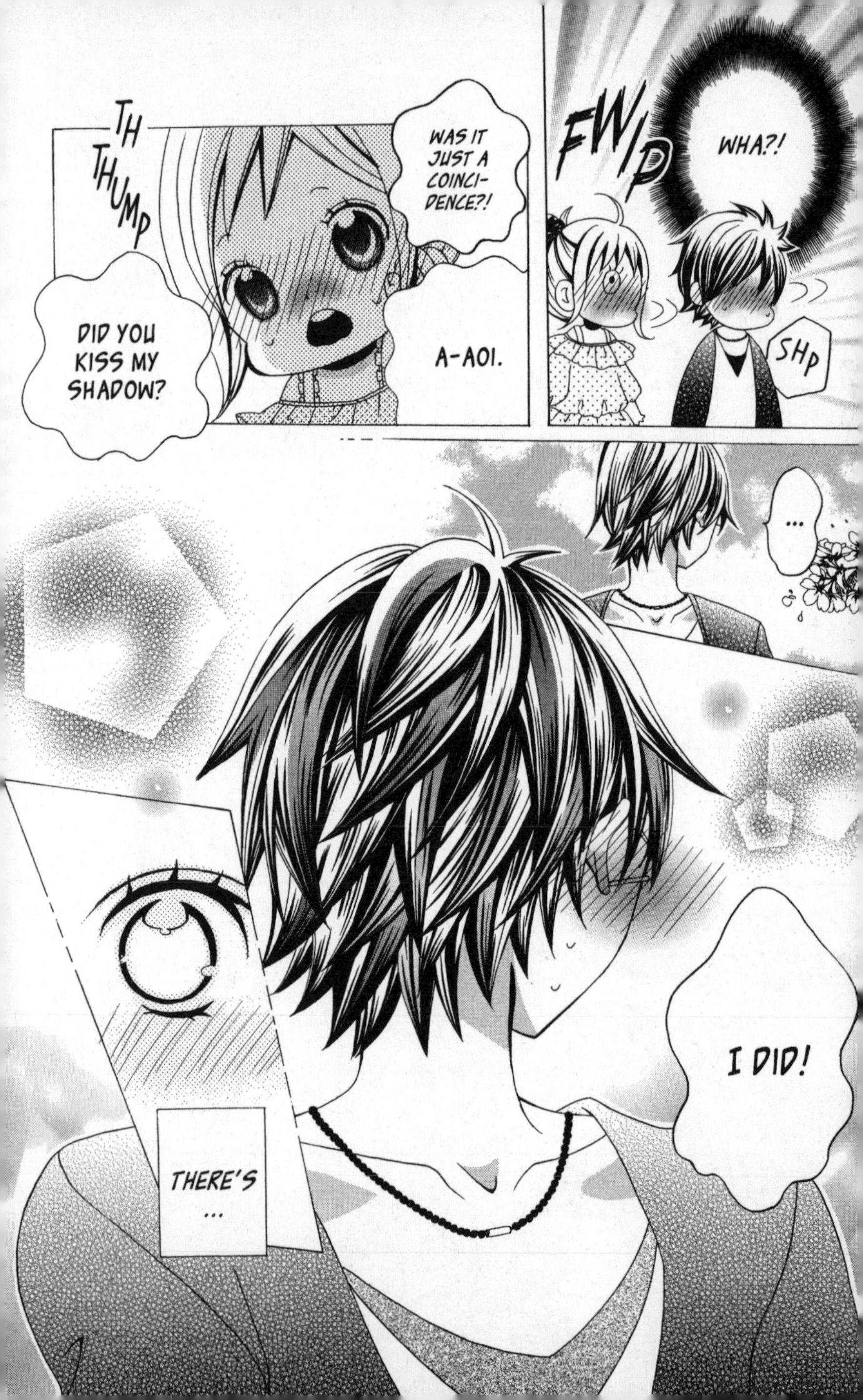
FWIP
WHA?!
SHP
WAS IT JUST A COINCIDENCE?!
TH THUMP
A-AOI.
DID YOU KISS MY SHADOW?
...
I DID!
THERE'S ...

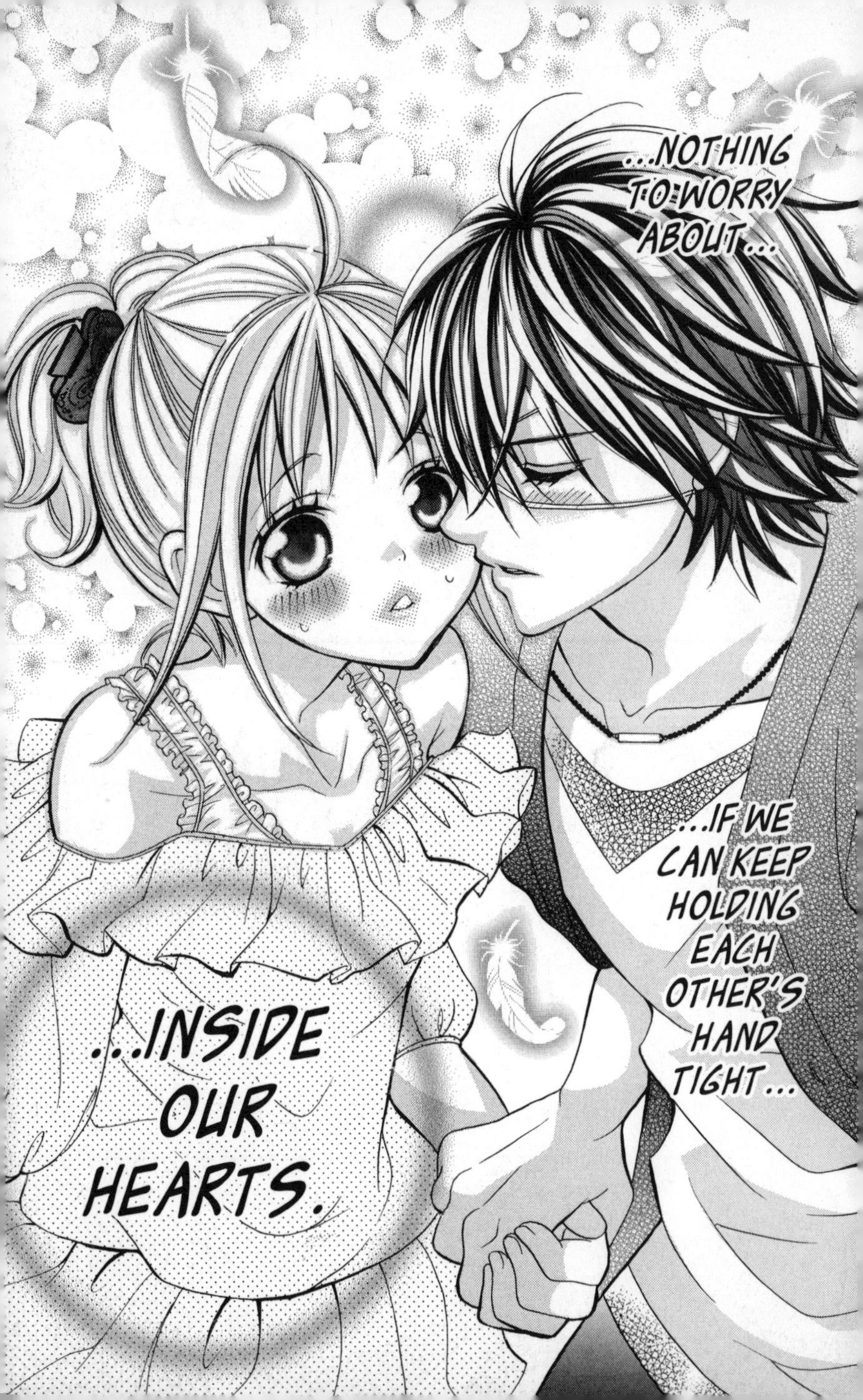
...NOTHING TO WORRY ABOUT...
...IF WE CAN KEEP HOLDING EACH OTHER'S HAND TIGHT...
...INSIDE OUR HEARTS.

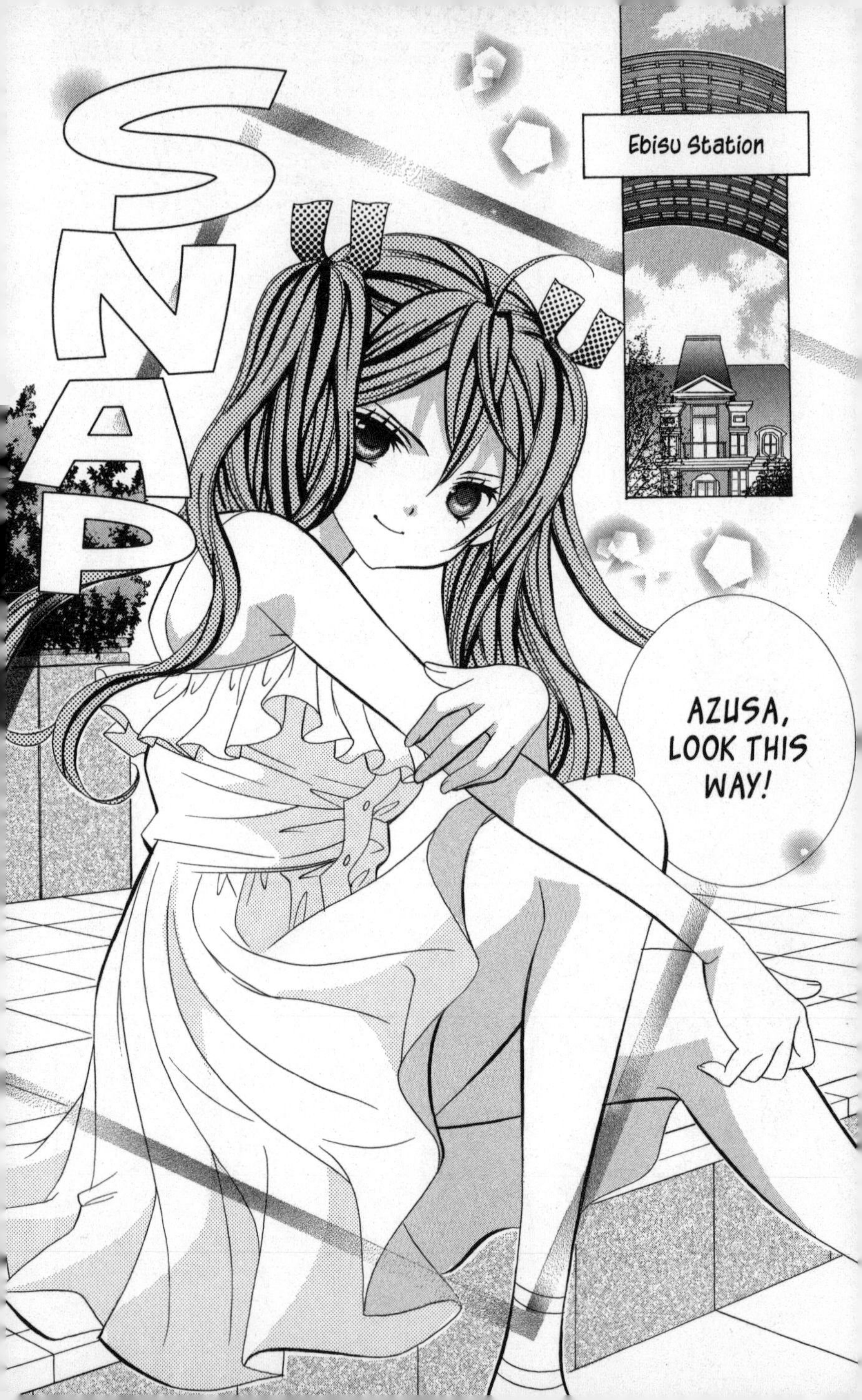
Ebisu Station
AZUSA, LOOK THIS WAY!
SNAP

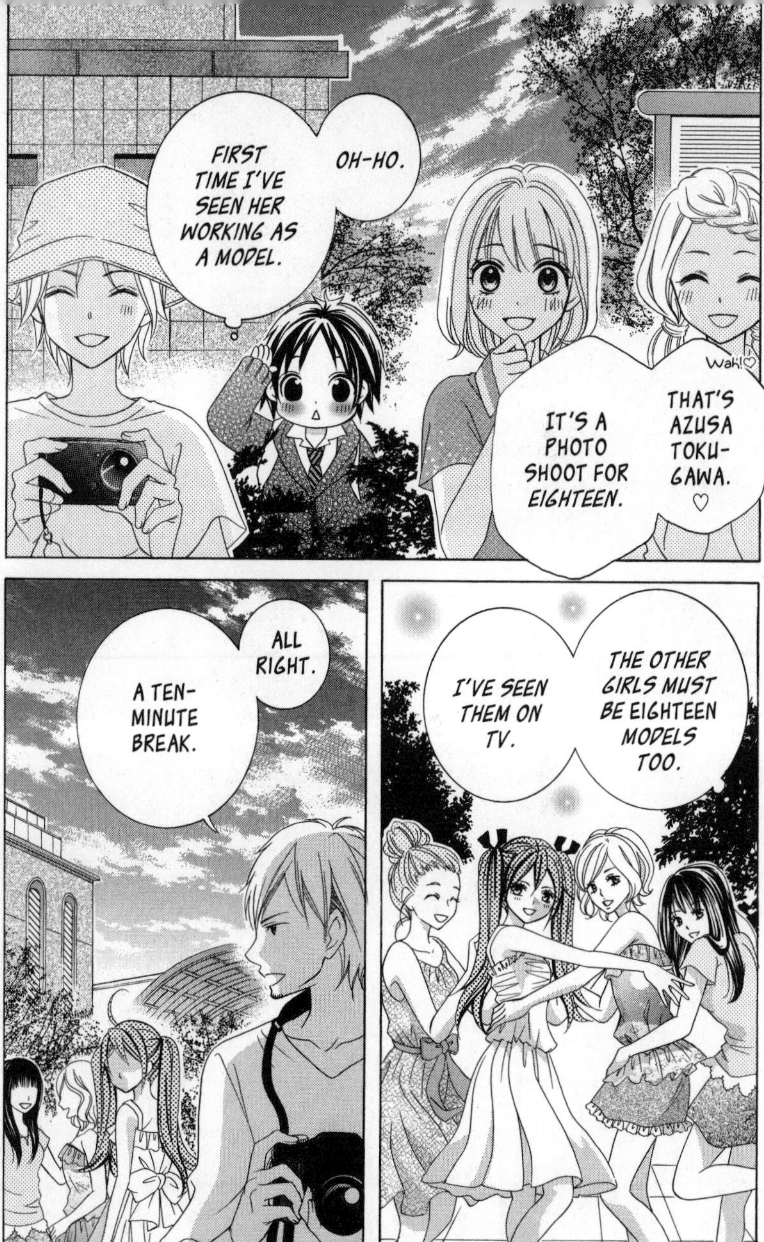
OH-HO.
FIRST TIME I'VE SEEN HER WORKING AS A MODEL.
Wah!♡
THAT'S AZUSA TOKU-GAWA. ♡
IT'S A PHOTO SHOOT FOR EIGHTEEN.
THE OTHER GIRLS MUST BE EIGHTEEN MODELS TOO.
I'VE SEEN THEM ON TV.
ALL RIGHT.
A TEN-MINUTE BREAK.

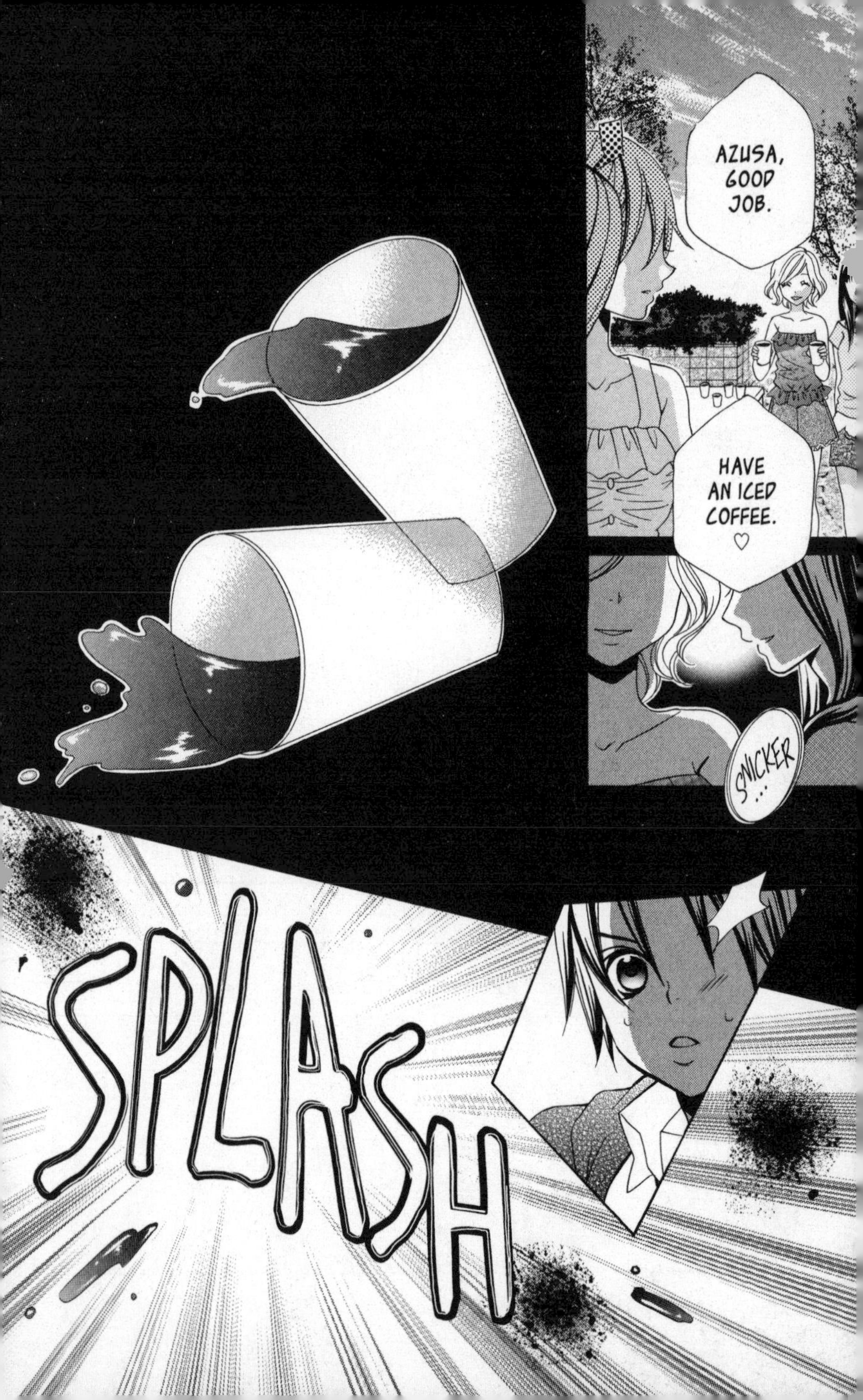
AZUSA, GOOD JOB.
HAVE AN ICED COFFEE. ♡
SNICKER...
SPLASH

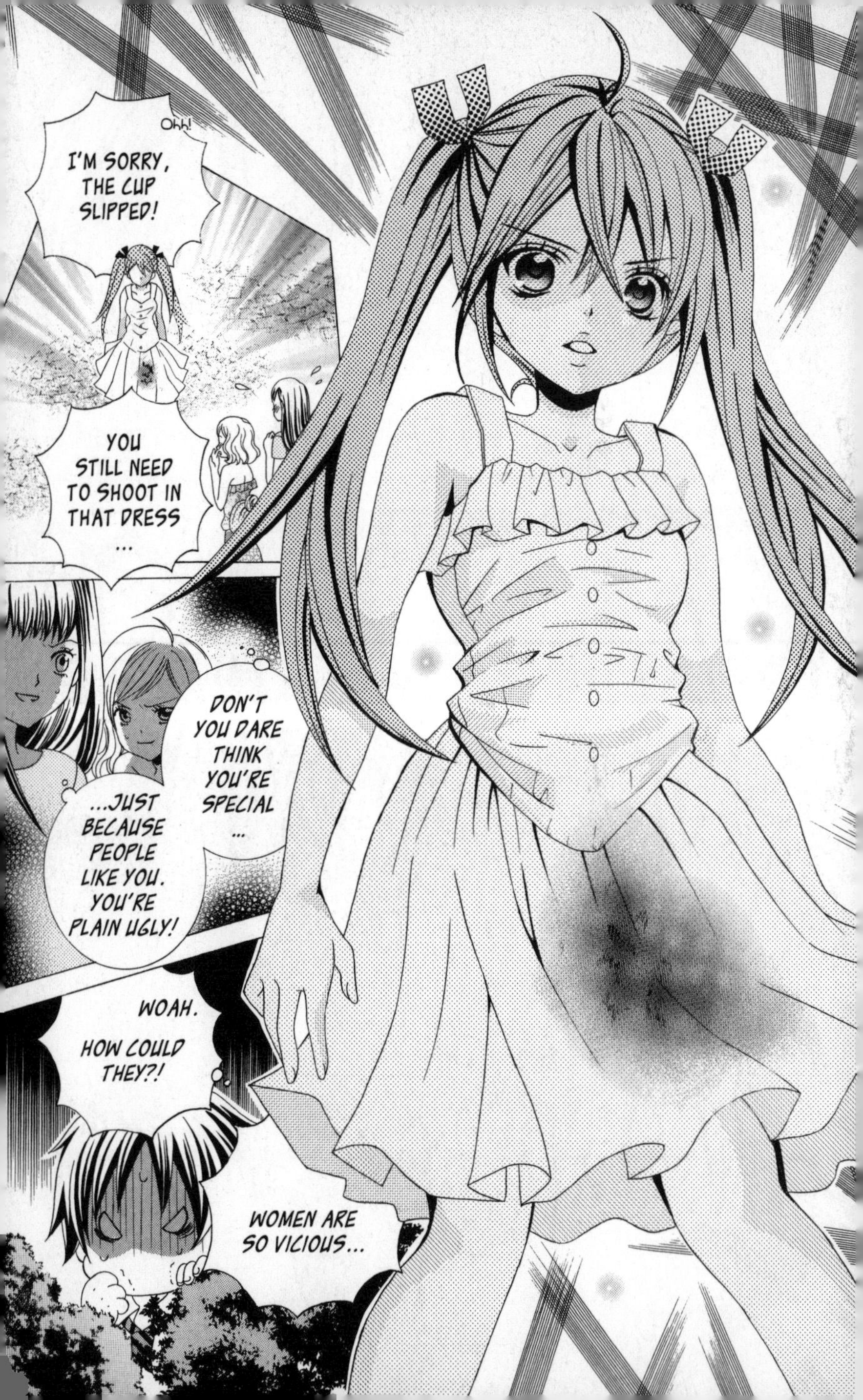
Ohh!
I'M SORRY, THE CUP SLIPPED!
YOU STILL NEED TO SHOOT IN THAT DRESS ...
DON'T YOU DARE THINK YOU'RE SPECIAL ...
...JUST BECAUSE PEOPLE LIKE YOU. YOU'RE PLAIN UGLY!
WOAH.
HOW COULD THEY?!
WOMEN ARE SO VICIOUS...

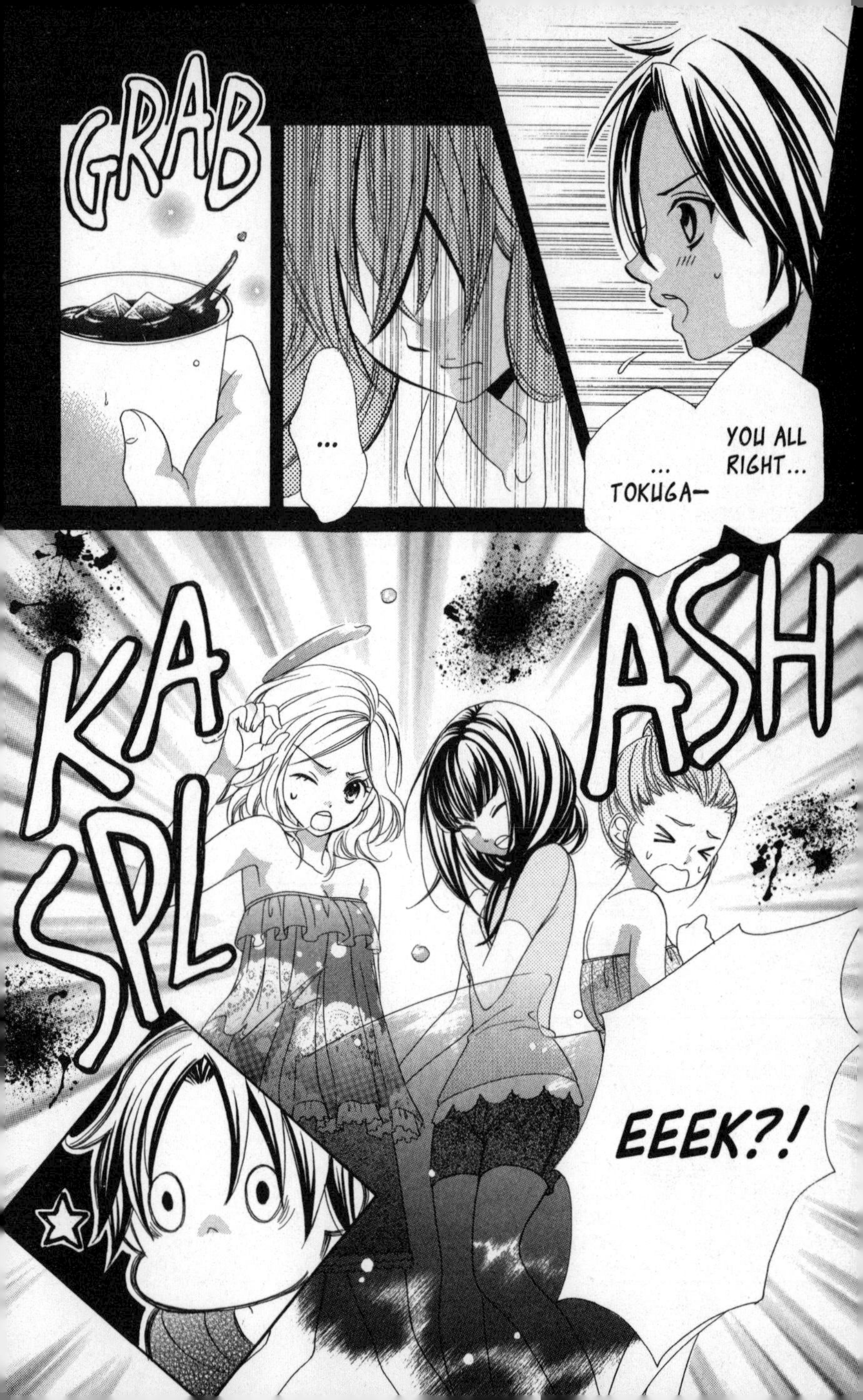
YOU ALL RIGHT... ...TOKUGA—
...
GRAB
KA
SPL
ASH
EEEK?!

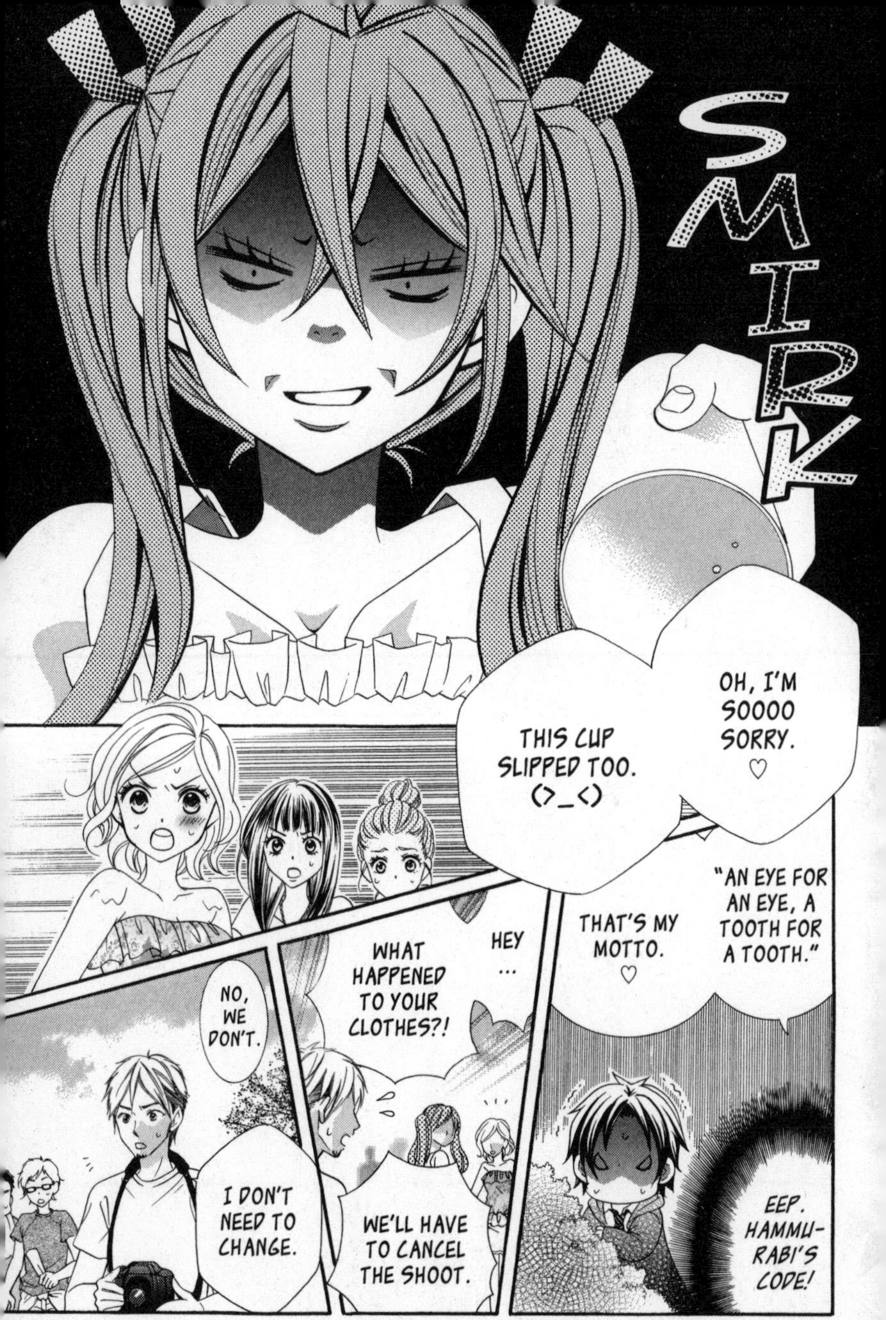
SMIRK
OH, I'M SOOOO SORRY. ♡
THIS CUP SLIPPED TOO. (>_<)
"AN EYE FOR AN EYE, A TOOTH FOR A TOOTH."
THAT'S MY MOTTO. ♡
EEP. HAMMU-RABI'S CODE!
HEY...
WHAT HAPPENED TO YOUR CLOTHES?!
WE'LL HAVE TO CANCEL THE SHOOT.
NO, WE DON'T.
I DON'T NEED TO CHANGE.

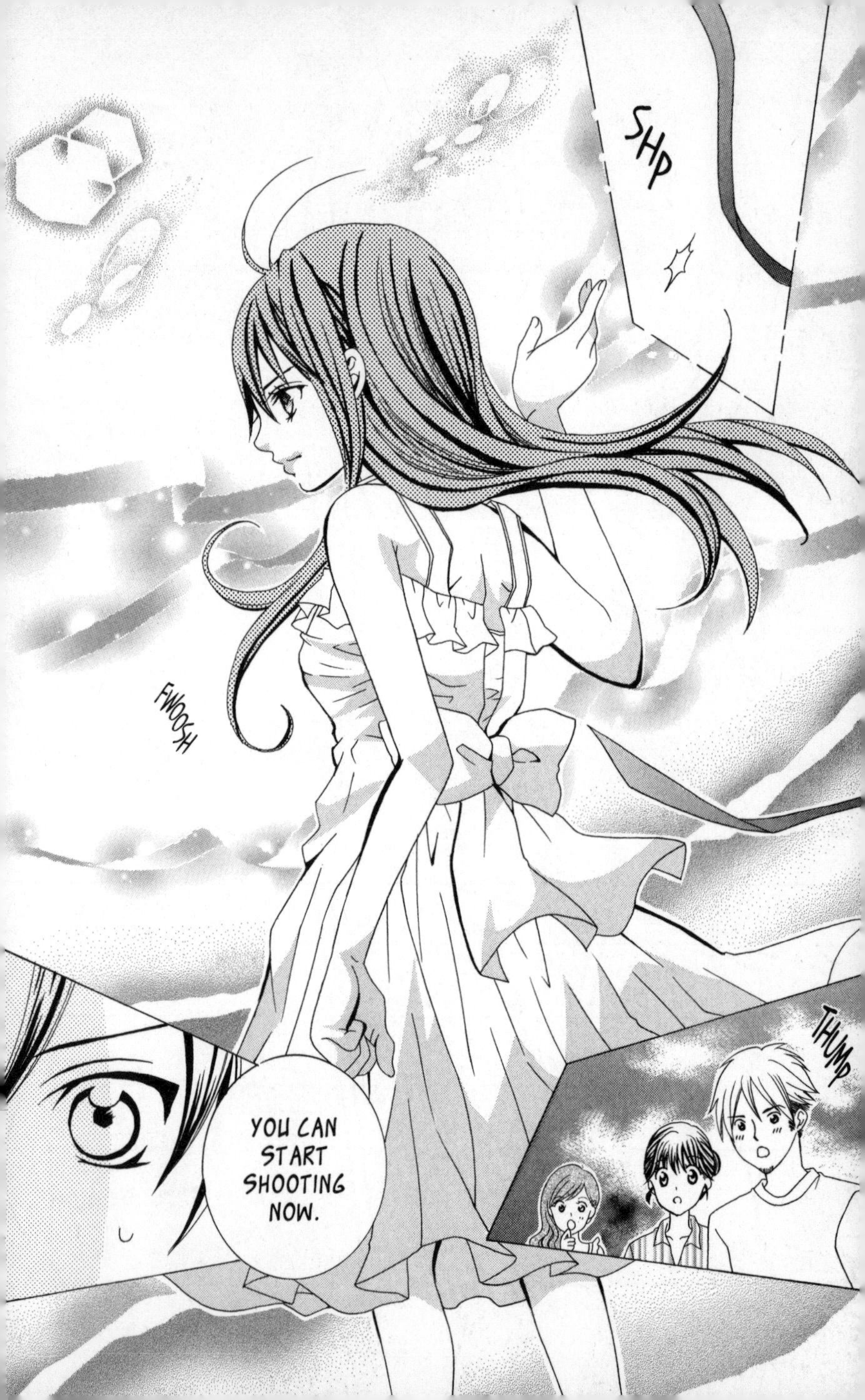
SHP
FWOOSH
THUMP
YOU CAN START SHOOTING NOW.

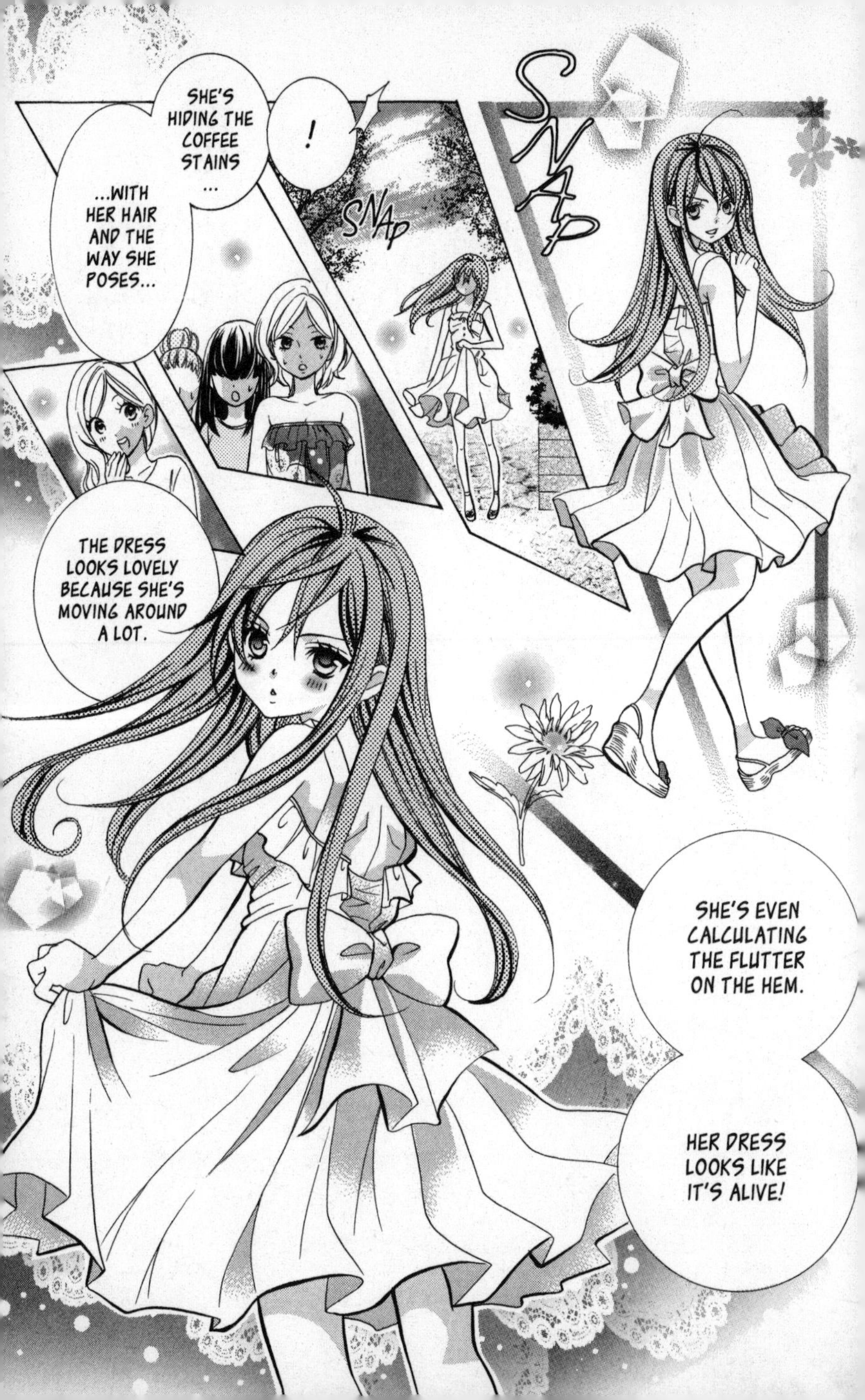
SNAP
!
SNAP
SHE'S HIDING THE COFFEE STAINS ...
...WITH HER HAIR AND THE WAY SHE POSES...
THE DRESS LOOKS LOVELY BECAUSE SHE'S MOVING AROUND A LOT.
SHE'S EVEN CALCULATING THE FLUTTER ON THE HEM.
HER DRESS LOOKS LIKE IT'S ALIVE!

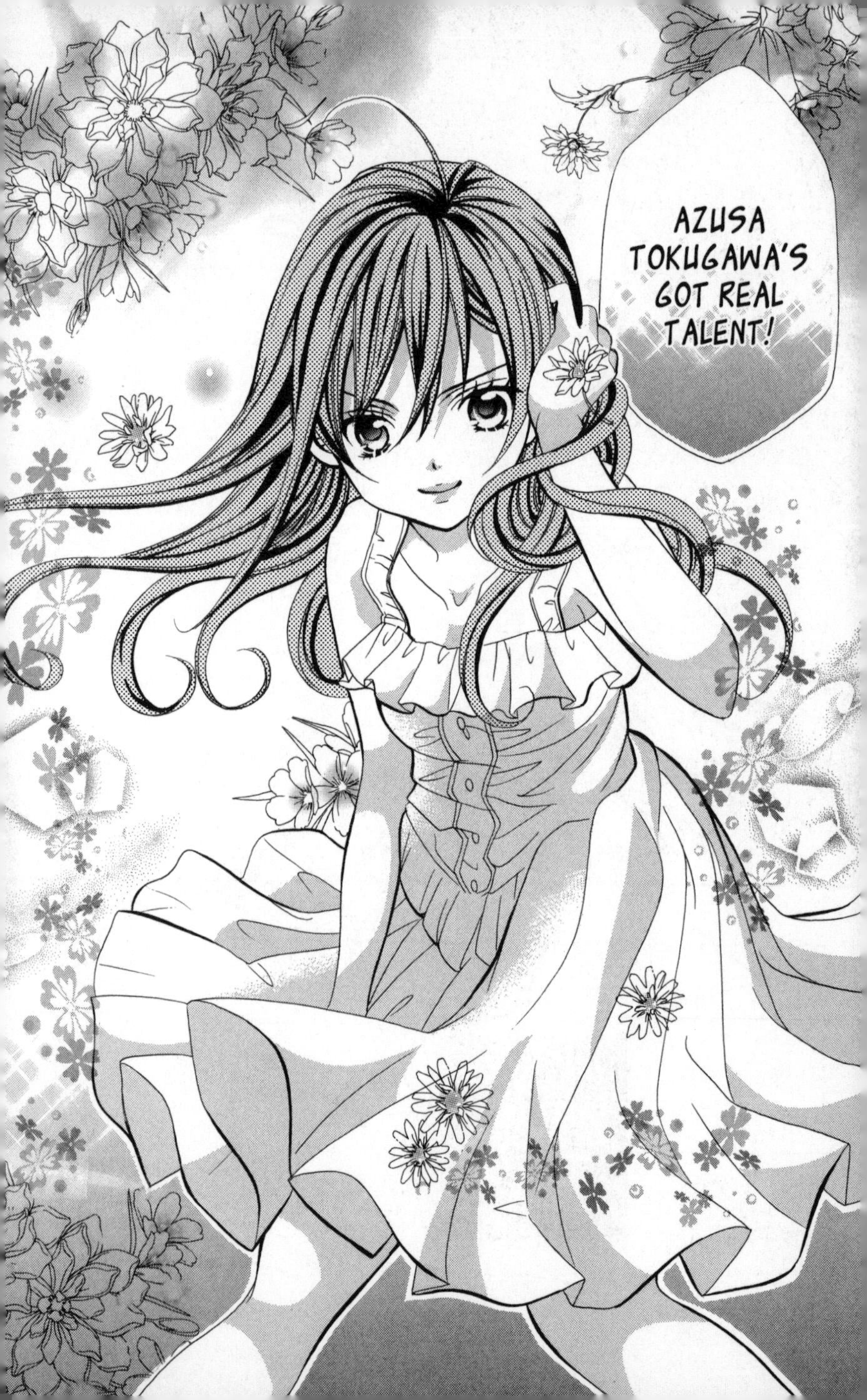
AZUSA TOKUGAWA'S GOT REAL TALENT!

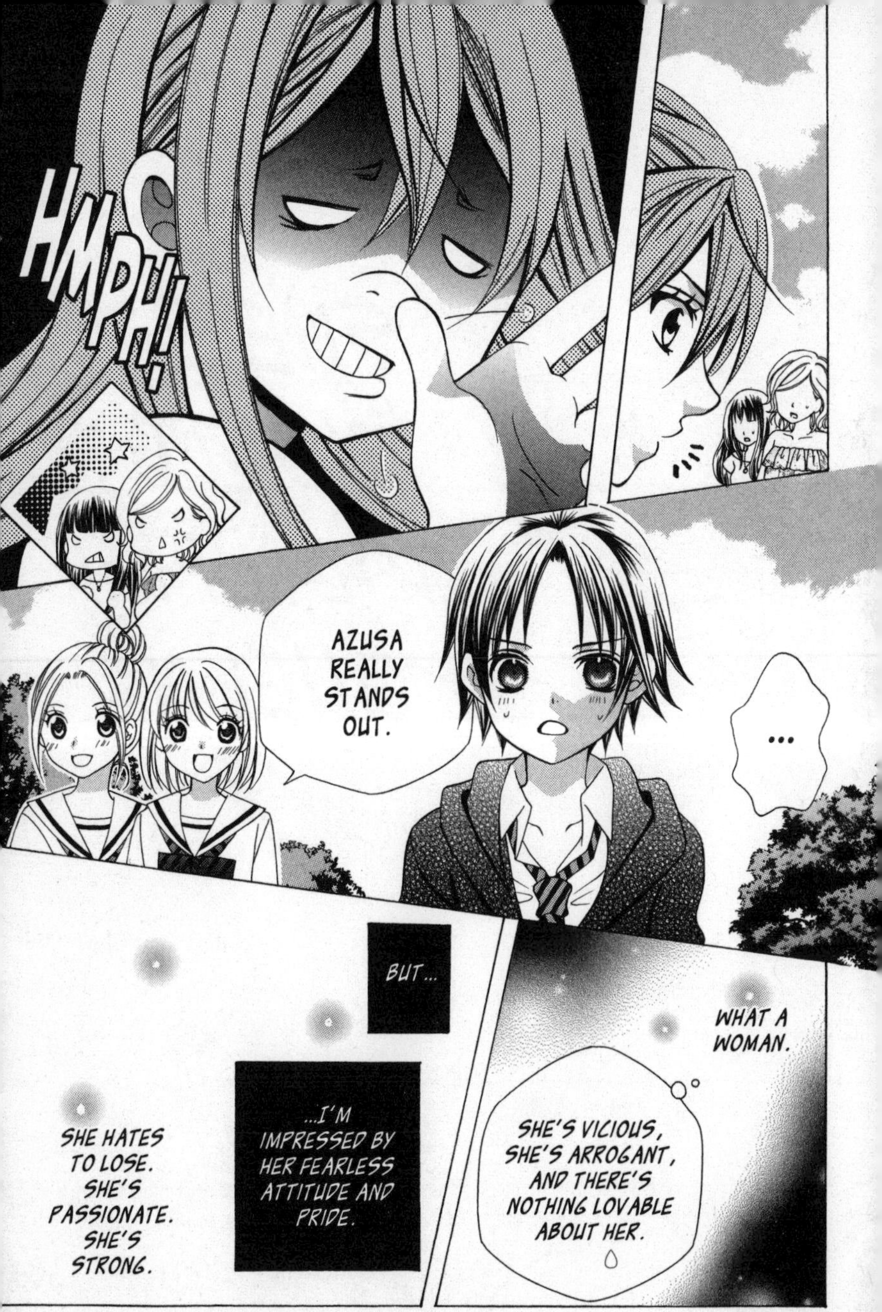
HMPH!
AZUSA REALLY STANDS OUT.
...
WHAT A WOMAN.
SHE'S VICIOUS, SHE'S ARROGANT, AND THERE'S NOTHING LOVABLE ABOUT HER.
BUT...
...I'M IMPRESSED BY HER FEARLESS ATTITUDE AND PRIDE.
SHE HATES TO LOSE. SHE'S PASSIONATE. SHE'S STRONG.

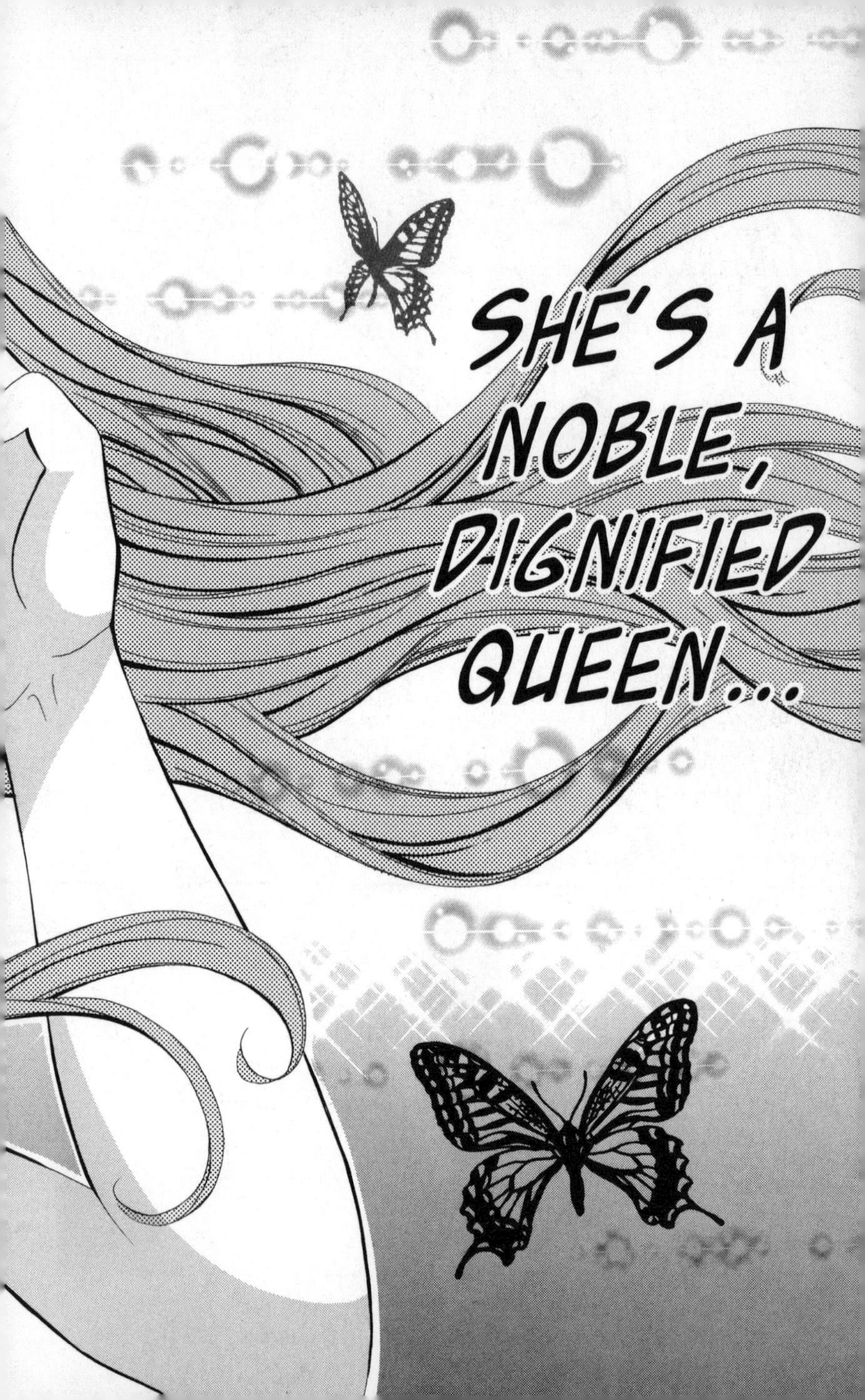
SHE'S A NOBLE, DIGNIFIED QUEEN...

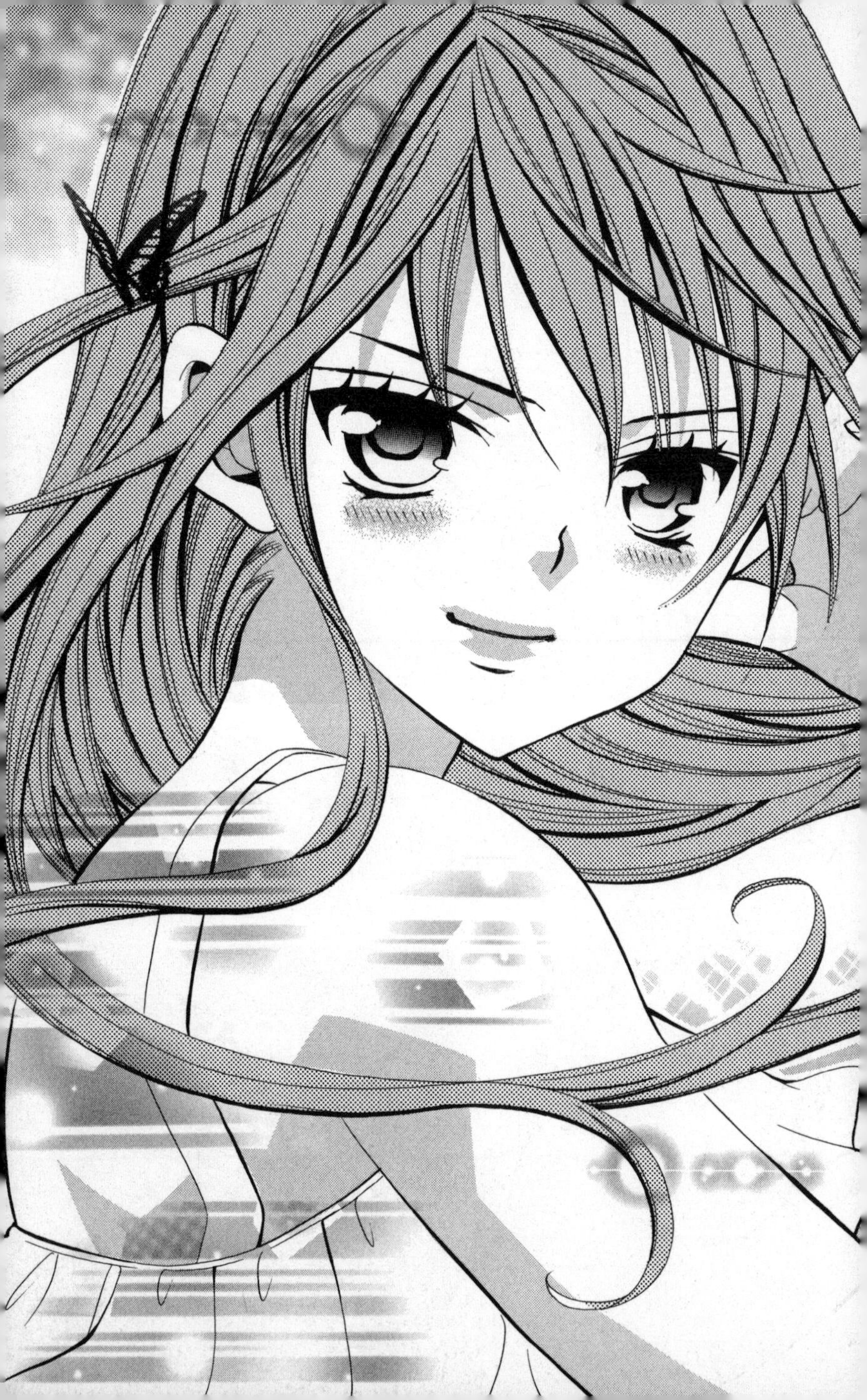

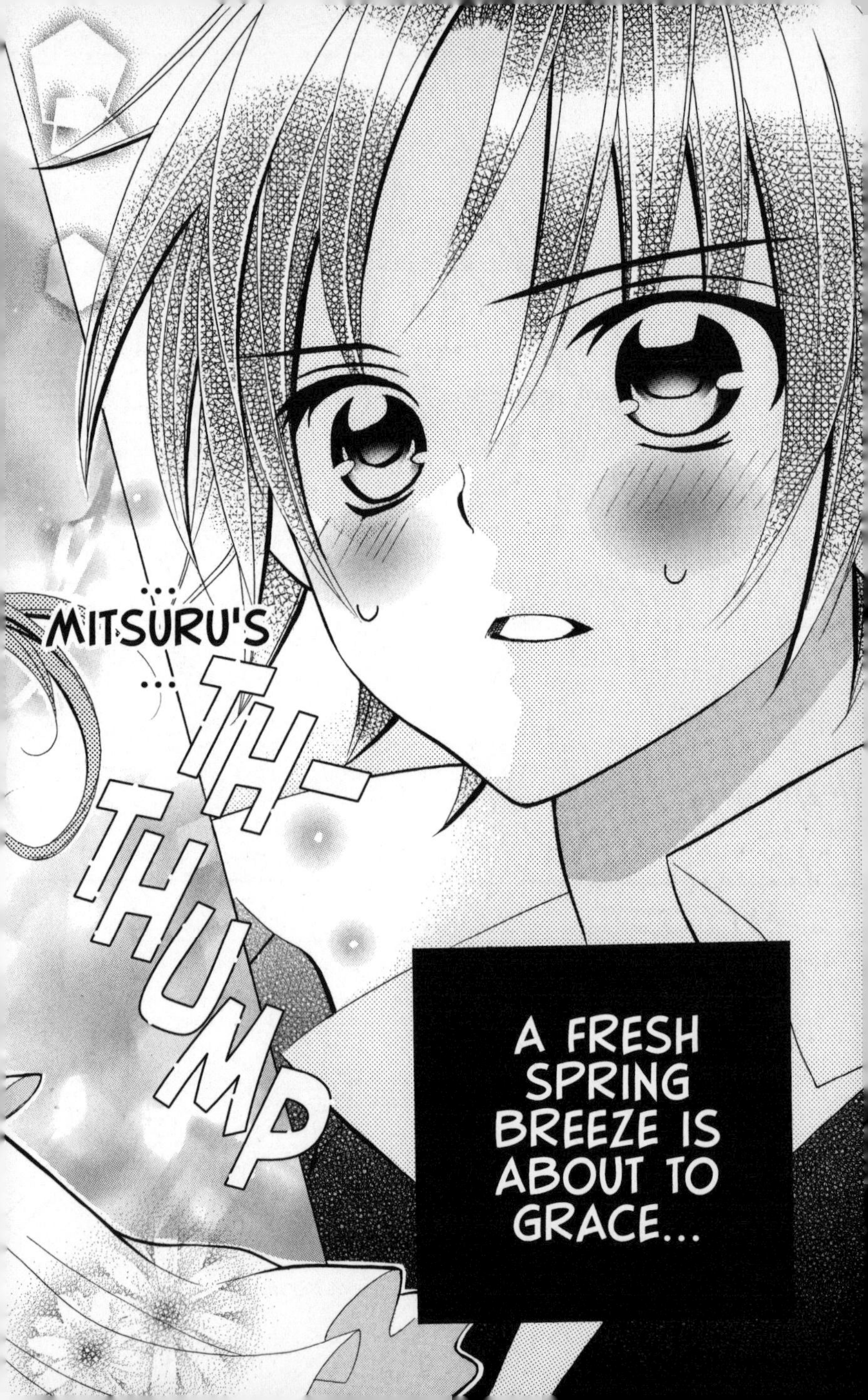
...MITSURU'S
...TH-THUMP
A FRESH SPRING BREEZE IS ABOUT TO GRACE...

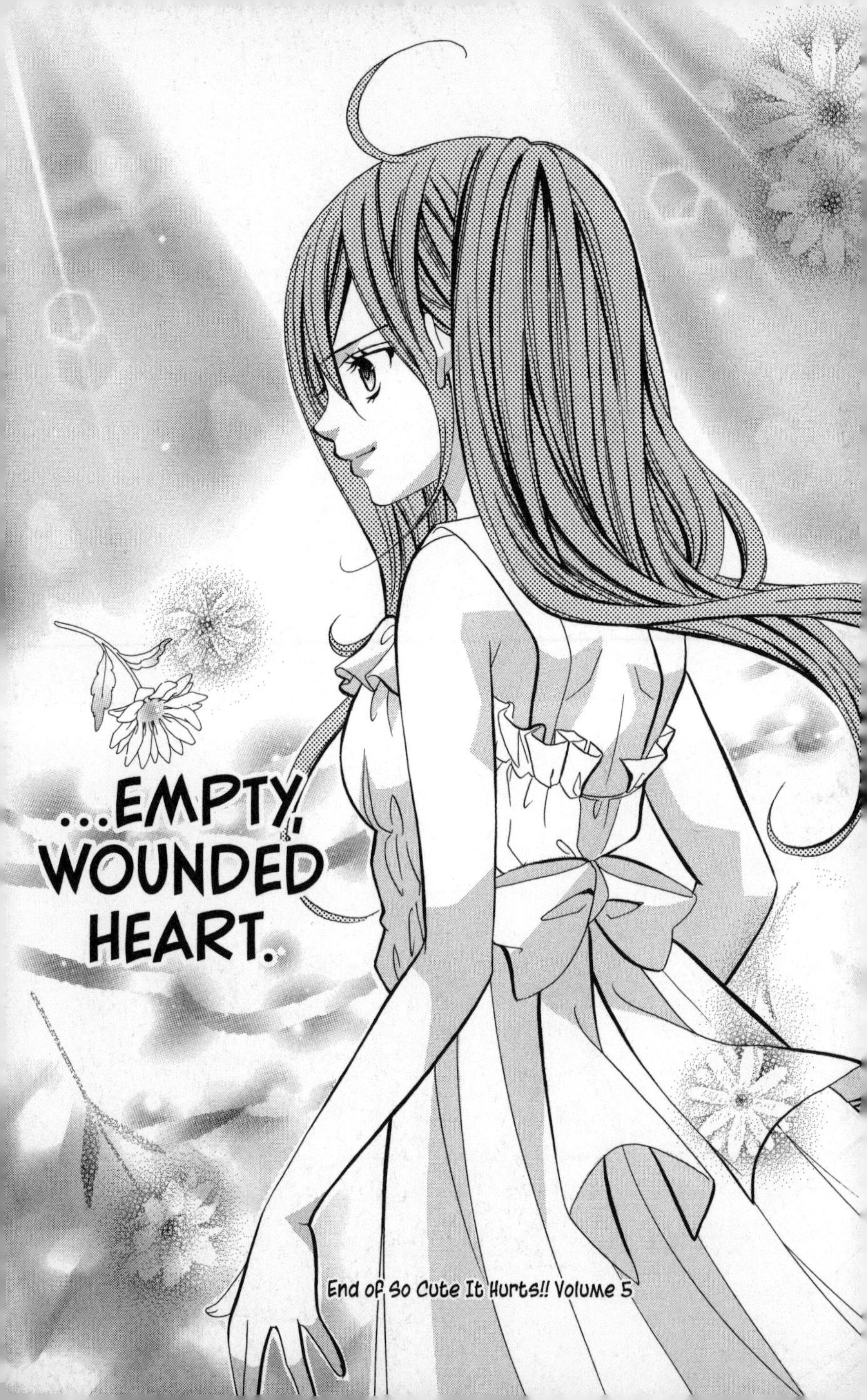
...EMPTY, WOUNDED HEART.
End of So Cute It Hurts!! Volume 5

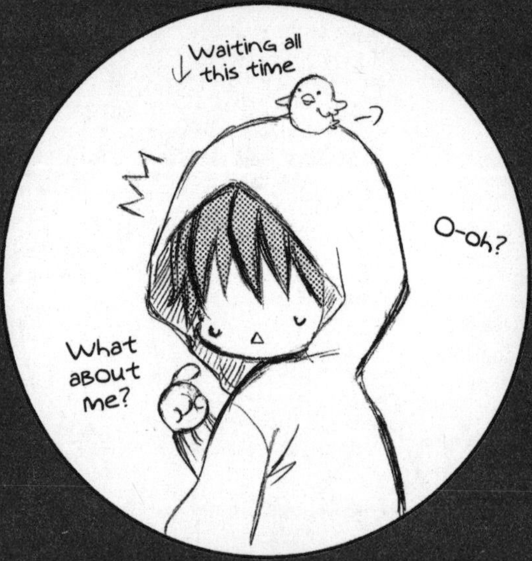
Waiting all this time
O-oh?
What about me?

You'll find out who he is in volume 6!

GLOSSARY

Page 72, note: Moe
Moe means to have an affection for or an attraction to something. It is often used in referring to anime, manga and game characters.

Page 79, panel 1: Cheerleading
In Japan, there are male cheerleading squads as well as female ones. That is why Moyuyu is confused when Megumu comes out dressed as a girl. He was expecting a male cheerleader outfit.

Page 118, author note: Hakama
A Japanese garment tied at the waist and worn over kimono. Divided *hakama* resemble pants in that they have two separate legs and were worn when riding horses. The undivided hakama do not have separate legs.

Page 122, panel 2: Otaku
Otaku are superfans or hobbyists, and would be called nerds or geeks in North America.

Page 130, panel 3: Day duty
In Japanese schools, students take turns being responsible for certain classroom chores, including recording daily details in the logbook.

Page 159, panel 1: Takoyaki
Fried octopus balls, a popular festival food. *Tako* means "octopus" in Japanese.

AUTHOR BIO

They made a lot of *So Cute!* goodies for this year's Summer Festival! (^O^) My favorites are the eye-patch-penguin strap and extra-large handkerchief (the one Mego wrapped around her head in volume 3, LOL). I use them too! ♪♪ (//∇//)

Volume 6 will come with an anime DVD in Japan. The story is a new one, and production is already in progress! I'm excited about it because the story seems to be a very merry one! I hope everyone is looking forward to it too!! (^O^)

Go Ikeyamada is a Gemini from Miyagi Prefecture whose hobbies include taking naps and watching movies. Her debut manga *Get Love!!* appeared in *Shojo Comic* in 2002, and her current work *So Cute It Hurts!!* (*Kobayashi ga Kawai Suguite Tsurai!!*) is being published by VIZ Media.